FIFTY YEARS OF

COLLECTIBLE

GLASS

1920-1970

EASY IDENTIFICATION
AND PRICE GUIDE

VOLUME II:
STEMWARE, DECORATIONS,
DECORATIVE ACCESSORIES

ISBN: 1-58221-001-2
Library of Congress Catalog Card Number: 97-74599

Editor: Kyle Husfloen
Assistant Editor: Ruth Willis
Editorial Assistant: Nancy Crowley
Designers: Lynn Bradshaw, Virginia Hill
Design Assistant: Janell Edwards
Cover Design: Lynn Bradshaw

Front Cover: Left to right: U.S. Glass/Tiffin Cordelia
etching on No. 17067 goblet, Fostoria Glass Co.
No. 2250 candy jars. Top: Viking Glass Co. Prelude
etching on sherbet. Bottom: Westmoreland blue satin
dog doorstop

Back Cover: Top: Morgantown Glass Co. No. 7643 Golf
Ball stems in various color combinations.
Bottom: Economy Tumbler Co. (Morgantown)
Art Moderne stemware

Please Note: Though listings have been double-checked and every effort
has been made to assure accuracy, neither the editors nor the publisher
can assume responsibility for any losses that might be incurred as a result
of consulting this guide, or for errors, typographical or otherwise.

Printed in the United States of America

To order additional copies of this
book or a catalog please contact:

Antique Trader Books
700 E. State Street
Iola, WI 54990-0001
1-800-258-0929

 Antique Trader Books
A Division of Krause Publications

CONTENTS

FOREWORD

This volume is the second (in a 2-volume set) presenting information about stemware, decorations and accessory items. Volume I covered tableware patterns, kitchenware and barware—often made by machine-made glass companies. Machine-made glass was made cheaply, often cheaply enough to be used as free gifts at movies, gas stations, etc.

Hand-made glass companies manufactured products of higher quality with more hand finishing than those of machine-made companies. Thus, in this book, most of the emphasis is on hand-made glass companies such as Morgantown, Duncan & Miller, Heisey, Cambridge and others. Because these companies were producing glass for a higher-end market than the machine-made companies, many of their products were hand manipulated (crimped edges, rolled edges, etc.). This better quality glass lent itself to decorations such as etchings and cuttings in a wide variety—both in motif and quality.

Most companies also made decorative glass, sometimes with specific uses in mind, such as vases, or simply decorative pieces, such as figurines. Many of these form collecting categories in themselves, some even limited to specific companies.

We have continued the format we began in Volume I of listing related items in chapters. For stemware we have grouped patterns with the same type of stem portion together and often subdivided the list into shapes of goblet bowls. Decorations have been listed by the distinct motif of the pattern. The chapter on accessories simply presents several categories of items that are collected today. Only a few of the possibilities are listed, but we have included items made by several companies to give an overview of the scope of these collecting categories.

Finally, we have included a chapter strictly to help in identification. This contains catalog pages, ads, and other material just too good to ignore. The items in this chapter are not priced or presented with extensive lists. We were inundated with masses of information, and chose this way to present as much as possible.

Happy Glass Collecting!
Neila and Tom Bredehoft

SPECIAL THANKS

We are greatly indebted to many friends for information, permission to photograph pieces, advice on pricing and general help in writing this book. Without help such as this, we would not have been able to present such a complete book.

Susan and Lee Allen
Larry Baker
French Batten
Dave Bush
Joan and Odie Finchum
Mart Groesser
Kyle Husfloen
Leora and Jim Leasure
Dean Six
Weston Area Glass History and Study Group, Weston, WV

INTRODUCTION

During the Victorian era, American stemware usually consisted of pressed lines, usually quite plain or made in standard designs. As large patterns of pressed glass were developed, often a matching goblet and wine were made. A few companies made hand-blown stemware during this period, but pressed-ware companies far outnumbered them. Since sales are dependent on innovation, early in the 1910s the emphasis of production was changed to lightweight blown stemware. Companies that had only produced pressed ware added blown-ware shops to their factories. Other companies sprang up that made blown ware exclusively. The first stems made were quite plain when compared to their later cousins.

Companies sold their stem lines either plain or decorated. Companies added decorating departments to their factories, primarily etching and cutting shops. It soon became apparent that decorated stemware would sell readily to housewives, and etchings and cuttings were designed in abundance. By the 1920s color made its appearance in American glass and also in stemware. At this time, little colored stemware was decorated. However, this all changed in the 1930s when entire table services of pressed ware in color were decorated with etchings or cuttings. Stemware in color was etched or cut to match. Both stemware and decorations reached the pinnacle of design, intricacy and quality in the 1930s. Companies such as Fostoria, Heisey, Cambridge, Tiffin, Duncan & Miller, plus many less well-known companies developed new stem lines and decorations on a regular basis. All introduced new lines at the annual January glass show in Pittsburgh where salesmen displayed their wares and took orders for glass. On hand were examples of the latest stems with their decorations. Often, if no sales were written for a decoration, it was abandoned after the show. For instance, it is documented that some Heisey cuttings new in the 1940s had notations and dates indicating "no orders" with mid-January discontinued dates. So some of these are extremely rare today since only samples were made. Other factories almost certainly did the same thing. In later years a mid-year show in Chicago was also held. Companies usually had new patterns at both shows. So several decorations could be introduced in January, and several more introduced in July or August. The effect was a plethora of patterns available. In addition to decorations done by glass manufacturers, many decorating companies bought glass blanks and applied many types of decorations.

Also in the 1930s other major changes in stemware occurred. The stem portion itself became artistic, with elaborate pressed patterns resulting in a sculptured appearance. Libbey introduced the Douglas Nash series of stems and decorations, including the Silhouette animal stemmed line. Nash also created some very innovative colors and optics for stemware. Other companies also developed wonderfully elaborate cuttings and etchings. With national advertising in many women's magazines, among other venues, a popular decoration was often expanded to 100 pieces or more. During the 1930s and early 1940s such major lines as Cambridge's *Rose Point*, Fostoria's *June*, Heisey's *Orchid* and Duncan's *First Love* were extremely popular.

By the 1940s fewer stems and decorations were developed. Partly due to World War II with the shortages of materials and manpower, production of stemware was curtailed or severely cut back. Color was abandoned almost completely. After the war ended, the industry had difficulty regaining its momentum in sales. After all, many women worked in factories during the war and retained their jobs. Elegant entertaining with a full set of stemware and formal table settings was too time-consuming and did not fit into the lifestyle of a working woman. Casual lines were in demand. Cuttings and etchings continued to be produced, but at a slower pace, and usually with much simpler execution.

The 1950s saw the demise of many of the handmade glass companies that produced stemware and decorations. Combinations of the difficulties listed above plus the increasing cost of materials and rising wages were the primary reasons companies closed. Most often, companies with popular lines were bought by other, more solvent, companies and the lines were continued at the new factory. When Tiffin bought out Duncan & Miller, its first catalogs capitalized on the Duncan name by calling the ware Duncan by Tiffin. Much the same occurred when Imperial acquired Heisey and Cambridge.

By the 1960s fewer companies were making stemware and the decorations done were less elaborate than before. Some of the companies still in business were Tiffin, Bryce, Seneca and Morgantown. By the 1970s most of these companies were out of business or were barely managing to survive.

At the present time, there is little choice if you want American-made blown stemware. Almost all stemware now available in this country is imported.

tradition in crystal...

Plantation Ivy...
hospitality's
traditional warmth
captured in
boldly etched
hand blown crystal

the finest in glassware, made in America by hand

Heisey
HAND-WROUGHT CRYSTAL

Part I
STEMWARE

Identifying stemware is sometimes a daunting task. But proper identification is possible for a large number of stems. There are hundreds and hundreds of different stems. The subject is so large that books have been written on only one company's stems. It was difficult to select which stems to include in this book. Hundreds more could have been included if not for space limitations.

Groups of stemware are presented, making it easier for collectors to identify stems. The primary groups or chapters are based on the shape of the stem portion of the piece, i.e., does it have a twist?, does it have an animal? or is it plain or have some other recognizable characteristic? The following chapters group stems with like attributes together.

Note: For easier reference look at the chapter headings at the top of each page. Bowl shapes are noted below these.

Common definitions are needed to make the study of stemware easier. The following definitions are used in these chapters.

Bowl—the upper part of a stemmed item that actually contains the liquid.

Flute—one of several flat areas around a stem, usually concave.

Foot—the base of stemware upon which the item rests.

Knop—a bulge or finger grip, usually in the middle of the stem, making it easier to grasp.

Optic—a decorative effect that is done while making the bowl. It imparts a delicate pattern to the bowl. Many different optics were used: diamond, wide, wire, loop, peacock, narrow and others.

Panel—one of several flat areas around a stem.

Stem—this can be used in two ways. 1. The middle portion of a piece of stemware, the column that supports the bowl. 2. The entire item of stemware.

We have arranged stems into the following categories: Animals, Beads, Flutes & Panels, Knops, Miscellaneous, Naturalistic, Nudes, Plain, Reeded, Sculptured, and Twist.

Recognizing the motif of the stem portion solves only half the problem of stemware identification. The other half is identifying the bowl shape. This is more of a problem than identifying the stems themselves. Bowls do have common shapes, such as bell, tapered, ovoid, etc. It is important to categorize the bowl shapes when identifying stemware since stems and bowls could be interchanged to make new and different lines. This was a cost-saving measure by glass companies. Most chapters are divided into sub-categories, using some or all of the bowl shapes as guidelines.

The following are basic shapes in this book:

Bell—a round-bottomed bowl with a flared top.

Cupped—a round bowl smaller at the top than at the widest point.

Flared—usually a tapered bowl with the upper edge flared outward.

Ovoid—an oval or egg-shaped bowl.

Straight—a bowl shape in which the sides are parallel.

Tapered—a cone-shaped or V-shaped bowl.

Touraine—a bowl with a specific complex curve, forming a double bulge in the bowl.

Tulip—a round-bottomed bowl with the top first cupped in and then flared out, usually fairly sharply.

Plain stemware causes the most confusion for those trying to identify a specific line. Plain stems can be either pressed or simply pulled from the bottom of the bowl when it is blown. If a horizontal joint line can be seen between the bowl and the stem, then it was pressed and the bowl attached to it. (An exception to this is when the entire piece is pressed.) On both styles a foot is applied and formed by hand.

Some plain stemware is easily identified because of unique bowl shapes, but often many of these stems are practically the same from company to company. Since most glass companies made many types of plain stems, the best way to identify them is by a decoration on the piece.

Another facet of identifying stemware is determining the specific piece. When all stems of a pattern are almost identical in shape and

Attaching a foot to a goblet

1

the capacity varies only by an ounce, sometimes less, it is quite difficult to decide which piece is which. To help decide, remember that stem lines are based on the goblet shape. Shapes of other pieces in the line conform to the goblet shape or to a standard industry shape, i.e. sherries often have a trumpet-shaped bowl with a slight flare at the top, regardless of the goblet shape. Learn the goblet shape. Become familiar with the sizes of pieces listed. A stem with the goblet shape but only about half the capacity of a goblet is probably a claret. Further, if the piece holds only about a third of a full goblet, it is a wine. The following will help in identifying specific stems and will give the original purpose of each item.

Goblet—the standard shape with which to compare other stems in the line. Originally used for water at a formal table setting.

Claret—the same shape as a goblet, but holding only about half as much. Made for claret or other wines, as the name implies.

Wine—the same shape as a goblet, but holding only about a third as much. Used for various wines.

Cordial—the same shape as a goblet, but holding only about 1 ounce. Used for cordials.

Saucer Champagne—has a broader and shallower bowl than a goblet. Used for serving champagne. Sometimes sold for a dual purpose as a high-stemmed sherbet.

Cocktail—has a short, broad bowl. Used for mixed drinks.

Parfait—has a slender elongated bowl just wide enough to accept a dessert spoon. Sometimes also used for juice.

Oyster Cocktail or Seafood Cocktail—a fairly broad bowl. It has little or no stem portion.

Sherbet—similar in shape to the Saucer Champagne, but on a low stem.

Sherry—a small bowled stem, containing less than an ounce to 2 ounces. Shape of bowl may vary from the rest of the stem line, usually being fairly deep and flared. Used for sherry wine.

Brandy—a small bowled stem holding an ounce or less. Used for serving brandies.

There are a few other stems which have various names.

Footed Juice—has a tall slender bowl, short stem, and holds about 4 ounces. Used for juice. Some companies at first called these "sodas" and sometimes other names such as "seltzers."

Footed Iced Tea—has a tall bowl holding about 12 to 13 oz., with a short stem. Originally used for serving iced tea. Other original names include "footed soda."

Today's collectors have changed the purpose of some stems. For instance, goblets today are often used to serve wine. What formerly was a footed iced tea is then used for serving water. Saucer champagnes have gone out of favor with today's hostess, who usually prefers to serve champagne from tall, narrow bowled champagne flutes.

Below are examples of typical stem lines to help identify specific pieces.

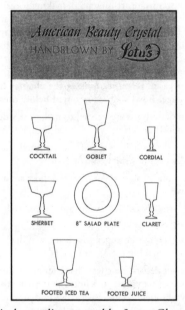

Typical stem line as used by Lotus Glass Co., from original flyer

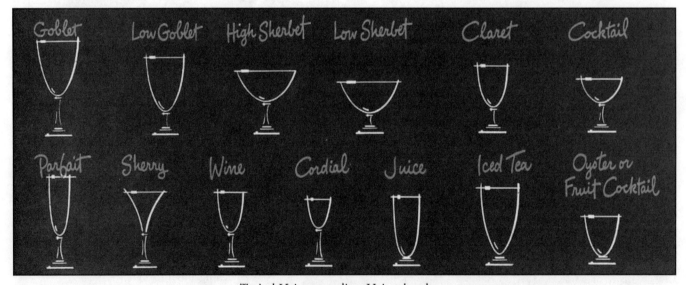

Typical Heisey stem line, Heisey brochure

*This chapter contains several of the animal figural stems made by several companies. Libbey Glass began this trend with its Silhouette pattern, designed by Douglas Nash. Other companies such as Heisey and Morgantown followed with a few specialized items of their own. **The following prices are for undecorated items.***

BANTAM ROOSTER

Date: 1951

Manufacturer: A.H. Heisey & Co., Newark, OH

Colors: Crystal

Notes: One of three rooster stems made to match No. 4225 Cobel cocktail shakers with rooster-head stoppers.

    Cocktail $500.00

CHANTICLEER, NO. 5038

Date: 1942

Manufacturer: A.H. Heisey & Co., Newark, OH

Colors: Crystal

Decorations: No. 9012 Victory etching, "Me" or "You" to match a cocktail shaker engraved "Us," No. 904 Rialto cutting, No. 926 George VI cutting, No. 980 Moonglo cutting

Notes: One of the Roosters used with the Heisey No. 4225 Cocktail shaker with rooster-head stopper.

    Cocktail, 3½ oz. $70.00
    Cocktail with Victory etching 85.00

GOOSE

Date: 1948

Manufacturer: A.H. Heisey & Co., Newark, OH

Colors: Crystal. Rare with Amber stem, crystal bowl

Decorations: Goose may be satin-finished. No. 941 Barcelona cutting

Notes: Heisey made a matching Goose decanter.

    Cocktail, 4 oz. $175.00
    Cordial, 1 oz. 350.00
    Sherry, 2 oz. 350.00
    Wine, 3 oz. 225.00

HORSE HEAD, NO. 5066

Date: 1948

Manufacturer: A.H. Heisey & Co., Newark, OH

Colors: Crystal only

Decorations: No. 980 Moonglo cutting

Notes: Blown bowl, pressed stem. Made to match the No. 4225 Cobel cocktail shaker with a horse-head stopper.

    Cocktail $400.00
    Sherry 500.00

L to R: Goose stem sherry, Barcelona Cut; Bantam Rooster cocktail; Chanticleer cocktail with Victory etch; Rooster Head cocktail with special, unknown cutting; Horse Head sherry. Colt (not illustrated) was made in a cocktail in crystal, 1951. All by Heisey.

ROOSTER HEAD, NO. 5048

Date: 1947

Manufacturer: A.H. Heisey & Co., Newark, OH

Colors: Crystal, Crystal bowl with Amber stem

Decorations: No. 467 Tally Ho etching. No. 980 Moonglo cutting. Occasionally found with elaborate Heisey cuttings.

Notes: The easiest to find rooster stem made to match Heisey's No. 4225 Cobel cocktail shaker with rooster-head stopper.

    Cocktail, 3½ oz. $65.00

SEA HORSE

Date: 1950

Manufacturer: A.H. Heisey & Co., Newark, OH

Colors: Crystal, Crystal bowl Amber stem

Notes: Blown bowl, pressed stem. Some have a wide swirl optic in the bowl.

    Cocktail, crystal $150.00
    Cocktail, amber stem 600.00

ANIMALS & HUMANS (continued)

Jockey cocktail,
Crystal bowl, Amber stem

Rooster cocktail

Rooster Head cocktail

Silhouette sherry,
Monkey stem, Moonstone

Original Ad: Top Hat cocktail

JOCKEY

Date: Unknown

Manufacturer: Morgantown Glass, Morgantown, WV

Colors: Crystal, Crystal bowl with Amber stem and foot

Notes: Made for Gulfstream race track. Some Morgantown items have peacock optic bowls. The stems were continued by Imperial Glass Co.

Cocktail $95.00

ROOSTER

Date: 1930s

Manufacturer: Morgantown Glass, Morgantown, WV

Colors: Crystal. Various colors in combination with Crystal

Notes: Cocktail shakers with the rooster as a stopper were also made. For colors add 100% to 200%.

Cocktail, Crystal $22.00

ROOSTER HEAD

Date: Unknown

Manufacturer: Unknown

Colors: Crystal. Various color combinations, mostly pastels, combined with Crystal

Notes: We have been unsuccessful in determining the maker of these attractive cocktails. They are usually of moderate quality, but the various colors make them very pretty.

Cocktail, any color with crystal $35.00

SILHOUETTE

Date: Ca. 1933

Manufacturer: Libbey Glass Co., Toledo, OH

Colors: Crystal bowls with stems in Black, Moonstone (opalescent)

Decorations: None known

Notes: Blown bowl, pressed stem. No optic. Designed by A. Douglas Nash, Libbey's designer. Each stem is a different animal, listed below.

Bowl, Center (elephant) . . . . $700.00+
Candlesticks, pr. (camel) . . . . 1000.00+
Champagne (squirrel) 200.00
Champagne, Hollow Stem (squirrel) 200.00
Claret (bear) 175.00
Cocktail (kangaroo) 175.00
Compote, 6" (giraffe) . . . . 700.00+
Cordial (greyhound) 300.00
Goblet (cat) 300.00
Sherbet (rabbit) 115.00
Sherry (monkey) 160.00

TOP HAT

Date: 1942

Manufacturer: Morgantown Glass, Morgantown, WV

Colors: Crystal, Crystal stem and foot with bowls in Stiegel Green, Ritz Blue, Spanish Red and various pastels, Amber stem and foot with Crystal bowl

Notes: Made for New York's Knickerbocker Hotel. This ad appeared in September 1942 and referred to them as Hi-Hat cocktails.

Cocktail $140.00

Chapter 2
BEADS

Several companies used beads or balls to good effect in designing stems. The following are a sampling of those that may be found today. **The following prices are for undecorated items.**

BELL SHAPED BOWL

CANDLEWICK, NO. 3400

Date: 1936

Manufacturer: Imperial Glass Corp., Bellaire, OH

Colors: Crystal

Decorations: No. 108 cutting, No. 279 cutting

Notes: Blown bowl, pressed stem. Made to match Candlewick tableware.

Claret, 5 oz..	$50.00
Cocktail, 4 oz.	18.00
Cordial, 1 oz..	42.00
Finger Bowl, Footed.	30.00
Goblet, 9 oz. (4-Bead Stem)	25.00
Oyster Cocktail, 4 oz. (1-Bead Stem)	18.00
Parfait, 6 oz. (1-Bead Stem)	42.00
Saucer Champagne or Sherbet, 6 oz.	16.00
Seafood Icer or Fruit Cocktail with insert (1-Bead)	75.00
Sherbet, Low, 5 oz. (1-Bead Stem)	14.00
Tumbler, Footed, 9 oz. (1-Bead Stem).	22.00
Tumbler, Iced Tea, Footed, 12 oz. (1-Bead Stem).	17.00
Tumbler, Water, Footed, 10 oz. (1-Bead Stem)	17.00
Wine, 4 oz.	24.00

Candlewick No. 3400 Goblet and Saucer Champagne

OVOID BOWL

NO. 1025

Date: 1931

Manufacturer: Seneca Glass Co., Morgantown, WV

Colors: Dark Blue, Light Blue, Dark Green, Light Green, Amber, Amethyst

Decorations: Unknown

Notes: Blown bowl, pressed stem. Prices are for Crystal. Add 50% for colors.

Brandy	$40.00
Cordial	50.00
Goblet.	20.00
Cocktail	18.00

Original Ad: No. 1025 stemware

OVOID BOWL *(continued)*

Tear Drop No. 5301
Liquor Cocktail

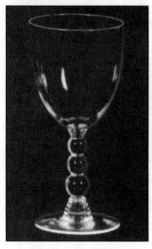

Terrace No.5111½ Terrace
Tall Stem Goblet

No. 4024 Victorian Goblet
with Embassy Cutting

TEAR DROP, NO. 5301

Date: 1935

Manufacturer: Duncan & Miller Glass Co.,
Washington, PA

Colors: Crystal

Notes: Blown bowl, pressed stem. Made to
match Tear Drop tableware.

Claret, 4 oz., 5½" tall	$15.00
Cocktail, Liquor, 3½ oz., 4½" tall	15.00
Cordial, 1 oz., 4" tall	25.00
Finger Bowl, 4½"	12.00
Goblet, Ale, 8 oz., 6¼" tall	20.00
Goblet, 9 oz., 7" tall	10.00
Goblet, Luncheon, 9 oz., 5¾" tall	10.00
Ice Cream (sherbet), 4 oz. or 5 oz., 3½" tall	8.00
Iced Tea or Hi-ball, 12 oz., 5½" tall or 14 oz., 6" tall	10.00
Juice, Orange, Footed, 4½ oz., 4" tall	10.00
Oyster Cocktail, Footed, 3½ oz., 2¾" tall	10.00
Saucer Champagne or Tall Sherbet, 5 oz., 5" tall	10.00
Sherbet, Footed, 5 oz., 2½" tall	8.00
Sherry, 1¾ oz., 4½" tall	25.00
Split or Party Glass, Footed, 8 oz., 5" tall	10.00
Tumbler, Footed, 9 oz., 4½" tall	10.00
Whiskey or Cocktail, Footed, 3 oz., 3" tall	12.00
Whiskey, Footed, 2 oz., 2¾" tall	15.00
Wine, 3 oz., 4¾" tall	15.00

TERRACE, NO. 5111½

Date: 1935

Manufacturer: Duncan & Miller Glass Co.,
Washington, PA

Colors: Crystal

Decorations: First Love etching

Notes: Blown bowl, pressed stem. Made to
match Terrace tableware.

Claret, Tall Stem, 4½ oz., 6" tall	$17.00
Cocktail, Liquor, 3½ oz., 4½" tall	17.00
Cordial, 1 oz., 3¾" tall	30.00
Finger Bowl, 4"	12.00
Goblet, Luncheon, Low, 10 oz., 5¾" tall	12.00
Goblet, Tall Stem, 10 oz., 6¾" tall	18.00
Ice Cream, Short Stem, Footed (sherbet), 5 oz., 4" tall	8.00
Iced Tea, Footed, 12 oz., 6½" tall	12.00
Iced Tea, Footed, 14 oz., 6¾" tall	15.00
Orange Juice, Footed, 5 oz., 5¼" tall	12.00
Oyster Cocktail, 4 oz., 3¾" tall	8.00
Pousse Café, 1 oz., 3¾" tall	30.00
Saucer Champagne, Tall Stem, 5 oz., 5" tall	15.00
Whiskey, Footed, 3 oz., 4½" tall	15.00
Wine, 3 oz., 5¼" tall	17.00

VICTORIAN, NO. 4024

Date: 1933

Manufacturer: Fostoria Glass Co.,
Moundsville, WV

Colors: Crystal. Crystal stem and foot with
colored bowls in: Burgundy, Empire Green,
Regal Blue, Ruby

Decorations: Silver Mist (satin), No. 89
Elsinore double needle etching, No. 725
Manhattan rock crystal cutting, No. 726
Meteor cutting, No. 727 National cutting,
No. 728 Embassy cutting, No. 732 Seaweed
cutting, No. 733 Marquette rock crystal cutting

Notes: Blown bowl, pressed stem and foot.

	Crystal	Colors
Claret-Wine, 3½ oz., 4½" tall	$27.00	$32.00
Cocktail, 4 oz., 3⅝" tall	20.00	26.00
Cordial, 1 oz., 3⅛" tall	35.00	60.00
Goblet, 10 oz., 5⅝" tall	27.00	32.00
Goblet, 11 oz., 6⅞" tall	27.00	32.00
Iced Tea, Footed, 12 oz., 5½" tall	27.00	32.00
Juice, Footed, 5 oz., 4¼" tall	22.00	28.00
Oyster Cocktail, 4 oz., 3⅜" tall	15.00	20.00
Rhine Wine, 3½ oz., 5⅞" tall	27.00	32.00
Saucer Champagne, 6½ oz., 4½" tall	24.00	30.00
Sherbet, 5½ oz., 3⅞" tall	18.00	24.00
Sherry, 2 oz., 3⅞" tall	27.00	32.00
Tumbler, Footed, 8 oz., 4¾" tall	22.00	28.00
Whiskey, Footed, 1½ oz., 2½" tall	22.00	27.00

(continued) OVOID BOWL

WESTCHESTER, NO. 6012

Date: 1934

Manufacturer: Fostoria Glass Co., Moundsville, WV

Colors: Crystal. Crystal stem and foot with Colored bowl: Burgundy, Empire Green, Regal Blue, Ruby

Decorations: No. 318 Springtime, No. 323 Rambler etching. Rambler etching with gold trim is No. 615 etching. No. 738 Festoon cutting, No. 739 Rock Garden cutting, No. 740 Rondeau cutting, No. 741 Watercress cutting, No. 742 Orbit cutting, No. 743 Heraldry cutting, No. 744 Regency cutting, No. 745 Ivy rock crystal cutting, No. 746 Gossamer cutting, No. 763 Cyrene cutting, No. 764 Pierette rock crystal cutting, No. 616 St. Regis cut and gold encrusted rim. Mother of Pearl iridescence on crystal bowl.

Notes: Blown bowl, pressed stem, plain. Used for plate etchings, cuttings and gold bands. For cuttings add about 25% to crystal prices.

Brandy, 1 oz., 4" tall	$30.00
Claret, 4½ oz., 5¾" tall	24.00
Cocktail, 3 oz.,4⅝" tall	21.00
Cordial, 1 oz., 3½" tall	30.00
Creme de Menthe, 2 oz., 4½" tall	23.00
Goblet, 10 oz., 6⅞" tall	24.00
Oyster Cocktail, Footed, 4 oz., 3½" tall	14.00
Rhine Wine, 4½ oz.	24.00
Saucer Champagne, 5½ oz., 5" (high sherbet)	22.00
Sherbet, Low, 5½ oz., 4" tall	15.00
Sherry, 2 oz., 4½" tall	24.00
Wine, 3 oz., 5¼" tall	24.00
Tumbler, Footed, 5 oz., 4¼" tall (juice)	15.00
Tumbler, Footed, 10 oz., 5⅜" tall (water)	17.00
Tumbler, Footed, 13 oz., 5¾" tall (iced tea)	21.00

Original Catalog Illustration: No. 6012 Westchester stems with No. 323 Rambler etching

STRAIGHT BOWL

GASCONY, NO. 3397

Date: 1932

Manufacturer: A.H. Heisey & Co., Newark, OH

Colors: Crystal, Sahara. Crystal foot with Tangerine bowl. Some with crystal foot and Stiegel Blue bowl (cobalt)

Decorations: Etchings: No. 448 Old Colony, No. 452 Ambassador, No. 453 Inca, No. 455 Sportsman, No. 456 Titania, No. 457 Springtime, No. 458 Olympiad, No. 459 Fisherman, No. 460 Club Drinking Scene, No. 462 Fox Chase, No. 465 Golf Scene, No. 467 Tally Ho

Notes: Blown bowl, pressed foot. For Sahara, add 100%. For Tangerine, add 600-700%.

Cocktail, 3 oz.	$15.00
Decanter & Stopper, Footed, 1 pt.	125.00
Goblet, Low Footed, 11 oz.	40.00
Oyster Cocktail, 4 oz.	15.00
Pitcher, Tomato Juice	90.00
Saucer Champagne, 6 oz.	25.00
Sherbet, 6 oz.	15.00
Soda, Footed, 5 oz.	15.00
Soda, Footed, 10 oz.	20.00
Soda, Footed, 12 oz.	25.00
Soda, Footed, 14 oz.	30.00
Soda, Footed, 18 oz.	40.00
Tumbler, Footed, 10 oz.	30.00
Wine, 2½ oz.	40.00

No. 3397 Gascony soda with No. 458 Olympiad etching

TOURAINE SHAPED BOWL

NO. 503

Date: 1930s

Manufacturer: Duncan & Miller Glass Co., Washington, PA

Colors: Crystal

Decorations: No. 640 Laurel Wreath cutting, No. 782 Bridal Bow cutting

Notes: Blown bowl, pressed stem.

Cigarette Holder, 3¼" tall	$12.00
Claret, 5 oz., 5½" tall	15.00
Cocktail, Liquor, 3½ oz., 4½" tall	15.00
Cordial, 1 oz., 3½" tall	25.00
Creme de Menthe, 2 oz., 4" tall	15.00
Goblet, 10 oz., 6½" tall	15.00
Goblet, 9 oz., 6¾" tall	15.00
Goblet, Luncheon, 10 oz., 5" tall	12.00
Ice Cream (sherbet), 5 oz., 3½" tall	8.00
Iced Tea, Footed, 12 oz., 6½" tall	10.00
Juice, Orange, Footed, 5 oz., 4¼" tall	10.00
Oyster Cocktail, 3½ oz., 3¾" tall	8.00
Saucer Champagne, 5 oz., 4¾" tall	12.00
Sherry, 2 oz., 4¾" tall	15.00
Tumbler, Footed, 9 oz., 5½" tall	10.00
Whiskey, Footed, 2 oz., 3¼" tall	15.00
Wine, 2½ oz., 4¾" tall	15.00

Original Catalog Illustration: No. 503 Touraine Saucer Champagne

Chapter 3
FLUTES OR PANELS

Flutes and panels are primarily flat surfaces made up to form a stem, but variations can have slight hollows in the panels. This type of stem is very old, as it has been made almost since stems were created. The following prices are for undecorated items.

BELL SHAPED BOWL

Original Catalog Illustration: No. 5375 goblet, saucer champagne and claret

DIAMOND, NO. 5375

Date: 1940

Manufacturer: Duncan & Miller Glass Co., Washington, PA

Colors: Crystal, Ruby bowl with crystal stem

Decorations: Charmaine Rose etching, No. 697 Chantilly cutting, No. 706 Florentine cutting, No. 776 Queen's Lace cutting, No. 778 Garland cutting

Notes: Blown bowl, pressed stem. Made to match No. 75 Diamond pattern of tableware brought out to celebrate the 75th anniversary. Designed by Robert A. May. For Ruby add 50%.

Cocktail, Liquor, 3½ oz., 5" tall	$12.00
Cordial, 1 oz., 4¼" tall	45.00
Goblet, 9 oz., 7¼" tall	18.00
Iced Tea, 12 oz., 6½" tall	18.00
Orange Juice, 5 oz., 4¾" tall	12.00
Oyster Cocktail, 4½ oz., 3¾" tall	9.00
Saucer Champagne, 5½ oz., 5½" tall	18.00
Wine, 3 oz., 5¾" tall	20.00

KENT, NO. 33

Date: Ca. 1930s

Manufacturer: Duncan & Miller Glass Co., Washington, PA

Colors: Crystal

Decorations: No. 628 Marlborough cutting, No. 629 Wellington cutting, No. 720 Palmetto cutting

Notes: Blown bowl, pressed stem.

Claret, 4½ oz., 6¾" high	$15.00
Cocktail, 4 oz., 6" high	12.00
Cordial, 1 oz., 3¾" high	45.00
Finger Bowl, 4½"	8.00
Goblet, 10 oz., 7¾" high	18.00
Iced Tea, Footed, 12 oz., 7" high	18.00
Orange Juice, Footed, 6 oz., 5¼" tall	12.00
Oyster Cocktail, 4 oz., 4" high	9.00
Saucer Champagne, 6 oz., 6¾" high	18.00
Wine, 3 oz., 6" high	20.00

Original Catalog Illustration: No. 33 Kent stemware,
No. 628 Marlborough cutting and No. 629 Wellington cutting

(continued) BELL SHAPED BOWL

KIMBERLY, NO. 4091

Date: 1937

Manufacturer: A.H. Heisey & Co., Newark, OH

Colors: Crystal. Rare in Zircon bowl with Crystal stem and foot.

Decorations: Etchings: No. 495 Polo Player, No. 496 Skier, No. 497 Rosalie. Cuttings: No. 844½ Cromwell, No. 893 Carlton, No. 895 Waterford, No. 896 Sungate, No. 919 Laurel Wreath, No. 920 Gray Laurel Wreath, No. 941 Barcelona, No. 943 Belfast, No. 944 Courtship, No. 945 Virginia, No. 956 Everest, No. 973 Ceylon, No. 1015 Dolly Madison Rose, No. 1016 Botticelli

Notes: Blown bowl, pressed stem. Made plain or with Saturn optic. Used with No. 1488 Kohinoor table accessories.

Claret, 4½ oz.	$25.00
Cocktail, 3 oz.	22.00
Cordial, 1 oz.	75.00
Finger Bowl (No. 3335)	10.00
Goblet, 10 oz.	28.00
Goblet, Low Foot, 10 oz.	24.00
Oyster Cocktail, 4½ oz. (No. 3542)	10.00
Saucer Champagne, 5½ oz.	20.00
Sherbet, 5½ oz.	15.00
Soda, Footed, 5 oz. (No. 4091½)	15.00
Soda, Footed, 12 oz. (No. 4091½)	15.00
Wine, 2 oz.	40.00

Original Catalog Illustration:
No. 4091 Kimberly
saucer champagne

NO. 6010

Date: 1933

Manufacturer: Fostoria Glass Co., Moundsville, WV

Colors: Crystal

Decorations: No. 317 Sheraton etching, No. 722 Wellington rock crystal cutting, No. 722½ Leicester rock crystal cutting, No. 723 Westminster rock crystal cutting

Notes: Blown bowl, pressed stem. Made in regular optic.

Claret-Wine, 4¼ oz.	$25.00
Cocktail, 4 oz.	18.00
Cordial, 1 oz.	50.00
Goblet, 9 oz.	20.00
Oyster Cocktail, 5½ oz.	12.00
Sherbet, High, 5½ oz.	18.00
Sherbet, Low, 5½ oz.	12.00
Tumbler, Footed, 5 oz. (juice)	18.00
Tumbler, Footed, 9 oz. (water)	18.00
Tumbler, Footed, 12 oz. (iced tea)	20.00

Original Catalog Illustration:
No. 6010 cocktail with
No. 317 Sheraton etching

OLD GLORY, NO. 3333

Date: 1919

Manufacturer: A.H. Heisey & Co., Newark, OH

Colors: Crystal, Hawthorne

Decorations: Several needle etchings. No. 161 Somerset pantograph etching. No. 366 Peacock etching, No. 413 Renaissance etching, No. 425 Dogwood etching, No. 456 Titania, No. 457 Springtime. Cuttings: No. 657 Liberty, No. 679 Windsor, No. 864 Blue Willow, No. 880 Salem, No. 887 Southampton, No. 906 Windemere, No. 907 Cheerio

Notes: Blown bowl, pressed stem. Josef Balda designed Renaissance etching and probably Old Glory stemware for Heisey. Add 150% for Hawthorne.

Burgundy, 3 oz.	$22.00
Claret, 4½ oz.	22.00
Cocktail, 3 oz. or 2½ oz.	22.00
Comport, High Footed, 6"	55.00
Cordial, 1 oz.	45.00
Finger Bowl (No. 3309)	10.00
Goblet, 8 oz. or 9 oz.	24.00
Grape Fruit, Footed	25.00
Grape Juice, 6 oz.	28.00
Iced Tea, Footed, Handled, 12 oz. (No. 3476)	28.00
Oyster Cocktail, 4½ oz. (No. 3542)	10.00
Parfait, 4½ oz.	25.00
Pousse Café, ¾ oz.	55.00
Saucer Champagne, 5½ oz.	20.00
Sherry, 2 oz.	27.00
Soda, Footed 12 oz. (No. 3476)	20.00
Sundae or Sherbet, 5½ oz.	12.00
Wine, 2 oz.	25.00

Original Catalog Illustration:
No. 3333 Old Glory goblet
and parfait

BELL SHAPED BOWL *(continued)*

Original Heisey Pattern Folder:
No. 341 Old Williamsburg goblet

OLD WILLIAMSBURG, NO. 341

Date: The pattern first appeared in the early 1900s. Stemware listed here became popular in the 1930s and 1940s.

Manufacturer: A.H. Heisey & Co., Newark, OH

Colors: Crystal. Rare in Cobalt, Dawn (gray), Alexandrite, Amber, Limelight. Other colors were made by Imperial Glass Corp. after 1957.

Notes: All pressed. Originally this stem line was No. 373 introduced by Heisey about 1912. Later it replaced the original No. 341 stem line and became Old Williamsburg. Due to its long life, other pieces were made. Made to match No. 341 Old Williamsburg table ware, a large colonial line.

Claret	$24.00
Cocktail, 3 oz.	20.00
Goblet, 9 oz.	25.00
Goblet, Low Footed	25.00
Iced Tea, Footed, 12 oz.	22.00
Juice, Footed	15.00
Oyster Cocktail	10.00
Sherbet, Low, 4½ oz.	10.00
Sherbet, Tall, 5 oz.	10.00
Wine, 2 oz.	18.00

Original Catalog Illustration:
No. 5321 Trianon stemware,
No. 683 Tiara cutting

TRIANON, NO. 5321

Date: 1930s

Manufacturer: Duncan & Miller Glass Co., Washington, PA

Colors: Crystal

Decorations: Adoration etching, No. 683 Tiara cutting, No. 695 Viceroy cutting, No. 705 Blossom Time cutting.

Notes: Blown bowl, pressed stem.

Claret, 5 oz., 6¾" tall $15.00
Cocktail, Liquor, 3 oz., 5½" high 12.00

Cordial, 1 oz., 4½" tall	45.00
Finger Bowl, 4½"	8.00
Goblet, 10 oz., 7½" tall	18.00
Ice Cream, Footed, 6 oz., 3½" tall (sherbet)	9.00
Iced Tea, Footed, 13 oz., 6¼" tall	18.00
Oyster Cocktail, 4½ oz., 3½" tall	12.00
Saucer Champagne or Tall Sherbet, 6 oz., 6" high	18.00
Wine, 3 oz., 6¼" tall	20.00

No. 5331 Victory stems with
Eternally Yours cutting

VICTORY, NO. 5331

Date: 1930s

Manufacturer: Duncan & Miller Glass Co., Washington, PA

Colors: Crystal

Decorations: Language of Flowers etching, No. 763 Prelude cutting, No. 765 Eternally Yours cutting, No. 764 Lexington cutting, No. 772 Victory cutting

Notes: Blown bowl, pressed stem.

Claret, 5 oz., 6" high $15.00
Cocktail, Liquor, 3½ oz., 4½" high 12.00

Cordial, 1 oz., 4¼" tall	45.00
Finger Bowl, 4½"	8.00
Goblet, 10 oz., 7½" high	18.00
Ice Cream, Footed, 5 oz., 6¾" tall (sherbet)	9.00
Iced Tea, Footed, 13 oz., 7½" tall	18.00
Orange Juice, Footed, 5 oz., 5½" tall	12.00
Oyster Cocktail, 4½ oz., 4¾" tall	9.00
Saucer Champagne or Tall Sherbet, 6 oz., 4¾" high	18.00
Sherry, 2 oz., 4¾" tall	30.00
Tumbler, Footed, 10 oz., 7" tall	12.00
Wine, 3 oz., 5¾" high	20.00

CUPPED BOWL

KING ARTHUR, NO. 3357

Date: 1925

Manufacturer: A.H. Heisey & Co., Newark, OH

Colors: Crystal, Flamingo. Crystal bowl with Moongleam or Flamingo stem and foot.

Decorations: No. 168 Adam etching, No. 170 Cleopatra etching, No. 442 Diana etching

Notes: Blown bowl, pressed stem. Made with diamond optic or plain. A similar stemware line is No. 3355 Fairacre, which has a small flared rim but is otherwise the same as King Arthur.

Cocktail, 4 oz.	$22.00
Cordial, 1 oz.	60.00
Finger Bowl	8.00
Goblet, 10 oz.	22.00
Goblet, Luncheon, 10 oz.	22.00
Iced Tea, Footed, 12 oz.	18.00
Oyster Cocktail, 3¾ oz.	12.00
Parfait, 5 oz.	20.00
Saucer Champagne, 6½ oz.	18.00
Sherbet, 6½ oz.	15.00
Wine, 2½ oz.	30.00

Original Catalog Illustration:
No. 3357 King Arthur
saucer champagne

OLD DOMINION, NO. 3380

Date: 1930

Manufacturer: A.H. Heisey & Co., Newark, OH

Colors: Crystal, Flamingo, Sahara. Crystal stem and foot with Marigold or Moongleam bowl. Crystal bowl with Alexandrite or Moongleam stem and foot.

Decorations: No. 447 Empress etching, No. 448 Old Colony etching, No. 456 Titania etching

Notes: Blown bowl, pressed stem. For Flamingo, Moongleam and Sahara, add 100%. For Marigold, add 125%. For Alexandrite, add 500%.

Bar, 1 oz.	$25.00
Bar, 2 oz.	22.00
Claret, 4 oz.	20.00

Cocktail, 3 oz.	15.00
Cordial, 1 oz.	55.00
Finger Bowl (4075)	12.00
Goblet, Short Stem, 10 oz.	22.00
Goblet, Tall Stem, 10 oz.	22.00
Grape Fruit, Footed	25.00
Oyster Cocktail	12.00
Parfait, 5 oz.	20.00
Saucer Champagne, Short Stem, 6 oz.	20.00
Saucer Champagne, Tall Stem, 6 oz.	20.00
Sherbet, 6 oz.	12.00
Soda or Iced Tea, 12 oz.	18.00
Soda, 5 oz.	15.00
Soda, 8 oz.	15.00
Soda, 16 oz.	20.00
Tumbler, Footed, 10 oz.	12.00
Wine, 2½ oz.	22.00

No. 3380 Old Dominion goblet

FLARED BOWL

ALBEMARLE, NO. 3368

Date: 1928

Manufacturer: A.H. Heisey & Co., Newark, OH

Colors: Crystal, Flamingo, Crystal with Moongleam stem and foot, Marigold with Crystal stem and foot.

Decorations: No. 447 Trojan double plate etching. No. 867 Chateau cutting, No. 904 Rialto cutting, No. 909 Champlain

Notes: Blown bowl, pressed stem. Made with diamond optic bowls. Marked on the stem below the knop. Add 50% for Flamingo and Moongleam. Add 125% for Marigold.

Bar, Footed, 1½ oz.	$18.00
Claret, 4 oz.	18.00
Cocktail, 3 oz.	12.00
Comport, High Footed, 7"	50.00
Cordial, 1 oz.	50.00
Finger Bowl (3309)	10.00
Goblet, 8 oz.	22.00
Oyster Cocktail, 3 oz.	10.00
Parfait, 4½ oz.	24.00
Saucer Champagne, 5 oz.	22.00
Sherbet, 5 oz.	12.00
Soda, 5 oz.	12.00
Soda, 8 oz.	15.00
Soda or Iced Tea, 12 oz.	15.00
Tumbler, Footed, 10 oz.	15.00
Wine, 2½ oz.	20.00

Original Catalog Illustration:
No. 3368 Albemarle
goblet and claret

FLARED BOWL *(continued)*

No. 1953 Sherbet

CATHEDRAL, No. 1953

Date: 1953

Manufacturer: Cambridge Glass Co., Cambridge, OH

Colors: Crystal

Decorations: Ambassador rock crystal engraving, Joan of Arc rock crystal engraving, Old Master rock crystal engraving, No. 10 Old English rock crystal engraving, Silver Wheat rock crystal engraving, No. 1084 rock crystal engraving.

Notes: Blown bowl, pressed stem

Cocktail	$20.00
Goblet	18.00
Sherbet	9.00
Tumbler, Footed, 5 oz.	9.00
Tumbler, Footed, 12 oz.	18.00

Original Catalog Illustration: No. A56 Today goblet

TODAY, No. A56

Date: Ca. 1953

Manufacturer: Cambridge Glass Co., Cambridge, OH

Colors: Crystal

Decorations: Formal rock crystal engraving, No. 2P Roses rock crystal engraving, No. 8P Tomorrow rock crystal engraving.

Notes: Blown bowl, pressed stem

Claret	$20.00
Cocktail	12.00
Cordial	48.00
Goblet	18.00
Iced Tea, Footed, 12 oz.	18.00
Sherbet	8.00
Tumbler, Footed, 5 oz. (juice)	9.00
Wine	30.00

OVOID BOWL

Original Catalog Illustration: No. 3750 Charleston goblet

CHARLESTON, No. 3750

Date: Ca. 1940

Manufacturer: Cambridge Glass Co., Cambridge, OH

Colors: Crystal

Decorations: No. 1014 Bexley rock crystal engraving, No. 1053 Harvest rock crystal engraving, Euclid rock crystal engraving, Fuchsia rock crystal engraving, Hanover rock crystal engraving, Ivy rock crystal engraving, Meadow Rose rock crystal engraving, Minton Wreath rock crystal engraving. Gold band with hairline, D/460.

Notes: Blown bowl, pressed stem.

Claret, 4½ oz.	$20.00
Cocktail, 3½ oz.	12.00
Cordial, 1 oz.	48.00
Goblet, 10 oz.	18.00
Iced Tea, Footed, 12 oz.	18.00
Oyster Cocktail, 5 oz.	8.00
Sherbet, Low	8.00
Sherbet, Tall, 6 oz.	9.00
Tumbler, Footed, 5 oz. (juice)	9.00
Wine, 3 oz.	30.00

MOONSTONE, NO. 2882

Date: 1974

Manufacturer: Fostoria Glass Co., Moundsville, WV

Colors: Crystal, Apple Green, Pink, Blue, Yellow, Dark Blue, Brown

Decorations: None known

Notes: All pressed.

Goblet, 10 oz., 6½"	15.00
Highball, 15 oz., 5½"	15.00
Iced Tea, Footed, 13 oz., 6½" tall	15.00
Old Fashioned, Double, 12 oz., 4"	15.00
Sherbet, 7 oz., 5½"	12.00
Wine, 5 oz., 5⅛"	15.00

No. 2882 Moonstone wine

NO. 3135

Date: 1930

Manufacturer: Cambridge Glass Co., Cambridge, OH

Colors: Crystal, Amber, Emerald, Gold Krystol, Peach-Blo, Willow Blue

Decorations: No. 744 Apple Blossom etching, No. 746 Gloria etching

Notes: Blown bowl, pressed stem. Optic.

Cordial, 1 oz.	$55.00
Finger Bowl	9.00
Fruit Salad, 6 oz.	9.00
Goblet, 8 oz.	18.00
Oyster Cocktail, 4½ oz.	8.00
Plate, Finger Bowl	6.00
Sherbet, Low, 6 oz.	8.00
Sherbet, Tall, 6 oz.	9.00
Tumbler, Footed, 5 oz. (juice)	9.00
Tumbler, Footed, 10 oz. (water)	15.00
Tumbler, Footed, 12 oz. (iced tea)	18.00

Original Catalog Illustration: No. 3135 cocktail with No. 744 Apple Blossom etching

NO. 5098

Date: 1928

Manufacturer: Fostoria Glass Co., Moundsville, WV

Colors: Crystal, Azure, Gold Tint, Green, Rose. Crystal stem & foot with colored bowls: Amber, Azure, Gold Tint, Green, Rose, Topaz, Wisteria. Also made with Azure bowl and mother-of-pearl iridescence.

Decorations: No. 84 Camden needle etching, No. 278 Versailles etching, No. 279 June etching, No. 282 Acanthus plate etching, No. 305 Fern etching, No. 188 Berry cutting, No. 199 Delphine cutting, No. 41 Kingston gold band with Camden N.E.

Notes: Blown bowl, pressed stem. Made in regular optic. Prices are for crystal. For Amber, Green, Topaz, Gold Tint add 25%. For Rose or Azure add 75%. For Wisteria add 100%.

Claret, 4 oz., 6" tall	$18.00
Cocktail, 3 oz., 5⅛" tall	16.00
Cordial, ¾ oz., 3⅞" tall	32.00
Goblet, 10 oz., 8¼" tall	18.00
Oyster Cocktail, 5 oz., 3¾" tall	10.00
Parfait, 6 oz., 5¼" tall	18.00
Sherbet, High, 6 oz., 6" tall	17.00
Sherbet, Low, 6 oz., 4⅛" tall	11.00
Wine, 2½ oz., 5⅜" tall	18.00
Tumbler, Footed, 5 oz., 4⅜" tall (juice)	13.00
Tumbler, Footed, 9 oz., 5¼" tall (water)	13.00
Tumbler, Footed, 12 oz., 6" tall (iced tea)	18.00
Whiskey, Footed, 2½ oz., 2⅞" tall	18.00

Original Catalog Illustration: No. 5098 goblet with No. 278 Versailles etching

OVOID BOWL *(continued)*

No. 3350 Wabash goblet with
No. 440 Frontenac etching

WABASH, NO. 3350

Date: 1922

Manufacturer: A.H. Heisey & Co.,
Newark, OH

Colors: Crystal, Flamingo, Hawthorne, Crystal
stem and foot with Marigold bowl, Moongleam
stem and foot with Crystal bowl

Decorations: No. 166 Mayflower pantograph
etching, No. 439 Pied Piper double plate
etching, No. 440 Frontenac etching. No. 741
Chantilly cutting, No. 746 Mt. Vernon cutting,
No. 833 Royal York cutting, No. 941 Barcelona
cutting, No. 990 Mystic cutting.

Notes: Blown bowl, pressed stem. Patented by
Josef Balda for Heisey in 1926. Be aware that
Fenton made an all-pressed stem line very
similar to Wabash. Add 100% for Moongleam
or Flamingo. Add 400% for Hawthorne
or Marigold.

Claret, 4 oz.	$25.00
Cocktail, 3 oz.	18.00
Comport & Cover, 6"	60.00
Cordial, 1 oz.	60.00
Finger Bowl (2 styles)	12.00
Goblet, 10 oz.	25.00
Grape Fruit, Footed	25.00
Iced Tea, Footed & Handled, 12 oz.	27.00
Iced Tea, Footed, 12 oz.	20.00
Jug, Squat, 3 pt.	120.00
Oyster Cocktail, 4 oz.	12.00
Parfait, 5 oz.	22.00
Plate, 6" (pressed)	6.00
Saucer Champagne, 6 oz.	20.00
Sherbet, 6 oz.	14.00
Tankard, 3 pt.	120.00
Tumbler, Footed, 10 oz.	18.00

TAPERED BOWL

Original Catalog Illustration:
No. 3700 Dunkirk goblet

DUNKIRK, NO. 3700

Date: 1939

Manufacturer: Cambridge Glass Co.,
Cambridge, OH

Colors: Crystal

Decorations: No. 1005 Ardsley rock crystal
engraving (cut flutes at base of bowl), No. 1074
Cambridge Rose rock crystal engraving,
No. 821 King Edward rock crystal engraving,
Laurel Wreath rock crystal engraving, Manor
rock crystal engraving, Montrose rock crystal
engraving, Plymouth rock crystal engraving,
Strathmore rock crystal engraving, Tempo rock
crystal engraving, Wedding Band—gold band
with hairline

Notes: Blown bowl, pressed stem.

Claret, 4½ oz.	$15.00
Cocktail, 3 oz.	12.00
Cordial, 1 oz.	45.00
Goblet, 9 oz.	18.00
Iced Tea, Footed, 12 oz.	18.00
Oyster Cocktail, 4½ oz.	9.00
Sherbet, Low, 6 oz.	9.00
Sherbet, Tall, 6 oz.	9.00
Tumbler, Footed, 5 oz.	12.00
Tumbler, Footed, 10 oz.	12.00
Wine, 2½ oz.	20.00

No. 5082 goblet and high sherbet
with Eilene needle etching

NO. 5082

Date: 1924

Manufacturer: Fostoria Glass Co.,
Moundsville, WV

Colors: Crystal, Green. Crystal stem and foot
with colored bowls: Azure, Green, Rose. Crystal
bowl with colored stems: Amber, Blue, Green

Decorations: No. 74 Richmond needle etching,
No. 83 Eilene needle etching, No. 269 Rogene
etching, No. 270½ Mystic plate etching,
No. 272 Delphian plate etching, No. 167
Kenmore cutting, No. 43 Princess gold band of
Richmond N.E., No. 51 Duchess gold band of
Delphian P.E.

Notes: Blown bowl, pressed stem. Made in
regular, loop or spiral optics. Prices are for
Crystal. For Amber or Green add 20%. For
Rose, Azure or Blue add 75%.

Claret, 4½ oz., 5¾" tall	$22.00
Cocktail, 3 oz., 4½ oz. tall	17.00
Cordial, ¾ oz., 3¾" tall	35.00
Fruit, 5 oz., 3¾" tall (low sherbet)	22.00
Goblet, 9 oz., 7⅝" tall	18.00
Parfait, 6 oz.	22.00
Saucer Champagne, 5 oz., 5¼" tall	18.00
Wine, 2¾ oz., 5⅛" tall	22.00

STARDUST

Date: 1950

Manufacturer: Libbey Glass Co., Toledo, OH

Colors: Crystal

Decorations: Unknown

Notes: Blown bowl, pressed stem. Low priced stemware at $1.50 for four items in 1950. Rims have Libbey's patented safety rim called Safedge.

Champagne or Sherbet	$6.00
Goblet or Beverage	8.00
Juice or Parfait	5.00
Wine or Cocktail	6.00

Original Ad: Stardust

TIMELESS, No. 352

Date: 1953

Manufacturer: Seneca Glass Co., Morgantown, WV

Colors: Crystal

Decorations: No. 352-1 cutting, No. 352-2 cutting, No. 803 cutting, No. 1227 Fleur de Lis cutting, No. 1229 Caprice cutting, No. 1230 Marlboro cutting, No. 1231 cutting, No. 1252 cutting, No. 1254 Coronation cutting, No. 1262 Ardis cutting, No. 1263 Westwind cutting, No. 1330½ cutting, No. 1345½ cutting, No. 1380 cut flutes and notched stem "J" cutting

Notes: Blown bowl, pressed stem. There is a interior air trap teardrop at the top of the stem. Other pieces were no doubt made but are undocumented.

Goblet	$25.00

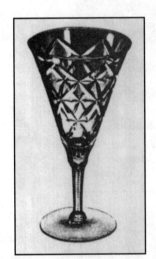

Original Catalog Illustration: No. 352 Timeless goblet

WINDSOR, No. 31

Date: 1930s

Manufacturer: Duncan & Miller Glass Co., Washington, PA

Colors: Crystal

Decorations: No. 645 Sherwood cutting, No. 717 Chesterfield cutting, No. 803 Bristol Diamond cutting

Notes: Blown bowl, pressed stem.

Claret, 4 oz., 5¾" tall	$15.00
Cocktail, Liquor, 3 oz., 4¾" tall	12.00
Cordial, 1 oz., 3¾" tall	45.00
Finger Bowl, 4¼"	8.00
Goblet, 9 oz., 7" tall	18.00
Iced Tea, Footed, 12 oz., 6½" tall	18.00
Orange Juice, Footed, 5 oz., 4¾" tall	12.00
Oyster Cocktail, 4 oz., 4" tall	9.00
Saucer Champagne, 5 oz., 4½" tall	18.00
Wine, 3 oz., 5½" tall	20.00

Original Catalog Illustration: No. 31 Windsor saucer champagne and liquor cocktail

Chapter 4
KNOPS

Knops in stemware refer to the bulge, button or sphere which is usually located in the middle of the stem to make it easier to hold the glass. **The following prices are for undecorated items.**

CUPPED BOWL

Original Catalog Illustration:
No. 3390 Carcassonne
goblet with tall stem

CARCASSONNE, NO. 3390

Date: 1930

Manufacturer: A.H. Heisey & Co., Newark, OH

Colors: Crystal, Crystal bowl with Moongleam stem and foot, Flamingo, Sahara, Steigel Blue bowl with Crystal stem and foot, Alexandrite bowl with Crystal stem and foot

Decorations: Etchings: No. 448 Old Colony, No. 450½ Formal Chintz, No. 451 Lafayette, No. 456 Titania, No. 457 Springtime, No. 458 Olympiad, No. 9010 Pan. Classic etching by Lotus Glass Co.

Notes: Blown bowl, pressed stem. May be marked with Diamond H on underside of foot. For Moongleam, Flamingo and Sahara, add 100%. For Steigel Blue (Cobalt) and Alexandrite, add 600%.

Bar, Footed, 2 oz.	$25.00
Cigarette Holder	22.00
Claret, 4 oz.	18.00
Cocktail, 3 oz.	17.00
Cordial, 1 oz.	50.00
Decanter, Footed, 1 pt.	110.00
Finger Bowl, Footed	12.00
Flagon, 12 oz.	45.00
Goblet, Short Stem, 11 oz.	22.00
Goblet, Tall Stem, 11 oz.	24.00
Jug, Footed, 3 pt.	150.00
Morning After, 10½ oz.	30.00
Oyster Cocktail, 3 oz.	15.00
Saucer Champagne, 6 oz.	17.00
Sherbet, 6 oz.	15.00
Soda, Footed, 5 oz.	15.00
Soda, Footed, 8 oz.	18.00
Soda or Iced Tea, 12 oz.	18.00
Vase, Footed, 8"	45.00
Wine, 2½ oz.	27.00

Original Catalog Illustration:
No. 1402 Tally Ho
lunch goblet and juice

TALLY HO, NO. 1402

Date: 1932

Manufacturer: Cambridge Glass Co., Cambridge, OH

Colors: Crystal, Amber, Amethyst, Carmen, Forest Green, Gold Krystol, Royal Blue

Decorations: Catawba etching, Grape etching, Imperial Hunt etching, No. 690 rock crystal engraving

Notes: All pressed. There are two other styles of Tally Ho stemware which are also listed in this book. On this line the decorations are known only on Crystal at this time. For other colors, add 75% to Crystal prices.

	Crystal	Carmen Royal Blue
Claret, 4½ oz.	$9.00	$26.00
Cocktail or Oyster Cocktail, Low Stem, 4 oz.	8.00	24.00
Cocktail, 3 oz.	9.00	24.00
Cordial, 1 oz.	18.00	55.00
Goblet, 10 oz.	12.00	30.00
Goblet, 14 oz.	14.00	35.00
Goblet, 18 oz.	20.00	45.00
Goblet, Lunch, 10 oz.	10.00	24.00
Juice, Tomato or Orange, Tall Stem, 6 oz.	7.00	24.00
Sherbet, Low, 6½ oz.	7.00	20.00
Sherbet, Tall, 7½ oz.	9.00	25.00
Wine, 2½ oz.	10.00	27.00

CUPPED BOWL

TALLY HO, NO. 1402/100

Date: 1932

Manufacturer: Cambridge Glass Co., Cambridge, OH

Colors: Crystal. The following colors with Crystal stem and foot and colored bowls: Amber, Amethyst, Carmen, Forest Green, Gold Krystol, Royal Blue

Decorations: Elaine etching, Minerva etching, Valencia etching, Lace Design No. D/1007 (silk screen in various colors), Yukon (etched bands), Platinum band. Elaine (D/1014), Minerva and Valencia are also known gold encrusted.

Notes: Blown bowl, pressed stem. For colors, add 75% to Crystal prices.

	Crystal	Carmen, Royal Blue
Brandy Inhaler, Tall	$18.00	$45.00
Claret	15.00	35.00
Cocktail	15.00	32.00
Cordial	18.00	38.00
Goblet	18.00	45.00
Oyster Cocktail	9.00	25.00
Sherbet, Low	9.00	25.00
Sherbet, Tall	12.00	30.00
Wine	15.00	38.00

Original Catalog Illustration:
No. 1402/100 Tally Ho low sherbet, goblet, oyster cocktail

TALLY HO, NO. 1402/200

Date: Ca. 1934

Manufacturer: Cambridge Glass Co., Cambridge, OH

Colors: Crystal

Decorations: Chintz etching, Vichy etching

Notes: Blown bowl, pressed stem.

Cocktail, 3½ oz.	$10.00
Pousse Café, 1 oz.	45.00
Sherbet, Low, 6 oz.	8.00
Tumbler, Footed, 3 oz.	12.00
Tumbler, Footed, 5 oz.	9.00
Tumbler, Footed, 10 oz.	10.00

Original Catalog Illustration: No. 1402/200
Tally Ho stemware Chintz etching 10 oz. footed tumbler,
5 oz. footed tumbler and low sherbet

WHIRLPOOL, NO. 1506

Date: 1938

Manufacturer: A.H. Heisey & Co., Newark, OH

Colors: Crystal, Zircon. Other colors such as Ruby, Verde Green, Blue and more were made by Imperial Glass Corp. after 1957.

Decorations: None known

Notes: All pressed. When portions of this pattern were resurrected by Heisey in later years, the name was changed to Provincial. Add 400% to 500% for pieces in Zircon (blue-green). For Imperial colors add 15% to Crystal prices.

Goblet, 10 oz.	$15.00
Juice, Footed, 5 oz.	18.00
Oyster Cocktail, 5 oz.	10.00
Saucer Champagne or Sherbet	10.00
Soda, Footed, 12 oz. (Iced Tea)	20.00
Tumbler, Footed, 9 oz.	20.00
Wine, 3¼ oz	12.00

Original Heisey Pattern Folder:
No. 1506 Whirlpool goblet

CUPPED BOWL *(continued)*

Original Catalog Illustration:
No. 30 York goblet with No. 632 Warwick cutting

YORK, NO. 30

Date: 1930s

Manufacturer: Duncan & Miller Glass Co., Washington, PA

Colors: Crystal

Decorations: No. 632 Warwick cutting

Notes: Blown bowl, pressed stem. Designed by Robert A. May.

Cocktail, Liquor	$12.00
Goblet	18.00
Iced Tea, Footed	18.00
Oyster Cocktail	9.00
Saucer Champagne or Tall Sherbet	18.00
Wine	20.00

FLARED BOWL

No. 17578 goblet,
Wistaria bowl

Original Catalog
Illustration: No. D1
Mandarin goblet with
Governor Clinton cutting

MANDARIN, D1

Date: 1940s

Manufacturer: Duncan & Miller Glass Co., Washington, PA

Colors: Crystal

Decorations: Made with Satin stem. Athena cutting, Chinese Garden cutting, Fern cutting, Governor Clinton cutting, Spring Glory cutting.

Notes: Blown bowl, pressed stem. Designed by Robert A. May.

Cocktail, Liquor, 3½ oz.	$12.00
Goblet, 11 oz.	18.00
Iced Tea, Footed, 14 oz.	18.00
Orange Juice, Footed, 5 oz.	12.00
Oyster Cocktail, Footed, 4½ oz.	9.00
Saucer Champagne or Tall Sherbet, 5 oz.	18.00
Wine or Claret, 4 oz.	20.00

No. 17578

Date: 1940s or 1950s

Manufacturer: Tiffin Glass Co., Tiffin, OH

Colors: Crystal, Wistaria bowl with Crystal stem and foot, Twilight

Decorations: Cuttings: Heritage, Monticello, Princeton, Kohinoor, Lexington

Notes: For Wistaria or Twilight, add 150%.

Goblet	$20.00
Sherbet/Saucer Champagne	17.00

Catalog Illustration:
No. 5089 Princess with
No. 1076 Nonchalance cutting

PRINCESS, NO. 5089

Date: 1952

Manufacturer: A.H. Heisey & Co., Newark, OH

Colors: Crystal

Decorations: No. 507 Orchid etching. No. 1062 Bridal Lace cutting, No. 1063 Wood Violet cutting, No. 1064 Provincial Wreath cutting, No. 1065 Baroness cutting, No. 1073 Serenade cutting, No. 1076 Nonchalance cutting

Notes: Blown bowl, pressed stem. A late stem line with limited success, but when found is usually decorated.

Claret, 4 oz	$15.00
Cocktail, 3½ oz.	12.00
Cordial, 1 oz	35.00
Goblet, 10 oz.	18.00
Iced Tea, Footed, 12 oz.	18.00
Juice, Footed, 5 oz.	15.00
Saucer Champagne, 5½ oz.	16.00
Wine, 2½ oz	18.00

OVOID BOWL

AURORA, NO. 1066

Date: 1931

Manufacturer: Cambridge Glass Co., Cambridge, OH

Colors: Crystal, Mandarin Gold, Moonlight (blue). Colored bowl with Crystal stem and foot: Amber, Amethyst, Carmen, Emerald, Dark Emerald, Dianthus Pink, Forest Green, Gold Krystol, Moonlight, Peach-Blo, Royal Blue

Decorations: Apple Blossom etching, Diane etching, Elaine etching, Gloria etching, Portia etching. Laurel Wreath cutting, Newport cutting, No. 622 cutting, No. 629 cutting, No. 690 cutting. Hunt Scene, D/990 (enameled).

Notes: Blown bowl, pressed stem. Made in plain or optic. For colors, add 100–150%.

Brandy, ¾ oz	$25.00
Claret, 4½ oz	12.00
Cocktail, Low, 3 oz	10.00
Cocktail, Tall, 3½ oz	10.00
Cordial, 1 oz	35.00
Goblet, 11 oz	12.00
Oyster Cocktail, 5 oz	9.00
Parfait, Café, 5 oz	22.00
Pousse Café, 1 oz	25.00
Sherbet, Low, 7 oz	8.00
Sherbet, Tall, 7 oz	10.00
Sherry, 2 oz	22.00
Wine, 3 oz	20.00
Tumbler, Footed, 3 oz	7.00
Tumbler, Footed, 5 oz	8.00
Tumbler, Footed, 9 oz	8.00
Tumbler, Footed, 12 oz	9.00

Catalog Illustration:
No. 1066 Aurora stemware

CABOCHON, NO. 6091

Date: 1951

Manufacturer: A.H. Heisey & Co., Newark, OH

Colors: Crystal

Decorations: Cuttings: No. 1051 Hollyhock, No. 1052 Silver Iris, No. 1053 Cat-Tail, No. 1060 Starlight, No. 1066 Debutante, No. 1071 Baroque, No. 1072 Southwind, No. 1081 Wedding Band

Notes: Blown bowl, pressed stem. Also made in pressed tableware, No. 1951. Designed by Horace King. Numbers in parentheses refer to the catalog illustration for piece shapes.

Cocktail, 4 oz	$12.00
Goblet, 10 oz	20.00
Iced Tea, Footed, 12 oz	20.00
Juice, Footed, 5 oz	17.00
Oyster Cocktail, 3 oz	10.00
Sherbet, 5½ oz	10.00
Wine, 3 oz	20.00

Catalog Illustration:
No. 6091 Cabochon stems with
No. 1052 Silver Iris and
No. 1066 Debutante cuttings

CABOT, NO. 6025

Date: 1939

Manufacturer: Fostoria Glass Co., Moundsville, WV

Colors: Crystal

Decorations: No. 336 Plymouth etching, No. 337 Sampler etching, No. 789 Suffolk rock crystal cutting, No. 790 Hawthorn rock crystal cutting, No. 791 Georgian rock crystal cutting (cut flutes), No. 826 Minuet rock crystal and gray cutting.

Notes: Blown bowl, pressed stem. Made plain or with dimple optic. Used for plate etchings and rock crystal cuttings. Dimple optic stems may be slightly higher, approximately 10-15%.

Wine, 4 oz., 4" tall	$16.00
Cocktail, 3½ oz., 3½" tall	12.00
Cordial, 1 oz., 2⅞" tall	35.00
Goblet, 10 oz., 5½" tall	18.00
Oyster Cocktail, 4 oz., 3½" tall	9.00
Sherbet, 6 oz., 3¾" tall	9.00
Tumbler, Footed, 5 oz., 4¼" tall	9.00
Tumbler, Footed, 12 oz., 5⅝" tall	14.00

Original Catalog Illustration:
No. 6025 Cabot goblet with
No. 336 Plymouth etching

DOVER, NO. 5330

Date: 1930s

Manufacturer: Duncan & Miller Glass Co., Washington, PA

Colors: Crystal, Ruby bowl with crystal stem and foot.

Decorations: No. 767 Wilshire cutting, No. 768 Sheffield cutting, No. 769 Saratoga cutting, No. 775 Nobility cutting

Notes: Blown bowl, pressed stem. Designed by Robert A. May. For Ruby add 50%.

Claret, 5 oz., 5¼" tall	$15.00
Cocktail, Liquor, 3½ oz., 4"	12.00
Cordial, 1 oz., 3½" tall	45.00
Finger Bowl, 4¼"	8.00
Goblet, 10 oz., 5¾" tall	18.00
Ice Cream (sherbet), 5 oz., 3½" tall	9.00
Iced Tea, Footed, 13 oz., 6½" tall	18.00
Juice, Orange, Footed, 5 oz., 4½" tall	12.00
Oyster Cocktail, 4½ oz., 3½" tall	9.00
Saucer Champagne or Tall Sherbet, 6 oz., 4½" tall	18.00
Tumbler, Footed, 10 oz., 5⅞" tall	10.00
Wine, 3 oz., 4¾" tall	20.00

Original Catalog Illustration:
No. 5330 Dover saucer
champagne and claret

19

OVOID BOWL *(continued)*

Original Catalog Illustration: No. 064 stems

No. 064

Date: 1930s

Manufacturer: U.S. Glass Co., Tiffin, OH

Colors: Crystal or Crystal with Black Trim in regular optic. Mandarin with Crystal Trim or Crystal with Amber Trim in festoon optic

Notes: Blown bowl, pressed foot. Made regular or festoon optic. For festoon optic, add 25%.

Cocktail	$20.00
Goblet	30.00
Iced Tea	28.00
Saucer Champagne	25.00
Table (tumbler)	20.00
Wine	30.00

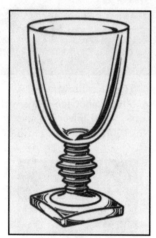

Original Catalog Illustration: No. 4020 claret

No. 4020

Date: 1929

Manufacturer: Fostoria Glass Co., Moundsville, WV

Colors: Crystal. Crystal bowl with colored stem and foot in: Green, Amber, Ebony. Colored bowl with crystal stem and foot in: Rose, Topaz/Gold Tint, Wisteria.

Decorations: No. 283 Kashmir plate etching, No. 284 New Garland plate etching, No. 285 Minuet plate etching, No. 305 Fern plate etching, No. 306 Queen Ann plate etching, No. 307 Fountain plate etching, No. 195 Millefleur cutting, No. 700 Formal Garden cutting, No. 701 Tapestry cutting, No. 702 Comet cutting, No. 703 New Yorker cutting, No. 773 Rhythm rock crystal cutting, No. 783 Chelsea rock crystal cutting. Also decorated with various colored bands and dots called Club Design.

Notes: Blown bowl, pressed stem. Made plain. For Wisteria add 50-75%. For other colors add 25%.

Claret, 4 oz	$24.00
Cocktail, (low) 3½ oz., 2½" tall	15.00
Cocktail, 4 oz., 3⅝" tall	18.00
Goblet, 11 oz., 5¾" tall	24.00
Iced Tea, Footed, 16 oz., 6" tall	25.00
Juice, Footed, 5 oz., 4⅛" tall	18.00
Sherbet, Low, 5 oz., 2⅞" tall	15.00
Sherbet, Low, 7 oz. 3" tall	15.00
Sherbet, Tall, 7 oz., 4⅜" tall	20.00
Tumbler, Footed, 10 oz., 5" tall	20.00
Tumbler, Footed, 13 oz., 5¼" tall	24.00
Whiskey, 2 oz., 2⅛" tall	20.00
Wine, 3 oz.	24.00

Original Catalog Illustration: Pristine goblet

PRISTINE

Date: 1936

Manufacturer: Cambridge Glass Co., Cambridge, OH

Colors: Crystal

Decorations: Firenze etching, Laurel etching, Rose Point etching, Daffodil etching, Wildflower etching. American Star rock crystal engraving, Broadmoor rock crystal engraving, Belfast rock crystal engraving, Cranston rock crystal engraving, Chesterfield rock crystal engraving, Courtship rock crystal engraving, Etruscan rock crystal engraving, Fantasy rock crystal engraving, Grecian rock crystal engraving, Killarney rock crystal engraving, Neo-Classic rock crystal engraving, Pine Tree rock crystal engraving, Straw Flower rock crystal engraving, The Pines rock crystal engraving, Whitehall rock crystal engraving. Laurel and Rose Point with gold encrustation. Astoria (gold band)

Brandy, ¾ oz	$35.00
Claret, 4½ oz.	12.00
Cocktail, 3½ oz.	12.00
Cordial, 1 oz	30.00
Goblet, 11 oz.	12.00
Oyster Cocktail, 5 oz.	9.00
Sherbet, Low, 6 oz.	7.00
Sherbet, Tall, 6 oz.	9.00
Sherry, 2 oz	15.00
Wine, 3 oz.	12.00
Tumbler, Footed, 5 oz.	9.00
Tumbler, Footed, 10 oz. or 12 oz.	12.00

(continued) # OVOID BOWL

VICTORIAN

Date: Ca. 1930s

Manufacturer: Duncan & Miller Glass Co., Washington, PA

Colors: Crystal

Notes: All pressed.

Cocktail or Wine, 2½ oz. $18.00
Finger Bowl 9.00
Goblet, 9 oz. 18.00
Hi Ball, 13 oz 16.00

Ice Cream, 4 oz. (sherbet). 9.00
Iced Tea, Footed, 12 oz. 17.00
Juice, Orange, Footed, 5 oz. 12.00
Old Fashioned, 7 oz. 9.00
Parfait, 5 oz 15.00
Plate, Finger Bowl 6.00
Saucer Champagne, 5 oz. 15.00
Tumbler, Footed, 2 oz. (bar) 22.00
Tumbler, Footed, 9 oz. 15.00

Original Catalog Illustration:
Victorian goblet and ice cream

TAPERED BOWL

ALDEN, NO. 5323

Date: 1940s

Manufacturer: Duncan & Miller Glass Co., Washington, PA

Colors: Crystal. Crystal bowl, light blue stem and foot.

Decorations: No. 686 Killarney cutting; No. 701 Concord cutting, No. 703 Virginia cutting (cut flutes) and No. 734 Belfast cutting

Notes: Blown bowl, pressed stem. Designed by Robert A. May.

Claret, 5 oz., 5¼" tall $15.00
Cocktail, Liquor, 3½ oz., 4¼" tall 12.00
Finger Bowl, 4½" 8.00
Goblet, 10 oz., 6" tall 18.00
Ice Cream, Footed, 6 oz.,
    3" tall (sherbet) 9.00
Iced Tea, Footed, 13 oz., 5¾" tall 18.00
Orange Juice, Footed, 5 oz., 4¼" tall. . . 12.00
Oyster Cocktail, 4½ oz., 3¼" tall 9.00
Saucer Champagne or Tall Sherbet,
    6 oz., 4¼" tall 18.00
Wine, 3 oz., 4¾" tall 20.00

Original Catalog Illustration:
No. 5323 Alden goblet
and ice cream

CAMBRIDGE SQUARE, NO. 3798

Date: 1951

Manufacturer: Cambridge Glass Co., Cambridge, OH

Colors: Crystal

Decorations: Triumph (Platinum band)

Notes: Blown bowl, pressed stem.

Cocktail $24.00
Cordial 50.00
Goblet. 30.00
Iced Tea, 12 oz. 28.00
Juice, 5 oz 22.00
Sherbet 18.00
Wine. 30.00

Original Catalog Illustration:
No. 3798 Cambridge
Square goblet

DUNCAN PHYFE, D1

Date: 1950s

Manufacturer: Duncan & Miller Glass Co., Washington, PA

Colors: Crystal

Decorations: Holiday cutting, Pickwick cutting, Wild Rose cutting, Willow cutting

Notes: Blown bowl, pressed stem. Designed by James Rosati.

Cocktail, Liquor, 3½ oz. $12.00
Goblet, 10 oz 18.00
Iced Tea, Footed, 14 oz. 18.00
Orange Juice, Footed, 5 oz. 12.00
Oyster Cocktail, Footed, 4½ oz. 9.00
Saucer Champagne or Tall
    Sherbet, 5 oz. 18.00
Wine or Claret, 4 oz. 20.00

Original Catalog Illustration:
No. D1 Duncan Phyfe goblet
with Holiday cutting

TAPERED BOWL *(continued)*

Original Catalog Illustration:
No. 5322 Erin goblet
and saucer champagne

ERIN, NO. 5322

Date: 1930s

Manufacturer: Duncan & Miller Glass Co.,
Washington, PA

Colors: Crystal

Decorations: No. 690 Kohinoor cutting,
No. 691 Sun Ray cutting, No. 702 Berkeley
cutting, No. 733 Laurel Diamond cutting

Notes: Blown bowl, pressed stem. Designed by
Robert A. May.

Claret, 4½ oz., 5¼" tall	$15.00
Cocktail, 3½ oz., 4¼" tall	12.00
Finger Bowl, 4¼"	8.00
Goblet, 9 oz., 6" tall	18.00
Ice Cream, Footed, 6 oz., 3¼" tall (sherbet)	9.00
Iced Tea, Footed, 13 oz., 6" tall	18.00
Orange Juice, Footed, 5 oz., 4½" tall	12.00
Oyster Cocktail, 4½ oz., 3½" tall	9.00
Saucer Champagne or Tall Sherbet, 6 oz., 4½" tall	18.00
Wine, 3 oz., 4¾" tall	20.00

Original Catalog Illustration:
No. 504 Granada saucer
champagne and cocktail

GRANADA, NO. 504

Date: 1930s

Manufacturer: Duncan & Miller Glass Co.,
Washington, PA

Colors: Crystal, Ruby bowl with crystal stem
and foot

Decorations: No. 607 Alhambra cutting;
No. 635 Locksley cutting; No. 689
Stratford cutting.

Notes: Blown bowl, pressed stem. Compare
this stem line to Heisey's No. 3404 Spanish
listed later. Designed by Robert A. May.

	Crystal	Ruby
Claret, 5 oz.	$20.00	$30.00
Cordial, 1 oz.	50.00	52.00
Goblet, 10 oz.	22.00	32.00
Ice Cream, Footed, 5 oz.	10.00	18.00
Iced Tea, Footed, 12 oz.	22.00	28.00
Liquor Cocktail, 3½ oz.	17.00	27.00
Orange Juice, Footed, 5 oz.	15.00	20.00
Oyster Cocktail, 4½ oz.	10.00	17.00
Saucer Champagne, 5 oz.	22.00	27.00
Sherry, 2 oz.	25.00	35.00
Tumbler, Footed, 10 oz.	10.00	20.00
Whiskey, Footed, 3 oz.	20.00	22.00
Wine, 3½ oz.	25.00	32.00

Original Catalog Illustration:
No. 3400 lunch goblet with
No. 744 Apple Blossom etching

NO. 3400

Date: 1930

Manufacturer: Cambridge Glass Co.,
Cambridge, OH

Colors: Crystal, Amber, Emerald, Gold Krystol,
Peach-Blo, Willow Blue. Crystal stem and foot
with Ebony bowl.

Decorations: Apple Blossom etching,
Gloria etching

	Crystal	Colors
Goblet, Lunch, 9 oz.	$15.00	$30.00
Sherbet, Footed, 6 oz.	9.00	18.00
Tumbler, Footed, 2½ oz. (whiskey)	18.00	50.00
Tumbler, Footed, 9 oz.	12.00	27.00
Tumbler, Footed, 12 oz.	15.00	30.00

Original Catalog Illustration:
No. 6000 with goblet, plate, cup
& saucer & saucer champagne
No. 309 Legion etching saucer

NO. 6000

Date: 1933

Manufacturer: Fostoria Glass Co.,
Moundsville, WV

Colors: Crystal, Amber, Gold Tint, Green,
Rose, Topaz

Decorations: No. 309 Legion plate etching,
No. 712 Waterbury rock crystal cutting,
No. 749 Celebrity rock crystal cutting,
No. 750 Memories rock crystal cutting.

Notes: Blown bowl, pressed stem. Made in
regular optic.

Cocktail, 3½ oz., 3¾" tall	$13.00
Goblet, 10 oz., 6¼" tall	18.00
Oyster Cocktail, 4 oz., 2⅞" tall	9.00
Saucer Champagne, 6 oz., 4¾" tall	16.00
Sherbet, Low, 6 oz., 3⅞" tall	12.00
Tumbler, Footed, 5 oz., 3⅝" tall	10.00
Tumbler, Footed, 13 oz., 5¼" tall	15.00
Wine, 3 oz., 4¼" tall	17.00

TAPERED BOWL

OXFORD, NO. 5024

Date: 1940

Manufacturer: A.H. Heisey & Co., Newark, OH

Colors: Crystal

Decorations: No. 957 Oriental cutting, No. 958 Ping Pong cutting, No. 964 Maryland cutting, No. 976 St. George Waterford cutting, No. 1055 Westminster cutting, No 1067 Yorktown cutting, No. 1068 Victoria cutting, No. 1074 Inspiration cutting, No. 1077 Fanfare cutting

Notes: Blown bowl, pressed stem. Other companies made very similar stemware lines. Heisey made a similar line with an extra heavy sham in the same forms called No. 5011

Yorktown. "Heisey's Oxford, the oldest type of English and Irish design, truly exemplifies simple beauty that is ageless."—From Heisey pattern folder.

Claret, 4½ oz	$18.00
Cocktail, 3½ oz	15.00
Cocktail, Double, 6 oz	17.00
Cordial, 1 oz	50.00
Goblet, 9 oz	20.00
Goblet, 11 oz	20.00
Iced Tea, Footed, 12 oz	18.00
Juice, Footed, 5 oz	14.00
Oyster Cocktail, 4 oz	9.00
Saucer Champagne, 6½ oz	16.00
Wine, 3 oz	20.00

Original Pattern Folder: No. 5024 Oxford goblet

SPANISH, NO. 3404

Date: 1933

Manufacturer: A.H. Heisey & Co., Newark, OH

Colors: Crystal, Steigel Blue with Crystal stem and foot, Tangerine with Crystal stem and foot, Sahara with Crystal stem and foot.

Decorations: Etchings: No. 456 Titania, No. 457 Springtime, No. 458 Olympiad, No. 461 Concord. Cuttings: No. 789 Aberdeen, No. 793 Monterrey, No. 794 Riviere, No. 797 Killarney, No. 798 Malta, No. 847 Streamline, No. 865 Florentine, No. 879 Da Vinci, No. 941 Barcelona, No. 966 Picket.

Notes: Blown bowl, Pressed stem. Compare this stem line with Duncan's Granada, listed previously. May be marked with the Diamond H on the stem near the base just above the rings. Made in wide optic. For Sahara, add 350%. For Steigel Blue (Cobalt), add 300%. For Tangerine, add 800%.

Claret, 4 oz	$35.00
Cocktail, 3½ oz	38.00
Comport, 6"	95.00
Cordial, 1 oz	120.00
Finger Bowl (No. 3335)	10.00
Goblet, 10 oz	45.00
Oyster Cocktail, 3½ oz	30.00
Saucer Champagne, 5½ oz	32.00
Sherbet 5½ oz	18.00
Soda, Footed, 5 oz	20.00
Soda, Footed, 12 oz	22.00
Tumbler, Footed, 10 oz	22.00
Wine, 2½ oz	60.00

Original Catalog Illustration: No. 3404 Spanish goblet & claret

WATERFORD, NO. 102

Date: 1930s

Manufacturer: Duncan & Miller Glass Co., Washington, PA

Colors: Crystal

Decorations: Amber stain

Notes: All pressed. Even though the bowl design looks like a cutting, it is a pressed design.

Cocktail or Wine, 3 oz	$18.00
Finger Bowl	12.00

Goblet, 9 oz	18.00
Hi Ball, 7½ oz	14.00
Ice Cream, 6 oz. (sherbet)	10.00
Iced Tea, 12 oz.	16.00
Iced Tea, 14 oz.	16.00
Jug, ½ gal.	65.00
Juice, Orange, 5 oz.	14.00
Parfait, 5 oz.	16.00
Saucer Champagne, 6 oz.	15.00
Tumbler, 2 oz. (bar)	20.00
Tumbler, Table, 9 oz.	15.00

Original Catalog Illustration: No. 102 Waterford goblet

Stems listed in this category defy description by ordinary glass stem terms. Included are some open-work stems and others that have distinctive shapes. **The following prices are for undecorated items.**

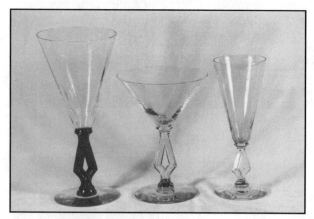

Art Moderne stems

ART MODERNE

Date: 1929

Manufacturer: Economy Tumbler Co. (Morgantown), Morgantown, WV

Colors: Crystal, Rose, Green. Crystal bowl with Black stem and foot. Ritz Blue bowl, Crystal stem and foot. Topaz bowl with Crystal stem and foot.

Notes: Blown bowl, pressed stem. For Rose, Green or Topaz, add 50%. For Ritz Blue or Black, add 75%.

Cordial	$110.00
Goblet	95.00
Iced Tea	80.00
Saucer Champagne	85.00
Tumbler, Footed	70.00
Wine	95.00

Catalog Illustration:
No. 15017 Beehive claret

BEEHIVE, NO. 15017

Date: 1920s

Manufacturer: U.S. Glass Co., Tiffin OH

Colors: Crystal, Crystal with Amber Trim, Crystal with Green Trim, Rose

Notes: Researcher and author Fred Bickenheuser states more than 50 pieces were made in this line. Made in wide optic.

Claret	$45.00
Cordial	85.00

Goblet, 10 oz.	45.00
Iced Tea, Footed, 14 oz.	35.00
Jug & Cover, Footed	250.00
Parfait	40.00
Saucer Champagne	40.00
Seltzer, Footed, 5 oz. (juice)	20.00
Sundae (sherbet)	22.00
Table, Footed, 8 oz. (tumbler)	30.00
Whiskey, Footed	40.00
Wine	45.00

Original Ad: Filament stems

FILAMENT STEMS BY MORGANTOWN

Morgantown made many innovative stems in the 1930s. The most unusual were the filament stems, which have a thin stripe of color encased in crystal glass to form the stems. This gives the illusion of a very thin colored stem, but the crystal shell makes them as sturdy as other stemware. Morgantown made many of its lines with various filaments in colors such as: Ritz blue, Spanish Red, Green, Topaz and Black. The following are some of the filament stems available. Most of these stems are valued at about $100, with some variation for color and rarity of stem. Naturally, decorations add to this value.

MISCELLANEOUS

L to R: No. 7606½ Athena,
No. 7533 Walpole (2 examples), No. 770 Salem

No. 7720 Palazzo

L to R: No. 7684 Maypole,
No. 7662 Majesty, No. 7654 Lorna,
No. 7673 Lexington (2 examples)

L to R: No. 7620 Fontanne, No. 7701 Fischer,
No. 7880 Carlos, No. 7659½ Lenox

L to R: No. 7779½ Maypole,
No. 7880 Carlos (2 examples)

L to R: No. 7938½ Mecca
No. 7616½ Wescott

GOLF BALL, No. 7643

Date: 1930s

Manufacturer: Morgantown Glass Co., Morgantown, WV

Colors: Crystal. Color combinations in Spanish Red, Topaz, Stiegel Green, Amethyst, Ritz Blue and Pink, Milk Glass and possibly other Morgantown colors.

Notes: This golf ball-shaped stem was used with different shaped bowls to make new stemlines. Golf Ball remained popular for several years, resulting in a wide variety of pieces and colors.

Goblet, Spanish Red $80.00
Goblet, Ritz Blue 80.00
Goblet, Stiegel Green 60.00

No. 7643 Golf Ball stems in various color combinations

SENECA WINE

Little is known about this stem other than that it has a Seneca original label. Seneca made at least two other bowl shapes on this stem.

Wine $50.00

SQUARE, No. 7636

Date: 1928

Manufacturer: Morgantown Glass Works, Morgantown, WV

Colors: Crystal, Crystal with Ebony stem, Anna Rose Pink, and more.

Goblet $200.00

Catalog Illustration:
No. 7643 Golf Ball
goblet with cutting

Seneca Wine

Square goblet from
patent drawing

Chapter 6
NATURALISTIC

Naturalistic stems comprise natural shapes, such as the knot-like loop of Lariat and the Lily of the Valley-shaped stem of Duncan. **The following prices are for undecorated items.**

BELL SHAPED BOWL

Original Pamphlet:
No. 5040 Lariat goblet

LARIAT, NO. 5040

Date: 1941

Manufacturer: A.H. Heisey & Co., Newark, OH

Colors: Crystal

Decorations: No. 980 Moonglo cutting, No. 1003 Ivy engraving, No. 1009 Mexicali Rose, No. 1039 Desert Flower

Notes: Blown bowl, pressed stem. Made to match Lariat tableware.

Claret, 4 oz.	$20.00
Cocktail, 3½ oz.	20.00
Cordial, Low Stem, 1 oz.	120.00
Cordial, Tall Stem, 1 oz.	180.00
Goblet, 10 oz.	25.00
Iced Tea, Footed, 12 oz.	25.00
Juice, Footed, 5 oz.	22.00
Oyster Cocktail, 4½ oz.	18.00
Saucer Champagne, 5½ oz.	22.00

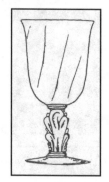

Original Drawing:
No. 5019 Waverly goblet

WAVERLY, NO. 5019

Date: 1940

Manufacturer: A.H. Heisey & Co., Newark, OH

Colors: Crystal

Decorations: No. 9015 English Ivy etching, No. 9019 Easter Lily etching. No. 1020 Burgundy cutting, No. 1021 Melrose cutting, No. 1042 Wood Lily cutting

Notes: Blown bowl, pressed stem. Burgundy and Melrose were made to match silverware patterns. Made to match No. 1519 Waverly tableware.

Cocktail, 3½ oz.	$12.00
Cordial, 1 oz.	65.00
Goblet, 10 oz.	17.00
Iced Tea, Footed, 13 oz.	15.00
Juice, Footed, 5 oz.	15.00
Sherbet or Saucer Champagne, 5½ oz.	12.00
Wine or Claret, 3 oz.	15.00

Original Catalog Illustration:
D4 Lily of the Valley goblet

LILY OF THE VALLEY, D4

Date: 1940s

Manufacturer: Duncan & Miller Glass Co., Washington, PA

Colors: Crystal

Decorations: Satin stem. Lily of the Valley cutting

Notes: Blown bowl, pressed stem. Designed by Robert A. May. Made to match Lily of the Valley tableware.

Cocktail, Liquor, 3½ oz.	$30.00
Goblet, 10 oz.	35.00
Iced Tea, Footed, 14 oz.	30.00
Orange Juice, Footed, 5 oz.	22.00
Oyster Cocktail, 4½ oz.	17.00
Saucer Champagne or Tall Sherbet, 5 oz.	28.00
Wine or Claret, 4 oz.	32.00

FLARED BOWL

PLANTATION, NO. 1567

Date: 1948

Manufacturer: A.H. Heisey & Co., Newark, OH

Colors: Crystal

Notes: All pressed. Designed by Horace King. See also No. 5067 Plantation for blown stemware.

Claret, 4 oz.	$85.00
Cocktail, 3½ oz.	45.00
Goblet, 10 oz.	60.00
Iced Tea, Footed, 12 oz.	60.00
Juice, Footed.	55.00
Oyster Cocktail, 3½ oz.	23.00
Sherbet, 5 oz.	28.00
Wine, 2 oz.	85.00

Original Pamphlet:
No. 1567 Plantation stems

MISCELLANEOUS BOWL

MAI TAI

Date: 1960s

Manufacturer: Morgantown Glass, Morgantown, WV

Colors: Crystal bowl with Amber stem

Notes: The pattern is a representation of South Seas carving. Some early examples have peacock optic bowls. Imperial Glass eventually obtained the contract with Trader Vic's restaurants and marketed the pieces, but all were made at Morgantown. This was a private mold owned by Trader Vic's. Bowl shapes vary according to piece (cocktail, champagne, etc.).

Champagne	$45.00
Cocktail	45.00

Mai Tai cocktail, amber stem

OVOID BOWL

LARIAT, NO. 1540

Date: 1941

Manufacturer: A.H. Heisey & Co., Newark, OH

Colors: Crystal

Decorations: No. 981 Moon Beam cutting, No. 982 Moon Gleam cutting, No. 999 Carolina cutting

Notes: All pressed. See previous Bell Shaped bowl for blown Lariat, No. 5040.

Cocktail, 3½ oz.	$20.00
Goblet, 9 oz.	22.00
Iced Tea, Footed, 12 oz.	20.00
Juice, Footed, 5 oz.	18.00
Sherbet, Low, 6 oz.	15.00
Wine, 3½ oz.	22.00

Catalog Illustration: No. 1540
Lariat stems

TAPERED BOWL

PLANTATION, NO. 5067

Date: 1949

Manufacturer: A.H. Heisey & Co., Newark, OH

Colors: Crystal

Decorations: No. 516 Plantation Ivy etching, No. 1038 Pine cutting

Notes: Blown bowl, pressed stem. Designed by Horace King. Amber stemmed pieces were made by Imperial Glass. See above for pressed Plantation, No. 1567.

Claret	$35.00
Cocktail, 4½ oz.	25.00
Cordial, 1 oz.	140.00
Goblet, 10 oz.	35.00
Oyster Cocktail, 4 oz.	20.00
Sherbet, 6½ oz.	25.00
Soda, 12 oz. (iced tea)	35.00
Soda, 5 oz. (juice)	30.00
Wine, 3 oz.	35.00

Original Pamphlet: No. 5067
Plantation goblet

Chapter 7

NUDES

CAMBRIDGE NUDE, NO. 3011

Date: 1936

Manufacturer: Cambridge Glass Co., Cambridge, OH

Colors: Crystal, Carmen bowl with Crystal stem, Royal Blue bowl with Crystal stem, Crown Tuscan, Crown Tuscan stem with various colored bowls, Crystal with Heatherbloom bowl, possibly others.

Notes: Many other pieces are known in this stemware line including candlesticks, comports, ashtrays, cigarette boxes and others. Only the stem line is included here. Prices can vary widely with the item and/or the color combination. It is possible that not all pieces were made in all colors or color combinations.

No. 3011 Cambridge Nude
cordial and cocktial

	Crystal	Carmen, Royal Blue
Brandy, 1 oz.	$95.00	$135.00
Claret, 4½ oz.	90.00	135.00
Cocktail, 3 oz. (tapered bowl)	135.00	195.00
Cocktail, 3 oz.	185.00	245.00
Cocktail, 3 oz.	95.00	125.00
Cordial, 1 oz.	195.00	270.00
Goblet, Banquet	195.00	315.00
Goblet, Table	120.00	165.00
Hoch, 6 oz.	195.00	315.00
Roemer, 5 oz.	185.00	310.00
Saucer Champagne	110.00	135.00
Wine, 3 oz.	110.00	140.00

DRAPED NUDE, NO. 15078

Date: 1934

Manufacturer: U.S. Glass Co., Tiffin, OH

Colors: Crystal bowl with stem & foot in: Crystal, Green, Royal Blue

Decorations: Fuchsia etching

Notes: Blown bowl, pressed stem. Made plain (no optic), although some examples are known with optic. This nude stem is tastefully draped in a toga-like garment.

No. 15078 Draped Nude stems

	Crystal, Satin	Green	Blue
Champagne, 5½ oz.	$170.00	$225.00	$250.00
Claret, 4 oz.	170.00	225.00	250.00
Cocktail, 3 oz.	170.00	225.00	250.00
Cordial, Large, 1¼ oz.	200.00	250.00	275.00
Cordial, Small, 1 oz.	200.00	250.00	275.00
Goblet, 9 oz.	185.00	220.00	250.00
Saucer Champagne, 5½ oz.	180.00	225.00	250.00
Wine, Large, 3½ oz.	170.00	225.00	250.00
Wine, Small, 2½ oz.	170.00	225.00	250.00

SENECA NUDE

Date: Unknown

Manufacturer: Seneca Glass Co., Morgontown WV

Colors: Crystal, possibly colors combined with Crystal

Decorations: None known

Notes: Illustrations of this stem are not available, but Seneca did make a nude stem in several crystal and color combinations. The figure is lacking in detail and simply a straight stem with arms held tightly against the body. Due to rarity all examples are valued at least $100.00. Be aware that recent production by an individual is made in a crystal/cobalt blue combination.

Chapter 8
PLAIN

Plain stems are the most common and simplest of stemware, having no design features in the stem. In blown ware, plain stem portions can be pressed; in these you can see the joint between the bowl and stem. In a pulled stem, the bowl is blown with extra glass at the far end. This extra glass is literally pulled and drawn into a stem onto which a foot is applied.

*Included is a variation of plain stems called lady leg. In these the stem, again, is very plain with no design, but there is a bulge just below the top. **The following prices are for undecorated items.***

BELL SHAPED BOWL

No. 40

Date: Ca. 1927

Maker: Louie Glass Co., Weston, WV

Colors: Crystal

Decorations: Mother-of-pearl iridescence

Notes: Blown bowl, pulled stem. Lady leg type. This company, along with its sister company, West Virginia Glass Specialty, made many rather plain stem lines, vases, pitchers and tumblers often found today as "unknown depression era glassware."

Claret, 4 oz.	$12.00
Cocktail, 3 oz.	10.00
Cordial, 1 oz.	30.00
Goblet, 9 oz.	12.00
Saucer Champagne, 6 oz.	10.00
Sherbet, 6 oz.	8.00
Wine, 3 oz.	12.00

No. 40 goblet, iridized bowl

No. 766

Date: Ca. 1896

Manufacturer: Fostoria Glass Co., Moundsville, WV

Colors: Crystal

Decorations: No. 36 Irish Lace needle etching, No. 42 Chain needle etching, No. 232 Lotus plate etching, No. 237 Garland plate etching, No. 250 Oriental plate etching, No. 255 Modern Vintage etching, No. 257 Victory plate etching, No. 4 rock crystal cutting, No. 125 cutting, No. 130 Priscilla cutting, No. 142 Arrow rock crystal cutting, No. 8 Cascade (gold encrustation), No. 9 Newport (gold band), No. 15 (gold band), No. 31 Laurel (gold encrustation), No. 32 Regent (gold encrustation), Amber iridescent, Mother-of-pearl iridescent

Notes: Blown bowl, pulled stem. Regular, narrow optic or plain. This stem line was continued by Fostoria for many years.

Brandy, ¾ oz., 3¾" tall (also pousse café)	$15.00
Burgundy, 2 oz., 4⅝" tall	14.00
Claret, 4¼ oz., 5⅝" tall	11.00
Cocktail, 3 oz.	9.00
Cordial, ¾ oz., 3⁷⁄₁₆" tall	18.00
Creme de Menthe, 2 oz.	14.00
Fruit, 4½ oz. (sherbet), 3¼" tall	8.00
Goblet, 7 oz.	10.00
Goblet, 9 oz., 7" tall	12.00
Parfait, 6 oz., 5¾ " tall	12.00
Rhine Wine, 4 oz.	14.00
Saucer Champagne, 5 oz., 4⅜" tall	10.00
Sherbet, 2⅝"	8.00
Sherry	14.00
Sorbet	14.00
Tumbler, Handled & Footed, 12 oz., 5¼" tall	14.00
Whiskey	18.00
Wine, 2¾ oz., 5" tall	12.00

Original Catalog Illustration: No. 766 stems with No. 255 Modern Vintage etching

BELL SHAPED BOWL *(continued)*

Original Catalog Illustration:
No. 877 goblet with
No. 197 Chatteris cutting

No. 877

Date: 1927

Manufacturer: Fostoria Glass Co., Moundsville, WV

Colors: Crystal, Amber, Azure, Empire Green, Green, Orchid, Regal Blue

Decorations: No. 82 Cordelia needle etching, No. 277 Vernon etching, No. 290 Oak Leaf Brocade etching, No. 196 Lattice cutting, No. 197 Chatteris rock crystal cutting, No. 72 Oakwood—brocade with all over iridescence with gold edge

Notes: Blown bowl, pressed stem (lady leg shape). Made plain or with regular optic. Prices given are for crystal. For amber or green add 20%. For orchid, azure, empire green or regal blue add 100%.

Claret, 4 oz.	$15.00
Cocktail, 3½ oz.	12.00
Cordial, ¾ oz.	25.00
Goblet, 10 oz., 7⅞" tall	18.00
Oyster Cocktail, 4½ oz., 3¾ " tall	10.00
Parfait	15.00
Sherbet, High, 6 oz., 6⅛" tall	15.00
Sherbet, Low, 6 oz., 4" tall	10.00
Tumbler, Footed, 5 oz. (juice)	10.00
Tumbler, Footed, 9 oz. (water)	10.00
Tumbler, Footed, 12 oz. (iced tea)	15.00
Whiskey, Footed, 2½ oz.	11.00
Wine, 2¾ oz.	15.00

Original Catalog Illustration:
No. 3060 goblet with
No. 704 etching

No. 3060

Date: 1925

Manufacturer: Cambridge Glass Co., Cambridge, OH

Colors: Crystal. Crystal stem with Colored bowls in: Amber, Emerald, Gold Krystol, Peach-Blo (pink)

Decorations: Cleo etching, No. 520 etching, No. 704 etching

Notes: Blown bowl, pulled stem. This style of stemware was made by many companies, so a distinctive decoration is needed to properly identify this. Add 50% for etched pieces.

	Crystal	Colors
Cocktail, 2½ oz.	$6.00	$14.00
Finger Bowl	5.00	10.00
Fruit Salad, 7 oz.	6.00	12.00
Goblet, 9 oz.	10.00	15.00
Sherbet, Tall, 6 oz.	8.00	12.00
Tumbler, Footed, 3 oz.	6.00	12.00
Tumbler, Footed, 5 oz.	6.00	12.00
Tumbler, Footed, 10 oz.	7.00	12.00
Wine, 2½ oz.	7.00	14.00

No. 5093

Date: 1926

Manufacturer: Fostoria Glass Co., Moundsville, WV

Colors: Amber, Green, Blue. Crystal bowl with colored stem & foot: Amber, Azure, Blue, Green, Rose. Also made with Amber stem and foot with mother-of-pearl iridescent bowls.

Decorations: No. 85 Avalon needle etching, No. 275 Vesper etching

Notes: Blown bowl, pressed stem (lady leg shape). Made with regular, loop or spiral optics. Prices given are for Amber or Green. For Rose, Azure or Blue add 25%.

Claret, 4½ oz., 5⅝" tall	$22.00
Cocktail, 3 oz., 4½" tall	20.00
Cordial, ¾ oz., 3⅜" tall	35.00
Goblet, 9 oz., 7⅛" tall	22.00
Parfait	22.00
Sherbet, High, 6 oz., 5" tall	22.00
Sherbet, Low, 6 oz., 4" tall	15.00
Wine, 2¾ oz., 4¾" tall	22.00

Original Catalog Illustration: No. 5093 high sherbet and low sherbet with No. 275 Vesper etching

(continued) BELL SHAPED BOWL

NO. 6004

Date: 1933

Manufacturer: Fostoria Glass Co., Moundsville, WV

Colors: Crystal. Crystal bowl with Green or Wisteria base

Decorations: No. 310 Fuchsia, No. 707 Staunton rock crystal cutting, No. 708 Nairn rock crystal cutting

Notes: Blown bowl, pressed stem. Made with regular or loop optics. Prices given are for Crystal or Green. For Wisteria add 100%.

Claret, 4 oz.	$22.00
Cocktail, 3 oz.	18.00
Cordial, ¾ oz.	35.00
Goblet, 9 oz.	20.00
Oyster Cocktail, 4½ oz.	10.00
Parfait, 5½ oz.	32.00
Saucer Champagne, 5½ oz. (high sherbet)	17.00
Sherbet, Low, 5½ oz.	12.00
Wine, 2½ oz.	24.00
Tumbler, Footed, 2½ oz. (bar or whiskey)	17.00
Tumbler, Footed, 5 oz. (juice)	12.00
Tumbler, Footed, 9 oz. (water)	12.00
Tumbler, Footed, 12 oz. (iced tea)	18.00

Original Catalog Illustration: No. 6004 stems with No. 310 Fuchsia etching

NO. 14180

Date: Ca. 1914

Manufacturer: U.S. Glass Co., Tiffin, OH

Colors: Crystal

Decorations: Oneida etching, Roses etching, Thistle etching, Vintage etching, Vera cutting, Virginia cutting, No. 155 cutting, No. 156 cutting, No. 388 cutting, No. 203 etching, No. 201 needle etching

Notes: Made in wide optic. Blown bowl with a plain pulled stem.

Claret, 4 oz.	$20.00
Cocktail, 3½ oz.	15.00
Cordial, 1 oz.	45.00
Goblet, 9 oz.	20.00
Parfait, Café, 5¾ oz.	18.00
Saucer Champagne, 6½ oz.	18.00
Sundae, 6½ oz. (sherbet)	10.00
Wine, 2½ oz.	20.00

Original Catalog Illustration: No. 14180 claret with Rose etching

NO. 14196

Date: Ca. 1915

Manufacturer: U.S. Glass Co., Tiffin, OH

Colors: Crystal, Amber, Green, Rose, Lilac, Mandarin, Blue with Canary combination.

Decorations: Charmian etching with gold filling, Poppy etching, Diana etching, Apollo-Diana etching with gold border, Pauline etching, Rambler Rose etching—gold band, Special Vintage etching, Laurel Gold-Encrusted Band, Minton Gold-Encrusted Band, Valencia Gold-Encrusted Band and various needle etchings

Notes: Blown bowl, pulled stem. Made in wide optic.

Café Parfait	$18.00
Claret	22.00
Cocktail	15.00
Finger Bowl	8.00
Goblet	22.00
Oyster Cocktail	8.00
Saucer Champagne	20.00
Sundae (sherbet)	12.00
Tumbler, Footed & Handled, 12 oz.	25.00
Wine, 2 oz.	22.00

Catalog Illustration: No. 14196 goblet with gold encrusted Apollo Diana design

BELL SHAPED BOWL *(continued)*

Original Catalog Illustration: No. 3790 Simplicity goblet, sherbet and wine with Lynbrook rock crystal engraving

Original Catalog Illustration:
No. 83 Tavern flared goblet, parfait, and luncheon goblet

SIMPLICITY, NO. 3790

Date: 1950

Manufacturer: Cambridge Glass Co., Cambridge, OH

Colors: Crystal. Crystal stem and foot with colored bowls in: Carmen, Moonlight (blue), Smoke

Decorations: Magnolia etching, Autumn rock crystal engraving, No. 32P Blue Danube rock crystal engraving, No. 6P Crown rock crystal engraving, Festoon rock crystal engraving, No. 3P Flight rock crystal engraving, Lily of the Valley rock crystal engraving, Lynbrook rock crystal engraving, Miss Flowers rock crystal engraving, No. 1P Orion rock crystal engraving, No. 10P Starlite rock crystal engraving, No. 4P Starburst rock crystal engraving, Tropical rock crystal engraving

Notes: Blown bowl, pressed stem.

Claret	$15.00
Cocktail	10.00
Cordial	40.00
Goblet	15.00
Oyster Cocktail	8.00
Sherbet	8.00
Tumbler, Footed, 5 oz.	9.00
Tumbler, Footed, 12 oz.	12.00
Wine	15.00

TAVERN, NO. 83

Date: Ca. mid-1910s

Manufacturer: Duncan & Miller Glass Co., Washington, PA

Colors: Crystal

Notes: All pressed. Made to match a large line of pressed tableware and accessories. Due to its long production (20 years or more), more stems than those listed below were made.

Cocktail, 3 oz, (83½)	$14.00
Goblet, Flared, 9 oz.	18.00
Goblet, Luncheon, 9 oz. (83½)	18.00
Ice Cream, 5 oz., 4"	12.00
Ice Cream, 5 oz. (83-945)	12.00
Ice Cream, Sherbet, 5 oz. (83-943)	12.00
Ice Cream, Flared, 5 oz. (83-941)	12.00
Parfait, 5 oz.	15.00

CUPPED BOWL

Original Illustration: No. 15043 goblet with Luciana etching

NO. 15043

Date: 1925

Manufacturer: U.S. Glass Co., Tiffin, OH

Colors: Crystal, Crystal with Black Trim, Crystal with Amber Trim

Decorations: Luciana etching

Notes: Blown bowl, pulled stem. Made in regular optic.

Goblet	$25.00
Parfait, Café	22.00
Sundae (sherbet)	18.00
Wine	25.00

(continued) CUPPED BOWL

No. 661

Date: 1922

Manufacturer: Fostoria Glass Co., Moundsville, WV

Colors: Crystal

Decorations: No. 91 Ballet needle etching, No. 265 Orient plate etching, No. 267 Virginia etching, No. 268 Melrose plate etching, No. 168 Louisa cutting, No. 170 Cynthia cutting, No. 29 Empress gold band, No. 40 Nome gold band, No. 42 Miami gold band with cutting

Notes: Blown bowl, pulled stem. Made with regular optic.

> Claret, 5½ oz. $7.00
> Cocktail, 3 oz. 6.00
> Cordial, ¾ oz. 12.00
> Fruit, 6 oz., 3½" tall (low sherbet). 5.00
> Goblet, 9 oz., 7" tall. 8.00
> Parfait, 5½ oz. 6" tall. 7.00
> Saucer Champagne, 6 oz., 4⅞" tall 7.00
> Wine, 2 oz., 4¾" tall 7.00

Original Catalog Illustration: No. 661 saucer champagne, claret, and goblet with No. 267 Virginia etching

MISCELLANEOUS SHAPED BOWL

No. 2809

Date: 1924

Manufacturer: U.S. Glass Co., Tiffin, OH

Colors: Crystal, Green, Pink

Decorations: Deerwood etching

Notes: Blown bowl, pulled stem.

> Cocktail. $25.00
> Goblet. 35.00
> Saucer Champagne. 30.00
> Wine. 35.00

No. 6005

Date: 1933

Manufacturer: Fostoria Glass Co., Moundsville, WV

Colors: Crystal. Crystal bowl with Topaz base, Gold Tint base, Green base

Decorations: Mother-of-pearl iridescence with amber base, No. 311 Florentine etching, No. 312 Mayday plate etching

Notes: Blown bowl, pressed stem (lady leg shape). Made in regular optic. Prices are for crystal. For colors add 50%.

> Claret, 5 oz. $22.00
> Cocktail, 4 oz. 16.00
> Cordial, 1 oz. 32.00
> Goblet, 9 oz. 18.00
> Oyster Cocktail, 6 oz. 10.00
> Parfait 22.00
> Saucer Champagne, 5½ oz. (tall sherbet). 17.00
> Sherbet, Low, 7 oz. 12.00
> Wine, 3 oz. 22.00
> Tumbler, Footed, 2½ oz. (bar or whiskey). 18.00
> Tumbler, Footed, 5 oz. (juice) 12.00
> Tumbler, Footed, 9 oz. (water) 12.00
> Tumbler, Footed, 12 oz. (iced tea). 14.00

Original Catalog Illustration: No. 2809 goblet and saucer champagne with Deerwood etching

Original Catalog Illustration: No. 6005 stems with No. 311 Florentine etching

MISCELLANEOUS SHAPED BOWL

No. 15028 goblet, diamond optic

No. 15028

Date: 1930s

Manufacturer: U.S. Glass Co. Tiffin, OH

Colors: Crystal, Green, Rose, Twilite

Decorations: No. 421 cutting

Notes: Blown bowl, pulled stem. Made in a full line of stems. For Rose or Green, add 100%, for Twilite add 200%

Café Parfait	$18.00
Claret, 6 oz.	20.00
Cocktail, 5 oz.	15.00
Cordial 1¾ oz.	45.00
Goblet, 10 oz.	20.00
Saucer Champagne, 6 oz.	18.00
Sundae (sherbet)	9.00
Wine, 4 oz.	20.00

Original Catalog Illustration:
Nova goblet

NOVA

Date: 1928

Manufacturer: Huntington Tumbler Co., Huntington, WV

Colors: Crystal. Others unknown, but Huntington made many.

Decorations: Unknown

Notes: Blown bowl, pressed stem (lady leg). This has a very unusual octagonal bowl shape.

Goblet	$25.00

OVOID BOWL

Original Catalog Illustration:
No. 863 goblet with No. 167
Fairfax cutting

Catalog Illustration: No. 14194
goblet with Eldorado etching

No. 863

Date: 1898

Manufacturer: Fostoria Glass Co., Moundsville, WV

Colors: Crystal

Decorations: No. 38½ Block needle etching, No. 42 Chain needle etching, No. 67 Small Cloverleaf needle etching, No. 204 Vintage plate etching, No. 210, plate etching, No. 212 plate etching, No. 214 plate etching, No. 227 New Vintage plate etching, No. 237 Garland plate etching, No. 253 Persian plate etching, No. 4 cutting, No. 81 Large Sunburst Star rock crystal cutting, No. 110 cutting, No. 116 Mission cutting, No. 118 Billow cutting, No. 125 cutting, No. 129 cutting, No. 132 Clover cutting, No. 133 Chrysanthemum cutting, No. 135 Geneva cutting, No. 138 Apple Blossom cutting, No. 167 Fairfax cutting

Notes: Blown bowl, pulled stem. Made plain or with narrow optic. This stem line was continued by Fostoria for many years, thus its inclusion here.

Brandy (pousse café)	$10.00
Café Parfait	10.00
Champagne, Hollow Stem (cut flutes)	10.00
Champagne, Tall	10.00
Claret	10.00
Cocktail, 3½ oz. or 3 oz.	12.00
Cordial	15.00
Creme de Menthe	10.00
Fruit	9.00
Goblet, 5½ oz. or 10½ oz.	10.00
Goblet, Long Stem, 7 oz.	10.00
Goblet, Short Stem, 9 oz.	10.00
Rhine Wine or Sherry	10.00
Roemer, 4½ oz or 5½ oz.	12.00
Saucer Champagne	9.00

No. 14194

Date: 1920

Manufacturer: U.S. Glass Co., Tiffin, OH

Colors: Crystal

Decorations: Beatrice etching, Eldorado etching, Elinor etching, Psyche etching, No. 278 needle etching, No. SB684 cutting

Notes: Blown bowl, pulled stem (lady leg shape). Made in wide optic.

Cocktail, 3 oz. or Parfait, Café	$15.00
Goblet, 9 oz.	20.00
Iced Tea, Footed & Handled, 12 oz.	18.00
Jug & Cover, Footed, 2 qt.	65.00
Juice, Footed, 5 oz.	12.00
Juice, Footed & Handled, 5 oz.	16.00
Oyster Cocktail or Sundae (sherbet)	9.00
Saucer Champagne	18.00
Tumbler, Footed, 12 oz.	15.00
Tumbler, Table, 10 oz.	15.00
Wine, 2½ oz.	20.00

STRAIGHT BOWL

No. 880

Date: Ca. 1899

Manufacturer: Fostoria Glass Co., Moundsville, WV

Colors: Crystal

Decorations: No. 36 Irish Lace needle etching, No. 45 Greek needle etching, No. 227 New Vintage plate etching, No. 234 Kornflower plate etching, No. 237 Garland plate etching, No. 249 Rosilyn plate etching, No. 81 Large Sunburst Star cutting, No. 135 Geneva cutting, No. 175 Airdale cutting

Notes: Blown bowl, pulled stem. Made plain or with narrow optic. Made for many years.

Ale, Tall	$9.00
Brandy (pousse café), ¾ oz. or 1 oz.	11.00
Champagne, Hollow Stem	9.00
Champagne, Tall	8.00
Claret, 4½ oz. or 6½ oz.	9.00
Cocktail, 3 oz. or 3½ oz.	8.00
Cordial, ¾ oz. or 1 oz.	15.00
Creme de Menthe	9.00
Goblet, 8, 9, 10 or 11 oz.	9.00
Grapefruit, Short	9.00
Grapefruit, Tall	9.00
Hot Whiskey	8.00
Rhine Wine	9.00
Saucer Champagne, 5½ oz. or 7 oz.	9.00
Sherbet	7.00
Sherry	9.00
Wine, 2½ oz. or 3½ oz.	9.00

Original Catalog Illustration:
No. 880 goblet with No. 175
Airdale cutting

TAPERED BOWL

No. 3106

Date: 1934

Manufacturer: Cambridge Glass Co., Cambridge, OH

Colors: Crystal

Decorations: Diane etching, Elaine etching, Lily of the Valley etching, Rose Point etching. Brentwood cutting, Laurel Wreath cutting, Stafford cutting, Sunnybrook cutting.

Notes: Blown bowl, pressed stem. The footed tumblers listed actually appear to be a shorter stemmed version of the regular pieces. For decorated pieces, add 50 to 65% to crystal prices.

Brandy, ¾ oz.	$38.00
Claret, 4½ oz.	11.00
Cocktail, 3 oz.	11.00

Cordial, 1 oz.	38.00
Creme de Menthe, 2½ oz.	12.00
Finger Bowl	15.00
Goblet, Low Bowl, 10 oz.	12.00
Goblet, Tall Bowl, 9 oz.	12.00
Oyster Cocktail, 5 oz.	9.00
Pousse Café, 1 oz.	38.00
Sherbet, Low, 7 oz.	7.00
Sherbet, Tall, 7 oz.	9.00
Sherry, 2 oz.	12.00
Tumbler, Footed, 3 oz.	12.00
Tumbler, Footed, 5 oz.	12.00
Tumbler, Footed, 9 oz.	12.00
Tumbler, Footed, 12 oz.	12.00
Wine, 2½ oz.	11.00

Original Catalog Illustration:
No. 3106 low bowl goblet, low
sherbet and high bowl goblet
with Diane etching

No. 14187

Date: 1922

Manufacturer: U.S. Glass Co., Tiffin, OH

Colors: Crystal. Green stem and foot with Crystal bowl.

Decorations: Isabella Etching, No. 404 cutting

Notes: Blown bowl, pressed stem (lady leg shape). Made in wide optic and spiral optic.

Bonbon, 4" high	$12.00
Claret	18.00
Cocktail, 3 oz.	15.00
Goblet, 9 oz.	18.00
Oyster Cocktail	9.00
Parfait, Café	15.00
Saucer Champagne	18.00
Sundae (sherbet)	9.00
Wine, 2½ oz.	18.00

Original Catalog Illustration:
No. 14187 goblet with
Isabella etching

TULIP SHAPED BOWL

Original Catalog Illustration:
No. 3308 Bob White goblet

BOB WHITE, NO. 3308

Date: Ca. 1916

Manufacturer: A.H. Heisey & Co.,
Newark, OH

Colors: Crystal

Decorations: No. 366 Peacock etching, No. 403 etching, No. 430 etching, No. 432 etching, No. 455 Sportsman etching, No. 459 Fisherman etching, No. 460 Club Drinking Scene etching, No. 462 Fox Chase etching, No. 694 Balboa cutting

Notes: Blown bowl, pulled stem.

Burgundy, 3 oz.	$16.00
Claret, 4½ oz.	16.00
Cocktail, 3 oz.	16.00
Cordial, 1 oz.	25.00
Finger Bowl.	10.00
Goblet, 11 oz.	22.00
Goblet, 7 oz. or 9 oz.	18.00
Grape Juice, 4½ oz.	16.00
Parfait, 4½ oz.	18.00
Pousse Café.	25.00
Saucer Champagne, 6 oz.	12.00
Sherbet, Footed, 6 oz.	10.00
Sherry, 2 oz.	18.00
Sundae, Footed, 6 oz.	10.00
Wine, 2 oz.	18.00

Original Catalog Illustration:
No. 14178 goblet with
Adam etching

NO. 14178

Date: 1920s

Manufacturer: U.S. Glass Co., Tiffin, OH

Colors: Crystal

Decorations: Adam etching, Florentine cutting, No. 313 cutting, No. 360 cutting, No. 310 needle etching

Notes: Blown bowl, pulled stem. Made in wide optic. Discontinued by early 1934.

Café Parfait.	$7.00
Claret.	8.00
Cocktail, 3 oz.	6.00
Cordial.	12.00
Finger Bowl	5.00
Goblet, 10 oz.	9.00
Oyster Cocktail	5.00
Pousse Café	12.00
Saucer Champagne	8.00
Sundae.	5.00
Wine, 2½ oz.	9.00

Original Catalog Illustration:
No. 858 claret and goblet with
No. 73 Lenore etching

NO. 858

Date: 1904

Manufacturer: Fostoria Glass Co.,
Moundsville, WV

Colors: Crystal

Decorations: No. 47 Large Cloverleaf needle etching, No. 73 Lenore needle etching, No. 204 Vintage plate etching, No. 205 Blackberry plate etching, No. 215 plate etching, No. 227 New Vintage plate etching, No. 238 Empire plate etching, No. 241 Lily of the Valley plate etching, No. 252 New Adam plate etching, No. 256 Florid plate etching, No. 77 cutting, No. 81 Large Sunburst Star rock crystal cutting, No. 104 cutting, No. 116 Mission cutting, No. 118 Billow cutting,

Notes: Blown bowl, pulled stem. Made for many years.

Ale.	$17.00
Brandy.	10.00
Champagne, Hollow Stem	9.00
Champagne, Long Stem	17.00
Champagne, Tall.	9.00
Claret, 4½ oz.	10.00
Claret, 6½ oz.	10.00
Cocktail.	9.00
Cordial.	15.00
Creme de Menthe.	9.00
Fruit.	8.00
Goblet, 8 oz.	9.00
Goblet, 9 oz.	9.00
Goblet, 10 oz.	10.00
Goblet, 11 oz.	10.00
Hot Whiskey	10.00
Oyster Cocktail	6.00
Parfait	9.00
Saucer Champagne, 5½ oz.	8.00
Saucer Champagne, 7 oz.	8.00
Sherbet.	8.00
Sherry	10.00
Wine, 2¾ oz.	10.00
Wine, 3½ oz.	10.00

Reeded stems are comprised of small vertical ridges giving the impression of bundles of reeds. The following prices are for undecorated items.

BELL SHAPED BOWL

FONTAINE, NO. 5320

Date: 1930s

Manufacturer: Duncan & Miller Glass Co., Washington, PA

Colors: Crystal

Decorations: No. 684 Kimberly cutting

Notes: Blown bowl, pressed stem. Designed by Robert A. May.

Goblet. $18.00

No. 5320 Fontaine goblet with No. 684 Kimberly cutting

NO. 3130

Date: Ca. 1929

Manufacturer: Cambridge Glass Co., Cambridge, OH

Colors: Crystal. Crystal stem and foot with colored bowls in: Amber, Dianthus Pink, Emerald, Gold Krystol, Moonlight (blue), Peach-Blo, Willow Blue. Crystal bowl with Carmen stem and foot. Crystal bowl with Ebony stem and foot.

Decorations: Apple Blossom etching, Elaine etching, Gloria etching, Portia etching, No. 731 etching, No. 732 etching, No. 739 etching, No. 540 etching, Auburn rock crystal engraving, Cordelia rock crystal engraving, Glendale rock crystal engraving, Ravenna rock crystal engraving, Wedding Rose rock crystal engraving, Winthrop rock crystal engraving, No. 538 rock crystal engraving, No. 541 rock crystal engraving, No. 652 rock crystal engraving, No. 656 rock crystal engraving, No. 657 rock crystal engraving

Claret, 4½ oz.. . . . . $26.00
Cocktail, 3 oz. 16.00
Cordial, 1 oz. 50.00
Fruit Salad, 6 oz.. . . . . 9.00
Goblet, 8 oz. or 9 oz. 18.00
Oyster Cocktail, 4½ oz. 8.00
Sherbet, Low, 6 oz.. . . . . 8.00
Sherbet, Low, 7 oz. 8.00
Sherbet, Tall, 6 oz. 9.00
Sherbet, Tall, 7 oz. 9.00
Tumbler, Footed, 2½ oz. (whiskey) . . 28.00
Tumbler, Footed, 5 oz. (juice) 9.00
Tumbler, Footed, 8 oz. (water). 14.00
Tumbler, Footed, 10 oz. (water). 15.00
Tumbler, Footed, 12 oz. (iced tea) . . . 18.00
Tumbler, Footed with stem, 12 oz.. . . . 20.00
Wine, 2½ oz. 30.00

Original Catalog Illustration: No. 3130 goblet, tall sherbet and low sherbet with No. 538 rock crystal engraving

NO. 5299

Date: 1928

Manufacturer: Fostoria Glass Co., Moundsville, WV

Colors: Crystal stem & foot with colored bowl: Azure, Gold Tint, Green, Topaz, Wisteria

Decorations: No. 278 Versailles etching, No. 280 Trojan etching, No. 283 Kashmir plate etching

Notes: Blown bowl, pressed stem. Made in regular optic. Prices for all colors except Wisteria. For Wisteria, add about 50–60%.

Claret, 4 oz., 6" tall. $35.00
Cocktail, 3 oz., 5⅛" tall 26.00
Cordial, ¾ oz., 3⅞" tall 68.00
Goblet, 9 oz., 8¼" tall 28.00
Iced Tea, Footed, 12 oz., 5⅞" tall . . . 27.00
Juice, Footed, 5 oz., 4½" tall 17.00
Oyster Cocktail, 4½ oz., 3½" tall . . . 12.00
Parfait, 5½ oz. 28.00
Sherbet, High, 6 oz., 6⅛" tall 24.00
Sherbet, Low, 6 oz., 4¼" tall 16.00
Tumbler, Footed, 9 oz., 5⅜" tall 17.00
Whiskey, Footed, 2½ oz., 3" tall 42.00
Wine, 2½ oz., 5½" tall 38.00

Original Catalog Illustration: No. 5299 goblet and high sherbet with Trojan etching

BELL SHAPED BOWL *(continued)*

No. 51 goblet with crystal stem and Blue bowl

Original Catalog Illustration: No. 6014 goblet, saucer
champagne and low sherbet with No. 326 Arcady etching

Original Catalog Illustration: No. 15024 Goblet
with Flanders etching

NO. 51

Date: 1930s

Manufacturer: Seneca Glass Co.,
Morgantown, WV

Colors: Crystal, Crystal stem and foot with Blue bowl

Decorations: Unknown

Goblet, blue bowl. $45.00

NO. 6014

Date: 1935

Manufacturer: Fostoria Glass Co.,
Moundsville, WV

Colors: Crystal. Crystal stem and foot with Azure or Gold Tint bowl

Decorations: No. 325 Corsage plate etching, No. 326 Arcady plate
etching, No. 754 Cavendish rock crystal cutting, No. 755 Palmetto
rock crystal cutting, No. 758 Bordeaux cutting, No. 759 Weylin
cutting

Notes: Blown bowl, pressed stem. Made regular or loop optic.

	Crystal	Colors
Claret	$27.00	$37.00
Cocktail.	20.00	25.00
Cordial	38.00	58.00
Goblet	24.00	32.00
Iced Tea, Footed.	22.00	26.00
Juice, Footed	18.00	22.00
Oyster Cocktail	12.00	20.00
Saucer Champagne	22.00	26.00
Sherbet, Low	15.00	22.00
Tumbler, Footed, 9 oz. (water)	18.00	24.00
Wine.	27.00	37.00

NO. 15024

Date: Ca. 1913 into the 1920s

Manufacturer: U.S. Glass Co., Tiffin, OH

Colors: Crystal

Decorations: Classic etching, Flanders etching

Notes: Blown bowl, pressed stem.

Café Parfait $15.00
Claret 22.00
Cocktail. 15.00
Finger Bowl 9.00
Goblet. 22.00
Saucer Champagne. 20.00
Sundae (sherbet) 10.00
Wine. 22.00

(continued) # BELL SHAPED BOWL

SCEPTRE, NO. 6017

Date: 1937

Manufacturer: Fostoria Glass Co., Moundsville, WV

Colors: Crystal. Crystal stem and foot, Azure bowl or Gold Tint bowl

Decorations: No. 329 Lido etching, No. 330 Lenox etching, No. 331 Shirley etching, No. 341 Romance etching, No. 766 Ripple cutting, No. 767 Beacon rock crystal cutting, No. 768 Bridal Shower cutting, No. 776 Laurel cutting, No. 777 Raynel rock crystal cutting, No. 778 Lucerne rock crystal cutting, No. 784 Drape rock crystal cutting, No. 785 Cynthia cutting, No. 618 Simplicity gold band

Notes: Blown bowl, pressed stem. Made plain. Used for plate etchings and cuttings. "A thin-blown bowl of perfect symmetry, a sparkling rosette, a slender fluted stem unite to achieve this flashing table gem of clearest crystal." —From Fostoria ad, 1937.

	Crystal	Colors
Claret, 4 oz., 5⅞" tall	$27.00	$35.00
Cocktail, 3½ oz., 4⅞" tall	22.00	25.00
Cordial, ¾ oz., 3⅞" tall	40.00	50.00
Goblet, 9 oz., 7⅜" tall	24.00	30.00
Oyster Cocktail, 4 oz., 3⅝" tall	15.00	18.00
Saucer Champagne, 6 oz., 5½" tall (high sherbet)	22.00	24.00
Sherbet, Low, 6 oz., 4½" tall	20.00	22.00
Tumbler, Footed, 5 oz., 4¾" tall (juice)	15.00	18.00
Tumbler, Footed, 9 oz., 5½" tall (water)	15.00	18.00
Tumbler, Footed, 12 oz., 6" tall (iced tea)	22.00	25.00
Tumbler, Footed, 14 oz., 6½" tall (iced tea)	22.00	25.00
Wine, 3 oz., 5½" tall	27.00	35.00

Original Catalog Illustration: No. 6017 Sceptre goblet and champagne with Lido etching

CUPPED BOWL

NEO CLASSIC, NO. 6011

Date: 1934

Manufacturer: Fostoria Glass Co., Moundsville, WV

Colors: Crystal. Crystal stem and foot with colored bowl: Amethyst, Burgundy, Empire Green, Regal Blue, Ruby. Crystal bowl with Amber stem and foot.

Decorations: No. 322 Nectar etching. Mother-of-pearl iridescent bowl. Silver Mist (satin) stem. No. 729 Rocket cutting (stars), No. 730 Whirlpool cutting, No. 731 Celestial cutting, No. 734 Planet cutting, No. 735 Shooting Stars cutting, No. 736 Directoire cutting, No. 737 Quinfoil cutting, No. 765 Mardi Gras cutting, No. 770 Athenian cutting

Notes: Blown bowl, pressed stem. Made plain. Used for plate etchings and modernistic cuttings.

Original Catalog Illustration: No. 6011 Neo Classic stems with No. 729 Rocket cutting

	Crystal	Amber Burgundy Amethyst Empire Green	Regal Blue Ruby
Brandy, 1 oz., 4" tall	$25.00	$30.00	$40.00
Claret, 4½ oz., 5⅝" tall	20.00	32.00	50.00
Cocktail, 3 oz., 4⅝" tall	15.00	30.00	42.00
Cordial, 1 oz., 3¼" tall	32.00	40.00	58.00
Creme de Menthe, 2 oz., 4½" tall	15.00	27.00	38.00
Goblet, 10 oz., 6⅜" tall	18.00	32.00	47.00
Oyster Cocktail, 4 oz., 3¼" tall	10.00	22.00	25.00
Rhine Wine, 4½ oz., 6" tall	20.00	32.00	48.00
Saucer Champagne, 5½ oz., 4¾" tall	15.00	28.00	42.00
Sherbet, Low, 5½ oz., 3¼" tall	10.00	27.00	27.00
Sherry, 2 oz., 4⅝" tall	15.00	28.00	40.00
Wine, 3 oz., 5" tall	22.00	32.00	50.00
Tumbler, Footed, 2 oz., 2¾" tall (whiskey or bar)	18.00	25.00	38.00
Tumbler, Footed, 5 oz., 3⅞" tall (juice)	10.00	22.00	32.00
Tumbler, Footed, 10 oz., 4½" tall (water)	11.00	22.00	32.00
Tumbler, Footed, 13 oz., 5⅜" tall (iced tea)	15.00	27.00	42.00

FLARED BOWL

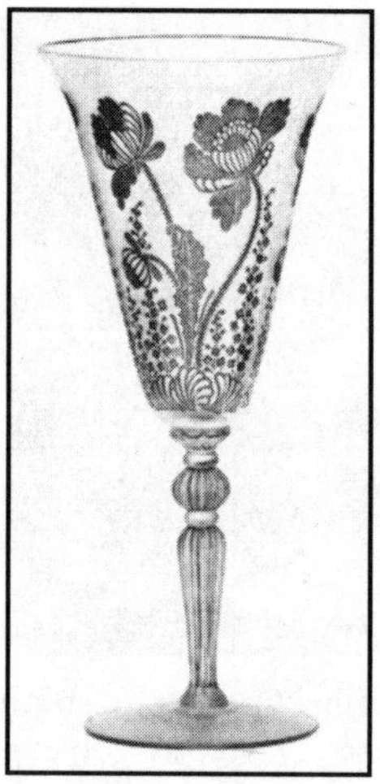

Original Catalog Illustration:
No. 3035 goblet with
No. 746 Gloria etching

NO. 3035

Date: 1931

Manufacturer: Cambridge Glass Co., Cambridge, OH

Colors: Crystal. The following Crystal stem with colored bowls: Amber, Amethyst, Carmen, Dianthus Pink, Forest Green, Gold Krystol, Heatherbloom, Peach-Blo

Decorations: Apple Blossom etching, Brettone etching, Elaine etching, Gloria etching, Lorna etching, Portia etching, No. 731 etching. No. 560 rock crystal engraving, No. 613 rock crystal engraving, No. 614 rock crystal engraving, No. 616 rock crystal engraving, No. 621 rock crystal engraving

Notes: Blown bowl, pressed stem. Made in plain or optic. For decorated pieces, add 50%

	Crystal	Pastels
Claret, 4½ oz.	$15.00	$25.00
Cocktail, 3 oz.	12.00	16.00
Cordial, 1 oz.	30.00	50.00
Fruit Salad, 6 oz.	9.00	14.00
Goblet, 9 oz.	15.00	18.00
Oyster Cocktail, 4½ oz.	9.00	14.00
Sherbet, Low, 6 oz.	9.00	15.00
Sherbet, Tall, 6 oz.	11.00	16.00
Tumbler, Footed, 2½ oz.	9.00	11.00
Tumbler, Footed, 5 oz.	11.00	14.00
Tumbler, Footed, 8 oz.	11.00	14.00
Tumbler, Footed, 10 oz.	12.00	16.00
Tumbler, Footed, 12 oz.	12.00	16.00
Wine, 2½ oz.	15.00	25.00

MISCELLANEOUS SHAPED BOWL

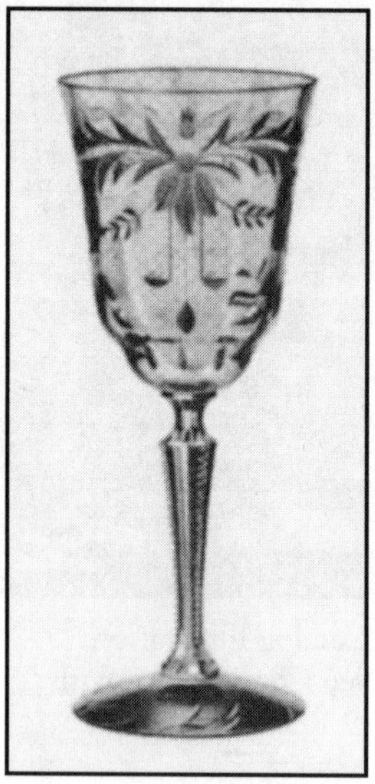

Original Catalog Illustration:
No. 6009 Camelot goblet with
No. 718 Doncaster cutting

CAMELOT, NO. 6009

Date: 1933

Manufacturer: Fostoria Glass Co., Moundsville, WV

Colors: Crystal, Amber. Crystal stem and foot with colored bowl: Rose (1933), Blue (1979)

Decorations: No. 316 Midnight Rose etching, No. 88 Cameo double needle etch, Grand Majesty plate etching, No. 718 Doncaster rock crystal cutting, No. 719 Lancaster rock crystal cutting, No. 720 Nottingham rock crystal cutting, No. 721 Buckingham rock crystal cutting

Notes: Blown bowl, pressed stem. Made in regular optic. Used for needle etchings, plate etchings and rock crystal cuttings. Reintroduced by Fostoria in 1979 as Camelot. The pieces marked * were current production at that time.

	Crystal	Colors
Claret-Wine, 3¾ oz., 5⅜" tall	$25.00	$32.00
Cocktail, 3¾ oz., 4¾" tall	18.00	22.00
Cordial, 1 oz., 3¾" tall	35.00	45.00
Dessert/Champagne, 9 oz., 6⅜" tall *	17.00	24.00
Goblet, 9 oz., 7⅝" tall	20.00	25.00
Goblet, 13 oz., 8³⁄₁₆" tall *	20.00	27.00
Iced Tea, Footed, 12 oz., 5⅞" tall	18.00	22.00
Iced Tea, Footed, 16 oz., 6¾" tall *	18.00	27.00
Magnum, 16 oz. 7¾" tall *	38.00	45.00
Oyster Cocktail, 4¾ oz., 3¾" tall	12.00	18.00
Saucer Champagne, 5½ oz., 5⅝" tall (high sherbet)	18.00	24.00
Sherbet, Low, 5½ oz., 4⅜" tall	14.00	17.00
Tumbler, Footed, 5 oz., 4⅜" tall (juice)	13.00	17.00
Tumbler, Footed, 9 oz., 5¼" tall (water)	14.00	18.00
Wine, 9 oz., 7⅜" tall *	24.00	35.00

MISCELLANEOUS SHAPED BOWL
(continued)

No. 15018

Date: 1930s

Manufacturer: U.S. Glass Co., Tiffin, OH

Colors: Crystal, All Rose, Crystal bowl with Green stem and foot, Green

Decorations: Empire etching

Notes: Blown bowl, pressed stem. Made in regular optic or wide optic.

Claret	$22.00
Cocktail	15.00
Goblet	22.00
Parfait, Café	15.00
Saucer Champagne	20.00
Sundae (sherbet)	10.00
Wine	22.00

Original Catalog Illustration:
No. 15018 goblet with
Empire etching

OVOID

MADEMOISELLE, NO. 6033

Date: 1949

Manufacturer: Fostoria Glass Co., Moundsville, WV

Colors: Crystal

Decorations: No. 342 Boquet etching, No. 821 Spinet cutting, No. 823 Sprite cutting, No. 625 Reflection-platinum band

Notes: Blown bowl, pressed stem. For cuttings and etchings add about 20%.

Claret or Wine, 4 oz.	$25.00
Cocktail, 4 oz.	20.00
Cordial, 1 oz.	40.00
Goblet, 10 oz.	24.00
Iced Tea, Footed, 13 oz.	18.00
Juice, Footed, 5 oz.	15.00
Oyster Cocktail, 4 oz.	9.00
Parfait, 6 oz.	18.00
Sherbet, High, 6 oz.	19.00
Sherbet, Low, 6 oz.	10.00

Original Ad: No. 6033
Mademoiselle stems

No. 15079

Date: 1934

Manufacturer: U.S. Glass Co., (Tiffin), Tiffin, OH

Colors: Crystal bowl with stems and feet in colors: Amber, Green, Royal Blue

Decorations: Unknown

Notes: Blown bowl, pressed stem. Made plain (no optic). For colors add 50%.

Café Parfait, 5½ oz.	$15.00
Champagne, 5 oz.	15.00
Cocktail, 3½ oz.	15.00

Cordial, 1 oz.	45.00
Goblet, 9 oz.	22.00
Iced Tea, Footed, 12½ oz.	20.00
Pousse Café, 1 oz.	45.00
Saucer Champagne, 5½ oz.	20.00
Seltzer, Footed, 4½ oz. (juice)	15.00
Sherry, 2 oz.	40.00
Sundae, 5½ oz. (sherbet)	10.00
Table, Footed, 9½ oz. (tumbler)	18.00
Whiskey, Footed, 2¼ oz.	22.00
Wine, 2½ oz.	22.00

Original Catalog Illustration:
No. 15079 goblet

Chapter 10
SCULPTURED

Sculptured stems include the fancy, exquisitely intricate stems made by many companies in the mid-1930s and with some continuation later. Typically these stems are made up of many motifs and are indeed small sculptures. **The following prices are for undecorated items.**

BELL SHAPED BOWL

Original Catalog Illustration:
No. 5317 Cathay Goblet

CATHAY, NO. 5317

Date: 1930s

Manufacturer: Duncan & Miller Glass Co., Washington, PA

Colors: Crystal

Decorations: No. 651 Rhapsody cutting, No. 652 Lucerne cutting, No. 681 Lovelace cutting, No. 682 Coronet cutting, No. 688 Juno cutting, No. 713 Minuet cutting

Notes: Blown bowl, pressed stem. Designed by Robert A. May.

Claret, 5 oz., 5¾" tall	$15.00
Cocktail, Liquor, 3½ oz., 4" tall	12.00
Cordial, 1 oz., 3½" tall	45.00
Finger Bowl, 4½"	8.00
Goblet, 10 oz., 6¼" tall	18.00
Ice Cream, Footed (sherbet), 5 oz., 3½" tall	9.00
Iced Tea, Footed, 12 oz., 6½" tall	18.00
Juice, Orange, Footed, 5 oz., 4¾" tall	12.00
Oyster Cocktail, 4½ oz., 3½" tall	9.00
Saucer Champagne, 5 oz., 4½" tall	18.00
Tumbler, Footed, 9 oz., 5½" tall	14.00
Wine, 3 oz., 5" tall	20.00

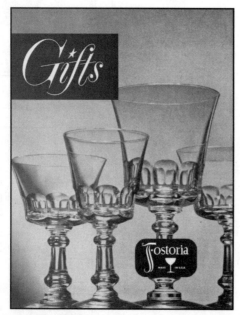

Original Advertisement: No. 6023 Colfax stems with
No. 786 Dolly Madison cutting (cut flutes)

COLFAX, NO. 6023

Date: 1940

Manufacturer: Fostoria Glass Co., Moundsville, WV

Colors: Crystal

Decorations: No. 94 Spencerian tracing, No. 334 Colonial Mirror plate etching, No. 335 Willow plate etching, No. 786 Dolly Madison rock crystal cutting (cut flutes), No. 787 Pilgrim rock crystal cutting, No. 788 Chippendale rock crystal cutting, No. 792 Cathedral rock crystal cutting, No. 793 Spire rock crystal cutting, No. 801 Brighton rock crystal cutting, No. 802 Wentworth rock crystal cutting, No. 820 Wakefield rock crystal cutting, No. 825 Revere rock crystal cutting

Notes: Blown bowl, pressed stem. Made plain (without optic).

Claret-Wine, 4 oz., 4¾" tall	$15.00
Cocktail, 3¾ oz., 4⅜" tall	14.00
Cordial, 1 oz., 3⅜" tall	28.00
Goblet, 9 oz., 6⅜" tall	17.00
Iced Tea, 12 oz., 4¾" tall	15.00
Juice, Footed, 5 oz., 4½" tall	14.00
Oyster Cocktail, 4 oz., 3⅝" tall	9.00
Saucer Champagne, 6 oz., 4⅞" tall	15.00
Sherbet, Low, 6 oz., 4⅛" tall	9.00
Tumbler, Footed, 9 oz., 5⅛" tall	12.00

(continued) # BELL SHAPED BOWL

DEAUVILLE, NO. 5326

Date: 1930s

Manufacturer: Duncan & Miller Glass Co., Washington, PA

Colors: Crystal

Decorations: Indian Tree etching, No. 777 Burgundy cutting, No. 783 Francis First cutting

Notes: Blown bowl, pressed stem.

Claret, 4½ oz., 6¾" high $15.00
Cocktail, Liquor, 3½ oz., 5¼" high 12.00
Cordial, 1 oz., 5" high 45.00
Finger Bowl, 4½". 8.00
Goblet, 9 oz., 7¾" high 18.00
Goblet, Luncheon, 9 oz., 6" high 18.00
Ice Cream, 6 oz. (sherbet), 3¾" high 9.00
Iced Tea, Footed, 13 oz., 6¾" high 18.00
Orange Juice, Footed, 5 oz., 4¾" high 12.00
Oyster Cocktail, 4½ oz., 4¼" high 9.00
Plate, Finger Bowl, 6" 5.00
Saucer Champagne, 6 oz., 6" high 18.00
Wine, 3 oz., 6¼" high 20.00

Original Catalog Illustration:
No. 5326 Deauville Claret

DUNCAN SCROLL, NO. D5

Date: 1950s

Manufacturer: Duncan & Miller Glass Co., Washington, PA

Colors: Crystal

Decorations: Dawn cutting, Cretan cutting, Spring Beauty cutting, Fleur-de-lis cutting, Hawthorne cutting

Notes: Blown bowl, pressed stem.

Cocktail, Liquor $12.00
Goblet. 20.00
Iced Tea, Footed 18.00
Juice, Footed 12.00
Saucer Champagne or Tall Sherbet 18.00
Seafood Cocktail 9.00
Wine or Claret 20.00

Original Catalog Illustration:
No. D5 Duncan Scroll goblet with Spring Beauty cutting

ETERNAL LIFE, D6

Date: 1950s

Manufacturer: Duncan & Miller Glass Co., Washington, PA

Colors: Crystal

Decorations: Belvidere cutting, Concerto cutting, Wildflower cutting

Notes: Blown bowl, pressed stem.

Cocktail, Liquor. $12.00
Goblet. 18.00
Iced Tea, Footed. 18.00
Juice, Footed 12.00
Saucer Champagne or Tall Sherbet 18.00
Seafood Cocktail 9.00
Wine or Claret. 20.00

Original Catalog Illustration:
No. D6 Eternal Life goblet with Concerto cutting

BELL SHAPED BOWL *(continued)*

No. 3411 Monte Cristo goblet with
No. 456 Titania etching

Original Catalog Illustration:
No. 3411 Monte Cristo wine

Original Catalog Illustration:
No. 3408 Jamestown goblet

MONTE CRISTO, NO. 3411

Date: 1933

Manufacturer: A.H. Heisey & Co., Newark, OH

Colors: Crystal

Decorations: No. 456 Titania etching, No. 458 Olympiad etching, No. 801 Waikiki cutting, No. 802 Manchester cutting, No. 839 Bonnie Briar cutting, No. 848 Botticelli cutting, No. 851 Kalarama cutting, No. 861 Neapolitan cutting, No. 863 Contessa cutting, No. 898 Trafalgar cutting

Notes: Blown bowl, pressed stem.

Cocktail, 3½ oz.	$25.00
Comport, 7"	65.00
Cordial, 1 oz.	85.00
Finger Bowl	12.00
Goblet, 9 oz.	35.00
Oyster Cocktail, 4½ oz.	12.00
Saucer Champagne, 6 oz.	25.00
Sherbet, 6 oz.	15.00
Sherry, 1½ oz.	70.00
Soda, Footed, 5 oz. (juice)	12.00
Soda, Footed, 12 oz. (iced tea)	18.00
Tumbler, Footed, 9 oz.	17.00
Wine, 2½ oz.	60.00

JAMESTOWN, NO. 3408

Date: 1933

Manufacturer: A.H. Heisey & Co., Newark, OH

Colors: Crystal, Sahara (rare)

Decorations: No. 497 Rosalie etching, No. 500 Belvedere etching. Cuttings: No. 803 Hialeah, No. 812 Sweet Briar, No. 816 Palmetto, No. 829 Roxy, No. 831 Valencia, No. 833 Bavaria, No. 835 Larkspur, No. 837 Cristobal, No. 855 Fuchsia, No. 866 Kent, No. 939 Festoon Wreath, No. 941 Barcelona, No. 965 Narcissus, No. 984 Lancaster, No. 985 Sheffield

Notes: Blown bowl, pressed stem. Made in wide optic. Very similar to No. 3360 Penn Charter, which has a different shaped bowl.

Claret, 4½ oz.	$22.00
Cocktail, 3 oz.	18.00
Cordial, 1 oz.	55.00
Finger Bowl	12.00
Goblet, 9 oz.	25.00
Saucer Champagne, 6 oz.	15.00
Sherbet, 6 oz.	12.00
Sherry, 1½ oz.	45.00
Soda, Footed, 13 oz. (iced tea)	15.00
Tumbler, Footed, 9 oz.	18.00
Vase, 9"	60.00
Wine, 2 oz.	27.00

(continued) BELL SHAPED BOWL

NO. 3121

Date: 1931

Manufacturer: Cambridge Glass Co., Cambridge, OH

Colors: Crystal. Crystal stem and foot with colored bowls in: Amber, Forest Green, Gold Krystol

Decorations: Elaine etching, Portia etching, Rose Point etching, Wildflower etching, No. 640 rock crystal engraving, No. 654 rock crystal engraving, No. 655 rock crystal engraving, Achilles rock crystal engraving, Kenmore rock crystal engraving. The following etchings were also available with gold encrustation: No. D/1014 Elaine, No. D/1001 Portia, No. D/1041 Rose Point.

Notes: Blown bowl, pressed stem. Made plain or optic.

Claret, 4½ oz.	$30.00
Cocktail, 3 oz.	26.00
Comport, Blown, 5⅜"	75.00
Cordial, 1 oz.	60.00
Goblet, 10 oz.	30.00
Iced Tea, Footed, 12 oz.	24.00
Oyster Cocktail, 4½ oz.	15.00
Sherbet, Low, 6 oz.	18.00
Sherbet, Tall, 6 oz.	24.00
Tumbler, Footed, 5 oz.	18.00
Tumbler, Footed, 10 oz.	22.00
Wine, 3½ oz.	30.00

Original Catalog Illustration:
No. 3121 cocktail, goblet, and tall sherbet with Portia etching

NO. 3124

Date: 1932

Manufacturer: Cambridge Glass Co., Cambridge, OH

Colors: Crystal. Gold Krystol bowl, Crystal stem and foot.

Decorations: Apple Blossom etching, Minerva etching, Portia etching, No. 611 rock crystal engraving, No. 615 rock crystal engraving, No. 618 rock crystal engraving, No. 619 rock crystal engraving, No. 639 rock crystal engraving

Notes: Blown bowl, pressed stem. See also No. 3122 for the same stem with a differently shaped bowl. For items in color, add 50%.

Claret, 4½ oz.	$22.00
Cocktail, 3 oz.	25.00
Goblet, 10 oz.	18.00
Oyster Cocktail, 4½ oz.	8.00
Sherbet, Low, 7 oz.	8.00
Sherbet, Tall, 7 oz.	9.00
Tumbler, Footed, 3 oz.	28.00
Tumbler, Footed, 5 oz.	10.00
Tumbler, Footed, 10 oz.	15.00
Tumbler, Footed, 12 oz.	16.00
Wine, 3 oz.	30.00

Original Catalog Illustration:
No. 3124 goblet with
Portia etching

RUTLEDGE, NO. 6036

Date: 1951

Manufacturer: Fostoria Glass Co., Moundsville, WV

Colors: Crystal

Decorations: No. 344 Camelia plate etching, No. 827 Rose cutting, No. 828 Ballet rock crystal cutting, No. 829 Chatham rock crystal cutting

Notes: Blown bowl, pressed stem. Made plain (no optic).

Claret, Wine, 3¼ oz., 4¾" tall	$22.00
Cocktail, 3½ oz., 4⅛" tall	18.00
Cordial, 1 oz., 3¼" tall	35.00
Goblet, 9½ oz., 6⅞" tall	22.00
Iced Tea, Footed, 12 oz., 6⅛" tall	20.00
Juice, Footed, 5 oz., 4⅝" tall	13.00
Oyster Cocktail, 4 oz., 3¾" tall	11.00
Parfait, 5½ oz., 5⅞" tall	20.00
Sherbet, High, 6 oz., 4¾" tall	20.00
Sherbet, Low, 6 oz., 4⅛" tall	15.00

Original Company Ad: No. 6036
Rutledge assortment with
No. 827 Rose cutting

BELL SHAPED BOWL *(continued)*

Original Company Ad: No. 6037 Silver Flutes stems with
No. 343 Heather etching

Original Catalog Illustration: Stradivari stems

Original Brochure: No. 5010 Symphone goblet with
No. 921 Danish Princess cutting

SILVER FLUTES, No. 6037

Date: 1949

Manufacturer: Fostoria Glass Co., Moundsville, WV

Colors: Crystal

Decorations: No. 343 Heather etching

Notes: Blown bowl, pressed stem.

Cocktail, 4 oz., 5" tall	$22.00
Cordial, 1 oz., 4" tall	55.00
Goblet, 9 oz., 7⅞" tall	25.00
Goblet, Low, 9 oz., 6⅜" tall	22.00
Iced Tea, Footed, 12 oz., 6⅛" tall	22.00
Juice, Footed, 5 oz., 4⅞" tall	18.00
Oyster Cocktail, 4½ oz., 4" tall	14.00
Parfait, 6 oz., 6⅛" tall	28.00
Sherbet, High, 7 oz., 6" tall	22.00
Sherbet, Low, 7 oz., 4¾" tall	15.00
Wine, 4 oz., 6" tall	35.00

STRADIVARI

Date: Ca. 1936

Manufacturer: Cambridge Glass Co., Cambridge, OH

Colors: Crystal

Decorations: Diane etching, Portia etching. Celestial cutting, Melody cutting, Symphony cutting, No. 940 cutting

Notes: Blown bowl, pressed stem. Also called Regency in later years.

Claret, 4½ oz.	$25.00
Cocktail, 3½ oz.	15.00
Cordial, 1 oz.	55.00
Goblet, 10 oz.	20.00
Oyster Cocktail, 4½ oz.	10.00
Sherbet, Low, 7 oz.	10.00
Sherbet, Tall, 7 oz.	14.00
Tumbler, Footed, 5 oz.	12.00
Tumbler, Footed, 10 oz.	15.00
Tumbler, Footed, 12 oz.	16.00
Wine, 3 oz.	35.00

SYMPHONE, No. 5010

Date: 1939

Manufacturer: A.H. Heisey & Co., Newark, OH

Colors: Crystal

Decorations: No. 502 Crinoline etching, No. 503 Minuet etching, No. 921 Danish Princess cutting, No. 983 Lady Astor cutting

Notes: Blown bowl, pressed stem

Claret, 4 oz.	$30.00
Cocktail, 3½ oz.	25.00
Comport, 5½"	65.00
Cordial, 1 oz.	85.00
Finger Bowl	12.00
Goblet, 9 oz.	35.00
Goblet, Low Foot, 9 oz,.	30.00
Oyster Cocktail, 4½ oz.	12.00
Saucer Champagne, 6 oz.	25.99
Sherbet, 6 oz.	15.00
Soda, Footed, 5 oz. (juice)	12.00
Soda, Footed, 12 oz. (iced tea)	18.00
Wine, 2½ oz.	60.00

(continued) Bell Shaped Bowl

Wilma, No. 6016

Date: 1936

Manufacturer: Fostoria Glass Co., Moundsville, WV

Colors: Crystal. Crystal stem and foot with colored bowl: Azure, Blue, Pink

Decorations: No. 327 Navarre etching, No. 328 Meadow Rose etching, No. 761 Melba rock crystal cutting, No. 762 Cumberland rock crystal cutting, No. 515 Richelieu etching with gold filling, No. 696 Victoria (platinum band), No. 697 Regis (gold band)

Notes: Blown bowl, pressed stem. Made in regular optic. Volume sizes were readjusted in original Fostoria catalogs (an asterisk (*) indicates the larger sizes were made in the 1970s and later.) Cuttings are priced about 25% higher than crystal prices.

Original Catalog Illustration: No. 6016 Wilma stem pieces with Navarre etching

	Crystal	Colors
Brandy Inhaler, 15 oz., 5½" tall *	$32.00	$50.00
Champagne, Continental, 5 oz., 8⅛" tall	32.00	50.00
Claret, 4 oz. or 4½ oz., 6" tall	22.00	30.00
Claret, Large, 6½ oz., 6¼" tall *	25.00	32.00
Cocktail, 3½ oz., 5¼" tall	18.00	25.00
Cocktail/Sherry, 6 oz., 6³⁄₁₆" tall *	30.00	45.00
Cordial, ¾ oz. or 1 oz., 3⅞" tall	35.00	50.00
Goblet, 9 oz. or 10 oz., 7⅝" tall	22.00	30.00
Magnum, 16 oz., 7¼" tall *	35.00	30.00
Oyster Cocktail, 4 oz., 3⅝" tall	15.00	20.00
Saucer Champagne, 5½ oz. or 6 oz., 5⅝" tall	18.00	25.00
Sherbet, Low, 5½ oz. or 6 oz., 4⅜" tall	15.00	20.00
Tumbler, Footed, 5 oz., 4⅝" tall (juice)	18.00	25.00
Tumbler, Footed, 10 oz., 5⅜" tall (water)	18.00	25.00
Tumbler, Footed, 13 oz., 5⅞" tall (iced tea)	22.00	30.00
Wine, 3 oz. or 3¼ oz., 5¼" tall	25.00	32.00

Wistar, No. 5329

Date: 1930s

Manufacturer: Duncan & Miller Glass Co., Washington, PA

Colors: Crystal

Decorations: No. 758 Exeter cutting, No. 760 Andover cutting

Notes: Blown bowl, pressed stem. Designed by Robert A. May.

Claret, 5 oz., 7" tall	$15.00
Cocktail, Liquor, 3½ oz., 5½" tall	12.00
Cordial, 1 oz., 4¾" tall	45.00
Finger Bowl, 4½"	8.00
Goblet, 10 oz., 7¾" tall	20.00
Ice Cream, Footed (sherbet), 6 oz., 3½" tall	9.00
Iced Tea, Footed, 13 oz., 6½" tall	18.00
Juice, Orange, Footed, 5 oz., 4½" tall	12.00
Oyster Cocktail, 4½ oz., 4" tall	9.00
Saucer Champagne or Tall Sherbet, 6 oz., 6¼" tall	18.00
Tumbler, Footed, or Luncheon Goblet, 9 oz., 5½" tall	16.00
Wine, 3 oz., 6½" tall	20.00

Original Catalog Illustration: No. 5329 Wistar goblet and champagne

Cupped Bowl

Legionnaire, No. 5077

Date: 1950

Manufacturer: A.H. Heisey & Co., Newark, OH

Colors: Crystal, Crystal bowl with Amber stem

Decorations: No. 9016 Poppy etching, No. 1024 Hawthorne cutting, No. 1025 Arcadia cutting, No. 1026 Bellevue cutting, No. 1027 Fremont cutting, No. 1028 Hibiscus cutting, No. 1029 Evening Star cutting, No. 1035 Cornflower cutting, No. 1036 Beau Knot cutting, No. 1037 June cutting, No. 1041 Lily cutting, No. 1082 Rosebud cutting

Notes: Blown bowl, pressed stem. Similar to Crystolite, No. 5003

Claret, 3½ oz.	$12.00
Cocktail, 3½ oz.	10.00
Cordial, 1 oz.	50.00
Goblet, 10 oz.	15.00
Iced Tea, Footed, 12 oz.	12.00
Juice, Footed, 5 oz.	10.00
Oyster Cocktail, 3½ oz.	8.00
Sherbet, 6 oz.	7.00

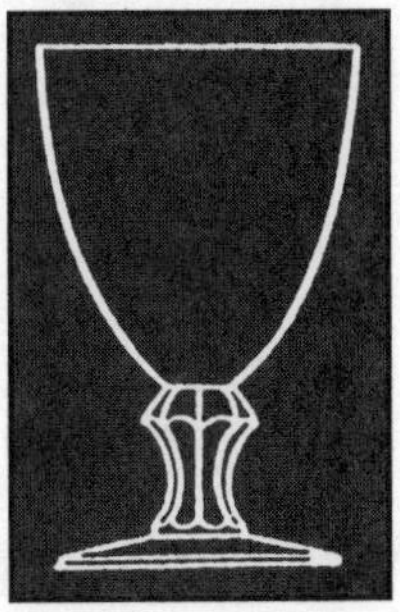

Original Catalog Illustration: No. 5077 Legionnaire goblet

CUPPED BOWL *(continued)*

Original Catalog Illustration:
No. 15016 claret with Luciana etching

No. 15016

Date: 1925

Manufacturer: U.S. Glass Co., Tiffin, OH

Colors: Crystal, Crystal with Black Trim, Crystal with Amber Trim

Decorations: Luciana etching, Psyche etching, Classic etching, No. 406 cutting

Notes: Blown bowl, pressed stem. Made in regular optic.

Claret	$22.00
Cocktail, 3 oz.	15.00
Goblet, 11 oz.	22.00
Parfait	15.00
Saucer Champagne	20.00
Sundae (sherbet)	10.00
Wine, 2½ oz.	22.00

FLARED BOWL

Original Catalog Illustration:
No. 2630 Century goblet

CENTURY, NO. 2630

Date: 1950

Manufacturer: Fostoria Glass Co., Moundsville, WV

Colors: Crystal

Decorations: None known

Notes: Blown bowl, pressed stem. Made to match the pressed Century pattern of tableware.

Cocktail, 3½ oz.	$15.00
Goblet, 10½ oz.	22.00
Iced Tea Tumbler, Footed, 12 oz.	24.00
Juice Tumbler, Footed, 5 oz.	15.00
Sherbet, 5½ oz.	12.00
Wine, 3½ oz.	28.00

CHALICE, NO. D7

Date: 1950s

Manufacturer: Duncan & Miller Glass Co., Washington, PA

Colors: Crystal

Decorations: Sundown rock crystal cutting,

Notes: Blown bowl, pressed stem.

Cocktail, Liquor	$12.00
Goblet	20.00
Saucer Champagne or Tall Sherbet	18.00
Seafood Cocktail	9.00
Tumbler, Footed (iced tea)	18.00
Tumbler, Footed (juice)	12.00
Wine or Claret	20.00

L to R: Original Catalog Illustrations: No. D7 Chalice goblet
with Sundown cutting and No. 75 Diamond goblet

DIAMOND, NO. 75

Date: 1940

Manufacturer: Duncan & Miller Glass Co., Washington, PA

Colors: Crystal. Ruby bowl, Crystal stem.

Decorations: None known

Notes: All pressed. Made to match a full pressed table line. Ruby, add 50%.

Claret or Wine, 4 oz.	$15.00
Cocktail, 3½ oz.	15.00
Goblet, 9 oz.	17.00
Iced Tea, Footed, 12 oz.	16.00
Juice, Orange, Footed, 5 oz.	10.00
Oyster Cocktail, 4½ oz.	15.00
Saucer Champagne/Tall Sherbet, 6 oz.	15.00
Wine, 3½ oz.	15.00

(continued) **FLARED BOWL**

No. 17477

Date: 1940s or 1950s

Manufacturer: Tiffin Glass Co., Tiffin, OH

Colors: Crystal, Wisteria bowl with Crystal stem and foot

Decorations: Cuttings: April, Arcadia, Astral, Autumn, Balsam, Brilliance, Brookmar, Calais, Carmel—platinum, Chapel Bells, Cherry Blossom, Coronet, Enchanted, Eugenia, Georgette, Jupiter—gold or platinum, Karen, Lenox Belvedere, Lenox Country Garden, Lenox Rhodora, Lenox Rutledge, Marigold, Ming, Monte Carlo, Nancy, Oakwood, Old Master, Pamela, Peach Tree, Piccadily, Pine Tree, Poinsettia, Prince Charming, Rose Leaf, Rutledge, Seville, Shooting Star, Silhouette, Southern Garden, Syncopation, Tiffin Rhodora, Willow Leaf. Etchings: Damask Rose, Gold Wreath—gold encrusted, Magnolia, Minton Wisteria—gold encrusted, Rose, Silver Wreath—platinum band, Sunnyvale, Anniversary gold bands. Pink Rain sand carving (Wisteria), Rain sand carving (crystal).

Notes: Blown bowl, pressed stem. For Wisteria, add 150%. Only a few decorations are found on Wisteria pieces.

Goblet. $20.00
Sherbet, Tall/Saucer Champagne. . 17.00

No. 17477 sherbet and goblet, Wisteria bowls

MISCELLANEOUS SHAPED BOWL

GADROON, No. 3500

Date: 1933

Manufacturer: Cambridge Glass Co., Cambridge, OH

Colors: Crystal. Crystal stem & foot with colored bowls: Amber, Amethyst, Carmen, Forest Green, Gold Krystol, Royal Blue

Decorations: Diane etching, Elaine etching, Minerva etching, Rose Point etching, Valencia etching. Adonis cutting, Croesus cutting, Harvest cutting, Victory Wreath cutting. Elaine and Rose Point also with gold encrustation.

Notes: Blown bowl, pressed stem. Optic or plain. Patented in 1933.

	Crystal	Colors or Decorated
Claret, 4½ oz.	$10.00	$28.00
Cocktail	9.00	28.00
Cordial, 1 oz.	35.00	75.00
Finger Bowl	8.00	20.00
Finger Bowl, Footed	10.00	22.00
Goblet, Long Bowl	10.00	30.00
Goblet, Short Bowl	10.00	35.00
Oyster Cocktail	8.00	22.00
Parfait, Café, 5 oz.	10.00	25.00
Sherbet, Low, 7 oz.	8.00	22.00
Sherbet, Tall, 7 oz.	9.00	25.00
Tumbler, 2½ oz.	8.00	22.00
Tumbler, Footed, 5 oz.	8.00	22.00
Tumbler, Footed, 10 oz.	8.00	24.00
Tumbler, Footed, 13 oz.	9.00	25.00
Wine, 2½ oz.	10.00	30.00
Wine, Low, 2½ oz.	10.00	30.00

Original Catalog Illustration: No. 3500 Gadroon long bowl goblet

No. 3126

Date: 1931

Manufacturer: Cambridge Glass Co., Cambridge, OH

Colors: Crystal. Colored bowls with Crystal stem and foot in: Amber, Amethyst, Carmen, Forest Green, Heatherbloom, Royal Blue

Decorations: Elaine etching, Portia etching, Valencia etching, D/1001 Portia etching with gold encrustation

Notes: Blown bowl, pressed stem. Made plain or optic

Claret, 4½ oz.	$18.00
Cocktail, 3 oz.	15.00
Cordial, 1 oz.	40.00
Goblet, 9 oz.	20.00
Oyster Cocktail, 4½ oz.	10.00
Sherbet, Low, 7 oz.	10.00
Sherbet, Tall, 7 oz.	15.00
Tumbler, Footed, 2½ oz. (bar)	25.00
Tumbler, Footed, 5 oz. (juice)	15.00
Tumbler, Footed, 9 oz. (water)	16.00
Tumbler, Footed, Short, 12 oz. (iced tea)	18.00
Tumbler, Footed, Tall, 12 oz. (iced tea)	18.00
Wine, 2½ oz.	20.00

Original Catalog Illustration: No. 3126 sherbet with Portia etching

MISCELLANEOUS SHAPED BOWL *(continued)*

Original Catalog Illustration:
No. 3600 goblet

NO. 3600

Date: 1938

Manufacturer: Cambridge Glass Co., Cambridge, OH

Colors: Crystal

Decorations: Chantilly etching, Minuet rock crystal, Marquis rock crystal, Petite rock crystal, Rosemarie rock crystal. Chantilly was also available with gold encrustation, designated as D/1061

Notes: Blown bowl, pressed stem. No. 3625 is a very similar stem with a slightly different shaped bowl.

Brandy, 1 oz.	$45.00
Claret, 4½ oz.	25.00
Cocktail, 3 oz.	15.00
Cordial, 1 oz.	55.00
Goblet, 10 oz.	18.00
Iced Tea, Footed, 12 oz.	18.00
Oyster Cocktail, 4½ oz.	8.00
Sherbet, Low, 7 oz.	8.00
Sherbet, Tall, 7 oz.	9.00
Tumbler, Footed, 5 oz. (juice)	9.00
Tumbler, Footed, 10 oz. (water)	15.00
Wine, 2½ oz.	32.00

Original Catalog Illustration:
No. 6007 goblet, plate and
cup and saucer with
No. 286 Manor etching

NO. 6007

Date: 1931

Manufacturer: Fostoria Glass Co., Moundsville, WV

Colors: Crystal. Crystal bowl with Amber base. Crystal stem and foot with colored bowl: Gold Tint, Green, Topaz, Wisteria.

Decorations: No. 87 Castle needle etching, No. 286 Manor plate etching, No. 313 Morning Glory etching, No. 709 York rock crystal cutting, No. 710 Bristol rock crystal cutting, No. 711 Inverness rock crystal cutting, No. 713 Eaton rock crystal cutting, No. 714 Oxford rock crystal cutting

Notes: Blown bowl, pressed stem. Made in regular optic or loop optic. No. 6008 stem line uses the same stem but with a plain ovoid bowl. For colors add 20%, for Wisteria, add 80% to crystal prices.

Claret, 4 oz., 5⅜" tall	$24.00
Cocktail, 3½ oz., 4⅝" tall	20.00
Cordial, 1 oz., 3⅝" tall	32.00
Goblet, 10 oz., 7½" tall	22.00
Oyster Cocktail, 4½ oz., 3⅛" tall	10.00
Saucer Champagne, 5½ oz., 5⅜" tall (high sherbet)	20.00
Sherbet, Low, 5½ oz., 4" tall	15.00
Tumbler, Footed, 2 oz., 2¾" tall (bar or whiskey)	22.00
Tumbler, Footed, 5 oz., 4¼" tall (juice)	15.00
Tumbler, Footed, 9 oz., 5⅛" tall (water)	15.00
Tumbler, Footed, 12 oz., 5⅝" tall (iced tea)	20.00
Wine, 3 oz., 5" tall	26.00

OVOID BOWL

Original Catalog Illustration:
No. 3795 Allegro goblet

ALLEGRO, NO. 3795

Date: 1950s

Manufacturer: Cambridge Glass Co., Cambridge, OH

Colors: Crystal

Decorations: Paisley etching, Fascination rock crystal engraving, Fiesta rock crystal engraving, Spring rock crystal engraving

Notes: Blown bowl, pressed stem. There was another short-lived No. 3795 stemware line called Sweetheart, which has a heart-shaped stem, but this was undecorated.

Claret	$10.00
Cocktail	9.00
Cordial	35.00
Goblet	10.00
Sherbet	8.00
Tumbler, Footed, 12 oz.	8.00
Tumbler, Footed, 5 oz.	8.00
Wine	10.00

(continued) OVOID BOWL

AMERICAN LADY, NO. 5056

Date: 1933

Manufacturer: Fostoria Glass Co., Moundsville, WV

Colors: Crystal. Crystal base with colored bowl: Amethyst, Burgundy, Empire Green, Regal Blue

Decorations: None

Notes: Blown bowl, pressed stem. Made plain. Marketed as blown stemware to match the American pattern.

	Crystal	Amethyst, Burgundy	Regal Blue Empire Green
Claret, 3½ oz., 4⅝" tall	$22.00	$35.00	$80.00
Cocktail, 3½ oz., 4" tall	18.00	24.00	62.00
Cordial, 1 oz., 3⅛" tall	45.00	55.00	100.00
Goblet, 10 oz., 6½" tall	24.00	30.00	80.00
Oyster Cocktail	15.00	21.00	—
Sherbet, 5½ oz., 4½" tall	15.00	21.00	60.00
Tumbler, Footed, 5 oz., 4⅛" tall	21.00	22.00	60.00
Tumbler, Footed, 12 oz., 5½" tall (iced tea)	22.00	35.00	80.00
Wine, 2½ oz., 4½" tall	22.00	35.00	80.00

Original Ad: No. 5056 American Lady goblet, tumbler and sherbet

ASTRID, NO. 6030

Date: 1942

Manufacturer: Fostoria Glass Co., Moundsville, WV

Colors: Crystal

Decorations: No. 815 Holly cutting, No. 814 Christiana rock crystal cutting, No. 816 Gadroon rock crystal and gray cutting, No. 822 Trellis rock crystal and gray cutting, No. 340 Buttercup plate etching

Notes: Blown bowl, pressed stem. Made in plain or loop optic (then called Wavemere).

Claret, Wine, 3½ oz., 6" tall	$28.00
Cocktail, 3½ oz., 5¼" tall	17.00
Cordial, 1 oz., 3⅞" tall	40.00
Goblet, 10 oz., 7⅞" tall	25.00
Goblet, Low, 10 oz., 6⅜" tall	20.00
Iced Tea, Footed, 12 oz., 6" tall	22.00
Juice, Footed, 5 oz., 4⅝" tall	16.00
Oyster Cocktail, 4 oz., 3¾" tall	15.00
Saucer Champagne, 6 oz., 5⅜" tall	22.00
Sherbet, Low, 6 oz., 4⅜" tall	17.00

Original Catalog Illustration: No. 6030 Astrid goblet and saucer champagne with No. 816 Gadroon cutting

CELLINI

Date: 1947

Manufacturer: U.S. Glass Co., Tiffin, OH

Colors: Crystal

Notes: Blown bowl, hand-tooled stem.

Claret	$75.00
Cocktail	60.00
Goblet	75.00
Wine	75.00

Original Ad: Cellini stemware

CRYSTOLITE, NO. 5003

Date: 1938

Manufacturer: A.H. Heisey & Co., Newark, OH

Colors: Crystal

Decorations: No. 912 Sabrina cutting, No. 919 Laurel Wreath cutting

Notes: Blown bowl, pressed stem. Made in optic. Very similar to No. 5077 Legionnaire. Heisey made an extensive pressed tableware line in No. 1503 Crystolite.

Claret, 3½ oz.	$45.00
Cocktail	45.00
Cordial, 1 oz.	120.00
Goblet, 10 oz.	35.00
Oyster Cocktail	30.00
Sherbet or Saucer Champagne	35.00
Soda, 5 oz. (juice)	35.00
Soda, Footed, 12 oz. (iced tea)	35.00

Original Heisey Pamphlet: No. 5003 Crystolite goblet

OVOID BOWL *(continued)*

Duquesne goblet with cut design

DUQUESNE, NO. 3389

Date: 1930

Manufacturer: A.H. Heisey & Co., Newark, OH

Colors: Crystal, Sahara. Crystal stem and foot, Sahara bowl. Crystal stem and foot, Tangerine bowl.

Decorations: Etchings: No. 448 Old Colony, No. 449 Pompeii, No. 450 Chintz, No. 456 Titania, No. 457 Springtime, No. 458 Olympiad, No. 480 Normandie. Cuttings: No. 790 Fleur, No. 800 Graystone, No. 812 Sweet Briar, No. 832 Continental, No. 834 Moulin Rouge, No. 843 Tahiti, No. 848 Botticelli, No. 868 Minaret, No. 905 Rosemont, No. 913 Everglade

Notes: Blown bowl, pressed stem. For Sahara, add 75%. For Tangerine, add 100%.

Claret, 4 oz.	$18.00
Cocktail, 3 oz.	15.00
Cordial, 1 oz.	55.00
Finger Bowl (4071)	8.00
Goblet, 9 oz.	20.00
Grape Fruit, Footed	20.00
Oyster Cocktail, 4 oz.	10.00
Parfait, 5 oz.	20.00
Saucer Champagne, 5 oz.	18.00
Sherbet, 5 oz.	12.00
Soda, Footed, 5 oz.	8.00
Soda, Footed, 8 oz.	9.00
Tumbler, Footed, 10 oz.	8.00
Wine, 2½ oz.	20.00

Catalog Illustration: No. 6026 Greenbriar tall and short goblets with No. 338 Chintz etching

GREENBRIAR, NO. 6026

Date: 1940

Manufacturer: Fostoria Glass Co., Moundsville, WV

Colors: Crystal.

Decorations: No. 338 Chintz etching, No. 799 Mulberry rock crystal cutting, No. 800 Selma rock crystal cutting, No. 803 Rheims rock crystal cutting

Notes: Blown bowl, pressed stem. Made in regular optic or Niagara (diamond) optic.

Claret-Wine, 4½ oz., 5⅜" tall	$22.00
Cocktail, 4 oz., 5" tall	17.00
Cocktail, Footed, 4 oz., 3⅝" tall	15.00
Cordial, 1 oz., 3⅞" tall	40.00
Goblet, 9 oz., 7⅝" tall	22.00
Goblet, Low, 9 oz., 6⅞" tall	18.00
Oyster Cocktail, 4 oz., 3⅝" tall	10.00
Saucer Champagne, 6 oz., 5½" tall	18.00
Sherbet, Low, 6 oz., 4⅜" tall	15.00
Tumbler, Footed, 5 oz., 4¾" tall (juice)	14.00
Tumbler, Footed, 13 oz., 6" tall (iced tea)	18.00

STRAIGHT BOWL

Catalog Illustration: No. 4055 Park Lane claret

PARK LANE, NO. 4055

Date: 1935

Manufacturer: A. H. Heisey & Co., Newark, OH

Colors: Crystal

Decorations: Cuttings: No. 812 Sweet Briar, No. 838 St. Moritz, No. 840 Briar Cliff, No. 842 Singapore, No. 844 Piccadilly, No. 849 Nomad, No. 850 Del Monte, No. 854 Lombardy, No. 859 Cohassett, No. 860 Vienna, No. 862 Monaco, No. 870 St. Albans, No. 876 Honolulu, No. 962 Punties

Notes: Blown bowl, pressed stem.

Claret, 4 oz.	$25.00
Cocktail, 3 oz.	22.00
Cordial, 1 oz.	80.00
Finger Bowl	10.00
Goblet, 10 oz.	30.00
Oyster Cocktail, 3 oz.	12.00
Saucer Champagne, 6 oz.	18.00
Sherbet, 6 oz.	12.00
Sherry, 1½ oz.	40.00
Soda, Footed, 5 oz. (juice)	15.00
Soda, Footed, 9 oz. (tumbler)	18.00
Soda, Footed, 13 oz. (iced tea)	18.00
Wine, 2½ oz.	45.00

TAPERED BOWL

NO. 3122

Date: 1931

Manufacturer: Cambridge Glass Co., Cambridge, OH

Colors: Crystal. Crystal stem and foot with colored bowls: Amber, Carmen, Emerald, Forest Green, Gold Krystol, Heatherbloom, Peach-Blo, Royal Blue

Decorations: Diane etching, Portia etching. No. 603 rock crystal engraving, No. 608 rock crystal engraving, No. 621 rock crystal engraving, No. 623 rock crystal engraving, No. 640 rock crystal engraving, No. 641 rock crystal engraving, No. 661 rock crystal engraving. Diane etching also with gold encrustation, D/1012.

Notes: Blown bowl, pressed stem. For stemware using the same stem but a different bowl shape, see No. 3124. Several sizes of tumblers, one to complement this stem line. All range in footed and one with sham bottom, were made value from $5.00 to $10.00. For items in color add 25%–35% to Crystal values listed below.

Claret, 4½ oz.	$25.00
Cocktail, Low, 3 oz.	140.00
Cocktail, Tall, 3½ oz.	15.00
Cordial, 1 oz.	50.00
Fruit Salad, 7 oz.	10.00
Goblet, 9 oz.	25.00
Goblet, 11 oz.	28.00
Oyster Cocktail, 4½ oz.	12.00
Sherbet, Low, 7 oz.	12.00
Sherbet, Tall, 7 oz.	15.00
Wine, 2½ oz.	25.00
Tumbler, Footed, 2½ oz.	24.00
Tumbler, Footed, 5 oz.	17.00
Tumbler, Footed, 7 oz. or 9 oz.	18.00
Tumbler, Footed, 12 oz.	20.00

Original Catalog Illustration:
No. 3122 sherbet with
No. 752 Diane etching

TULIP SHAPED BOWL

CANTERBURY, NO. 5115

Date: Ca. 1938

Manufacturer: Duncan & Miller Glass Co., Washington, PA

Colors: Crystal

Decorations: Remembrance etching, No. 622 Tristan rock crystal engraving, No. 621 Phoebus rock crystal engraving, No. 698 Maytime rock crystal engraving, No. 750 Tripole rock crystal engraving, No. 773 Chantilly rock crystal engraving

Notes: Blown bowl, pressed stem. Blown stemware to match No. 115 Canterbury pressed ware.

Claret, 5 oz., 6¾" tall	$15.00
Cocktail, Liquor, 3 oz., 5¼" tall	12.00
Cordial, 1 oz., 4¼" tall	45.00
Goblet, 10 oz., 7¼" tall	20.00
Ice Cream, Footed, 5 oz., 2¼" tall	9.00
Iced Tea, Footed, 12 oz., 5¾" tall	18.00
Orange Juice, Footed, 5 oz., 4¼" tall	12.00
Oyster Cocktail, Footed, 4 oz., 3¼" tall	9.00
Saucer Champagne, 5 oz., 5½" tall	18.00
Tumbler, Footed, 10 oz., 4½" tall	16.00
Wine, 3½ oz., 6" tall	20.00

Original Catalog Illustration:
No. 5115 Canterbury goblet
and saucer champagne

NO. 15033

Date: 1924

Manufacturer: U.S. Glass Co., Tiffin, OH

Colors: Crystal, Crystal bowl with Green stem and foot, Twilite, Twilite bowl with Crystal stem and foot, Rose

Decorations: Fontaine etching

Notes: Blown bowl, pressed stem. Made in wide optic.

Claret or Wine, 2½ oz.	$22.00
Cocktail or Parfait Café	15.00
Goblet	22.00
Saucer Champagne	20.00
Sundae (sherbet)	10.00

NO. 15039

Date: 1931 to 1946. Crystal only from 1951 to 1953

Manufacturer: A.H. Heisey & Co., Newark, OH

Colors: Crystal, Sahara, Flamingo, Moongleam. Limited production in Stiegel Blue (Cobalt)

Reproductions: Imperial Glass Corp. made candy jars and a bowl with a crimped edge (not originally made by Heisey) in several colors. These are found with and without the Diamond H.

Claret or Wine, 2½ oz.	$22.00
Cocktail or Parfait Café	15.00
Finger Bowl	8.00
Goblet	22.00
Saucer Champagne	20.00
Sundae (sherbet)	10.00

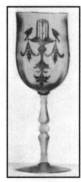 

L to R: Catalog Illustration:
No. 15033 goblet with
Fontaine etching, Catalog
Illustration: No. 15039 goblet

53

Chapter 11
TWIST

Twist stems in this chapter are pressed to resemble true hand twisted stems. **The following prices are for undecorated items.**

No. 77 cocktail

NO. 77

Date: Ca. 1930s

Manufacturer: Seneca Glass Co., Morgantown, WV

Colors: Crystal

Decorations: Unknown

Cocktail $20.00

Original Catalog Illustration: No. 15022 goblet, champagne and sundae

NO. 15022

Date: 1930s

Manufacturer: U.S. Glass Co. (Tiffin), Tiffin, OH

Colors: Crystal, Rose, Green. Crystal with green foot and cased button

Decorations: None known

Notes: Blown bowl, pressed stem. Button on stem may be cased with color. Made with wide or spiral optics. Designed by Virgil Loomis.

Cordial. $45.00
Goblet 22.00
Saucer Champagne 20.00
Sherbet. 10.00
Wine 22.00

Catalog Illustration: No. 15030 claret with Arcadian etching

NO. 15030

Date: 1930s

Manufacturer: U.S. Glass Co. (Tiffin), Tiffin, OH

Colors: Crystal, Crystal with Green trim

Decorations: Arcadian etching

Notes: Made in wide optic

Claret, 4½ oz.. . . . . $22.00
Cocktail, 3 oz. 15.00
Cordial, 1½ oz. 40.00
Goblet, 9 oz.. . . . . 22.00
Parfait, Café, 4½ oz.. . . . . 15.00
Saucer Champagne, 5½ oz.. 18.00
Sundae, 5½ oz. (sherbet). 10.00
Wine, 3 oz.. . . . . 22.0

(continued) TWIST

NO. 15037

Date: 1930s

Manufacturer: U.S. Glass Co., Tiffin, OH

Colors: Crystal, Rose, Green with Crystal trim, Black with Crystal trim.

Reproductions: Persian Pheasant etching, No. 406 Double Columbine cutting.

Notes: Blown bowl, pressed stem. Made in wide optic.

Café Parfait	$15.00
Claret	22.00
Cocktail	15.00
Cordial	45.00
Goblet	22.00
Saucer Champagne	20.00
Sundae (sherbet)	10.00
Table (tumbler)	10.00
Wine	22.00

Original Catalog Illustration: No. 15037 Goblet with Persian Pheasant etching

RIVIERA, D2

Date: 1950s

Manufacturer: Duncan & Miller Glass Co., Washington, PA

Colors: Crystal

Decorations: Ridgewood cutting, Mesa cutting

Notes: Blown bowl, pressed stem. Designed by James Rosati.

Brandy, 1½ oz.	$40.00
Cocktail, Liquor, 3½ oz.	12.00
Goblet, 10 oz.	18.00
Iced Tea, Footed, 14 oz.	18.00
Orange Juice, Footed, 5 oz.	12.00
Oyster Cocktail, Footed, 4½ oz.	9.00
Saucer Champagne or Tall Sherbet, 6 oz.	18.00
Wine or Claret, 4 oz.	20.00

Original Catalog Illustration: No. D2 Riviera goblet with Ridgewood cutting

TWIST

Date: 1910s

Manufacturer: Central Glass Co., Wheeling, WV. Continued by Imperial Glass Corporation, Bellaire, OH

Colors: Crystal. Colors a possibility.

Decorations: Unknown

Notes: A full line was made, but specific pieces are not known.

Goblet	$20.00

Original Catalog Cover: Twist stemware from Central Division of Imperial Glass Co.

TWISTED CRYSTAL, NO. 110

Date: 1950s

Manufacturer: Imperial Glass Corporation, Bellaire, OH

Colors: Crystal

Claret	$12.00
Cocktail	10.00
Comport or Mint, 4½"	10.00
Cordial	30.00
Finger Bowl	7.00
Goblet, 9 oz.	12.00
Iced Tea, Footed	10.00
Sherbet, Tall	7.00
Wine	12.00

Twisted Crystal Goblet and Tall Sherbet

Part II

DECORATIONS

Decorations and stemware go hand in hand. It could be said that decorations were designed to be placed on stemware. Often designers had specific lines of stemware in mind when designing the decorations. Thus Art Deco stems usually have Art Deco decorations.

Several decorating techniques will be discussed. First the glass item is made from molten glass and cooled, then the various decorations are applied.

Many people have difficulty distinguishing between etchings and gray cuttings. Etching is a chemical process using acid which erodes the surface of the glass, usually in highly detailed designs. Cutting is a mechanical process which grinds away some of the surface, leaving straight or curving lines cut into the glass. Most etchings are gray, satiny or even grainy in appearance. Cuttings can be gray or bright, depending on whether they have been polished. Most bright cuttings on stems were polished by immersion in acid, rather than the labor-intensive hand polishing of earlier periods. This acid polishing process is referred to as Rock Crystal.

Decorations on glass are done by many methods. The following are the most often found.

Etching transfer for a low goblet
of Daisy etching by Fostoria

Worker applying resist to stems after the
etching transfer has been applied

Etching—designs are made on glass by using hydrofluoric acid to eat into the surface of the glass. Pieces of glass to be etched are covered with a wax resist coating to protect the surface of the glass which is to remain undecorated. A design in the resist exposing the glass produces etched patterns. The items are then immersed in an acid bath. After the etching process, the articles are washed to remove the resist, cleaned and dried and are ready for sale. Artistic interpretation is always at the beginning of the process with the development of the design. Workers who actually etch the glass need not have artistic talents.

Satin Finish or Matte Finish—this is the simplest of etching decorations. An entire article is exposed to acid, resulting in a satiny, soft, semi-opaque finish. In some cases, companies used satin finish only on certain areas of the glass, producing interesting highlights.

Needle etching—this is a simple process, but is done by the use of a complicated machine. Goblets, for instance, are covered with wax resist. They are then put into a machine which uses needles to scratch a pre-ordained pattern (by use of cams) through the resist. Several goblets at a time can be prepared for etching. After the design is scratched into the wax, the items are placed in acid to produce the design. Needle etchings are composed of simple lines, loops, zigzags and other continuous line designs.

Typical needle etched design

Pantograph etching—this type of etching is a step more advanced than needle etching. A pantograph is a simple device by which a design can be traced and either enlarged or reduced. In the case of pantograph designs on glass, the stylus is traced over plates into which the etched design is greatly enlarged. This process also usually produces relatively simple designs composed of continuous lines. However, because the stylus can be raised or lowered over the tracing, smaller separate motifs may be produced also. Pantograph etchings are more intricate than needle etchings, with motifs such as flowers, bellflowers, arches and others possible. All pantograph etchings still appear as simple line designs with no variation in width of the outline.

Showing the transfer applied to a goblet to be plate etched

Typical sandblast carving showing multiple layers in the design

Plate etching—this is the most intricate and detailed etching done on glassware. In this type of etching, an artist produces a drawing which can be simple or elaborate, often very realistic in design. Lifelike flowers, birds and other motifs are possible. Plate etching requires many workers to produce a finished piece of glass—at least a dozen or more. The design is first etched into a large steel or copper plate, resulting in the design being lower than the surface. The wax resist is then rubbed into the design on the plate. A strong thin paper is placed over the resist in the design and rubbed into place. The paper is then removed with an alcohol solution, and the wax adheres to the goblet. The transfer is then placed on the piece to be decorated (sometimes several transfer pieces are needed to complete an article). At this time, the remainder of the piece of glass which is not to be etched is covered with wax resist. Workers brush on the wax over every surface which is to remain bright. The next process is to etch the item with acid. When this is finished, the piece is washed, cleaned and is ready for sale. This process produces the most intricate etching designs and those with the most artistry.

Double-plate etching—this is a refinement of plate etching. As the name implies, the glass article is etched twice. Double-plate etchings usually have satin medallions in which a small vignette is etched to enhance the appearance and draw attention to the design. The first etching puts on the satin finish for the medallions. Then the vignette design is carefully placed over the satin medallion and the same process as described in plate etching is done to complete the design. Many companies used this type of etching to produce small, delicate portraits on glass. This decoration requires two complete etching processes, adding considerably to the cost of manufacture.

Sandblast decoration—this type of decoration can look quite similar to etchings. In this process, the article of glass is covered with a rubbery material over the entire surface. A design is then cut through the rubber resist, exposing the glass beneath. Using a sandblasting nozzle, this area is then carved away, resulting in a design below the surface of the glass. Sometimes this is done in one level, but often more intricate carvings can be done which result in shallow sculptures with several levels.

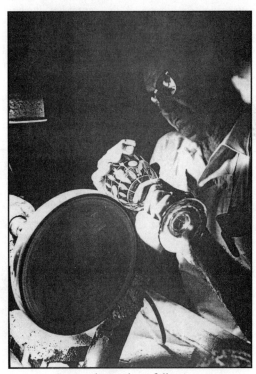

Cutting being done following a pre-marked design on a goblet

Cutting—cuttings are done individually by skilled workers removing glass by using a grinding wheel. In most cases, the cutter is given an example and uses his own artistic ability and skill to recreate the design in the piece of glass. The use of the abrasive cutting wheel imposes limits on the intricacy of the design. Motifs must be compatible to the types of cuts possible, such as slide cuts, punties, lines, and miters. Cutting designs may be simple or elaborate, depending on the artistry and skill of the cutter. Most cuttings are less elaborate than etchings because of the hand work involved. In contrast to etchings, cuttings rely heavily on the expertise and artistic talent of the cutter. Each piece is individually hand done. On the other hand, once etching plates have been prepared, each piece produced is exactly the same. Cuttings can be left gray as they come from the cutting wheel or can be polished to give an all-over bright surface. Sometimes only highlights are hand polished, giving an interesting and effective combination of gray and bright areas. More common are rock crystal cuttings in which the cut item is immersed in acid resulting in an entirely bright decoration on bright glass.

Engraving—a specialized and advanced type of cutting. Almost all engraving is done by using graduated sizes of copper wheels—from very tiny to about 3 or 4 inches in diameter. The copper wheels carry an abrasive slurry to the glass surface. Engraving can only be done by true artists. Engravers rarely have examples to copy, but create their own designs. Of all the decorating techniques discussed here, this type is the most elaborate and completely dependent on the skill of the engraver. Engravings are most effective when left gray, but sometimes have hand polished highlights. They are not mass produced because of the very labor intensive method of production. Often engravings are used for special items or presentation pieces where only one example or up to several dozen are produced. A special presentation piece may take up to several weeks or longer to be completed.

Other techniques were used to decorate glass. Most glass manufacturers had their own decorating shops and produced cuttings, etchings and other decorations. Many decorating companies, in addition to making cuttings and etchings, also applied enamels, silver, platinum, and gold decorations. These decorating companies bought blanks—undecorated glass from the glass makers—and decorated these with their own designs, sometimes mixing the products of several different glass companies. We have shown products of two such companies, Lotus Glass Co. and Cataract Sharpe Manufacturing Co. Hundreds of decorating companies existed during this 50 year period. Records and illustrations of most of these decorations do not exist today. This is one of the prime reasons that decorations are so difficult to properly attribute today.

Note: For easier reference check the titles at the very top of each page. Chapter names appear here while subcategories appear below the line.

Banding a goblet with gold or silver

Handpainted enamels on glass

Chapter 12

BANDS

DIAMONDS OR SQUARES

BEXLEY, NO. 1014

ROCK CRYSTAL ENGRAVING

Date: 1930s

Manufacturer: Cambridge Glass Co., Cambridge, OH

Colors: Crystal

STEMWARE:

NO. 3750 CHARLESTON

Claret, 4½ oz.	$20.00
Cocktail, 3½ oz.	15.00
Cordial, 1 oz.	50.00
Goblet, 10 oz.	20.00
Iced Tea, Footed, 12 oz.	18.00
Oyster Cocktail, 5 oz.	11.00
Sherbet, Low, 6 oz.	11.00
Sherbet, Tall, 6 oz.	15.00
Tumbler, Footed, 5 oz. (juice)	12.00
Wine, 3 oz.	20.00

ACCESSORIES:

Bowl, 11" (P384)	$42.00
Bowl, Salad, 10" (P427)	42.00
Candlesticks, 2-light, 6", pr. (647)	55.00
Candy Box & Cover (3900/165)	45.00
Celery & Relish, 3-part, 12" (3900/126)	37.00
Celery & Relish, 5-part, 12" (3900/120)	40.00
Comport, Blown (3121)	45.00
Cream (3900/41)	20.00
Jug, 76 oz. (3900/115)	80.00
Mayonnaise (3900/129)	25.00
Plate, Mayonnaise (3900/129)	12.00
Plate, Rolled Edge, 14" (3900/168)	45.00
Plate, Salad, 7½" (555)	15.00
Salt & Pepper, pr. (P360)	40.00
Sugar (3900/41)	20.00

Original Catalog Illustration: No. 1014 Bexley rock crystal engraving on No. 3750 Charleston goblet

BLUE DANUBE, NO. 32P

ROCK CRYSTAL ENGRAVING

Date: 1950s

Manufacturer: Cambridge Glass Co., Cambridge, OH

Colors: Crystal

STEMWARE:

NO. 3790 SIMPLICITY

Claret	$20.00
Cocktail	15.00
Cordial	45.00
Goblet	20.00
Iced Tea, Footed, 12 oz.	18.00
Juice, Footed, 5 oz.	12.00
Oyster Cocktail	10.00
Sherbet, Low	10.00
Wine	20.00

ACCESSORIES:

Plate, Salad, 8" (556)	$12.00

Original Catalog Illustration: No. 32P Blue Danube rock crystal engraving iced tea

DIAMONDS OR SQUARES *(continued)*

Original Catalog Illustration:
No. 682 Coronet cutting on
No. 5317 Cathay goblet and
saucer champagne

Original Catalog Illustration:
No. 6P Crown on No. 3790
Simplicity goblet

Original Catalog Illustration:
No. 1015 Hanover on
No. 3750 goblet

CORONET, NO. 682

ROCK CRYSTAL CUTTING

Date: 1940s

Manufacturer: Duncan & Miller Glass Co.,
Washington, PA

Colors: Crystal

STEMWARE:

NO. 5317 CATHAY

Claret, 5 oz., 5¾" tall	$30.00
Cocktail, Liquor, 3½ oz., 4" tall	30.00
Cordial, 1 oz., 3½" tall	70.00
Finger Bowl, 4½"	15.00
Goblet, 10 oz., 61/4" tall	45.00
Ice Cream, Footed (sherbet), 5 oz., 3½" tall	17.00
Iced Tea, Footed, 12 oz., 6½" tall	38.00
Juice, Orange, Footed, 5 oz., 4¾" tall	24.00
Oyster Cocktail, 4½ oz., 3½" tall	20.00
Saucer Champagne, 5 oz., 4½" tall	40.00
Tumbler, Footed, 9 oz., 5½" tall	35.00
Wine, 3 oz., 5" tall	45.00

ACCESSORIES:

Bowl, Deep Salad, 9" (33)	$55.00
Bowl, Flared, 12" (36)	68.00
Bowl, Low Foot, 13" (30)	68.00
Candlestick, Low, 3" pr. (115)	75.00
Candlesticks, 2-light, pr. (30)	115.00
Candy Box & Cover, 3-compartment, 6½" (106)	85.00
Celery & Relish, Oblong, 2-handled, 12" (30)	45.00
Comport, 6" (5317)	65.00
Comport, Tall, 7½" (8)	65.00
Cream (38)	40.00
Finger Bowl (30)	15.00
Iced Cocktail Set, 2 pc. or 3 pc. (30)	85.00
Mayonnaise Set (8)	85.00
Nappy, 2-handled, 6" (30)	35.00
Plate, 2-handled, 6" (30)	35.00
Plate, Bread & Butter, 6" (30½)	22.00
Plate, Dessert, 7½" (30½)	25.00
Plate, Salad, 8½" (30½)	25.00
Plate, Sandwich, 2-handled, 11" (30)	65.00
Plate, Torte, 13" (33)	80.00
Relish, 2-handled, 2-compartment, 6" (30)	35.00
Salad Dressing Set, 2-compartment, 6", 2 pc. (30)	55.00
Sugar (38)	40.00
Vase, 10" (506)	90.00
Vase, Flip, Flared 8" (30)	80.00

CROWN, NO. 6P

ROCK CRYSTAL ENGRAVING

Date: 1950s

Manufacturer: Cambridge Glass Co.,
Cambridge, OH

Colors: Crystal

STEMWARE:

NO. 3790 SIMPLICITY

Claret	$20.00
Cocktail	15.00
Cordial	45.00
Goblet	20.00
Iced Tea, Footed, 12 oz.	18.00
Oyster Cocktail	10.00
Sherbet, Low	10.00
Tumbler, Footed, 5 oz. (juice)	12.00
Wine	20.00

ACCESSORIES:

Plate, Salad, 8" (556)	$15.00

HANOVER, NO. 1015

ROCK CRYSTAL ENGRAVING

Date: 1930s

Manufacturer: Cambridge Glass Co.,
Cambridge, OH

Colors: Crystal

STEMWARE:

NO. 3750

Claret, 4½ oz.	$18.00
Cocktail, 3½ oz.	14.00
Cordial, 1 oz.	45.00
Goblet, 10 oz.	18.00
Iced Tea, Footed, 12 oz.	12.00
Oyster Cocktail, 5 oz.	9.00
Sherbet, Low, 6 oz.	9.00
Sherbet, Tall, 6 oz.	11.00
Tumbler, Footed, 5 oz. (juice)	10.00
Wine, 3 oz.	18.00

ACCESSORIES:

Plate, Salad, 7½" (555)	$10.00

(continued) DIAMONDS OR SQUARES

SHERWOOD, NO. 645

ROCK CRYSTAL CUTTING

Date: 1930s

Manufacturer: Duncan & Miller
Glass Co., Washington, PA

Colors: Crystal

STEMWARE:

NO. 31 WINDSOR

Claret, 4 oz., 5¾" tall	$30.00
Cocktail, Liquor, 3 oz., 4¾" tall	30.00
Cordial, 1 oz., 3¾" tall	70.00
Finger Bowl, 4¼"	15.00
Goblet, 9 oz., 7" tall	45.00
Iced Tea, Footed, 12 oz., 6½" tall	38.00
Orange Juice, Footed, 5 oz., 4¾" tall	24.00
Oyster Cocktail, 4 oz., 4" tall	20.00
Saucer Champagne, 5 oz., 4½" tall	40.00
Wine, 3 oz., 5½" tall	45.00

ACCESSORIES:

Bowl, Deep Salad, 9" (33)	$55.00
Bowl, Flared, 12" (36)	68.00
Bowl, Low Foot, 13" (30)	68.00
Candlestick, Low, 3" pr. (115)	75.00
Candlesticks, 2-light, pr. (30)	115.00
Candy Box & Cover, 3-compartment, 6½" (106)	85.00
Celery & Relish, Oblong, 2-handled, 12" (30)	45.00
Comport, 6" (5317)	65.00
Comport, Tall, 7½" (8)	65.00
Cream (38)	40.00
Finger Bowl (30)	15.00
Iced Cocktail Set, 2 pc. or 3 pc. (30)	85.00
Mayonnaise Set (8)	85.00
Nappy, 2-handled, 6" (30)	35.00
Plate, 2-handled, 6" (30)	35.00
Plate, Bread & Butter, 6" (30½)	22.00
Plate, Dessert, 7½" (30½)	25.00
Plate, Salad, 8½" (30½)	25.00
Plate, Sandwich, 2-handled, 11" (30)	65.00
Plate, Torte, 13" (33)	80.00
Relish, 2-handled, 2-compartment, 6" (30)	35.00
Salad Dressing Set, 2-compartment, 6", 2 pc. (30)	55.00
Sugar (38)	40.00
Vase, 10" (506)	90.00
Vase, Flip, Flared 8" (30)	80.00

Original Catalog Illustration:
No. 645 Sherwood cutting on
No. 31 Windsor goblet

STRATFORD, NO. 689

ROCK CRYSTAL CUTTING

Date: 1930s

Manufacturer: Duncan & Miller
& Co., Washington, PA

Colors: Crystal

STEMWARE:

NO. 504 GRANADA

Claret, 5 oz.	$45.00
Cordial, 1 oz.	70.00
Goblet, 10 oz.	45.00
Ice Cream, Footed, 5 oz.	17.00
Iced Tea, Footed, 12 oz.	38.00
Liquor Cocktail, 3½ oz.	17.00
Orange Juice, Footed, 5 oz.	24.00
Oyster Cocktail, 4½ oz.	17.00
Saucer Champagne, 5 oz.	40.00
Sherry, 2 oz.	55.00
Tumbler, Footed, 10 oz.	35.00
Whiskey, Footed, 3 oz.	30.00
Wine, 3½ oz.	45.00

ACCESSORIES:

Bowl, Deep Salad, 9" (33)	$55.00
Bowl, Flared, 12" (36)	68.00
Bowl, Low Foot, 13" (30)	68.00
Candlestick, Low, 3" pr. (115)	75.00
Candlesticks, 2-light, pr. (30)	115.00
Candy Box & Cover, 3-compartment, 6½" (106)	85.00
Celery & Relish, Oblong, 2-handled, 12" (30)	45.00
Comport, 6" (5317)	65.00
Comport, Tall, 7½" (8)	65.00
Cream (38)	40.00
Finger Bowl (30)	15.00
Iced Cocktail Set, 2 pc. or 3 pc. (30)	85.00
Mayonnaise Set (8)	85.00
Nappy, 2-handled, 6" (30)	35.00
Plate, 2-handled, 6" (30)	35.00
Plate, Bread & Butter, 6" (30½)	22.00
Plate, Dessert, 7½" (30½)	25.00
Plate, Salad, 8½" (30½)	25.00
Plate, Sandwich, 2-handled, 11" (30)	65.00
Plate, Torte, 13" (33)	80.00
Relish, 2-handled, 2-compartment, 6" (30)	35.00
Salad Dressing Set, 2-compartment, 6", 2 pc. (30)	55.00
Sugar (38)	40.00
Vase, 10" (506)	90.00
Vase, Flip, Flared 8" (30)	80.00

Original Catalog Illustration:
No. 689 Stratford cutting
on pressed ware

DIAMONDS OR SQUARES *(continued)*

Original Catalog Illustration:
No. 691 Sun Ray cutting on
No. 5322 Erin goblet

SUN RAY, NO. 691

ROCK CRYSTAL CUTTING

Date: 1940s

Manufacturer: Duncan & Miller Glass Co., Washington, PA

Colors: Crystal

STEMWARE:
NO. 5322 ERIN
Claret, 4½ oz., 5¼" tall	$30.00
Cocktail, 3½ oz., 4¼" tall	30.00
Finger Bowl, 4¼"	15.00
Goblet, 9 oz., 6" tall	45.00
Ice Cream, Footed, 6 oz., 3¼" tall (sherbet)	17.00
Iced Tea, Footed, 13 oz., 6" tall	38.00
Orange Juice, Footed, 5 oz., 4½" tall	24.00
Oyster Cocktail, 4½ oz., 3½" tall	17.00
Saucer Champagne or Tall Sherbet, 6 oz., 4½" tall	40.00
Wine, 3 oz., 4¾" tall	45.00

ACCESSORIES:
Bowl, Deep Salad, 9" (33)	$55.00
Bowl, Flared, 12" (36)	68.00
Bowl, Low Foot, 13" (30)	68.00
Candlestick, Low, 3" pr. (115)	75.00
Candlesticks, 2-light, pr. (30)	115.00
Candy Box & Cover, 3-compartment, 6½" (106)	85.00
Celery & Relish, Oblong, 2-handled, 12" (30)	45.00
Comport, 6" (5317)	65.00
Comport, Tall, 7½" (8)	65.00
Cream (38)	40.00
Finger Bowl (30)	15.00
Iced Cocktail Set, 2 pc. or 3 pc. (30)	85.00
Mayonnaise Set (8)	85.00
Nappy, 2-handled, 6" (30)	35.00
Plate, 2-handled, 6" (30)	35.00
Plate, Bread & Butter, 6" (30½)	22.00
Plate, Dessert, 7½" (30½)	25.00
Plate, Salad, 8½" (30½)	25.00
Plate, Sandwich, 2-handled, 11" (30)	65.00
Plate, Torte, 13" (33)	80.00
Relish, 2-handled, 2-compartment, 6" (30)	35.00
Salad Dressing Set, 2-compartment, 6", 2 pc. (30)	55.00
Sugar (38)	40.00
Vase, 10" (506)	90.00
Vase, Flip, Flared 8" (30)	80.00

FLOWERS

Original Catalog Illustration:
No. 705 Blossom Time cutting
on No. 5321 Trianon goblet

BLOSSOM TIME, NO. 705

ROCK CRYSTAL CUTTING

Date: 1940s

Manufacturer: Duncan & Miller Glass Co., Washington, PA

Colors: Crystal

STEMWARE:
NO. 5321 TRIANON
Claret, 5 oz., 6¾" tall	$30.00
Cocktail, Liquor, 3 oz., 5½" high	30.00
Cordial, 1 oz., 4½" tall	70.00
Finger Bowl, 4½"	15.00
Goblet, 10 oz., 7½" tall	45.00
Ice Cream, Footed, 6 oz., 3½" tall (sherbet)	17.00
Iced Tea, Footed, 13 oz., 6¼" tall	38.00
Oyster Cocktail, 4½ oz., 3½" tall	20.00
Saucer Champagne or Tall Sherbet, 6 oz., 6" high	40.00
Wine, 3 oz., 6¼" tall	45.00

ACCESSORIES:
Bowl, Deep Salad, 9" (33)	$55.00
Bowl, Flared, 12" (36)	68.00
Bowl, Low Foot, 13" (30)	68.00
Candlestick, Low, 3", pr. (115)	75.00
Candlesticks, 2-light, pr. (30)	115.00
Candy Box & Cover, 3-compartment, 6½" (106)	85.00
Celery & Relish, Oblong, 2-handled, 12" (30)	45.00
Comport, 6" (5317)	65.00
Comport, Tall, 7½" (8)	65.00
Cream (38)	40.00
Finger Bowl (30)	15.00
Iced Cocktail Set, 2 pc. or 3 pc. (30)	85.00
Mayonnaise Set (8)	85.00
Nappy, 2-handled, 6" (30)	35.00
Plate, 2-handled, 6" (30)	35.00
Plate, Bread & Butter, 6" (30½)	22.00
Plate, Dessert, 7½" (30½)	25.00
Plate, Salad, 8½" (30½)	25.00
Plate, Sandwich, 2-handled, 11" (30)	65.00
Plate, Torte, 13" (33)	80.00
Relish, 2-handled, 2-compartment, 6" (30)	35.00
Salad Dressing Set, 2-compartment, 6", 2 pc. (30)	55.00
Sugar (38)	40.00
Vase, 10" (506)	90.00
Vase, Flip, Flared 8" (30)	80.00

(continued) **FLOWERS**

CHANTILLY, NO. 697

ROCK CRYSTAL CUTTING

Date: 1940

Manufacturer: Duncan & Miller Glass Co., Washington, PA

Colors: Crystal

STEMWARE:
NO. 5375 DIAMOND
Cocktail, Liquor, 3½ oz., 5" tall $30.00
Cordial, 1 oz., 4¼" tall 70.00
Goblet, 9 oz., 7¼" tall 45.00
Iced Tea, 12 oz., 6½" tall 38.00
Orange Juice, 5 oz., 4¾" tall 24.00
Saucer Champagne, 5½ oz., 5½" tall . . . 45.00
Wine, 3 oz., 5¾" tall 45.00

ACCESSORIES:
Bowl, Deep Salad, 9" (33) $55.00
Bowl, Flared, 12" (36) 68.00
Bowl, Low Foot, 13" (30). 68.00
Candlestick, Low, 3", pr. (115). 75.00
Candlesticks, 2-light, pr. (30) 115.00

Candy Box & Cover, 3-compartment,
    6½" (106) 85.00
Celery & Relish, Oblong, 2-handled,
    12" (30). 45.00
Comport, 6" (5317). 65.00
Comport, Tall, 7½" (8) 65.00
Cream & Sugar, pr. (38). 80.00
Finger Bowl (30) 15.00
Iced Cocktail Set, 2 pc. or 3 pc. (30). . . 85.00
Mayonnaise Set (8) 85.00
Nappy or Plate, 2-handled, 6" (30) 35.00
Plate, Bread & Butter. 6", (30½) 22.00
Plate, Dessert, 7½" (30½) 25.00
Plate, Salad, 8½" (30½). 25.00
Plate, Sandwich, 2-handled, 11" (30) . . . 65.00
Plate, Torte, 13" (33) 80.00
Relish, 2-handled, 2-compartment,
    6" (30) 35.00
Salad Dressing Set, 2-compartment,
    6", 2 pc. (30) 55.00
Vase, 10" (506) 90.00
Vase, Flip, Flared 8" (30) 80.00

Original Catalog Illustration:
No. 697 Chantilly cutting on
No. 5375 Diamond goblet

COSMOS

HAND SCULPTURED

Date: 1947

Manufacturer: Chartiers Crystal–a division of Duncan & Miller, Washington, PA

Colors: Crystal

Notes: Chartiers was a "budget" line of Duncan & Miller.

Brandy $35.00
Cocktail, Liquor 18.00
Goblet 22.00
Iced Tea 20.00
Juice, Orange 15.00
Oyster Cocktail. 9.00
Sherbet. 9.00
Whiskey Sour 12.00
Wine 25.00

L to R: Original Ad: Cosmos hand sculptured decoration on
iced tea. Original Catalog Illustration: No. 170 Cynthia
cutting on candy jar

CYNTHIA, NO. 170

CUTTING

Date: 1924

Manufacturer: Fostoria Glass Co., Moundsville, WV

Colors: Crystal

STEMWARE:
NO. 877
Claret, 4 oz. $18.00
Cocktail, 3½ oz.. . . . . 15.00
Cordial, ¾ oz. 35.00
Goblet, 10 oz., 7⅞" tall 21.00
Oyster Cocktail, 4½ oz., 3¾" tall . . . 12.00
Parfait 18.00
Sherbet, High, 6 oz., 6⅛" tall 18.00

Sherbet, Low, 6 oz., 4" tall 12.00
Tumbler, Footed, 5 oz. (juice) 12.00
Tumbler, Footed, 9 oz. (water). 12.00
Tumbler, Footed, 12 oz. (iced tea) . . . 18.00
Whiskey, Footed, 2½ oz.. . . . . 15.00
Wine, 2¾ oz.. . . . . 21.00

ACCESSORIES:
Bedroom Set, 2 pc. (1697)
    (tumble up). $65.00
Candy Jar & Cover, ½ lb. (2250) . . . 45.00
Cream (2133) 36.00
Decanter, qt., Cut Flutes (800) 65.00
Finger Bowl (1769). 9.00

Grapefruit (945½) 15.00
Jug & Cover (2270) 65.00
Jug (1852-6). 55.00
Jug (303-3). 45.00
Jug (724-7). 55.00
Marmalade & Cover (4087) 35.00
Mayonnaise (1769) 18.00
Oil & Stopper, 5 oz. (1485) 35.00
Plate, Mayonnaise. 10.00
Plate, Salad, 7" (1897)
    or 8¼" (2238) 10.00
Plate, Sandwich, 9" (1848) 12.00
Salt & Pepper, pr. (2235) 35.00
Sugar (2133). 18.00

FLOWERS *(continued)*

Original Catalog Illustration:
No. 706 Florentine on
No. 5375 Diamond goblet

FLORENTINE, No. 706
ROCK CRYSTAL CUTTING

Date: 1940s

Manufacturer: Duncan & Miller Glass Co.,
Washington, PA

Colors: Crystal

STEMWARE:

No. 5375 DIAMOND

Cocktail, Liquor, 3½ oz., 5" tall	$30.00
Cordial, 1 oz., 4¼" tall	70.00
Goblet, 9 oz., 7¼" tall	45.00
Iced Tea, 12 oz., 6½" tall	38.00
Orange Juice, 5 oz., 4¾" tall	24.00
Oyster Cocktail, 4½ oz., 3¾" tall	20.00
Saucer Champagne, 5½ oz., 5½" tall	40.00
Wine, 3 oz., 5¾" tall	45.00

ACCESSORIES:

Bowl, Deep Salad, 9" (33)	$55.00
Bowl, Flared, 12" (36)	68.00
Bowl, Low Foot, 13" (30)	68.00
Candlestick, Low, 3" pr. (115)	75.00

Candlesticks, 2-light, pr. (30)	115.00
Candy Box & Cover, 3-compartment, 6½" (106)	85.00
Celery & Relish, Oblong, 2-handled, 12" (30)	45.00
Comport, 6" (5317)	65.00
Comport, Tall, 7½" (8)	65.00
Cream & Sugar, pr. (38)	80.00
Finger Bowl (30)	15.00
Iced Cocktail Set, 2 pc. or 3 pc. (30)	85.00
Mayonnaise Set (8)	85.00
Nappy or Plate, 2-handled, 6" (30)	35.00
Plate, Bread & Butter, 6" (30½)	22.00
Plate, Dessert, 7½" (30½)	25.00
Plate, Salad, 8½" (30½)	25.00
Plate, Sandwich, 2-handled, 11" (30)	65.00
Plate, Torte, 13" (33)	80.00
Relish, 2-handled, 2-compartment, 6" (30)	35.00
Salad Dressing Set, 2-compartment, 6", 2 pc. (30)	55.00
Vase, 10" (506)	90.00
Vase, Flip, Flared 8" (30)	80.00

Original Ad: Glenmore
cutting on goblet

GLENMORE
GRAY CUTTING

Date: 1953

Manufacturer: Libbey Glass Co., Toledo, OH

Colors: Crystal

Notes: Designed by Freda Diamond. Made with Libbey's "safedge" rim.

Beverage, Footed (tumbler)	$9.00
Cocktail	10.00
Cordial	35.00
Goblet	15.00
Pilsner	18.00
Sherbet	9.00
Wine	15.00

Original Company Pamphlet:
Lynbrook rock crystal engraving
on No. 3790 Simplicity goblet

LYNBROOK
ROCK CRYSTAL ENGRAVING

Date: 1940s

Manufacturer: Cambridge Glass Co.,
Cambridge, OH

Colors: Crystal

STEMWARE:

No. 3790 SIMPLICITY

Claret	$14.00
Cocktail	14.00
Cordial	50.00
Goblet	18.00
Iced Tea, Footed, 12 oz.	16.00
Oyster Cocktail	10.00
Sherbet, Low	10.00
Tumbler, Footed 5 oz. (juice)	14.00
Wine	18.00

ACCESSORIES:

Bonbon, 2-handled, 5½" (1180)	$22.00
Bowl, 12" (P430)	38.00
Candlesticks, 2-light, 6", pr. (3600/495)	70.00
Candlesticks, 3½", pr. (628)	40.00

Candy Box & Cover, 6" (P306)	45.00
Celery, 11" (P247)	25.00
Cocktail Icer, 2 pc. (968)	80.00
Comport, 5½" (533)	30.00
Comport, Blown, 5" (3700)	32.00
Comport, Low, 6" (P54)	28.00
Cream & Sugar, pr. (P254)	40.00
Cream & Sugar, pr. (P253)	44.00
Jug, 76 oz. (3900/115)	80.00
Marmalade & Cover (P298)	32.00
Mayonnaise (1532)	28.00
Oil & Stopper, 6 oz. (P290)	52.00
Plate, Salad, 7½" (555)	12.00
Plate, 13½" (P166)	42.00
Plate, Crescent Salad (P454)	18.00
Plate, Footed, 8" (P56)	20.00
Plate, Mayonnaise (1532)	12.00
Plate, Salad, 7½" (555)	15.00
Relish, 2 pt., 6" (P1497)	18.00
Relish, 3 pt., 10" (P214)	30.00
Relish, 3 pt. (1498)	30.00
Salt & Pepper, pr. (P360)	45.00
Vase, 8" (6004)	58.00

MOONGLO, NO. 980

CUTTING

Date: 1942

Manufacturer: A.H. Heisey & Co., Newark, OH

Colors: Crystal

Notes: "If you have entertaining ideas, you'll welcome the unusual beauty of MOONGLO'S sculptured lines...for it lends itself to the inspired planning of original table settings.... This cosmopolitan pattern is obtainable in a complete assortment of stemware and beverage items complemented by hand-cast table accessories." —Original company brochure. Imperial Glass Corporation continued manufacture of a short line of Moonglo after 1957. No. 1540 refers to the Lariat pattern while the No. 1951 refers to Cabochon.

STEMWARE:

NO. 1540 LARIAT (PRESSED) OR
NO. 5040 LARIAT (BLOWN)

Cocktail	$35.00
Cordial, Low	120.00
Cordial, Tall	165.00
Finger Bowl	30.00
Goblet	48.00
Iced Tea, Footed	30.00
Juice, Footed	24.00
Saucer Champagne	40.00
Sherbet	18.00
Wine	48.00

ACCESSORIES:

Bar, 1½ oz. (4052)	$24.00
Bowl, Camellia, 9½" (1540)	55.00
Bowl, Floral, 11" (1951)	60.00
Bowl, Floral, 13" (1951)	65.00
Bowl, Floral, 9½" (398)	50.00
Bowl, Gardenia, 13" (1540)	75.00
Bowl, Gardenia, 13" (1951)	65.00
Bowl, Gardenia, 9" (1183)	50.00
Bowl, Oval, 13" (1540)	65.00
Bowl, Twin Dressing, 7" (1540)	55.00
Candelettes, 1 Light, pr. (1951)	75.00
Candleblocks, 1 Light, pr. (1540)	60.00
Candlestick, 3 Light, pr. (142)	175.00
Candlesticks, 2 Light, pr. (134)	125.00
Candlesticks, 2 Light, pr. (1540)	150.00
Candlesticks, 3 Light, pr. (1540)	170.00
Candy Box & Cover, 6½" (1951)	65.00
Candy Box & Cover, Plume Finial, 8½" (1540)	85.00
Candy Box & Cover, Small, 5" (1540)	75.00
Candy Dish, 7" (1540)	85.00
Caramel & Cover, 7" (1540)	95.00
Celery & Olive, 13" (1540)	45.00
Celery Tray (4044)	45.00
Celery Tray, 13" (1540)	45.00

Cheese & Cover, Footed, 5" (1540)	30.00
Cheese & Cracker, 14" (1540)	110.00
Cheese & Cracker, 14" (1951)	95.00
Cheese or Honey, Footed, 5¾" (1951)	30.00
Cocktail Shaker, 1 qt. (4036 or 4225)	120.00
Cocktail Shaker, 2 qt. (4225)	140.00
Cocktail, 3½ oz. (5038-Chanticleer)	120.00
Cocktail, 3½ oz. (5048-Rooster Head)	120.00
Cocktail, 3½ oz. (5066-Horse Head)	550.00
Comport & Cover, 6" (1540)	55.00
Comport & Cover, Footed, 10" (1540)	95.00
Cream (1540)	32.00
Cream (1951)	30.00
Cup & Saucer (1540)	65.00
Decanter, 1 pt. (4036½)	95.00
Dressing, Combination (1183)	40.00
Goblet (4052)	35.00
Jelly, Handled, 6" (1951)	28.00
Jelly, Handled, 7" (1540)	30.00
Jug, 72 oz. (5032)	135.00
Jug, Ice, 73 oz. (4164)	135.00
Mayonnaise, 5½" (1183 or 1540)	40.00
Mayonnaise, Divided, 5½" (1183)	40.00
Mayonnaise, Rolled End, 4½" (1567)	48.00
Mayonnaise, Small, 5" (1951)	35.00
Mint, Footed, 5¾" (1951)	30.00
Nappy, 5" (1951)	18.00
Nappy, 6" (1540)	22.00
Oil & Stopper, 3 oz. (1951)	120.00
Oil & Stopper, 4 oz. (1540)	150.00
Old Fashioned, 8 oz. (4052)	18.00
Plate, 10½" (1184)	110.00
Plate, 6" (1184 or 1540)	8.00
Plate, Buffet, 16" (1184)	75.00
Plate, Mayonnaise (1183, 1540 or 1951)	18.00
Plate, Punch Bowl (1540)	70.00
Plate, Salad, 7" or 8" (1184 or 1540)	18.00
Plate, Sandwich, 14" (1540 or 1951)	65.00
Plate, Torte, 14" (485 or 1951)	60.00
Punch Bowl (1540)	170.00
Punch Cup (1540)	15.00
Relish, 3-compartment, 9" (1951)	50.00
Relish, 3-compartment, Round, 10" (1540)	52.00
Relish, 4-compartment, Round, Handled, 8½" (1540)	52.00
Sandwich, Handled, 12" (1951)	55.00
Soda, 3 oz. or 5 oz. (4052)	20.00
Soda, 10 oz. or 12 oz. (4052)	24.00
Soda, 14 oz. (4052)	28.00
Sugar (1540)	32.00
Sugar (1951)	30.00
Sweetmeat, Handled (1540)	28.00
Tankard, 30 oz. (4054)	135.00
Tidbit, 7½" (1951)	65.00
Tray for Sugar & Cream (1951)	25.00
Vase, Fan, Footed, No. 2, 7" (1540)	80.00
Vase, Flared, 3½" (1951)	48.00

Original Pamphlet: No. 980
Moonglo cutting

Original Pamphlet: No. 980
Moonglo cutting

FLOWERS *(continued)*

Original Catalog Illustration:
No. 618 rock crystal engraving
on No. 3124 goblet

NO. 618

ROCK CRYSTAL ENGRAVING

Date: 1930s

Manufacturer: Cambridge Glass Company, Cambridge, OH

Colors: Crystal

NO. 3124

Claret, 4½ oz. $20.00
Cocktail, 3 oz. 15.00
Goblet, 10 oz. 20.00

Oyster Cocktail, 4½ oz. 12.00
Sherbet, Low, 7 oz. 12.00
Sherbet, Tall, 7 oz. 16.00
Wine, 3 oz. 20.00
Tumbler, Footed, 3 oz. 16.00
Tumbler, Footed, 5 oz. 16.00
Tumbler, Footed, 10 oz. 18.00
Tumbler, Footed, 12 oz. 18.00

NO. 621

ROCK CRYSTAL ENGRAVING

Date: 1930s

Manufacturer: Cambridge Glass Company, Cambridge, OH

Colors: Crystal

NO. 3035

Claret, 4½ oz. $20.00
Cocktail, 3 oz. 16.00
Cordial, 1 oz. 50.00
Fruit Salad, 6 oz. 14.00
Goblet, 9 oz. 20.00
Oyster Cocktail, 4½ oz. 14.00
Sherbet, Low, 6 oz. 15.00
Sherbet, Tall, 6 oz. 16.00
Tumbler, Footed, 2½ oz. 20.00
Tumbler, Footed, 5 oz. 14.00
Tumbler, Footed, 8oz. 14.00

Tumbler, Footed, 10 oz. 16.00
Tumbler, Footed, 12 oz. 16.00
Wine, 2½ oz. 20.00

NO. 3122

Claret, 4½ oz. $20.00
Cocktail, 3 oz. 15.00
Cordial, 1 oz. 50.00
Fruit Salad, 7 oz. 12.00
Goblet, 9 oz. 20.00
Oyster Cocktail, 4½ oz. 12.00
Sherbet, Low, 7 oz. 12.00
Sherbet, Tall, 7 oz. 16.00
Wine, 2½ oz. 20.00
Tumbler, Footed, 2½ oz. 20.00
Tumbler, Footed, 5 oz. or 7 oz. 15.00
Tumbler, Footed, 9 oz. or 12 oz. 18.00

Original Catalog Illustration:
No. 621 rock crystal engraving
on No. 3035 goblet

Original Catalog Illustration:
No. 622 rock crystal engraving on No. 1066 Aurora goblet

NO. 622

ROCK CRYSTAL ENGRAVING

Date: 1930s

Manufacturer: Cambridge Glass Company, Cambridge, OH

Colors: Crystal

NO. 1066 AURORA

Claret, 4½ oz. $20.00
Cocktail, 3½ oz. 15.00
Cordial, 1 oz. 50.00
Goblet 20.00
Iced Tea, Footed, 12 oz. 18.00
Sherbet, Tall, 7 oz. 12.00
Tumbler, Footed, 5 oz. 16.00
Wine, 3 oz. 20.00

NO. 623

ROCK CRYSTAL ENGRAVING

Date: 1930s

Manufacturer: Cambridge Glass Company, Cambridge, OH

Colors: Crystal

No. 3122
Claret, 4½ oz. $20.00
Cocktail, 3 oz. 15.00
Cordial, 1 oz. 50.00
Fruit Salad, 7 oz. 12.00

Goblet, 9 oz. 20.00
Oyster Cocktail, 4½ oz. 12.00
Sherbet, Low, 7 oz. 12.00
Sherbet, Tall, 7 oz. 16.00
Wine, 2½ oz. 20.00
Tumbler, Footed, 2½ oz. 12.00
Tumbler, Footed, 5 oz. 16.00
Tumbler, Footed, 7 oz. 16.00
Tumbler, Footed, 9 oz. 16.00
Tumbler, Footed, 12 oz. 18.00

Original Catalog Illustration:
No. 623 rock crystal engraving
on No. 3122 goblet

NO. 640

ROCK CRYSTAL ENGRAVING

Date: 1930s

Manufacturer: Cambridge Glass Company, Cambridge, OH

Colors: Crystal

STEMWARE:
No. 3121 OR No. 3122
Claret, 4½ oz. $20.00
Cocktail, 3 oz. 15.00
Comport, Blown, 5⅜" 50.00

Cordial, 1 oz. 60.00
Goblet, 10 oz. 20.00
Iced Tea, Footed, 12 oz. 18.00
Oyster Cocktail, 4½ oz. 12.00
Sherbet, Low, 6 oz. 12.00
Sherbet, Tall, 6 oz. 16.00
Tumbler, Footed, 5 oz. 16.00
Tumbler, Footed, 10 oz. 18.00
Wine, 3½ oz. 20.00

Original Catalog Illustration:
No. 640 rock crystal engraving
on No. 3121 goblet

NO. 654

ROCK CRYSTAL ENGRAVING

Date: 1930s

Manufacturer: Cambridge Glass Co., Cambridge, OH

Colors: Crystal

STEMWARE:
No. 3121
Claret, 4½ oz. $20.00
Cocktail, 3 oz. 16.00
Comport, Blown, 5⅜" 75.00

Cordial, 1 oz. 50.00
Goblet, 10 oz. 20.00
Iced Tea, Footed, 12 oz. 20.00
Oyster Cocktail, 4½ oz. 12.00
Sherbet, Low, 6 oz. 12.00
Sherbet, Tall, 6 oz. 16.00
Tumbler, Footed, 5 oz. 15.00
Tumbler, Footed, 10 oz. 18.00
Wine, 3½ oz. 20.00

Original Catalog Illustration:
No. 654 rock crystal engraving
on No. 3121 goblet

FLOWERS *(continued)*

Original Catalog Illustration:
No. 1P Orion cutting on
No. 3790 Simplicity goblet

ORION, NO. 1P

ROCK CRYSTAL ENGRAVING

Date: 1950s

Manufacturer: Cambridge Glass Co.,
Cambridge, OH

Colors: Crystal

STEMWARE:

NO. 3790 SIMPLICITY

Claret	$14.00
Cocktail	14.00
Cordial	50.00

Goblet	18.00
Iced Tea, Footed, 12 oz.	16.00
Oyster Cocktail	10.00
Sherbet, Low	10.00
Tumbler, Footed 5 oz. (juice)	14.00
Wine	18.00

ACCESSORIES:

Plate, Salad, 8" (556)	$15.00

Original Catalog Illustration:
No. 776 Queen's Lace cutting on
No. 5375 Diamond goblet

QUEEN'S LACE, NO. 776

ROCK CRYSTAL CUTTING

Date: 1940

Manufacturer: Duncan & Miller Glass Co.,
Washington, PA

Colors: Crystal

Notes: It is likely that pressed pieces were
made, especially plates, but we do not have
documentation for any.

STEMWARE:

NO. 5375 DIAMOND

Cocktail, Liquor, 3½ oz., 5" tall	$30.00
Cordial, 1 oz., 4¼" tall	70.00
Goblet, 9 oz., 7¼" tall	45.00
Iced Tea, 12 oz., 6½" tall	38.00
Orange Juice, 5 oz., 4¾" tall	24.00
Oyster Cocktail, 4½ oz., 3¾" tall	20.00
Saucer Champagne, 5½ oz., 5½" tall	40.00
Wine, 3 oz., 5¾" tall	45.00

ROSELAND, NO. 800

ETCHING

Date: Ca. 1927

Manufacturer: Monongah Glass Co., Fairmont, WV

Colors: Crystal

STEMWARE:

NO. 7814

Brandy	$55.00
Cocktail, 3½ oz.	18.00
Goblet, 10 oz.	22.00
Saucer Champagne or High Sherbet, 5½ oz.	20.00
Sherbet, 5 oz.	13.00
Wine	22.00

Original Catalog Illustration: No. 800 Roseland assortment

ACCESSORIES:

Comport, Footed, 7" (7783) (low)	$48.00
Confection Stand, 6" (high comport) (7806)	55.00
Cream	25.00
Decanter & Stopper	95.00
Finger Bowl (7806)	10.00
Grapefruit, 20 oz. (7975)	18.00
Iced Tea, 13 oz.	15.00
Jug, 67 oz. (91-7)	130.00

Parfait, 6 oz. (7815)	22.00
Plate, 5½" (10310)	8.00
Plate, 7" (10310)	9.00
Saucer Champagne or High Sherbet, 6 oz. (7815)	20.00
Sherbet, 6½ oz. (7815)	10.00
Sugar	25.00
Tumbler, 5 oz. (9011)	12.00
Tumbler, 9 oz. (9011)	15.00

(continued) **FLOWERS**

ROSES, NO. 2P

ROCK CRYSTAL ENGRAVING

Date: 1950s

Manufacturer: Cambridge Glass Co., Cambridge, OH

Colors: Crystal

STEMWARE:
NO. A56 TODAY
Claret $20.00
Cocktail 15.00
Cordial 45.00
Goblet or Wine 20.00
Iced Tea, Footed, 12 oz. 18.00
Juice, Footed, 5 oz. 12.00
Sherbet 10.00

ACCESSORIES:
Plate, Salad, 8" (556) $15.00

Original Catalog Illustration:
No. 2P Roses rock crystal engraving on No. A56 Today goblet

HONEYCOMB

BAGUETTE

POLISHED CUTTING

Date: 1952

Manufacturer: Libbey Glass Co., Toledo, OH

Colors: Crystal

Notes: Designed by Freda Diamond.

Cocktail $10.00
Cordial 35.00
Goblet 15.00
Sherbet 9.00
Wine. 15.00

Original Ad: Baguette cutting on goblet

LACE

NO. 615

ROCK CRYSTAL ENGRAVING

Date: 1930s

Manufacturer: Cambridge Glass Co., Cambridge, OH

Colors: Crystal

NO. 3124
Claret, 4½ oz. $20.00
Cocktail, 3 oz. 15.00
Goblet, 10 oz. 20.00
Oyster Cocktail, 4½ oz. 12.00
Sherbet, Low, 7 oz. 12.00
Sherbet, Tall, 7 oz. 16.00
Wine, 3 oz. 20.00
Tumbler, Footed, 3 oz. or 5 oz. 15.00
Tumbler, Footed, 10 oz. or 12 oz.. . . . . 18.00

Original Catalog Illustration:
No. 614 rock crystal engraving on No. 3124 goblet

LACE *(continued)*

Catalog Page: No. 436 Sheila etching on pressed ware

SHEILA, NO. 436

PLATE ETCHING

Date: 1931

Manufacturer: Central Glass Works, Wheeling, WV. Later by Imperial Glass Corporation, Bellaire, OH

Colors: Crystal. Others unknown.

Notes: While this is not a true band, it is included in this category for ease of comparison with other lacy designs. Name given by Hazel Marie Weatherman. Exact items made by Central are not known. This design was continued by Imperial Glass after they bought Central's assets. Imperial collectors know this pattern as Garden Arbor. The following list is from Imperial sources.

STEMWARE:

NO. 1470

Claret	$28.00
Cocktail	17.00
Cordial	65.00
Finger Bowl	15.00
Goblet	28.00
Iced Tea, 12 oz.	24.00
Juice, 5 oz.	18.00

Oyster Cocktail	17.00
Sherbet, Low	12.00
Sherbet, Tall	22.00
Water, 10 oz.	24.00
Wine	28.00

ACCESSORIES:

Bowl, Center, 12½" (148)	$90.00
Candlesticks, 5", pr. (148)	145.00

Celery, 10" (148)	50.00
Cream & Sugar, pr. (148)	100.00
Cup & Saucer (148)	75.00
Pickle Tray, 8" (148)	35.00
Plate, 5½" or 6½" (1484 & 1485)	30.00
Plate, 7½" or 8½" (1486 & 1487)	40.00
Plate, Oblong, 14" (1489)	65.00
Plate, Torte, 14" (148)	65.00
Tray, Pastry, Handled, 11" (center handle) (148)	60.00

Original Ad: No. 267 Virginia assortment

VIRGINIA, NO. 267

PLATE ETCHING

Date: Ca. 1925

Manufacturer: Fostoria Glass Co., Moundsville, WV

Colors: Crystal

STEMWARE:

NO. 661

Claret, 5½ oz.	$15.00
Cocktail, 3 oz.	12.00
Cordial, ¾ oz.	45.00
Fruit, 6 oz., 3½" tall (low sherbet)	10.00
Goblet, 9 oz., 7" tall	20.00
Parfait, 5½ oz., 6" tall	20.00
Saucer Champagne, 6 oz., 4⅞" tall	18.00
Wine, 2 oz., 4¾" tall	20.00

ACCESSORIES:

Bedroom Set, 2 pc. (tumble up) (1697)	$85.00
Bonbon (880)	25.00
Bottle, Salad (2083)	75.00
Bowl, Console, 9" (2267)	50.00
Candlesticks, 9½", pr. (2275)	95.00
Candy Jar & Cover, ¼ lb. (2250)	35.00
Candy Jar & Cover, ½ lb. (2250)	40.00
Cologne with Drip Stopper (2241)	65.00
Comport & Cover, 5" (5078)	55.00
Comport, 6" (5078)	35.00
Cream & Sugar, pr. (2133)	40.00
Decanter, Qt. (300)	85.00
Finger Bowl (1769)	12.00

Grapefruit & Liner (945½)	30.00
Jelly & Cover (825)	55.00
Jug & Cover (2270)	135.00
Jug (1852-6 & 303-3)	95.00
Jug, No. 7 (303 & 318)	95.00
Marmalade & Cover (4087)	60.00
Mayonnaise, Footed (2138)	30.00
Mustard & Cover (1831)	55.00
Nappy & Cover, 6" (5078)	35.00
Nappy, 5" (footed) (5078)	18.00
Nappy, 7" (footed) (5078)	24.00
Oil, 5 oz. (1465)	60.00
Plate, 5" (2283)	6.00
Plate, 7" or 8" (2283)	9.00
Plate, 9" (2283)	15.00
Plate, Finger Bowl, 6" (1769)	6.00
Plate, Mayonnaise	9.00
Salt & Pepper, pr. (2235)	65.00
Syrup, 8 oz. (2194)	55.00
Tumbler, 2½ oz. (4085)	20.00
Tumbler, 6 oz. (4085)	15.00
Tumbler, 13 oz. (4085)	22.00
Tumbler, Footed, 2½ oz. (4095)	20.00
Tumbler, Footed, 5 oz. (4095)	15.00
Tumbler, Footed, 10 oz. (4095)	20.00
Tumbler, Footed, 13 oz. (4095)	22.00
Tumbler, Handled, 12 oz. (869)	25.00
Tumbler, Handled, 13 oz. (4085)	25.00
Tumbler, Table (4085)	20.00
Vase (4055D)	40.00

LAUREL LEAF

HOLLY, NO. 815

CUTTING

Date: 1941

Manufacturer: Fostoria Glass Co., Moundsville, WV

Colors: Crystal

Notes: "There's nothing nicer to live with, nothing nicer to give than Holly. It's hand cut by skilled American craftsmen. So breathlessly lovely...from the long slender stem to the lucent wreath on a bell-toned bowl."—Original ad

STEMWARE:

NO. 6030

Claret-Wine, 3½ oz., 6" tall $55.00
Cocktail, 3½ oz., 5¼" tall 25.00
Cordial, 1 oz., 3⅞" tall 55.00
Goblet, 10 oz., 7⅞" tall 40.00
Goblet, Low, 10 oz., 6⅜" tall 40.00
Iced Tea, Footed, 12 oz., 6" tall 32.00
Juice, Footed, 5 oz., 4⅝" tall 30.00
Oyster Cocktail, 4 oz., 3¾" tall 28.00
Saucer Champagne, 6 oz., 5⅜" tall 38.00
Sherbet, Low, 6 oz., 4⅜" tall 28.00

ACCESSORIES:

Ashtray, Individual, Blown,
  2⅝" (2364) $18.00
Baked Apple, 6" (2364) 20.00

Bowl, Salad, 10½" (2364) 40.00
Bowl, Salad, 9" (2364) 35.00
Celery, 11" (2350) 30.00
Cheese & Cracker, 2 pt., 11¼" (2364) . . 55.00
Cigarette Holder, Blown, 2" (2364) 30.00
Comport, 8" (2364) 48.00
Cream, Footed, 3¼" (2350½) 32.00
Cup & Saucer 45.00
Finger Bowl, 4⅛" (1769) 15.00
Fruit, 5" (2364) 20.00
Jug, Footed, 53 oz., 8⅞" tall (6011) 90.00
Lunch Tray, Handled, 11¼" (2364) 48.00
Mayonnaise, 5" (2364) 40.00
Pickle, 8" (2350) 42.00
Plate, 6" or 7" (2337) 30.00
Plate, 8" (2337) 35.00
Plate, Mayonnaise, 6¾" (2364) 22.00
Plate, Sandwich, 11" (2364) 55.00
Plate, Torte, 14" (2364) 65.00
Plate, Torte, 16" (2364) 75.00
Relish, 2 pt., 6½" (2364) 40.00
Relish, 3 pt. (2364) 45.00
Salt & Pepper, 2¼", pr. (2364) 65.00
Soup, Rim, 8" (2364) 35.00
Sugar, Footed, 3⅛" (2350½) 32.00
Vase, 6", Ground Bottom (2619½) 48.00
Vase, 7½", Ground Bottom (2619½) . . . 60.00
Vase, 9½", Ground Bottom (2619½) . . . 85.00

Original Ad: No. 815 Holly cutting on No. 6030 stemware

LAUREL WREATH, NO. 640

ROCK CRYSTAL CUTTING

Date: 1930s

Manufacturer: Duncan & Miller Glass Co., Washington, PA

Colors: Crystal

STEMWARE:

NO. 503 TOURAINE

Cigarette Holder, 3¼" tall $30.00
Claret, 5 oz., 5½" tall 20.00
Cocktail, Liquor, 3½ oz., 4½" tall 20.00
Cordial, 1 oz., 3½" tall 60.00
Creme de Menthe, 2 oz., 4" tall 42.00
Goblet, 10 oz., 6½" tall 38.00
Goblet, 9 oz., 6¾" tall 35.00
Goblet, Luncheon, 10 oz., 5" tall 35.00
Ice Cream (sherbet), 5 oz., 3½" tall 15.00
Iced Tea, Footed, 12 oz., 6½" tall 32.00
Juice, Orange, Footed, 5 oz., 4¼" tall . . 20.00
Oyster Cocktail, 3½ oz., 3¾" tall 17.00
Saucer Champagne, 5 oz., 4¾" tall 35.00
Sherry, 2 oz., 4¾" tall 42.00
Tumbler, Footed, 9 oz., 5½" tall 30.00
Whiskey, Footed, 2 oz., 3¼" tall 40.00
Wine, 2½ oz., 4¾" tall 40.00

ACCESSORIES:

Bowl, Deep Salad, 9" (33) $55.00
Bowl, Flared, 12" (36) 68.00
Bowl, Low Foot, 13" (30) 68.00
Candlesticks, Low, 3" pr. (115) 75.00
Candlesticks, 2-light, pr. (30) 115.00
Candy Box & Cover, 3-compartment,
  6½" (106) 85.00
Celery & Relish, Oblong, 2-handled,
  12" (30) 45.00
Cream & Sugar, pr. (38) 80.00
Finger Bowl (30) 15.00
Iced Cocktail Set, 2 pc. or 3 pc. (30) . . . 85.00
Mayonnaise Set (8) 85.00
Nappy, 2-handled, 6" (30) 35.00
Plate, 2-handled, 6" (30) 35.00
Plate, Bread & Butter, 6" (30½) 22.00
Plate, Dessert, 7½" (30½) 25.00
Plate, Salad, 8½" (30½) 25.00
Plate, Sandwich, 2-handled, 11" (30) . . . 65.00
Plate, Torte, 13" (33) 80.00
Relish, 2-handled, 2-compartment,
  6" (30) 35.00
Vase, 10" (506) 90.00
Vase, Flip, Flared 8" (30) 80.00

Original Catalog Illustration: No. 640 Laurel Wreath on No. 503 Touraine goblet and saucer champagne

LAUREL LEAF *(continued)*

Original Catalog Illustration:
Laurel Wreath rock crystal
engraving assortment

Original Brochure:
Laurel Wreath engraving on
No. 3700 Dunkirk goblet

Original Catalog Illustration:
No. 1012 Minton Wreath on
No. 3750 stems

LAUREL WREATH

ROCK CRYSTAL ENGRAVING

Date: 1940s

Manufacturer: Cambridge Glass Co.,
Cambridge, OH

Colors: Crystal

STEMWARE:

NO. 3139

Claret, 4½ oz.	$18.00
Cocktail, 2½ oz.	14.00
Cordial, 1 oz.	60.00
Goblet, 10 oz.	18.00
Iced Tea, Footed, 12 oz.	16.00
Oyster Cocktail, 4½ oz.	10.00
Sherbet, Tall, 7 oz.	15.00
Sherry Wine, 2½ oz.	18.00
Tumbler, Footed, 5 oz. (juice)	12.00

NO. 3700 DUNKIRK

Claret, 4½ oz.	$18.00
Cocktail, 3 oz.	14.00
Cordial, 1 oz.	60.00
Goblet, 9 oz.	18.00
Iced Tea, Footed, 12 oz.	16.00
Oyster Cocktail, 4½ oz.	10.00
Sherbet, Low, 6 oz.	10.00
Sherbet, Tall, 6 oz.	15.00
Tumbler, Footed, 10 oz. (water)	14.00
Tumbler, Footed, 5 oz. (juice)	12.00
Wine, 2½ oz.	18.00

ACCESSORIES:

Bonbon (P56)	$22.00
Bonbon, 2-handled, 5½" (1180)	20.00
Bowl, Flared, 10" (P430)	35.00
Candlesticks, 2 Light, 6", pr. (3900/72)	65.00
Candlesticks, 3½", pr. (628)	50.00
Candy Box & Cover with Cut Knob, 6" (P306)	50.00
Celery & Relish, 5 pt., 12" (P418)	25.00
Celery (P247)	22.00
Comport, Blown, 5" (3700)	32.00
Comport, 5½" (533)	25.00
Comport, Low, 6" (P54)	25.00
Cream & Sugar, pr. (P253, P254)	36.00
Cocktail Icer, 2 pc. (968)	45.00
Jug, 76 oz. (3900/115)	70.00
Marmalade & Cover (P298)	40.00
Mayonnaise (1532)	25.00
Oil & Stopper (P290)	58.00
Old Fashioned Cocktail, 7 oz. (321)	16.00
Plate, Crescent Salad, 8" (P454)	18.00
Plate, Mayonnaise (1532)	12.00
Plate, Rolled Edge, 13½" (P166)	35.00
Plate, Salad, 7½" (555)	12.00
Plate, Salad, 8" (556)	12.00
Relish, 2 pc., 12" (P419)	30.00
Relish, 2 pt., 6" (1497)	20.00
Relish, 3 pt. (P1498)	22.00
Relish, 3 pt., 10" (P214)	28.00
Salt & Pepper, pr. (P360)	45.00
Tumbler, 1½ oz. (321)	15.00
Tumbler, 12 oz. or 14 oz. (497)	15.00
Vase, Footed, 8" (6004)	45.00

MINTON WREATH, NO. 1012

ROCK CRYSTAL ENGRAVING

Date: 1940s

Manufacturer: Cambridge Glass Co.,
Cambridge, OH

Colors: Crystal

STEMWARE:

NO. 3750

Claret, 4½ oz.	$30.00
Cocktail, 3½ oz.	20.00
Cordial, 1 oz.	90.00
Goblet, 10 oz.	30.00
Iced Tea, Footed, 12 oz.	30.00
Oyster Cocktail, 5 oz.	15.00
Sherbet, Low, 6 oz.	15.00
Sherbet, Tall, 6 oz.	24.00
Tumbler, Footed, 5 oz.	25.00
Wine, 3 oz.	30.00

ACCESSORIES:

Plate, Salad, 7½" (555)	$16.00

No. 3

ROCK CRYSTAL CUTTING

Date: 1947

Manufacturer: Chartiers Crystal—a division of Duncan & Miller, Washington, PA

Colors: Crystal

Notes: Chartiers was a "budget" line of Duncan & Miller.

Brandy	$35.00
Cocktail, Liquor	18.00
Goblet	22.00
Iced Tea	20.00
Juice, Orange	15.00
Oyster Cocktail	9.00
Sherbet	9.00
Whiskey Sour	12.00
Wine	25.00

Original Ad: No. 3 cutting on iced tea

NOBILITY, No. 775

ROCK CRYSTAL CUTTING

Date: 1940s

Manufacturer: Duncan & Miller Glass Co., Washington, PA

Colors: Crystal

STEMWARE:

No. 5330 DOVER

Claret, 5 oz., 5¼" tall	$30.00
Cocktail, Liquor, 3½ oz., 4"	30.00
Cordial, 1 oz., 3½" tall	70.00
Finger Bowl, 4¼"	15.00
Goblet, 10 oz., 5¾" tall	45.00
Ice Cream (sherbet), 5 oz., 3½" tall	17.00

Iced Tea, Footed, 13 oz., 6½" tall	38.00
Juice, Orange, Footed, 5 oz., 4½" tall	24.00
Oyster Cocktail, 4½ oz., 3½" tall	20.00
Saucer Champagne or Tall Sherbet, 6 oz., 4½" tall	40.00
Tumbler, Footed, 10 oz., 5⅞" tall	35.00
Wine, 3 oz., 4¾" tall	45.00

ACCESSORIES:

Plate, 6" (30½)	$15.00
Plate, 7½" (30½)	17.00
Plate, 8½" (30½)	17.00

Original Catalog Illustration: No. 775 Nobility cutting on No. 5330 Dover goblet

VICEROY, No. 695

ROCK CRYSTAL CUTTING

Date: 1940s

Manufacturer: Duncan & Miller Glass Co., Washington, PA

Colors: Crystal

STEMWARE:

No. 5321 TRIANON

Claret, 5 oz., 6¾" tall	$30.00
Cocktail, Liquor, 3 oz., 5½" high	30.00
Cordial, 1 oz., 4½" tall	70.00
Finger Bowl, 4½"	15.00
Goblet, 10 oz., 7½" tall	45.00
Ice Cream, Footed, 6 oz., 3½" tall (sherbet)	17.00
Iced Tea, Footed, 13 oz., 6¼" tall	38.00
Oyster Cocktail, 4½ oz., 3½" tall	20.00
Saucer Champagne or Tall Sherbet, 6 oz., 6" high	40.00
Wine, 3 oz., 6¼" tall	45.00

ACCESSORIES:

Bowl, Deep Salad, 9" (33)	$55.00
Bowl, Flared, 12" (36)	68.00
Bowl, Low Foot, 13" (30)	68.00
Candlesticks, Low, 3" pr. (115)	75.00
Candlesticks, 2-light, pr. (30)	115.00
Candy Box & Cover, 3-compartment, 6½" (106)	85.00
Celery & Relish, Oblong, 2-handled, 12" (30)	45.00
Comport, 6" (5317)	65.00
Comport, Tall, 7½" (8)	65.00
Cream (38)	40.00
Finger Bowl (30)	15.00
Iced Cocktail Set, 2 pc. or 3 pc. (30)	85.00
Mayonnaise Set (8)	85.00
Nappy, 2-handled, 6" (30)	35.00
Plate, 2-handled, 6" (30)	35.00
Plate, Bread & Butter, 6" (30½)	22.00
Plate, Dessert, 7½" (30½)	25.00
Plate, Salad, 8½" (30½)	25.00
Plate, Sandwich, 2-handled, 11" (30)	65.00
Plate, Torte, 13" (33)	80.00
Relish, 2-handled, 2-compartment, 6" (30)	35.00
Salad Dressing Set, 2-compartment, 6", 2 pc. (30)	55.00
Sugar (38)	40.00
Vase, 10" (506)	90.00
Vase, Flip, Flared 8" (30)	80.00

Original Catalog Illustration: No. 695 Viceroy cutting on No. 5321 Trianon goblet

LEAVES *(continued)*

Original Catalog Illustration:
Arcadia cutting on D7
Chalice goblet

Original Pattern Folder: No. 1025 Arcadia cutting on
No. 5077 Legionnaire goblet

ARCADIA, NO. 1025

ROCK CRYSTAL CUTTING

Date: 1950s

Manufacturer: Duncan & Miller Glass Co.,
Washington, PA

Colors: Crystal

Notes: It is likely that at least pressed plates
were made to match this pattern.

STEMWARE:

NO. D7 CHALICE

Cocktail, Liquor	$30.00
Goblet	45.00
Iced Tea, Footed	38.00
Juice, Footed	24.00
Saucer Champagne or Tall Sherbet	40.00
Seafood Cocktail	20.00
Wine or Claret	45.00

ARCADIA, NO. 1025

GRAY AND ROCK CRYSTAL CUTTING

Date: 1950

Manufacturer: A.H. Heisey & Co., Newark, OH

Colors: Crystal

Notes: Made to match Gladding-McBean's Franciscan china pattern also called Arcadia. No. 1183 refers to Revere and No. 1951 Cabochon.

STEMWARE:

NO. 5077 LEGIONNAIRE

Claret, 3½ oz.	$50.00
Cocktail, 3½ oz.	30.00
Cordial, 1 oz.	95.00
Goblet, Low, 10 oz.	50.00
Iced Tea, Footed, 12 oz.	45.00
Juice, Footed, 5 oz.	25.00
Oyster Cocktail, 3½ oz.	22.00
Sherbet, 6 oz.	22.00

ACCESSORIES:

Bar, 2 oz. (6060)	$24.00
Bonbon, Handled, 6" (1951)	25.00
Bowl, Floral or Gardenia, 13" (1951)	48.00
Bowl, Gardenia, 9" (1183)	40.00
Candellettes, 1 Light, pr. (1951)	85.00
Candy Box & Cover, 7¼" (1951)	85.00
Cheese or Honey, Footed, 5¾" (1951)	35.00
Cocktail Shaker, 1 qt. (6060)	95.00
Cream & Sugar, pr. (1951)	50.00
Cup & Saucer (1184)	55.00
Jelly, Handled, 6" (1951)	25.00
Jug, ½ gal. (3484)	110.00
Mayonnaise, 5½" (1183)	38.00
Mayonnaise, Small, 5" (1951)	38.00
Oil & Stopper, 3 oz. (1951)	75.00
Pitcher (6060)	110.00
Plate, Mayonnaise, 7" (1183 or 1951)	18.00
Plate, Sandwich, 14" (1951)	55.00
Plate, Torte, 14" (1183)	45.00
Relish, 3-compartment, 9" (1951)	40.00
Sandwich, Center-handled (1951)	95.00
Soda, 8 oz. or 10 oz. (6060)	20.00
Tid Bit, 7½" (1951)	45.00
Tray for Sugar & Cream (1951)	35.00
Vase, Flared, 3½" (1951)	35.00

LEAVES

BELVIDERE

ROCK CRYSTAL CUTTING

Date: 1950s

Manufacturer: Duncan & Miller Glass Co.,
Washington, PA

Colors: Crystal

STEMWARE:

NO. D6 ETERNAL LIFE

Cocktail, Liquor	$30.00
Goblet	45.00
Iced Tea, Footed	38.00

Juice, Footed	24.00
Saucer Champagne or Tall Sherbet	40.00
Seafood Cocktail	20.00
Wine or Claret	45.00

ACCESSORIES:

Plate, 7½" (30½)	15.00
Plate, 8½" (30½)	15.00

Original Catalog Illustration:
Belvidere cutting on No. D6
Eternal Life goblet

DOLORES

CUTTING

Date: Ca. 1950s

Manufacturer: Tiffin Art Glass Corp., Tiffin, OH

Colors: Crystal

Notes: "The graceful cutting complements the trend to china border patterns." —Original Tiffin Brochure.

STEMWARE:

NO. 17453

Champagne/Sherbet	$20.00
Claret	22.00
Cocktail	18.00
Cordial	45.00
Goblet	22.00
Iced Tea	22.00
Juice	18.00

ACCESSORIES:

Finger Bowl	10.00
Nappy, Dessert	16.00
Plate, Salad, 8"	12.00

Tiffin AMERICA'S PRESTIGE CRYSTAL

Original Tiffin Brochure: Dolores cutting on No. 17453 goblet

GARLAND, NO. 778

ROCK CRYSTAL CUTTING

Date: 1940

Manufacturer: Duncan & Miller Glass Co.,
Washington, PA

Colors: Crystal

STEMWARE:

NO. 5375 DIAMOND

Cocktail, Liquor, 3½ oz., 5" tall	$30.00
Cordial, 1 oz., 4¼" tall	70.00
Goblet, 9 oz., 7¼" tall	45.00

Iced Tea, 12 oz., 6½" tall	38.00
Orange Juice, 5 oz., 4¾" tall	24.00
Oyster Cocktail, 4½ oz., 3¾" tall	20.00
Saucer Champagne, 5½ oz., 5½" tall	40.00
Wine, 3 oz., 5¾" tall	45.00

ACCESSORIES:

Plate, 6" (30½)	$12.00
Plate, 7½" (30½)	15.00
Plate, 8½" (30½)	15.00

Original Catalog Illustration:
No. 778 Garland cutting on
No. 5375 Diamond goblet

LEAVES (continued)

Original Catalog Illustration:
No. 1059 Ivy cutting on
No. 3750 goblet

Original Tiffin Brochure: Lyndley
cutting with Platinum Band on
No. 17646 goblet

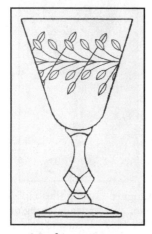

Mayfair cutting on
No.17525 goblet

IVY, NO. 1059

ROCK CRYSTAL ENGRAVING

Date: 1940s

Manufacturer: Cambridge Glass Co.,
Cambridge, OH

Colors: Crystal

STEMWARE:

NO. 3750

Claret, 4½ oz.	$20.00
Cocktail, 3½ oz.	17.00
Cordial, 1 oz.	55.00
Goblet, 10 oz.	20.00
Iced Tea, Footed, 12 oz.	17.00
Oyster Cocktail, 5 oz.	11.00
Sherbet, Low, 6 oz.	11.00
Sherbet, Tall, 6 oz.	17.00
Tumbler, Footed, 5 oz. (juice)	15.00
Wine, 3 oz.	20.00

ACCESSORIES:

Bowl, Deep Salad, 10" (P427)	$42.00
Bowl, Flower, 12" (P430)	38.00
Candlesticks, 2-light, 6", pr. (647)	70.00
Candy Box & Cover, 3-part, 7" (103)	48.00
Candy Box & Cover, 6" (P306)	42.00
Celery & Relish, 5-part, 10" (P212)	35.00
Comport, Tall, 6" (532)	48.00
Cream (138)	20.00
Plate, 14" (P125)	45.00
Plate, Salad Dressing	12.00
Plate, Salad, 7½" (555)	12.00
Salad Dressing, 2-part (1491)	32.00
Sugar (138)	20.00
Vase, Footed, 11" (278)	60.00

LYNDLEY

CUTTING

Date: 1950s

Manufacturer: Tiffin Art Glass Corp.,
Tiffin, OH

Colors: Crystal

Notes: "A stem of extraordinary dignity, to be highly prized for a lifetime." —Original Tiffin Brochure. Note the platinum rim. Tiffin used this quite effectively on many decorations, and also used gold rims.

STEMWARE:

NO. 17646

Champagne/Sherbet	$20.00
Claret	22.00
Cocktail	18.00
Cordial	45.00
Goblet	22.00
Iced Tea	22.00
Juice	16.00

ACCESSORIES:

Finger Bowl	$10.00
Nappy, Dessert	15.00
Plate, Salad, 8"	12.00

MAYFAIR

CUTTING

Date: 1952

Manufacturer: Tiffin Glass Co., Tiffin, OH

Colors: Crystal

Notes: "All stemware items available in this new pattern" —according to original ad.

STEMWARE:

NO. 17525

Goblet	$35.00

(continued) **LEAVES**

RIDGEWOOD

ROCK CRYSTAL CUTTING

Date: 1940s or 1950s

Manufacturer: Duncan & Miller Glass Co., Washington, PA

Colors: Crystal

STEMWARE:

NO. D2 RIVIERA

Brandy, 1½ oz.	$70.00
Cocktail, Liquor, 3½ oz.	30.00
Goblet, 10 oz.	45.00

Iced Tea, Footed, 14 oz.	38.00
Orange Juice, Footed, 5 oz.	24.00
Oyster Cocktail, Footed, 4½ oz.	20.00
Saucer Champagne or Tall Sherbet, 6 oz.	40.00
Wine or Claret, 4 oz.	45.00

ACCESSORIES:

Plate, 6" (30½)	$12.00
Plate, 7½" (30½)	15.00
Plate, 8½" (30½)	15.00

Original Catalog Illustration:
Ridgewood cutting on
No. D2 Riviera goblet

WOODMERE

CUTTING

Date: 1950s

Manufacturer: Tiffin Art Glass Corp., Tiffin, OH

Colors: Crystal

Notes: "For versatility and harmony; this rich combination of prism and scroll." —Original Tiffin Brochure.

STEMWARE:

NO. 17684

Champagne/Sherbet	$25.00
Claret	28.00

Cocktail	20.00
Cordial	50.00
Goblet	28.00
Iced Tea	22.00
Juice	20.00

ACCESSORIES:

Finger Bowl	$10.00
Nappy, Dessert	15.00
Plate, Salad, 8"	12.00

Original Tiffin Brochure:
Woodmere cutting on
No. 17684 goblet

MISCELLANEOUS

FLIGHT, NO. 3P

ROCK CRYSTAL ENGRAVING

Date: 1950s

Manufacturer: Cambridge Glass Co., Cambridge, OH

Colors: Crystal

STEMWARE:

NO. 3790 SIMPLICITY

Claret	$20.00
Cocktail	15.00

Cordial	45.00
Goblet	20.00
Iced Tea, Footed, 12 oz.	18.00
Oyster Cocktail	10.00
Sherbet, Low	10.00
Tumbler, Footed, 5 oz. (juice)	12.00
Wine	20.00

ACCESSORIES:

Plate, Salad, 8" (556)	$10.00c

Original Catalog Illustration:
No. 3P Flight on No. 3790
Simplicity goblet

NO. C970

CUTTING

Date: 1953

Manufacturer: Imperial Glass Corporation, Bellaire, OH

Colors: Crystal

Ice Bowl or Snack Bowl	$35.00
Pitchers (3 shapes)	40.00+
Tumblers (several sizes and styles)	10.00 to 20.00

Original ad: No. C970 cutting on tumblers

Chapter 13
BASKETS, CORNUCOPIAS & URNS

This chapter contains baskets, cornucopias or urns which are usually depicted holding bouquets of flowers. Sometimes these are not the primary motif of the decorations, but their presence rules out many strictly floral designs.

Adam etching on
No. 14178 goblet

ADAM

ETCHING

Date: 1920s

Manufacturer: U.S. Glass Co., Tiffin, OH

Colors: Crystal

STEMWARE:

NO. 14178
Café Parfait	$30.00
Champagne, Hollow Stem	30.00
Claret	35.00
Cocktail, 3 oz.	20.00
Cordial	70.00
Finger Bowl	15.00
Goblet, 10 oz.	35.00
Oyster Cocktail	15.00
Pousse Café	40.00
Saucer Champagne	25.00
Sundae	15.00
Wine, 2½ oz.	35.00

ACCESSORIES:
Cream (6)	$45.00
Decanter & Stopper (14179)	175.00
Grapefruit, Low (14251)	50.00
Jug, 2 qt. (102)	220.00
Oil Bottle & Stopper (14194)	145.00
Plate, Finger Bowl (8814)	10.00
Sugar (6)	45.00
Tumbler, 3 oz. (446)	40.00
Tumbler, 5 oz. (446)	26.00
Tumbler, Iced Tea, 12 oz. (446)	20.00
Tumbler, Iced Tea, Handled, 12 oz. (444)	26.00
Tumbler, Table, 10 oz. (446)	20.00
Vase, 10" (33)	130.00
Vase, 13" (6)	170.00

Bramble Rose etching on tumbler.

BRAMBLE ROSE

PLATE ETCHING

Date: Ca. 1918

Manufacturer: Morgantown Glass Works, Morgantown, WV

Colors: Crystal

Notes: Certainly other pieces were made, but we have not been able to document them.

Jug, 32 oz. (23)	$265.00
Tumbler, 10 oz. (9416)	25.00

(continued) BASKETS, CORNUCOPIAS & URNS

CLEO

PLATE ETCHING

Date: 1922

Manufacturer: Cambridge Glass Co., Cambridge, OH

Colors: Crystal, Amber, Dianthus Pink, Green, Mandarin Gold, Moonlight Blue

Notes: Most pressed pieces are part of the Decagon line. For Blue items, add 75%. For other colors add 50%.

Original Catalog Illustration: Cleo etching on Two-handled Bowl

STEMWARE:
NO. 3077
Cocktail, 2½ oz.	$35.00
Finger Bowl	24.00
Goblet, 9 oz.	45.00
Jug & Cover, 63 oz.	275.00
Plate, Finger Bowl	9.00
Sherbet, Low, 6"	10.00
Sherbet, Tall, 6 oz.	15.00
Tumbler, Footed, 5 oz.	18.00
Tumbler, Footed, 8 oz.	20.00
Tumbler, Footed, 10 oz.	25.00
Tumbler, Footed, 12 oz.	27.00

NO. 3115
Cocktail, 3½ oz.	$35.00
Comport, Tall, 7"	40.00
Finger Bowl	14.00
Goblet, 9 oz.	45.00
Plate, Finger Bowl	9.00
Sherbet, Tall, 6 oz.	15.00
Tumbler, Footed, 5 oz.	18.00
Tumbler, Footed, 8 oz.	20.00

Tumbler, Footed, 10 oz.	25.00
Tumbler, Footed, 12 oz.	27.00

ACCESSORIES:
Almond, Individual, 2½" (Decagon)	$100.00
Basket, 2-handled, 11" (977)	37.00
Basket, 2-handled, 7" (760)	15.00
Bonbon, 2-handled, 5½" (758)	12.00
Bonbon, 2-handled, 6¼" (749)	12.00
Bouillon, 2-handled (866)	18.00
Bowl, 11" (856)	52.00
Bowl, 2-handled, 10" (984)	42.00
Bowl, 2-handled, 8" (971)	40.00
Bowl, Oval, 15½" (841)	85.00
Candlesticks, 2-light (keyhole stem) (647)	55.00
Candlesticks, 4", pr. (627)	35.00
Candy Box & Cover (864)	110.00
Cereal, 6" (1011)	16.00
Comport, 4-toed, 6" (3400/13)	22.00
Cream & Sugar, pr. (867)	34.00
Cream Soup (1075)	20.00

Cup & Saucer (865)	18.00
Ice Pail (851)	70.00
Jug & Cover, 22 oz. (3077)	145.00
Jug & Cover, 68 oz. (124)	250.00
Mayonnaise, 5" (Footed) (983)	40.00
Oil & Stopper, 6 oz. (193)	65.00
Oil & Stopper, 6 oz. (tall) (197)	75.00
Pickle Tray, 9" (1082)	15.00
Plate for Sauce Boat (Stand) (1091)	20.00
Plate, 2-handled, 11" (972)	40.00
Plate, 2-handled, 7" (759)	9.00
Plate, Cream Soup (1075)	20.00
Plate, Dinner, 9½" (811)	60.00
Plate, Mayonnaise (983)	8.00
Relish, 2-handled, 2-compartment (3400/90)	40.00
Salt, Individual, 1½" (Decagon)	110.00
Sauce Boat (1091)	125.00
Syrup	125.00
Tray, Service, Oval, 12" (1078)	90.00
Tumbler, 12 oz. (9403)	32.00
Vase, 9½"	120.00
Vegetable, Oval, 9½" (1087)	35.00

CORSAGE, NO. 325

PLATE ETCHING

Date: 1937

Manufacturer: Fostoria Glass Co., Moundsville, WV

Colors: Crystal

Notes: "A bouquet on flashing crystal, flowers that never fade; always decorative for tables in the modern manner or correct for period appointments, too."—From Fostoria ad.

STEMWARE:
NO. 6014
Claret	$37.00
Cocktail	25.00
Cordial	58.00
Goblet	32.00
Iced Tea, Footed	26.00
Juice, Footed	22.00
Oyster Cocktail	20.00
Saucer Champagne	26.00
Sherbet, Low	22.00
Tumbler, Footed, 9 oz. (water)	24.00
Wine	37.00

ACCESSORIES:
Bonbon, 3-toed	$30.00
Bowl, Flared, 12"	80.00
Bowl, Handled, 9" or 10"	75.00
Candlesticks, 2-light, pr.	110.00
Candlesticks, 3-light, pr.	125.00
Candlesticks, 5½", pr.	95.00
Candy & Cover, 3-part	110.00
Celery	45.00
Compote, 4½"	50.00
Cream & Sugar. pr.	64.00
Cup & Saucer	40.00
Finger Bowl	30.00
Plate, Bread & Butter, 6"	22.00
Plate, Cake, Handled, 10"	55.00
Plate, Dinner, 9½"	60.00
Plate, Lunch, 8"	32.00
Plate, Salad, 7"	30.00
Plate, Torte, 13"	60.00
Relish, 3-part, 12"	60.00
Relish, 4- or 5-part	78.00
Vase, 8"	55.00

Corsage etching on No. 6014 stemware

79

BASKETS, CORNUCOPIAS & URNS *(continued)*

Original Catalog Illustration:
Athens-Diana etching on goblet
and parfait

DIANA

PLATE ETCHING

Date: 1920s

Manufacturer: U.S. Glass Co., Tiffin, OH

Colors: Crystal, Mandarin

Notes: Apollo-Diana has an added gold encrusted band about the top of pieces. Diana lacks this band. With a platinum encrusted band, the name is Athens-Diana. For colors or encrusted bands, add 50%.

STEMWARE:
NO. 14196 OR 15042
Café Parfait $28.00
Claret 30.00
Cocktail, 2½ oz. 28.00
Finger Bowl 18.00
Goblet 35.00
Oyster Cocktail 18.00
Saucer Champagne 30.00

Sundae (sherbet) 18.00
Tumbler, Footed & Handled, 12 oz. 30.00
Wine, 2 oz. 35.00

ACCESSORIES:
Grapefruit (14251) $50.00
Jug, 3 pt. (114) 125.00
Jug (128) 125.00
Nappy, Handled, 6" (5831) 30.00
Oil & Stopper (14194) 95.00
Oyster Cocktail (13630) 18.00
Plate, Finger Bowl (8814) 17.00
Plate, Salad, 8" (8833) 20.00
Tumbler, 5 oz. (354) 15.00
Tumbler, 12 oz. (354) 18.00
Tumbler, Handled, 12 oz. (354) 28.00
Tumbler, Table (354) 18.00
Vase, Bud 10" (9726) 45.00

Original Catalog Illustration:
No. 311 Florentine etching on
luncheon assortment

FLORENTINE, NO. 311

PLATE ETCHING

Date: 1931

Manufacturer: Fostoria Glass Co., Moundsville, WV

Colors: Crystal, Topaz (Gold Tint)

Notes: For Topaz, add 25% to 50%.

STEMWARE:
NO. 6005
Claret, 5 oz. $20.00
Cocktail, 4 oz. 16.00
Cordial, 1 oz. 50.00
Goblet, 9 oz. 25.00
Oyster Cocktail, 6 oz. 12.00
Saucer Champagne, 5½ oz. 20.00
Sherbet, Low, 7 oz. 12.00
Wine, 3 oz. 30.00
Tumbler, Footed, 2½ oz.
   (bar or whiskey) 24.00
Tumbler, Footed, 5 oz. (juice) 17.00
Tumbler, Footed, 9 oz. (water) 20.00
Tumbler, Footed, 12 oz. (iced tea) 24.00

ACCESSORIES:
Bonbon (2470) $20.00
Bowl, 10½" (2470½) 50.00
Bowl, 12" (2470) 58.00
Candlesticks, 2½", pr. (2470) 75.00
Candlesticks, 5½", pr. (2470½) 85.00
Comport, Low, 6" (2470) 25.00
Comport, Tall, 6" (2470) 40.00
Cream, Footed (2440) 32.00
Cup & Saucer (2440) 65.00
Dish, Lemon (2470) 24.00
Finger Bowl (869) 12.00
Plate, Bread & Butter, 6" (2440) 10.00
Plate, Cake, 10" (2470) 55.00
Plate, Dinner, 9" (2440) 85.00
Plate, Luncheon, 8" (2440) 20.00
Plate, Salad, 7" (2440) 20.00
Plate, Torte, 13" (2440) 55.00
Relish, 3-part Round (2470) 40.00
Sugar, Footed (2440) 32.00
Sweetmeat (2470) 25.00
Tray for Sugar & Cream (2470) 25.00
Tumbler, 2½ oz. or 12 oz. (4005) 24.00
Tumbler, 5 oz. (4005) 17.00
Tumbler, 9 oz. (4005) 20.00

(continued) BASKETS, CORNUCOPIAS & URNS

PORTIA

PLATE ETCHING

Date: Ca. 1932

Manufacturer: Cambridge Glass Co., Cambridge, OH

Colors: Crystal, Amber, Emerald, Heatherbloom, Mandarin Gold

Notes: Made for many years and thus on several stem lines and pressed lines. For colors add 50%. For Heatherbloom add 150%.

STEMWARE:

No. 3121
Claret, 4½ oz.	$32.00
Cocktail, 3 oz.	25.00
Cordial, 1 oz.	75.00
Goblet, 10 oz.	32.00
Oyster Cocktail, 4½ oz.	15.00
Sherbet, Low, 7 oz.	15.00
Sherbet, Tall, 7 oz.	18.00
Tumbler, Footed	20.00
Tumbler, Footed, 2½ oz. (whiskey)	42.00
Tumbler, Footed, 5 oz. (juice)	18.00
Tumbler, Footed, 10 oz. (water)	20.00
Tumbler, Footed, 12 oz. (iced tea)	27.00

No. 3124
Claret, 4½ oz.	$30.00
Cocktail, 3 oz.	20.00
Finger Bowl	18.00
Goblet, 10 oz.	24.00
Oyster Cocktail, 4½ oz.	15.00
Plate, Finger Bowl	9.00
Sherbet, Low, 7 oz.	15.00
Sherbet, Tall, 7 oz.	18.00
Tumbler, Footed, 3 oz. (whiskey)	22.00
Tumbler, Footed, 5 oz. (juice)	18.00
Tumbler, Footed, 10 oz. (water)	20.00
Tumbler, Footed, 12 oz. (iced tea)	27.00
Wine, 3 oz.	35.00

No. 3126
Brandy, 1 oz.	$62.00
Claret, 4½ oz.	32.00
Cocktail, 3 oz.	20.00
Cordial, 1 oz.	75.00
Finger Bowl	18.00
Goblet, 9 oz.	25.00
Oyster Cocktail, 4½ oz.	15.00
Plate, Finger Bowl	9.00
Sherbet, Low, 7 oz.	15.00
Sherbet, Tall, 7 oz.	18.00
Tumbler, Footed, 2½ oz. (whiskey)	42.00
Tumbler, Footed, 5 oz. (juice)	18.00
Tumbler, Footed, 10 oz. (water)	20.00
Tumbler, Footed, 13 oz. (iced tea)	25.00
Wine, 2½ oz.	45.00

No. 3130
Claret, 4½ oz.	$45.00
Cocktail, 3 oz.	20.00
Cordial, 1 oz.	75.00
Goblet, 9 oz.	28.00
Iced Tea, Footed, 12 oz.	25.00
Oyster Cocktail, 4½ oz.	17.00
Sherbet, Low, 7 oz.	15.00
Sherbet, Tall, 7 oz.	20.00
Tumbler, Footed, 5 oz.	20.00
Tumbler, Footed, 10 oz.	20.00
Wine, 2½ oz.	45.00

ACCESSORIES:
Basket, 2-handled, Footed, 6" (3500/55)	$28.00
Basket, 7" (119)	145.00
Bonbon, 2-handled, 5¼" (3400/1180)	25.00
Bonbon, Footed, 2-handled, 6" (3500/54)	24.00
Bonbon, Footed, 2-handled, 7" (3900/130)	30.00
Bowl, 2-handled, 11" (3400/1188)	45.00
Bowl, 2-handled, 11" (3900/34)	45.00
Bowl, 4-footed, Crimped, 11" (3400/160)	55.00
Bowl, 4-footed, Flared, 10" (3900/54)	50.00
Bowl, Footed, 11½" (3900/28)	48.00
Bowl, Grapefruit or Oyster, 6" (3400/109)	25.00
Candlesticks, 2-light, 6", pr. (3900/72)	85.00
Candlesticks, 3-light, 6" (3900.74)	110.00
Candlesticks, 1-light, 5", pr. (3900/67)	50.00
Candy Box & Cover (3900/165)	82.00
Celery & Relish, 3-part, 12" (3900/126)	50.00
Celery & Relish, 3-part, 9" (3900/125)	40.00
Celery & Relish, 5-part, 12" (3900/120)	48.00
Celery Tray, 11" (652)	38.00
Cocktail Icer, 2 pc. (968)	78.00
Cocktail Shaker, 32 oz. (P 191)	120.00
Cocktail Shaker, Ball, 80 oz. (3400/108)	200.00
Cocktail, 4 oz. (7801)	24.00
Cologne, 2 oz. (ball) (3400/97)	110.00
Comport, 5½" (3900/136)	38.00
Comport, Blown, 5⅜" (3121)	42.00
Comport, Tall (3121/1)	42.00
Cranberry, Round, 3½" (3400/49)	22.00
Cranberry, Square, 3½" (3400/80)	22.00
Cream (3900/41)	20.00
Cream, 8 oz. (ball) (3400/98)	37.00
Cream, Individual (3500/15)	20.00

Original Catalog Illustration: Portia etching on grapefruit or oyster bowl and cocktail icer

Original Catalog Illustration: Portia etching on No. 3126 footed tumbler

Original Catalog Illustration: Portia etching on No. 3124 tall sherbet

BASKETS, CORNUCOPIAS & URNS *(continued)*

Original Catalog Illustration:
Portia etching on 7" basket,
ivy ball and puff box

Original Catalog Illustration:
No. 317 Sheraton etching on
No. 6010 iced tea, claret-wine
and oyster cocktail.

Cream, Individual (3900/40) 20.00
Cup & Saucer, Square (3400/50,
    also 3900/17) 27.00
Decanter, Footed, 28 oz. (1321) 220.00
Hurricane Lamp (1603 or 1617). 195.00
Ice Bucket (3900/671) 85.00
Ivy Ball, 5½" (3400/93) 60.00
Jug, Ball (3400/38) 175.00
Mayonnaise (3900/129) 38.00
Mayonnaise (footed) (3900/19) 38.00
Mayonnaise, 2-compartment
    (3900/111) 40.00
Oil & Stopper, 6 oz. (193) 85.00
Oil & Stopper, 6 oz. (3900/100) 95.00
Oil & Stopper, 6 oz. (ball)
    (3400/99). 95.00
Pickle, 9½" (477) 32.00
Plate, 2-handled, 6" (3400/1181) 22.00
Plate, 2-handled, Footed,
    8" (3500/161) 22.00
Plate, 4-footed, 12" (3900/26) 50.00
Plate, Bonbon, Footed, 2-handled,
    8" (3900/131) 27.00
Plate, Bread & Butter,
    6½" (3900/20). 9.00
Plate, Dinner, 10½" (3900/24). 78.00
Plate, Mayonnaise (3900/129) 15.00
Plate, Rolled Edge, 14" (3900/166) 68.00
Plate, Salad, 8" (3900/22) 15.00
Plate, Salad, 8½" (round) (3400/62). . . . 15.00
Plate, Salad, 8½" (square)(3400/1176) . . 15.00

Plate, Torte, Rolled Edge, 4 Footed, 13"
    (3900/33). 50.00
Puff Box & Cover, 3½"
    (ball) (3400/94) 170.00
Relish or Pickle, 7" (3900/123) 30.00
Relish, 2-part, 6" (3400/90) 22.00
Relish, 2-part, 7" (3900/124) 25.00
Relish, 3-part, 3 Handles (3400/9) 30.00
Salt & Pepper, pr. (3900/1177). 40.00
Sherry, 2 oz. (7966) 45.00
Sugar (3900/41) 20.00
Sugar, 8 oz. (ball) (3400/98). 37.00
Sugar, Individual (3500/15) 20.00
Sugar, Individual (3900/40) 20.00
Tumbler, 13 oz. (3900/115) 22.00
Vase, "Flower Holder," Bud, 10" (274) . . 65.00
Vase, "Flower Holder," Footed,
    11" (1299) 78.00
Vase, "Flower Holder," Footed,
    13" (279) 125.00
Vase, "Flower Holder," Footed,
    13" (keyhole stem) (1238). 110.00
Vase, "Flower Holder," Footed,
    6" (6004) 58.00
Vase, "Flower Holder," Footed,
    8" (6004) 78.00
Vase, "Flower Holder," Footed,
    9" (keyhole stem) (1237). 90.00
Vase, "Flower Holder," Globe,
    5" (1309) 65.00
Vase, "Flower Holder," Footed (278). . . . 75.00

SHERATON, NO. 317

PLATE ETCHING

Date: 1933

Manufacturer: Fostoria Glass Co.,
Moundsville, WV

Colors: Crystal

Notes: Most likely more accessory pieces
were made.

STEMWARE:
No. 6010
Claret-Wine, 4¼ oz. $35.00
Cocktail, 4 oz. 22.00
Cordial, 1 oz. 55.00
Goblet, 9 oz. 25.00

Oyster Cocktail, 5½ oz. 14.00
Sherbet, High, 5½ oz. 22.00
Sherbet. Low, 5½ oz. 18.00
Tumbler, Footed, 5 oz. (juice). 17.00
Tumbler, Footed, 9 oz. (water) 18.00
Tumbler, Footed, 12 oz. (iced tea). 25.00

ACCESSORIES:
Finger Bowl (869) 12.00
Plate, R. O., 5" 10.00
Plate, R. O., 7" 12.00
Plate, R. O., 8" 15.00

Chapter 14
BIRDS

Birds are used in many decorations, primarily etchings. The birds are often quite stylized, but all make effective decorations for stemware and tableware.

ELDORADO

ETCHING

Date: 1920

Manufacturer: U.S. Glass Co., Tiffin, OH

Colors: Crystal

STEMWARE:

NO. 14194

Goblet, 9 oz. $32.00

Probably a full line was available.

ACCESSORIES:

Candy Jar & Cover, ½ lb. $65.00
Candy Jar & Cover, 1 lb. 75.00
Finger Bowl (8814) 17.00
Jug & Cover (14194) 295.00
Tankard & Cover, 1 qt. 350.00
Tumbler, 4½ oz. (juice) (520) 18.00
Tumbler, 12 oz. (Iced Tea) (517) 25.00
Tumbler, Handled, 12 oz. 35.00
Tumbler, Table, 10 oz. (580) 25.00

Original Catalog Illustration:
Eldorado etching
No. 14194 cocktail

EMPIRE

PLATE ETCHING

Date: 1920s

Manufacturer: U.S. Glass Co.

Colors: Crystal, All Rose

Notes: Prices listed are for Rose. For Crystal, deduct 25% to 50%.

STEMWARE:

NO. 15018

Goblet $75.00

Probably a full line was available.

ACCESSORIES:

Cream (6) $75.00
Cup & Saucer (8869) 60.00
Finger Bowl (185) 20.00
Jug & Cover, Footed (14194) 390.00
Plate, 8" (8833) 20.00
Sugar (6) 75.00
Tumbler, Table, 9 oz. (018) 40.00

Original Catalog Illustration:
Empire etching on covered jug

FONTAINE

ETCHING

Date: 1924

Manufacturer: U.S. Glass Co., Tiffin, OH

Colors: Crystal, All Twilite, All Rose, All Green. Twilite bowl with Crystal stem and foot

Notes: Prices given are for Rose or Green. For Crystal, deduct 25% to 50%. For Twilite, add 50%+.

STEMWARE:

NO. 15033

Cocktail. $35.00
Goblet. 40.00
Wine. 40.00

ACCESSORIES:

Candlesticks, Low, 5", pr. (9758) 175.00
Centerpiece, 13" (8153) 130.00
Cream & Sugar, pr. (4) 150.00
Cup & Saucer (8869) 60.00
Finger Bowl (002) 20.00
Grapefruit (251) 55.00
Jug & Cover (194) 375.00
Nappy, Deep, 8" (14194) 130.00
Plate, 6" (8814) 10.00
Plate, 8" (8833) 20.00
Plate, 10" (8818) 100.00
Tumbler, Table, 9 oz. (032) 40.00
Vase, 8" (2) 300.00
Vase, 9¼" (7) 300.00

Original Catalog Illustration:
Fontaine etching on grapefruit
and liner

BIRDS *(continued)*

Mallard Duck tumbler

MALLARD DUCK

ETCHING

Date: 1930s

Manufacturer: Duncan & Miller Glass Co., Washington, PA

Colors: Crystal

Notes: Barware items are usually found with colored bases in Amber, Green, Ruby, and Blue.

Ashtray, Oval, 3½" (32) $20.00
Ashtray, Oval, 5" x 3½" (32) 24.00
Ashtray, Oval, 7" (32) 35.00
Ashtray, Rectangular, 3½" (30) 20.00
Ashtray, Rectangular, 5" x 3¼"
   or 6½" (30) 24.00
Ashtray, Rectangular, 8" (30) 35.00
Ashtray, Rectangular, Oval Center,
   3½" (31) 20.00
Ashtray, Rectangular, Oval Center,
   5" (31) 24.00
Ashtray, Rectangular, Oval Center,
   6½" (31) 35.00
Cigarette Box & Cover,
   4½" x 3½" (30) 40.00
Cigarette Box & Cover, Oval,
   3½" (32) 40.00
Cigarette Box & Cover, Oval,
   4½" x 3½" (32) 45.00

Cigarette Box & Cover, Oval,
   7½" (32) 60.00
Cocktail Mixer, Handled, 32 oz.,
   10¾" tall (30) 95.00
Cocktail Shaker, 14 oz.,
   6½" tall or 18 oz. (5200) 110.00
Cocktail Shaker, 32 oz. (5200) 125.00
Cocktail, Footed, 4 oz.,
   3½" tall (520½) 35.00
Cocktail, Old Fashioned, 14 oz. (520) . . 22.00
Cocktail, Old Fashioned,
   6½ oz., 3¼" tall (520) 18.00
Highball, 11 oz., 5" tall (520) 18.00
Highball, 13 oz. (520) 20.00
Highball, 18 oz., 7½" tall (520) 24.00
Ice Tub, 6" (30) 55.00
Martini Mixer, 18 oz., 7¼" tall (5200) . . 95.00
Martini Mixer, 32 oz. (5200) 110.00
Old Fashioned, 7 oz., 2¼" tall (5200) . . . 22.00
Orange Juice, 5 oz., 3¼" tall (5200) 15.00
Tumbler, 10 oz. or 12 oz.,
   3¾" tall (5200) 17.00
Tumbler, 14 oz., 4¼" tall (5200) 18.00
Tumbler, 16 oz. or 18 oz. (5200) 20.00

Original Catalog Illustration:
No. 250 Oriental etching on jug
with tumbler

ORIENTAL, NO. 250

PLATE ETCHING

Date: Ca. 1918

Manufacturer: Fostoria Glass Co., Moundsville, WV

Colors: Crystal

Notes: Patent No. 50336 granted to this pattern.

STEMWARE:
NO. 766

Almond, 2" tall $25.00
Brandy, ¾ oz., 3¾" tall 65.00
Claret, 4 ½ oz., 5⅝" tall 35.00
Cordial, ¾ oz., 3⁷⁄₁₆" tall 65.00
Custard, 4 oz., 2¼" tall (punch cup) . . . 17.00
Finger Bowl, 2" tall 15.00
Fruit, 3¼" tall 14.00
Goblet, 9 oz., 7" tall 35.00

Parfait, 5 ½ oz., 7⅛" tall 40.00
Sherbet, 2⅝" tall 14.00
Sherry, 2 oz., 4⅜" tall 60.00
Wine, 3 ¾ oz., 5" tall 35.00

ACCESSORIES:
Bonbon, 5½" tall (880) $38.00
Bottle, Salad Dressing (2169) 85.00
Bottle, Salad Dressing, 7 oz. (2083) 85.00
Comport, 5", 6³⁄₁₆" tall (803) 50.00
Cream (2133) 45.00
Iced Tea, Handled, 14 oz. (701) 45.00
Jug & Cover (317½) 120.00
Jug with Tumbler Cover (2104) 170.00
Oyster Cocktail, 3⅝" tall (837) 20.00
Sugar (2133) 45.00
Tumbler, 8 oz., 4⅜" tall (4011) 25.00
Tumbler, 9 oz., 4" tall (837) 25.00

PEACOCK, NO. 366

PLATE ETCHING

Date: 1916

Manufacturer: A.H. Heisey & Co., Newark, OH

Colors: Crystal

STEMWARE:

NO. 3308 BOB WHITE

Burgundy, 3 oz.	$25.00
Claret, 4½ oz.	25.00
Cocktail, 3 oz.	22.00
Cordial, 1 oz.	65.00
Finger Bowl	15.00
Goblet, 11 oz.	35.00
Goblet, 7 oz. or 9 oz.	35.00
Grape Juice, 4½ oz.	22.00
Parfait, 4½ oz.	25.00
Pousse Café	40.00
Saucer Champagne, 6 oz.	25.00
Sherbet, Footed, 6 oz.	14.00
Sherry, 2 oz.	60.00
Sundae, Footed, 6 oz.	16.00
Wine, 2 oz.	35.00

NO. 3333 OLD GLORY

Burgundy, 3 oz.	$30.00
Claret, 4½ oz.	30.00
Cocktail, 3 oz. or 2½ oz.	30.00
Comport, High Footed, 6"	85.00

Cordial, 1 oz.	75.00
Finger Bowl (No. 3309)	20.00
Goblet, 8 oz. or 9 oz.	40.00
Grapefruit, Footed	50.00
Grape Juice, 6 oz.	45.00
Iced Tea, Footed, Handled, 12 oz. (No. 3476)	40.00
Oyster Cocktail, 4½ oz. (No. 3542)	16.00
Parfait, 4½ oz.	38.00
Pousse Café, ¾ oz.	70.00
Saucer Champagne, 5½ oz.	32.00
Sherry, 2 oz.	70.00
Soda, Footed, 12 oz. (No. 3476)	38.00
Sundae or Sherbet, 5½ oz.	18.00
Wine, 2 oz.	50.00

ACCESSORIES:

Iced Tea, Footed & Handled, 12 oz. (3476 or 3477)	$45.00
Jug, ½ gal. (4156 or 4160)	120.00
Jug, 73 oz. (4164)	120.00
Oyster Cocktail, 4½ oz. (3542)	20.00
Plate, 6", 7" or 8" (4182)	12.00
Soda or Iced Tea, 12 oz. (2351)	30.00
Soda, 8 oz. or 10 oz. (2351)	25.00
Soda, Taper, 5 oz. (2401)	20.00
Tankard, 54 oz. (4163)	120.00
Tumbler, 10 oz. (2930)	25.00

No. 366 Peacock etching on No. 3308 Bob White goblet

PERSIAN PHEASANT

PLATE ETCHING

Date: Ca. 1930

Manufacturer: U.S. Glass Co., Tiffin, OH

Colors: Crystal, Rose, Green with Crystal Trim.

STEMWARE:

NO. 15037, NO. 17358

Café Parfait	$32.00
Claret	38.00
Cocktail	30.00
Cordial	75.00
Goblet or Wine	38.00
Saucer Champagne	32.00
Sundae (sherbet)	20.00
Table (tumbler)	25.00

ACCESSORIES:

Bowl, Large (526)	$85.00
Bowl, Medium (526)	72.00
Bowl, Nut, 6" (5902)	65.00
Bowl, Salad, 10" (5902)	80.00
Bowl, Small (526)	110.00

Candleholders, pr. (9758)	95.00
Candlesticks, 2-light, pr. (5902)	140.00
Celery Tray (5902)	65.00
Centerpiece, 12" (8153)	95.00
Centerpiece, 12½" (cone shape) (5902)	110.00
Centerpiece, Crimped, 12" (5902)	95.00
Centerpiece, Shallow, 13" (5902)	95.00
Comport, High, 6" (004)	75.00
Comport, Low, 6" (185)	65.00
Comport, Tall (15082)	80.00
Cream (185 or 5902)	55.00
Cup & Saucer (8869)	60.00
Finger Bowl (002)	18.00
Grapefruit (251)	50.00
Jug & Cover, Footed (14194)	360.00
Jug (14194)	310.00
Jug, 60 oz. (5959)	310.00

Original Catalog Illustration: Persian Pheasant etching on No. 15037 covered pitcher

Mayonnaise (5902)	55.00
Nappy, 7" (5902)	45.00
Plate Lily or Floater (5902)	75.00
Plate, Cake, Center Handled (5909)	70.00
Plate, Handled Cake (5902)	65.00
Plate, Mayonnaise, 6" (5902)	20.00
Plate, Salad, 8" (5902)	20.00
Plate, Sandwich, 14" (5902)	50.00
Relish, 3-part, large (5902)	55.00
Relish, 3-part, small (5902)	40.00
Salt & Pepper, pr. (2)	100.00
Seafood Cocktail Set (6021)	95.00
Sugar (185)	55.00
Vase, Bud, 6" (14185)	90.00
Vase, Bud, 8" (14185)	110.00
Vase, Bud, 10" (14185)	125.00
Vase, Bud, 11" (15082)	130.00

Chapter 15

BOWS & RIBBONS

Original Catalog Illustration:
No. 782 Bridal Bow on No. 503
Touraine goblet

Original Catalog Illustration:
No. 867 Chateau cutting on
No. 3368 Albemarle goblet

BRIDAL BOW, NO. 782

ROCK CRYSTAL CUTTING

Date: 1930s

Manufacturer: Duncan & Miller Glass Co.,
Washington, PA

Colors: Crystal

STEMWARE:

NO. 503 TOURAINE

Cigarette Holder, 3¼" tall	$35.00
Claret, 5 oz., 5½" tall	30.00
Cocktail, Liquor, 3½ oz., 4½" tall	30.00
Cordial, 1 oz., 3½" tall	70.00
Creme de Menthe, 2 oz., 4" tall	45.00
Goblet, 10 oz., 6½" tall	45.00
Goblet, 9 oz., 6¾" tall	40.00
Goblet, Luncheon, 10 oz., 5" tall	40.00
Ice Cream (sherbet), 5 oz., 3½" tall	17.00
Iced Tea, Footed, 12 oz., 6½" tall	38.00
Juice, Orange, Footed, 5 oz., 4¼" tall	24.00
Oyster Cocktail, 3½ oz., 3¾" tall	20.00
Saucer Champagne, 5 oz., 4¾" tall	40.00
Sherry, 2 oz., 4¾" tall	55.00
Tumbler, Footed, 9 oz., 5½" tall	35.00
Whiskey, Footed, 2 oz., 3¼" tall	40.00
Wine, 2½ oz., 4¾" tall	45.00

ACCESSORIES:

Plate, 6" (30½)	$15.00
Plate, 7½" or 8½"(30½)	17.00

CHATEAU

ROCK CRYSTAL CUTTING WITH GRAY FLOWER

Date: 1935

Manufacturer: A.H Heisey & Co.,
Newark, OH

Colors: Crystal

Notes: "Truly regal, this exquisite rock crystal cutting by Heisey offers a complete choice of hand-blown stemware together with basic table accessories."—Heisey pattern folder.

STEMWARE:

NO. 3368 ALBEMARLE

Bar, Footed, 1½ oz.	$60.00
Claret, 4 oz.	85.00
Cocktail, 3 oz.	55.00
Comport, 7"	135.00
Cordial, 1 oz.	145.00
Finger Bowl	25.00
Goblet, 8 oz.	85.00
Oyster Cocktail, 3 oz.	25.00
Parfait, 4½ oz.	55.00
Saucer Champagne, 5 oz.	70.00
Sherbet, 5 oz.	25.00
Soda, Footed, 12 oz.	55.00
Soda, Footed, 5 oz.	45.00
Soda, Footed, 8 oz.	50.00
Tumbler, Footed, 10 oz.	50.00
Wine, 2½ oz.	85.00

ACCESSORIES:

Bar, 1½ oz. (2351)	$50.00
Bell, Dinner (3408)	225.00
Bottle, French Dressing, 8 oz. (5031)	135.00
Bowl, Floral, 10" (3397)	135.00
Bowl, Floral, 14" (1488)	185.00
Bowl, Floral, Dolphin Footed, 11" (1401 or 1509)	90.00
Bowl, Floral, Oval, Beaded Top, 11" (1429)	80.00
Bowl, Gardenia (485)	120.00
Bowl, Salad, 11" (4056)	120.00
Candelabra, 2-light, pr. (1483 or 4044)	475.00
Candelabra, 2-light, pr. (1488)	800.00
Candlesticks, 1-light, pr. (113)	110.00
Candlesticks, 2-light, pr. (134)	130.00
Candlesticks, 3-light, pr. (142)	145.00
Celery, 13" (1519)	60.00
Cigarette Holder (3390)	70.00
Cocktail Shaker, 2 Qt. (4225)	195.00
Comport, 6" (3404)	135.00
Comport, 7" (3411)	135.00
Cordial (5023)	125.00
Cream, Dolphin Footed (1509 or 1511)	60.00
Cup & Saucer (1509)	85.00

Decanter, 16 oz. (4026) 160.00
Grapefruit (3350) 75.00
Grapefruit, Low Footed (3801) 65.00
Ice Tub, Dolphin Footed (1509) 125.00
Jug, 73 oz. (4164) 175.00
Jug, Ice (4164) 175.00
Mayonnaise, Dolphin Footed,
   5½" (1509) 90.00
Mint, Footed, 6" (1509) 45.00
Oil & Stopper, 4 oz. (1509 or 1519) . . . 150.00
Old Fashioned, 8 oz. (2401) 30.00
Plate, 6" (1184) 18.00
Plate, 7" (1509) 22.00
Plate, 7" or 8" (1184) 24.00
Plate, 10½" (1184) 95.00

Plate, 10½" (1509) 150.00
Plate, 14" (1184) 55.00
Plate, Buffet, 16" (1184) 65.00
Plate, Sandwich, Round, 2-handled,
   12" (1509) 70.00
Plate, Torte, 18" (1184) 80.00
Relish, Five O'Clock, 11" (1509) 110.00
Relish, Triplex, 7" (1509) 65.00
Relish, Triplex, 10" (1509) 95.00
Salt & Pepper, pr. (10 or 1519) 95.00
Soda, 8 oz. (2401) 30.00
Soda, 12 oz. (2401) 38.00
Sugar, Dolphin Footed (1509 or 1511) . . 60.00
Tray, Variety, 12" (relish) (500) 95.00

CORSAGE, NO. 1075

ROCK CRYSTAL ENGRAVING

Date: 1950s

Manufacturer: Cambridge Glass Co.,
Cambridge, OH

Colors: Crystal

STEMWARE:

NO. 3116
Claret, 4½ oz. $20.00
Cocktail, 3 oz. 16.00

Cordial, 1 oz. 50.00
Goblet, 10 oz. 20.00
Iced Tea, Footed, 12 oz. 18.00
Oyster Cocktail, 4½ oz. 10.00
Sherbet, Low, 6 oz. 14.00
Sherbet, Tall, 6 oz. 16.00
Tumbler, Footed, 10 oz. (water) 15.00
Tumbler, Footed, 5 oz. (juice) 12.00
Wine, 3 oz. 20.00

Original Catalog Illustration:
No. 1075 Corsage rock crystal
engraving on goblet

JUNE, NO. 279

PLATE ETCHING

Date: 1928

Manufacturer: Fostoria Glass Co., Fostoria, OH

Colors: Crystal, Azure, Gold Tint/Topaz, Green, Rose

Notes: Most tableware pieces are in the No. 2375 Fairfax pattern. Patented: No. 76,373 and 76,455.

STEMWARE:

NO. 5098	Crystal	Gold Tint/Topaz Green	Azure, Rose
Claret, 4 oz., 6" tall	$40.00	$65.00	$70.00
Cocktail, 3 oz., 5⅛" tall	28.00	42.00	52.00
Cordial, ¾ oz., 3⅞" tall	85.00	125.00	150.00
Goblet, 9 oz., 8¼" tall	30.00	40.00	48.00
Iced Tea, Footed, 12 oz., 6" tall	34.00	42.00	50.00
Juice, Footed. 5 oz., 4⅜" tall	24.00	30.00	35.00
Oyster Cocktail, 5 oz., 3¾" tall	22.00	27.00	32.00
Parfait, 6 oz., 5¼" tall	32.00	60.00	78.00
Sherbet, High, 6 oz., 6" tall	28.00	35.00	40.00
Sherbet, Low, 6 oz., 4⅛" tall	22.00	30.00	35.00
Tumbler, Footed, 9 oz., 5¼" tall	24.00	32.00	35.00
Whiskey, Footed, 2½ oz., 2⅞" tall	35.00	55.00	60.00
Wine, 2½ oz., 5⅜" tall	35.00	60.00	125.00

Original Catalog Illustration:
No. 279 June etching on jug

BOWS & RIBBONS *(continued)*

Detail of No. 279 June etching

Original Catalog Illustration:
No. 279 June etching on
After Dinner cup and saucer

Original Catalog Illustration:
No. 279 June etching on
footed sugar and cover

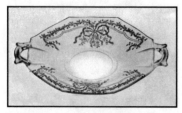

Original Catalog Illustration:
No. 279 June etching
on lemon plate

ACCESSORIES:	Crystal	Gold Tint/Topaz Green	Azure, Rose
Ashtray, Small (2350)	$28.00	$40.00	$60.00
Baker, 9" (2375)	40.00	85.00	145.00
Bonbon (2375)	15.00	28.00	40.00
Bottle, Salad Dressing (2375)	200.00	400.00+	900.00
Bouillon, Footed (2375)	15.00	28.00	45.00
Bowl, 10" (2395)	35.00	85.00	140.00
Bowl, 12" (2375)	45.00	65.00	125.00
Bowl, 12" "A" (2394)	45.00	65.00	125.00
Candlesticks, 2", pr. (2394)	35.00	50.00	75.00
Candlesticks, 3", pr. (2375)	48..00	75.00	130.00
Candlesticks, 5" pr. (2375½ or 2395½)	58.00	85.00	155.00
Celery, 11½" (2375)	30.00	55.00	115.00
Centerpiece, 12" (2375)	70.00	115.00	225.00
Cereal, 6" (2375)	22.00	40.00	60.00
Cheese & Cracker, 2-piece (2368)	48.00	78.00	125.00
Comport, 6" (2400)	24.00	40.00	75.00
Cream Soup, Footed (2375)	20.00	38.00	55.00
Cream, Footed (2375½)	18.00	24.00	65.00
Cream, Tea (2375½)	30.00	52.00	75.00
Cup & Saucer (2375½)	25.00	27.00	45.00
Cup & Saucer, After Dinner (2375)	32.00	60.00	110.00
Dessert, Large (2375)	35.00	75.00	135.00
Dish, Ice (2451)	30.00	48.00	70.00
Dish, Lemon (2375)	16.00	22.00	28.00
Fruit, 5" (2375)	18.00	24.00	32.00
Ice Bucket (2375)	65.00	95.00	200.00
Jug, Footed, 7" (5000)	250.00	380.00	700.00
Lunch Tray, Handled (2375)	24.00	58.00	45.00
Mayonnaise (footed) (2375)	24.00	35.00	65.00
Nappy, Round, 7" (2375—crystal only)	22.00	—	—
Oil & Stopper, Footed (2375)	230.00	375.00	660.00
Plate, Bread & Butter, 6" (2375)	6.00	9.00	15.00
Plate, Cake, 10" (2375)	24.00	48.00	72.00
Plate, Chop, 13" (2375)	25.00	62.00	85.00
Plate, Cream Soup (2375)	6.00	9.00	15.00
Plate, Dinner, 10" (2375)	45.00	78.00	140.00
Plate, Dinner, 9" (2375)	20.00	35.00	55.00
Plate, Luncheon, 8" (2375)	9.00	20.00	25.00
Plate, Mayonnaise (2375)	9.00	20.00	25.00
Plate, Salad, 7" (2375)	7.00	12.00	15.00
Plate, Torte, 13" (2440)	45.00	80.00	125.00
Platter, 12" (2375)	40.00	85.00	145.00
Platter, 15" (2375)	60.00	130.00	225.00
Relish, 8½" (2375)	25.00	42.00	—
Salt & Pepper, Footed, pr. (2375)	75.00	135.00	220.00
Soup, 7" (2375)	65.00	195.00	195.00
Sugar & Cover, Footed (2375½)	75.00	165.00	275.00
Sugar Pail	78.00	170.00	260.00
Sugar, Tea (2375½)	30.00	52.00	75.00
Sweetmeat (2375)	20.00	30.00	48.00
Whipped Cream (2375)	14.00	18.00	24.00
Whipped Cream Pail	85.00	160.00	245.00
Vase, 8"	85.00	160.00	295.00
Vase, Footed, Fan, 8½"	85.00	148.00	250.00

(continued) **BOWS & RIBBONS**

ROMANCE, NO. 341

PLATE ETCHING

Date: 1942

Manufacturer: Fostoria Glass Co., Moundsville, WV

Colors: Crystal

Notes: "It's one of many Fostoria 'Master-Etchings', superbly crafted, irresistibly beguiling. Romance is available in stemware as well as smart accent pieces to touch up any table setting."—Fostoria ad.

STEMWARE:

NO. 6017 SCEPTRE

Claret, 4 oz., 5⅞" tall. $35.00
Cocktail, 3½ oz., 4⅞" tall 24.00
Cordial, ¾ oz., 3⅞" tall 55.00
Goblet, 9 oz., 7⅜" tall 28.00
Oyster Cocktail, 4 oz., 3⅝" tall 15.00
Saucer Champagne, 6 oz., 5½" tall (high sherbet) 24.00
Sherbet, Low, 6 oz., 4½" tall 18.00
Tumbler, Footed, 5 oz., 4¾" tall (juice) 17.00
Tumbler, Footed, 9 oz., 5½" tall (water) 17.00
Tumbler, Footed, 12 oz. 6" tall (iced tea) 22.00
Tumbler, Footed, 14 oz., 6½" tall (iced tea) 22.00
Wine, 3 oz., 5½" tall 35.00

ACCESSORIES:

Ashtray, Individual, Blown, 2⅝" (2364) $22.00
Baked Apple, 6" (2364) 22.00
Bowl, Flared, 12" (2364) 85.00
Bowl, Footed, Blown, 9¼" (6023) 75.00
Bowl, Fruit, 13" (2364) 95.00
Bowl, Handled, 10" (2594) 80.00
Bowl, Oblong, Shallow, 11" (2596) . . . 110.00
Bowl, Salad, 10½" (2364) 75.00
Bowl, Salad, 9" (2364) 65.00
Candlesticks, 4", 1-light, pr. (2324) 70.00
Candlesticks, 5", 1-light, pr. (2596) 90.00
Candlesticks, 5½", 1-light, pr. (2594) . . . 90.00
Candlesticks, Duo, 5½", pr. (6023) . . . 110.00
Candlesticks, Trindle, 8", pr. (2594) . . . 135.00
Candy Box & Cover, Blown, 3¾" (2364) 145.00
Celery, 11" (2364) 55.00
Cheese & Cracker, 2 pc., 11¼" (2364) 68.00
Cigarette Holder, Blown, 2" (2364) 80.00
Comport, 5" (6030) 45.00
Comport, 8" (2364) 75.00
Cream 35.00
Cup & Saucer 45.00
Ice Bowl, 4¾"x 6" (4132) 75.00
Lily Pond, 12" (2364) 68.00
Lunch Tray, Handled, 11¼" (2364) 68.00
Mayonnaise, 5" (2364) 45.00
Pickle, 8" (2364) 40.00
Plate, Mayonnaise, 6¾" (2364) 20.00
Plate, Sandwich, 11" (2364) 65.00
Plate, Torte, 14" (2364) 75.00
Plate, Torte, 16" (2364) 115.00
Relish, 2 pt., 6½" (2364) 40.00
Relish, 3 pt., 10" (2364) 45.00
Salt & Pepper, pr. 85.00
Sugar 35.00
Vase, 10" (2470 or 2614) 115.00
Vase, 5" (4121) 60.00
Vase, 6", Ground Bottom (2619½) 65.00
Vase, 7½", Ground Bottom (2619½) . . . 85.00
Vase, 9½", Ground Bottom (2619½) . . 135.00
Vase, Bud, Footed, 6" (6021) 35.00
Vase, Footed, 6" (4143) 65.00
Vase, Footed, 7½" (4143) 75.00

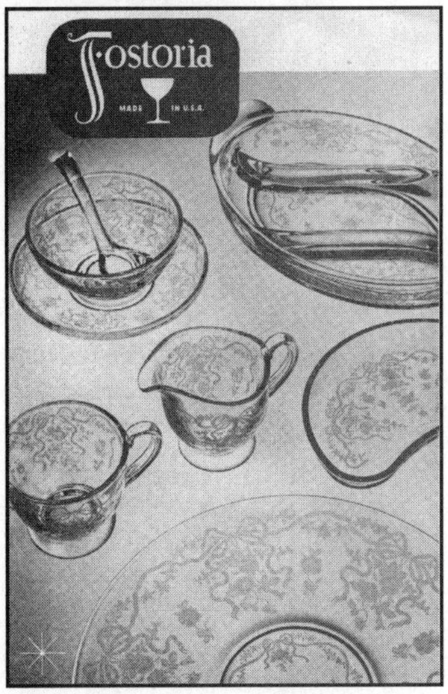

Original Ad: No. 341 Romance etching on pressed ware assortment

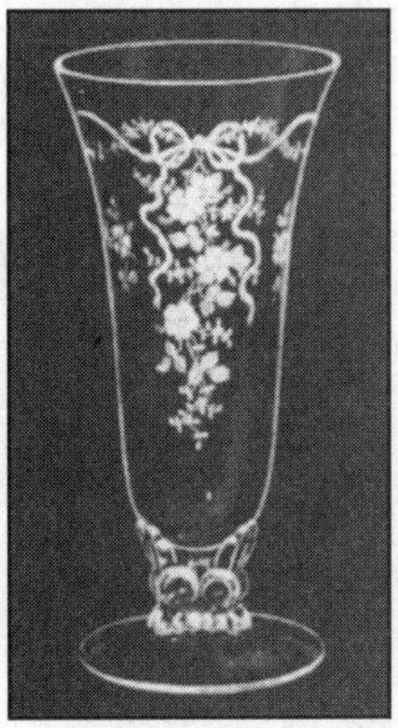

Original Catalog Illustration: No. 341 Romance etching on No. 2470 Vase

ROSE CLASSIC

ETCHED SATIN ROSES WITH 22K GOLD BOWS

Date: 1951

Manufacturer: Libbey Glass Co., Toledo, OH

Colors: Crystal

Cocktail $10.00
Cordial 35.00
Goblet 15.00
Sherbet 9.00
Wine 15.00

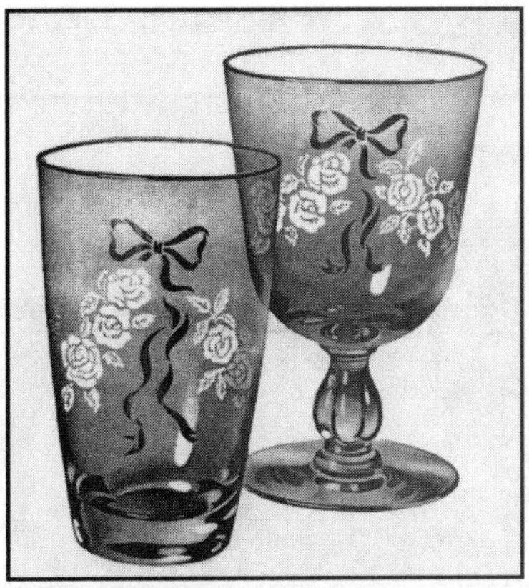

Original Ad: Rose Classic etching with Gold accents on iced tea and goblet

Chapter 16
BROCADE

Brocades are etchings covering the entire piece or almost the entire piece of glass, giving the appearance of brocade fabric with its woven patterns.

Original Catalog Illustration:
McKee Glass Co. Brocade etching assortment

U.S. Glass Co. Brocade dresser set

Catalog Illustration:
U.S. Glass Co. Brocade on "bright black glass"

BROCADE

ALL-OVER ETCHING

Date: 1930

Manufacturer: McKee Glass Co., Jeannette, PA

Colors: Crystal, Pink, Green

Notes: Probably more pieces were made than listed below. Add 50% for pieces in colors.

Bowl, Center, Flared Edge, 12"	$35.00
Bowl, Center, Roll Edge, 12"	35.00
Bowl, Nut, Handled (center handle)	25.00
Candlesticks, Low, pr.	45.00
Candy Box & Cover	35.00
Candy Jar & Cover	45.00
Cheese & Cracker, 2 pc.	35.00
Comport, Cone Shape	25.00
Comport, Flared Edge, 10"	35.00
Lunch Plate, Handled (center handle)	25.00
Mayonnaise Comport	25.00
Plate, Mayonnaise	15.00

BROCADE (FLOWER GARDEN & BUTTERFLY)

ETCHING

Date: 1920s

Manufacturer: U.S. Glass Co. (Tiffin), Tiffin, OH

Colors: Crystal, Amber, Blue, Canary, Green, Pink, Black

Notes: Many items were made, but not all appear to have been made in all colors. Black items especially are not known in other colors. Prices are for Crystal. For colors, add 25% to 50%.
Most collectors prefer Blue or Canary, but all items regardless of color are desirable.

Ashtray	$190.00
Candlesticks, 4", pr.	70.00
Candlesticks, 8", pr.	95.00
Candy Box & Cover, 6"	160.00
Candy Jar & Cover, 7½" (Conic)	100.00
Candy Box & Cover (Heart)	1000.00+
Cologne & Stopper, 7½ oz.	250.00
Comport, 4¾"	65.00
Comport, 10½"	55.00
Cream	90.00
Cup & Saucer	95.00
Mayonnaise, Footed	58.00
Plate, 7"	28.00
Plate, 8"	32.00
Plate, 10"	120.00

Powder Jar (3 styles, both
  footed and flat)............... 250.00
Sandwich Tray, Center-handled....... 150.00
Sugar......................... 90.00
Tray, Oval 70.00
Tray, Rectangular 80.00
Tumbler........................ 200.00
Vase, 6".......................... 85.00
Vase, 10½" 160.00

ITEMS IN BLACK:
Bowl & Base, Console, 9" (15320) $245.00
Bowl, Orange, Footed, 11" (8098) 245.00

GRAPE, No. 287

BROCADE PLATE ETCHING

Date: 1927

Manufacturer: Fostoria Glass Co.,
Moundsville, WV

Colors: Blue, Green Orchid

Bowl, 12" (2362)................. $85.00
Bowl, D, 7½" (2339).............. 75.00
Bowl, Deep, "E" (2297)........... 80.00
Bowl, Deep, 10½" (2397) 85.00
Bowl, Deep, 12" (2297)........... 85.00
Candle Blocks, 2", pr. (2372) 120.00

LACE

Date: 1922

Manufacturer: U.S. Glass Co. (Tiffin),
Tiffin, OH

Colors: Crystal with Amber, Blue or
Green Trim

OAK LEAF, No. 290

BROCADE PLATE ETCHING

Date: 1928

Manufacturer: Fostoria Glass Co.,
Moundsville, WV

Colors: Green, Rose, Crystal, Ebony

Notes: Not all pieces were made in all colors

STEMWARE:
No. 877
Goblet, 10 oz. $60.00
Oyster Cocktail, 4½ oz............. 40.00
Sherbet, High, 6 oz............... 45.00
Sherbet, Low, 6 oz................. 40.00
Tumbler, Footed, 5 oz. (juice)........ 30.00
Tumbler, Footed, 9 oz. (water) 40.00
Tumbler, Footed, 12 oz. (iced tea)..... 50.00

ACCESSORIES:
Bonbon (2375) $45.00
Bowl, 10" (2395)................. 85.00

Candles, "Summer Candles," pr....... 500.00
Candlesticks, 8", pr. (15319) 300.00
Candlesticks, 6" pr., (79) 500.00
Cologne, 1 oz. (5766) 360.00
Comport, High Foot, 7" (15320) 200.00
Comport, High Stem, 7" (15319)..... 125.00
Comport, Low Foot, 10" (15179).... 225.00
Comport, Tourraine, 10" (15179)..... 230.00
Vase, 2-handled, 10" (15319)........ 250.00
Vase, Dahlia, Cupped, 10½" (15151) 265.00
Vase, Dahlia, Cupped, 6" (15151) 140.00
Vase, Dahlia, Cupped, 8" (15151) 220.00
Vase, Wall (15320)............... 370.00

Candlesticks, 3", pr. (2362) 100.00
Candlesticks, 4", pr. (2324) 100.00
Centerpiece, 11" (bowl) (2329) 80.00
Centerpiece, Oval, 13" (2371) 90.00
Comport, 7" (2327)................ 120.00
Ice Bucket (2379) 110.00
Tray, Lunch, Center-handled (2287)...... 70.00
Vase, 8" (2292) 110.00
Vase, Optic, 5" (4103) 85.00
Vase, Optic, 6" (4100) 85.00

Notes: See also Tapestry and Wallpaper patterns
for similar Tiffin lines.

Iced Tea, 12 oz. (14185) $75.00
Jug & Cover, 2 qt. (14185) 550.00
Table (tumbler) (14185) 65.00
Vase, 10" (14185).............. 150.00

Bowl, 11" (cornucopia) (2398) 120.00
Bowl, 12" (2394)................. 85.00
Candlesticks, 2" (2394) 100.00
Candlesticks, 3", pr. (2395) 100.00
Cigarette Box & Cover, Large (2391) 85.00
Cigarette Box & Cover, Small (2391) 75.00
Comport, 8" (tall) (2400)........... 110.00
Confection & Cover (2380) 145.00
Jug (6000-7) 245.00
Mint, Footed, 4½" (2394) 45.00
Sugar Pail (2372) 110.00
Sweetmeat (2375) 45.00
Vase & Cover, Window, Small (2373).. 220.00
Vase, 8" (2387) 100.00
Vase, Fan, 8½" (2385) 120.00
Vase, Optic, 3" (4103) 50.00
Vase, Optic, 7" (2369) 90.00
Vase, Optic, 8" (4105) 90.00
Whipped Cream Pail (2376)........ 110.00

U.S. Glass Co. Brocade on
No. 79 candlestick with
glass candle

No. 287 Grape etching on bowl

Catalog Illustration: Lace etching
on tumblers

No. 290 Oak Leaf etching on
handled mint

Detail of Oak Leaf etching

BROCADE *(continued)*

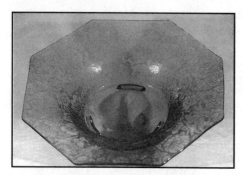

No. 289 Paradise etching

Detail of Paradise etching

Catalog Illustration: Tapestry etching on water set

Catalog Illustration: Wallpaper etching on water set

PARADISE, NO. 289

BROCADE PLATE ETCHING

Date: 1927

Manufacturer: Fostoria Glass Co., Moundsville, WV

Colors: Green, Orchid

Bowl, 12" (2342)	$85.00
Bowl, 12" (2362)	85.00
Bowl, Deep, "A," 12" (2297)	85.00
Bowl, Footed, "C" (2315)	85.00
Candle Blocks, 2", pr. (2372)	120.00
Candlesticks, 3", pr. (2362)	100.00
Candlesticks, 4", pr. (2324)	100.00
Candy Box & Cover, 3-part (2331)	130.00
Centerpiece, 11" (Bowl) (2329)	80.00
Centerpiece, Oval, 13" (2371)	90.00
Comport, 11" (2362)	140.00
Comport, 7" (2327)	120.00
Comport, 8" (2350)	120.00
Confection & Cover (2380)	130.00
Ice Bucket (2378)	110.00
Tray, Lunch, Center-handled, 12" (2342)	70.00
Vase, Optic, 5" (4103)	80.00
Vase, Optic, 7" (2369)	85.00
Vase, Optic, 8" (4100)	85.00

TAPESTRY

PLATE ETCHING

Date: 1922

Manufacturer: U.S. Glass Co. (Tiffin), Tiffin, OH

Colors: Crystal with Amber, Blue or Green Trim

Notes: See also Lace and Wallpaper for similar Tiffin lines.

Iced Tea, 12 oz. (14185)	$75.00
Jug & Cover, 2 qt. (14185)	550.00
Table (tumbler) (14185)	65.00
Vase, 10" (14185)	150.00

WALLPAPER

PLATE ETCHING

Date: 1922

Manufacturer: U.S. Glass Co. (Tiffin), Tiffin, OH

Colors: Crystal with Amber, Blue or Green Trim

Notes: See also Tapestry and Lace for similar Tiffin lines.

Iced Tea, 12 oz. (14185)	$75.00
Jug, & Cover, 2 qt. (14185)	550.00
Table (tumbler) (14185)	65.00
Vase, 10" (14185)	150.00

Chapter 17

CHRYSANTHEMUM

EMPRESS, NO. 447

PLATE ETCHING

Date: 1928

Manufacturer: A.H. Heisey & Co., Newark, OH

Colors: Crystal, Sahara, Moongleam, Flamingo, Marigold

Notes: Prices are for crystal items. For Sahara, Moongleam or Flamingo, add 100%. For Marigold, add 125%.

STEMWARE:

NO. 3380 OLD DOMINION

Bar, Footed, 1oz.	$30.00
Bar, Footed, 2oz.	28.00
Claret, 4 oz.	24.00
Cocktail, 3 oz.	18.00
Cordial, 1 oz.	60.00
Finger Bowl (4074)	15.00
Goblet, Short Stem or Tall Stem, 10 oz.	27.00
Grapefruit	27.00
Iced Tea, Footed, 12 oz.	20.00
Juice, Footed, 5 oz.	18.00
Oyster Cocktail, 4 oz.	15.00
Parfait, 5 oz.	24.00
Saucer Champagne, Short Stem or Tall Stem, 6 oz.	24.00
Sherbet, 6 oz.	15.00
Tumbler, Footed, 10 oz.	15.00
Water, Footed, 8 oz.	18.00
Wine, 2½ oz.	25.00

Original Ad: No. 447 Empress etching on
No. 3380 Old Dominion stemware

ACCESSORIES:

Bonbon, 2-handled, 6" (1229)	$22.00
Bouillon Cup, Footed (1184)	35.00
Candy Box & Cover, Deep, 6" (1184)	45.00
Celery Tray, 13" (1184)	28.00
Celery Tray, 9" (1184)	22.00
Cheese, 2-handled, 6" (1229)	22.00
Comport, Footed, 7" (3368)	75.00
Cream (1023)	25.00
Cream Soup & Plate (1509)	35.00
Cream Soup (1184)	25.00
Cup & Saucer (1184)	25.00
Cup & Saucer, After Dinner (1184)	45.00
Finger Bowl (4074)	10.00
Floral Bowl (135)	60.00
Floral Bowl, 14" (1184)	35.00
Goblet, 11 oz. (3386)	75.00
Grapefruit or Cereal, 6½" (1184)	18.00
Hors d'oeuvre, 2-handled, 13" (1229)	28.00
Ice Tub (500)	65.00
Jug, 73 oz. (4164)	135.00
Mayonnaise, Footed, 2-handled, 5½" (1229)	35.00
Mint & Cover, 7" (1253)	75.00
Mint, 2-handled, 6" (1229)	22.00
Oil, 4 oz. (1184)	70.00
Oval Baker, 9" (1184)	55.00
Plate, 10½" (1184)	45.00
Plate, 14" (1184)	35.00
Plate, 6" (3350)	10.00
Plate, 6" or 6½" (1184)	10.00
Plate, 7" or 8" (4182)	12.00
Plate, 8" or 9" (1184)	15.00
Plate, Oyster Cocktail, 8" (1184)	20.00
Plate, Sandwich, Center-handled, 10½" (1231)	30.00
Plate, Soup, 8" (1184)	15.00
Platter, 12" (1184)	75.00
Platter, 15" (1184)	45.00
Relish, 3-compartment, 13" (1184)	25.00
Salt & Pepper, pr. (42)	55.00
Sandwich Tray, 2-handled, 12" (1229)	28.00
Soda, 5 oz. (2401)	12.00
Soda, 8 oz., 10 oz. or 12 oz. (2351)	12.00
Soda, 14 oz. or 16 oz. (2351)	18.00
Sugar & Cover (1023)	30.00
Tumbler, 10 oz. (2930)	15.00
Vase, Bud (4205)	45.00

Chapter 18
DIAMONDS & PUNTIES

Original Catalog Illustration: No. 821 King Edward
rock crystal engraving

KING EDWARD, NO. 821

ROCK CRYSTAL ENGRAVING

Date: 1940s

Manufacturer: Cambridge Glass Co., Cambridge, OH

Colors: Crystal

Notes: The prefix P indicates pieces in Pristine pattern.

STEMWARE
No. 3700 DUNKIRK

Claret, 4½ oz.	$20.00
Cocktail, 3 oz.	18.00
Cordial, 1 oz.	55.00
Goblet, 9 oz.	20.00
Iced Tea, Footed, 12 oz.	17.00
Oyster Cocktail, 4½ oz.	11.00
Sherbet, Low, 6 oz.	11.00
Sherbet, Tall, 6 oz.	14.00
Tumbler, Footed, 5 oz. (juice)	14.00
Tumbler, Footed, 10 oz. (water)	15.00
Wine, 2½ oz.	20.00

ACCESSORIES

Bowl, 10" (P427)	$45.00
Bowl, Flared, 12" (P430)	45.00
Candlesticks, 2-light, 6", pr. (647)	65.00
Candlesticks, 3½", pr. (628)	45.00
Candy Box & Cover, 3 pt., 7" (103)	45.00
Celery & Relish, 5 pt., 10" (P212)	32.00
Celery & Relish, 5 pt., 12" (P418)	35.00
Celery, 11" (P247)	24.00
Cocktail Shaker, 32 oz. (P101)	90.00
Comport, Footed, 6" (533)	32.00
Comport, Tall, Footed, 6" (532)	45.00
Cream & Sugar, pr. (138 or P254)	48.00
Decanter, Footed, 28 oz. (1321)	100.00
Hurricane Lamp (1613)	110.00
Jug, 20 oz. (3900/117)	65.00
Jug, 76 oz. (3900/115)	95.00
Jug, Martini, 32 oz. (3900/114)	80.00
Mayonnaise (533)	32.00
Oil & Stopper, 6 oz. (P293)	58.00
Old Fashioned Cocktail, 7 oz. (321)	14.00
Plate, 13½" (1397)	50.00
Plate, Crescent Salad, 8" (P454)	20.00
Plate, Mayonnaise	12.00
Plate, Salad, 7½" or 8" (555 or 556)	15.00
Salad Dressing, 2 pt. (1491)	35.00
Tumbler, 12 oz. (497)	15.00
Whiskey, 1½ oz. (321)	25.00

Original Company Photo: No. 837 cutting

NO. 837

CUTTING

Date: 1968

Manufacturer: Imperial Glass Corp., Bellaire, OH

Colors: Crystal

Notes: Most pieces illustrated are on Heisey blanks. This cutting was done after Imperial bought out Heisey. The stemware was originally Heisey's Oxford line. Other Heisey patterns shown include the Revere mayonnaise and the Cabochon cream and sugar. The plates may also be from original Heisey molds.

STEMWARE:

Goblet	$24.00
Iced Tea	22.00
Saucer Champagne/Tall Sherbet	18.00
Wine/Claret	22.00

ACCESSORIES:

Bowl, Large	$25.00
Candy Jar & Cover	55.00
Cream & Sugar, pr.	36.00
Mayonnaise	28.00
Plate, Salad	15.00
Plate, Torte	32.00

(continued) DIAMONDS & PUNTIES

SHEFFIELD, NO. 768

ROCK CRYSTAL CUTTING

Date: 1940s

Manufacturer: Duncan & Miller Glass Co., Washington, PA

Colors: Crystal

Notes: While we have found no listing for pressed ware, it was likely made, especially plates.

STEMWARE:

NO. 5330 DOVER

Claret, 5 oz., 5¼" tall	$30.00
Cocktail, Liquor, 3½ oz., 4"	30.00
Cordial, 1 oz., 3½" tall	70.00
Finger Bowl, 4¼"	15.00
Goblet, 10 oz., 5¾" tall	45.00
Ice Cream (sherbet), 5 oz., 3½" tall	17.00
Iced Tea, Footed, 13 oz., 6½" tall	38.00
Juice, Orange, Footed, 5 oz., 4½" tall	24.00
Oyster Cocktail, 4½ oz., 3½" tall	20.00
Saucer Champagne or Tall Sherbet, 6 oz., 4½" tall	40.00
Tumbler, Footed, 10 oz., 5⅞" tall	35.00
Wine, 3 oz., 4¾" tall	45.00

Original Catalog Illustration: No. 768 Sheffield cutting on No. 5330 Dover goblet and champagne

WELLINGTON, NO. 629

ROCK CRYSTAL CUTTING

Date: 1930s

Manufacturer: Duncan & Miller Glass Co., Washington, PA

Colors: Crystal

STEMWARE:

NO. 33 KENT

Claret, 4½ oz., 6¾" high	$30.00
Cocktail, 4 oz., 6" high	30.00
Cordial, 1 oz., 3¾" high	70.00
Finger Bowl, 4½"	15.00
Goblet, 10 oz., 7¾" high	45.00
Iced Tea, Footed, 12 oz., 7" high	38.00
Orange Juice, Footed, 6 oz., 5¼" tall	24.00
Oyster Cocktail, 4 oz., 4" high	20.00
Saucer Champagne, 6 oz., 6¾" high	40.00
Wine, 3 oz., 6" high	45.00

ACCESSORIES:

Bowl, Deep Salad, 9" (33)	$55.00
Bowl, Flared, 12" (36)	68.00
Bowl, Low Foot, 13" (30)	68.00
Candlestick, Low, 3" pr. (115)	75.00
Candlesticks, 2-light, pr. (30)	115.00

Candy Box & Cover, 3-compartment, 6½" (106)	85.00
Celery & Relish, Oblong, 2-handled, 12" (30)	45.00
Comport, 6" (5317)	65.00
Comport, Tall, 7½" (8)	65.00
Cream (38)	40.00
Finger Bowl (30)	15.00
Iced Cocktail Set, 2 piece or 3 piece (30)	85.00
Mayonnaise Set (8)	82.00
Nappy, 2-handled, 6" (30)	35.00
Plate, 2-handled, 6" (30)	35.00
Plate, Bread & Butter, 6" (30½)	22.00
Plate, Dessert, 7½" (30½)	25.00
Plate, Salad, 8½" (30½)	25.00
Plate, Sandwich, 2-handled, 11" (30)	65.00
Plate, Torte, 13" (33)	80.00
Relish, 2-handled, 2-compartment, 6" (30)	35.00
Salad Dressing Set, 2-compartment, 6", 2 piece (30)	55.00
Sugar (38)	40.00
Vase, 10" (506)	90.00
Vase, Flip, Flared 8" (30)	80.00

Original Catalog Illustration: No. 629 Wellington cutting on No. 33 Kent goblet

Chapter 19
DIAMONDS OR SQUARES

Diamonds or square-shaped motifs are particularly adaptable to cuttings. These types of cuttings are often described as Waterford-type, after the prestigious Irish company.

Original Catalog Illustration: Athena cutting on No. D1 Mandarin goblet

ATHENA

ROCK CRYSTAL CUTTING

Date: 1950s

Manufacturer: Duncan & Miller Glass Co., Washington, PA

Colors: Crystal

STEMWARE:

NO. D1 MANDARIN
Cocktail, Liquor, 3½ oz.	$30.00
Goblet, 11 oz.	45.00
Iced Tea, Footed, 14 oz.	38.00
Orange Juice, Footed, 5 oz.	24.00
Oyster Cocktail, Footed, 4½ oz.	20.00
Saucer Champagne or Tall Sherbet, 5 oz.	40.00
Wine or Claret, 4 oz.	45.00

ACCESSORIES:
Plate, 6" (30½)	$15.00
Plate, 7½" (30½)	17.00
Plate, 8½" (30½)	17.00

BARCELONA, NO. 941

ROCK CRYSTAL CUTTING

Date: 1940

Manufacturer: A. H. Heisey & Co., Newark, OH

Colors: Crystal

Notes: "BARCELONA, brilliantly reflecting the gay grandeur of old Spain, offers a romantic blending of yesterday and today. A complete line of BARCELONA hand-blown rock crystal stemware and its complement of table accessories is ready to add glorious beauty to your table." —Original Ad. In 1956, several pieces of Barcelona were made for Tiffany's: a 142 candlestick, several pieces of 1183 Revere, and 4 items in Cabochon. No. 1509 refers to Queen Ann pattern; No. 1519, Waverly; and No. 1951, Cabochon.

STEMWARE:

NO. 3350 WABASH
Claret, 4 oz.	$45.00
Cocktail, 3 oz.	30.00
Cordial, 1 oz.	75.00
Finger Bowl	20.00
Goblet, 10 oz.	45.00
Grapefruit, 6"	35.00
Mayonnaise	35.00
Oyster Cocktail, 4 oz.	22.00
Parfait, 5 oz.	28.00
Saucer Champagne, 6 oz.	35.00
Sherbet, 6 oz.	22.00
Soda, Footed, 5 oz.	28.00
Soda, Footed, 8 oz.	30.00
Soda, Footed & Handled, 12 oz.	45.00
Soda, Footed, 12 oz.	32.00
Tumbler, Footed, 10 oz.	30.00
Wine, 2½ oz.	45.00

NO. 3404 SPANISH
Claret, 4 oz.	$55.00
Cocktail, 3½ oz.	35.00
Comport, 6"	48.00
Cordial, 1 oz.	90.00
Finger Bowl	20.00
Goblet, 10 oz.	55.00
Oyster Cocktail, 3 oz.	30.00
Saucer Champagne, 5½ oz.	38.00
Sherbet, 5½ oz.	30.00
Soda, Footed, 5 oz.	30.00
Soda, Footed, 8 oz. or 10 oz.	32.00
Soda, Footed, 12 oz.	35.00
Wine, 2½ oz.	55.00

NO. 3408 JAMESTOWN
Bell, Dinner	$185.00
Claret, 4½ oz.	45.00
Cocktail, 3 oz.	30.00
Cordial, 1 oz.	75.00
Finger Bowl	20.00
Goblet, 9 oz.	45.00
Iced Tea, Footed, 12 oz. (3408½)	32.00
Juice, Footed, 5 oz. (3408½)	25.00
Oyster Cocktail, 4 oz.	22.00
Parfait, 5 oz.	28.00
Saucer Champagne, 6 oz.	35.00

Original Brochure: No. 941 Barcelona cutting on No. 3408 Jamestown goblet

(continued) DIAMONDS OR SQUARES

Sherbet, 6 oz.. 22.00
Sherry, 1½ oz.. . . . . 75.00
Soda, 5 oz.. . . . . 25.00
Soda, 13 oz.. . . . . 32.00
Tumbler, 9 oz.. . . . . 28.00
Wine, 2 oz.. . . . . 45.00

NO. 4091 KIMBERLY
Bell, Dinner.. . . . . $185.00
Claret, 4½ oz.. . . . . 45.00
Cocktail, 3 oz.. . . . . 30.00
Cordial, 1 oz.. 75.00
Finger Bowl.. 20.00
Goblet, 10 oz.. . . . . 45.00
Goblet, Low Foot, 10 oz.. . . . . 40.00
Oyster Cocktail, 4½ oz.. . . . . 22.00
Saucer Champagne, 5½ oz.. . . . . 35.00
Sherbet, 5½ oz.. . . . . 22.00
Sherry, 1½ oz.. . . . . 75.00
Soda, Footed, 5 oz.. . . . . 28.00
Soda, Footed, 12 oz.. . . . . 32.00
Wine, 2 oz.. . . . . 45.00
Wine, Rhine, 6 oz.. . . . . 58.00

NO. 5024 OXFORD
Claret, 4 oz.. . . . . $45.00
Cocktail, 4 oz.. . . . . 30.00
Cordial, 1 oz.. . . . . 75.00
Finger Bowl.. 20.00
Goblet, 11 oz.. . . . . 45.00
Oyster Cocktail, 4 oz.. . . . . 22.00
Saucer Champagne, 6½ oz.. . . . . 35.00
Soda, Footed, 5 oz.. . . . . 28.00
Soda, Footed, 12 oz.. . . . . 32.00
Wine, 3 oz.. . . . . 45.00

ACCESSORIES:
Ashtray, Individual, 2¾" (1489). $12.00
Ashtray, Square, 4½" (1489). 16.00
Bar, 1½ oz. or 2 oz. (2351). 25.00
Bar, 3 oz. (2351). 18.00
Bottle, French Dressing, 8 oz. (5031). . . 95.00
Bottle, Rye (1489). 95.00
Bowl, 14" (1489). 85.00
Bowl, Combination Dressing,
　6½" (1509). 40.00
Bowl, Floral, 8½" (1509). 55.00
Bowl, Floral, 11" (1519). 60.00
Bowl, Floral, 13" (1951). 45.00
Bowl, Floral, Crimped, 13" (1519). . . . 65.00
Bowl, Floral, Dolphin Footed,
　11" (1509). 70.00
Bowl, Gardenia, 13" (485). 40.00
Bowl, Lily (1575). 45.00
Bowl, Salad, 9" or 11" (4056). 35.00
Candelabra, 1-light, 7½", pr. (1509). . . 150.00
Candelabra, 2-light, pr. (4044). 150.00
Candleblocks, 4", pr. (1489). 85.00
Candlesticks, 1-light, pr. (112). 55.00
Candlesticks, 2-light, pr. (134). 68.00
Candlesticks, 2-light, pr. (1519). 60.00
Candlesticks, 3-light, pr. (142). 78.00
Celery (1511). 25.00
Cigarette Box & Cover, 6" (1489). . . . 60.00
Cocktail Icer & Liner (3304). 75.00

Cocktail Shaker, 1 qt. (4036 or 4225). . 130.00
Comport, 6" (1951). 35.00
Comport, Oval, 7" (1509). 60.00
Cream & Sugar, pr. (1184). 70.00
Cream & Sugar, pr.
　(1511, 1540 or 1951). 50.00
Cream & Sugar, Dolphin-Footed,
　pr. (1509). 60.00
Cream, Individual (1519). 32.00
Custard (punch cup) (4058). 20.00
Decanter, 1 pt. (4036 or 4036½). 110.00
Decanter, 1 qt. (4036½). 130.00
Highball, 8 oz. (2351). 20.00
Honey, Footed, 7" (1519). 25.00
Ice Bucket, Dolphin-footed (1509). . . . 125.00
Jelly, 2-handled, Footed, 6" (1509). . . . 30.00
Jug, ½ gal. (6060). 125.00
Jug, 32 oz. (4161). 95.00
Jug, Ice, ½ gal. (3484 or 4164). 135.00
Marmalade & Cover (4121). 45.00
Mayonnaise (1496 or 1951). 32.00
Mayonnaise, Dolphin-footed,
　5½" (1509). 45.00
Mayonnaise, Twin (1495). 38.00
Mint, 5¾" (1951). 25.00
Mint, Dolphin-footed, 6" (1509). 35.00
Nappy, 4" or 5" (398). 12.00
Nappy, 8" (398). 25.00
Oil & Stopper (4043). 145.00
Oil & Stopper, 4 oz. (1509). 100.00
Old Fashioned, 8 oz. (2351). 18.00
Plate, 10½" (1184). 110.00
Plate, 10½" (1519). 125.00
Plate, 6" or 6½" (1184). 12.00
Plate, 7" or 8" (1184). 15.00
Plate, 8" (1951). 18.00
Plate, Buffet, 16" (1184). 100.00
Plate, Mayonnaise (1495). 18.00
Plate, Party or Torte, 14". 70.00
Plate, Sandwich, 14" (485). 45.00
Plate, Sandwich, Round,
　Center Handle, 12". 45.00
Plate, Torte, 14" (1519). 90.00
Plate, Torte, 14" (485). 45.00
Plate, Torte, 18" (1184). 120.00
Relish, 3-compartment,
　9½" or 11" (1509). 38.00
Relish, 3-compartment, 11" (1519). . . . 38.00
Relish, Five O'Clock, 11" (1509). 45.00
Relish, Oblong, 3-compartment,
　9" (1951). 38.00
Relish, Triplex, 7" (1509). 35.00
Salt & Pepper, Footed, pr. (1519). . . . 100.00
Salt & Pepper, pr. (57). 85.00
Sherry, Goose Stem (5058). 250.00
Soda, 5 oz. (2351). 18.00
Soda, 8 oz. or 10 oz. (2351). 20.00
Soda or Iced Tea, 12 oz. (2351). 22.00
Sugar, Individual (1519). 32.00
Tray, Sandwich, Center Handle (1519). . 45.00
Tray, Social Hour, 15" (1509 or 1519). . 100.00
Tray, Variety, 12" (relish) (500). 65.00
Tumbler, 10 oz. (2930). 25.00
Vase, Fan, No. 2 (1540). 65.00

Original Brochure:
No. 941 Barcelona cutting
on various pieces

DIAMONDS OR SQUARES *(continued)*

Original Catalog Illustration:
No. 702 Berkeley cutting on
No. 5322 Erin goblet

BERKELEY, NO. 702

ROCK CRYSTAL CUTTING

Date: 1940s

Manufacturer: Duncan & Miller Glass Co., Washington, PA

Colors: Crystal

STEMWARE:

NO. 5322 ERIN

Claret, 4½ oz., 5¼" tall	$30.00
Cocktail, 3½ oz., 4¼" tall	30.00
Finger Bowl, 4¼"	15.00
Goblet, 9 oz., 6" tall.	45.00
Ice Cream, Footed, 6 oz., 3¼" tall (sherbet)	17.00
Iced Tea, Footed, 13 oz., 6" tall	38.00
Orange Juice, Footed, 5 oz., 4½" tall . . .	24.00
Oyster Cocktail, 4½ oz., 3½" tall.	20.00
Saucer Champagne or Tall Sherbet, 6 oz., 4½" tall.	40.00
Wine, 3 oz., 4¾" tall	45.00

ACCESSORIES:

Bowl, Deep Salad, 9" (33)	$55.00
Bowl, Flared, 12" (36)	68.00
Bowl, Low Foot, 13" (30).	68.00
Candlestick, Low, 3" pr. (115)	75.00

Candlesticks, 2-light, pr. (30)	115.00
Candy Box & Cover, 3-compartment, 6½" (106)	85.00
Celery & Relish, Oblong, 2-handled, 12" (30)	45.00
Comport, 6" (5317).	65.00
Comport, Tall, 7½" (8)	65.00
Cream (38)	40.00
Finger Bowl (30)	15.00
Iced Cocktail Set, 2 piece or 3-piece (30)	85.00
Mayonnaise Set (8)	82.00
Nappy, 2-handled, 6" (30)	35.00
Plate, 2-handled, 6" (30)	35.00
Plate, Bread & Butter, 6" (30½)	22.00
Plate, Dessert, 7½" (30½)	25.00
Plate, Salad, 8½" (30½)	25.00
Plate, Sandwich, 2-handled, 11" (30) . . .	65.00
Plate, Torte, 13" (33)	80.00
Relish, 2-handled, 2-compartment, 6" (30)	35.00
Salad Dressing Set, 2-compartment 6", 2-piece (30)	55.00
Sugar (38)	40.00
Vase, 10" (506)	90.00
Vase, Flip, Flared 8" (30)	80.00

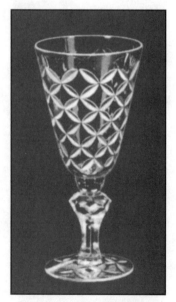

Original Catalog Illustration:
Bristol Diamond cutting on
No. 32 Windsor goblet

BRISTOL DIAMOND, NO. 803

ROCK CRYSTAL CUTTING

Date: 1930s

Manufacturer: Duncan & Miller Glass Co., Washington, PA

Colors: Crystal

STEMWARE:

NO. 32 WINDSOR

Claret, 4 oz., 5¾" tall.	$30.00
Cocktail, Liquor, 3 oz., 4¾" tall	30.00
Cordial, 1 oz., 3¾" tall	70.00
Finger Bowl, 4¼"	15.00
Goblet, 9 oz., 7" tall.	45.00
Iced Tea, Footed, 12 oz., 6½" tall	38.00
Orange Juice, Footed, 5 oz., 4¾" tall . . .	24.00
Oyster Cocktail, 4 oz., 4" tall	20.00
Saucer Champagne, 5 oz., 4½" tall. . . .	40.00
Wine, 3 oz., 5½" tall	45.00

ACCESSORIES:

Bowl, Deep Salad, 9" (33)	$55.00
Bowl, Flared, 12" (36)	68.00
Bowl, Low Foot, 13" (30).	68.00
Candlestick, Low, 3" pr. (115)	75.00
Candlesticks, 2-light, pr. (30)	115.00

Candy Box & Cover, 3-compartment, 6½" (106)	85.00
Celery & Relish, Oblong, 2-handled, 12" (30).	45.00
Comport, 6" (5317).	65.00
Comport, Tall, 7½" (8)	65.00
Cream (38)	40.00
Finger Bowl (30)	15.00
Iced Cocktail Set, 2-piece or 3-piece (30)	85.00
Mayonnaise Set (8)	82.00
Nappy, 2-handled, 6" (30)	35.00
Plate, 2-handled, 6" (30)	35.00
Plate, Bread & Butter, 6" (30½)	22.00
Plate, Dessert, 7½" (30½)	25.00
Plate, Salad, 8½" (30½).	25.00
Plate, Sandwich, 2-handled, 11" (30) . . .	65.00
Plate, Torte, 13" (33)	80.00
Relish, 2-handled, 2 compartment, 6" (30).	35.00
Salad Dressing Set, 2-compartment, 6", 2-piece (30).	55.00
Sugar (38)	40.00
Vase, 10" (506)	90.00
Vase, Flip, Flared 8" (30)	80.00

CANDLEWICK

ETCHING

Date: 1936

Manufacturer: Seneca Glass Co., Morgantown, WV

Colors: Crystal. Crystal bowl with colored bases in: Ruby, Green, Amber, Cobalt

Notes: "This captivating new stemware line is especially designed in style and colors to match harmoniously Candlewick dinner pattern of the Pope-Gosser China Company. An exact reproduction of the fluffy candlewick dot is etched by a special process into the clear crystal of the bowl."—Original Ad. Other pieces were certainly made but are undocumented at this time. For items in color add 50 to 75%.

STEMWARE:
No. 3600
Cocktail	$17.00
Goblet	20.00
Iced Tea	18.00
Sherbet	14.00

ACCESSORIES:
Plate, Salad	$17.00

Original Ad: Candlewick etching

CORONATION, NO. 1254

CUTTING

Date: 1953

Manufacturer: Seneca Glass Co., Morgantown, WV

Colors: Crystal

Notes: Coronation, a regal elegance achieved in fine handcut crystal. Undoubtedly other pieces were made but are now undocumented.

STEMWARE:
No. 352 TIMELESS
Goblet	$25.00

Original Ad: No. 1254 Coronation cutting on No. 352 Timeless goblet

DIAMOND CUT

Date: 1952

Manufacturer: Libbey Glass Co., Toledo, OH

Colors: Crystal

Beverage, 10 oz.	$7.00
Cocktail	10.00
Cordial	35.00
Goblet	15.00
Sherbet	9.00
Wine	15.00

Original Ad: Diamond Cut on goblet and 10 oz. beverage

DIAMONDS OR SQUARES *(continued)*

Original Catalog Illustration:
No. 684 Kimberly cutting on
No. 5320 Fontaine goblet

KIMBERLY, NO. 684

ROCK CRYSTAL CUTTING

Date: 1940s

Manufacturer: Duncan & Miller Glass Co.,
Washington, PA

Colors: Crystal

STEMWARE:

NO. 5320 FONTAINE
Goblet $45.00

ACCESSORIES:
Bowl, Deep Salad, 9" (33) $55.00
Bowl, Flared, 12" (36) 68.00
Bowl, Low Foot, 13" (30) 68.00
Candlesticks, Low, 3" pr. (115) 75.00
Candlesticks, 2-light, pr. (30) 115.00
Candy Box & Cover, 3-compartment,
   6½" (106) 85.00
Celery & Relish, Oblong, 2-handled,
   12" (30) 45.00

Comport, 6" (5317) 65.00
Comport, Tall, 7½" (8) 65.00
Cream (38) 40.00
Finger Bowl (30) 15.00
Iced Cocktail Set, 2- or 3-piece (30) 85.00
Mayonnaise Set (8) 82.00
Nappy, 2-handled, 6" (30) 35.00
Plate, 2-handled, 6" (30) 35.00
Plate, Bread & Butter, 6" (30½) 22.00
Plate, Dessert, 7½" (30½) 25.00
Plate, Salad, 8½" (30½) 25.00
Plate, Sandwich, 2-handled, 11" (30) . . . 65.00
Plate, Torte, 13" (33) 80.00
Relish, 2-handled, 2-compartment,
   6" (30) 35.00
Salad Dressing Set, -compartment,
   6", 2-piece (30) 55.00
Sugar (38) 40.00
Vase, 10" (506) 90.00
Vase, Flip, Flared 8" (30) 80.00

Original Catalog Illustration:
No. 690 Kohinoor cutting on
No. 5322 Erin goblet

KOHINOOR, NO. 690

ROCK CRYSTAL CUTTING

Date: 1940s

Manufacturer: Duncan & Miller Glass Co.,
Washington, PA

Colors: Crystal

STEMWARE:

NO. 5322 ERIN
Claret, 4½ oz., 5¼" tall $30.00
Cocktail, 3½ oz., 4¼" tall 30.00
Finger Bowl, 4¼" 15.00
Goblet, 9 oz., 6" tall 45.00
Ice Cream, Footed, 6 oz.,
   3¼" tall (sherbet) 17.00
Iced Tea, Footed, 13 oz., 6" tall 38.00
Orange Juice, Footed, 5 oz., 4½" tall . . . 24.00
Oyster Cocktail, 4½ oz., 3½" tall 20.00
Saucer Champagne or Tall Sherbet,
   6 oz., 4½" tall 40.00
Wine, 3 oz., 4¾" tall 45.00

ACCESSORIES:
Bowl, Deep Salad, 9" (33) $55.00
Bowl, Flared, 12" (36) 68.00
Bowl, Low Foot, 13" (30) 68.00
Candlesticks, Low, 3", pr. (115) 75.00

Candlesticks, 2-light, pr. (30) 115.00
Candy Box & Cover, 3-compartment,
   6½" (106) 85.00
Celery & Relish, Oblong, 2-handled,
   12" (30) 45.00
Comport, 6" (5317) 65.00
Comport, Tall, 7½" (8) 65.00
Cream (38) 40.00
Finger Bowl (30) 15.00
Iced Cocktail Set, 2 piece or
   3 piece (30) 85.00
Mayonnaise Set (8) 82.00
Nappy, 2-handled, 6" (30) 35.00
Plate, 2-handled, 6" (30) 35.00
Plate, Bread & Butter, 6" (30½) 22.00
Plate, Dessert, 7½" (30½) 25.00
Plate, Salad, 8½" (30½) 25.00
Plate, Sandwich, 2-handled, 11" (30) . . . 65.00
Plate, Torte, 13" (33) 80.00
Relish, 2-handled, 2-compartment,
   6" (30) 35.00
Salad Dressing Set, 2-compartment,
   6", 2-piece (30) 55.00
Sugar (38) 40.00
Vase, 10" (506) 90.00
Vase, Flip, Flared 8" (30) 80.00

(continued) DIAMONDS OR SQUARES

LOCKSLEY, NO. 635

ROCK CRYSTAL CUTTING

Date: 1930s

Manufacturer: Duncan & Miller Glass Co., Washington, PA

Colors: Crystal

STEMWARE:

NO. 504 GRANADA

Claret, 5 oz.	$30.00
Cocktail, Liquor, 3½ oz.	30.00
Cordial, 1 oz.	70.00
Goblet, 10 oz.	45.00
Ice Cream, footed, 5 oz.	17.00
Iced Tea, Footed, 12 oz.	38.00
Orange Juice, Footed., 5 oz.	24.00
Oyster Cocktail, 4½ oz.	20.00
Saucer Champagne, 5 oz.	40.00
Sherry, 2 oz.	55.00
Tumbler, footed, 10 oz.	35.00
Whiskey, footed., 3 oz.	40.00
Wine, 3½ oz.	45.00

ACCESSORIES:

Bowl, Deep Salad, 9" (33)	$55.00
Bowl, Flared, 12" (36)	68.00
Bowl, Low Foot, 13" (30)	68.00
Candlesticks, Low, 3" pr. (115)	75.00
Candlesticks, 2-light, pr. (30)	115.00
Candy Box & Cover, 3-compartment, 6½" (106)	85.00
Celery & Relish, Oblong, 2-handled, 12" (30)	45.00
Comport, 6" (5317)	65.00
Comport, Tall, 7½" (8)	65.00
Cream & Sugar, pr. (38)	80.00
Finger Bowl (30)	15.00
Iced Cocktail Set, 2-piece or 3-piece (30)	85.00
Mayonnaise Set (8)	82.00
Nappy, 2-handled, 6" (30)	35.00
Plate, 2-handled, 6" (30)	35.00
Plate, Bread & Butter, 6" (30½)	22.00
Plate, Dessert, 7½" (30½)	25.00
Plate, Salad, 8½" (30½)	25.00
Plate, Sandwich, 2-handled, 11" (30)	65.00
Plate, Torte, 13" (33)	80.00
Relish, 2-handled, 2-compartment, 6" (30)	35.00
Salad Dressing Set, 2-compartment, 6", 2-piece (30)	55.00
Vase, 10" (506)	90.00
Vase, Flip, Flared 8" (30)	80.00

Original Catalog Illustration: No. 635 Locksley cutting on No. 504 Granada goblet

MANHATTAN, NO. 725

ROCK CRYSTAL CUTTING

Date: 1933

Manufacturer: Fostoria Glass Co., Moundsville, WV

Colors: Crystal

Notes: Probably plates and accessory pieces were made to match.

STEMWARE:

NO. 4024 VICTORIAN

Claret-Wine, 3½ oz., 4½" tall	$32.00
Cocktail, 4 oz., 3⅝" tall	26.00
Cordial, 1 oz., 3⅛" tall	60.00
Goblet, 10 oz., 5⅝" tall	32.00
Goblet, 11 oz., 6⅞" tall	32.00
Iced Tea, Footed, 12 oz., 5½" tall	32.00
Juice, Footed, 5 oz., 4¼" tall	28.00
Oyster Cocktail, 4 oz., 3⅜" tall	20.00
Rhine Wine, 3½ oz., 5⅞" tall	32.00
Saucer Champagne, 6½ oz., 4½" tall	30.00
Sherbet, 5½ oz., 3⅞" tall	24.00
Sherry, 2 oz., 3⅞" tall	32.00
Tumbler, Footed, 8 oz., 4¾" tall	28.00
Whiskey, Footed, 1½ oz., 2½" tall	27.00

Original Catalog Illustration: No. 725 Manhattan cutting on No. 4024 Victorian goblet

DIAMONDS OR SQUARES *(continued)*

Original Catalog Illustration:
No. 1003 Manor cutting on
No. 3700 goblet

Original Catalog Illustration:
No. 964 Maryland cutting on
No. 5024 Oxford goblet

MANOR, NO. 1003

ROCK CRYSTAL CUTTING

Date: 1940s

Manufacturer: Cambridge Glass Co.,
Cambridge, OH

Colors: Crystal

STEMWARE:

NO. 3700
Claret, 4½ oz.	$18.00
Cocktail, 3 oz.	15.00
Cordial, 1 oz.	55.00
Goblet, 9 oz.	18.00
Ice Tea, Footed, 12 oz.	15.00
Oyster Cocktail, 4½ oz.	10.00
Sherbet, Low, 6 oz.	10.00
Sherbet, Tall, 6 oz.	15.00
Tumbler, Footed, 10 oz. (water)	12.00
Tumbler, Footed, 5 oz. (juice)	12.00
Wine, 2½ oz.	18.00

ACCESSORIES:
Bonbon, 2-handled, Footed (3900/130)	$20.00
Bowl, 4-footed, Flared, 12" (3900/62)	38.00
Candlesticks, 2-light, 6", pr. (3900/72)	65.00
Candy Box & Cover (3900/165)	42.00
Celery & Relish, 3-part, 8" (3900/125)	35.00
Celery & Relish, 5-part, 12" (3900/120)	40.00
Cocktail Icer, 2-piece (968)	60.00
Comport, 5½" (3900/136)	35.00
Cream & Sugar, pr. (3900/41)	40.00
Hurricane Lamp (1613)	145.00
Mayonnaise (3900/129)	32.00
Mayonnaise, 2-part (3900/111)	32.00
Plate, Bon Bon, 2-handled, Footed, 8" (3900/131)	18.00
Plate, Cake, 2-handled, 13½" (3900/35)	38.00
Plate, Mayonnaise	12.00
Plate, Rolled Edge, 14" (3900/166)	42.00
Plate, Salad, 8" (3900/22)	12.00
Vase, Footed, 11" (278)	55.00

MARYLAND, NO. 964

ROCK CRYSTAL CUTTING

Date: 1941

Manufacturer: A.H. Heisey & Co.,
Newark, OH

Colors: Crystal

Notes: "As distinguished and beautiful as its name, MARYLAND Hand-Blown Rock Crystal Cutting combines dignified grace with modern simplicity to make a perfect blending of the old and the new. You'll find this Heisey pattern in a complete line of stemware together with plates, bowls, hurricane lamps, candlesticks, compotes, and other lovely accessory pieces."—Original Ad. Beginning in 1959, Imperial Glass Corporation reproduced several stems in No. 5024 Oxford with Maryland cutting.

STEMWARE:

NO. 5024 OXFORD
Claret, 4½ oz.	$55.00
Cocktail, 3½ oz.	30.00
Cocktail, Double, 6 oz.	35.00
Comport, 6"	60.00
Cordial or Liquor, Footed 1 oz.	90.00
Cordial, Tall Stem, 1 oz.	100.00
Goblet, 9 oz.	50.00
Goblet, 11 oz.	55.00
Iced Tea, Footed, 12 oz.	50.00
Juice, Footed, 5 oz.	25.00
Oyster Cocktail, 4 oz.	20.00
Saucer Champagne, 6½ oz.	40.00
Sherbet, 6½ oz.	25.00
Wine, 3 oz.	50.00

ACCESSORIES:
Bar, 1½ or 2 oz. (2351)	$25.00
Bar, 2½ oz. (2355)	38.00
Bottle, French Dressing (1489)	70.00
Bottle, French Dressing, 8 oz. (5031)	95.00
Bowl, Oblong, 14" (1489)	80.00
Bowl, Salad, 9", with or without beaded edge (485)	45.00
Candleblocks, 4½", pr. (1489)	100.00
Cheese & Cracker, 15" (1495)	70.00
Cocktail Icer & Liner (3304)	100.00
Cocktail Shaker, 1 qt. (4036 or 4225)	110.00
Cocktail Shaker, 2 qt. (4225)	145.00
Comport, 6" (1951)	35.00
Cream & Sugar, pr. (1951)	50.00
Decanter, 1 pt. (4036½)	90.00
Decanter, 32 oz. (4035 or 4036)	95.00
Dish & Cover, Lemon, 6½" (1509)	85.00
Finger Bowl (3335)	30.00
Highball, 8 oz. (2351)	12.00
Hurricane Block, 1-light with Globe (1489)	250.00
Iced Tea, 12 oz. (2351)	15.00
Jug, 73 oz. (4164 or 6060)	145.00
Mayonnaise (1519)	35.00
Old Fashioned, 8 oz. (2351)	12.00
Old Fashioned, 8 oz. (2355)	35.00
Old Fashioned, Double, 13 oz. (2351)	15.00
Plate, Mayonnaise (1519)	15.00
Plate, Salad, 7" or 8" (1184)	15.00
Plate, Torte, 14" (485)	60.00
Relish, 3-compartment, Oblong, 9" (1951)	48.00
Relish, Five O'Clock, 11" (1509)	65.00
Salt & Pepper, pr. (57)	85.00
Sherry, 1 pt. (4036)	110.00
Soda, 5 oz. or 6 oz. (2355)	45.00
Soda, 8 oz. or Beverage, 10 oz. (2351)	12.00
Soda or Tumbler 10 oz. (2355)	50.00
Soda, 13 oz. (2355)	60.00
Soda, 14 oz. (2351)	15.00
Soda, 16 oz. (2355)	68.00

DIAMONDS & SQUARES
(continued)

No. 2

ROCK CRYSTAL CUTTING

Date: 1947

Manufacturer: Chartiers Crystal—a division of Duncan & Miller, Washington, PA

Colors: Crystal

Notes: Chartiers was a "budget" line of Duncan & Miller.

Brandy	$35.00
Cocktail, Liquor	18.00
Goblet	22.00
Iced Tea	20.00
Juice, Orange	15.00
Oyster Cocktail or Sherbet	9.00
Whiskey Sour	12.00
Wine	25.00

Original Ad: No. 2 cutting on iced tea

No. 731

PLATE ETCHING

Date: Ca. 1925

Manufacturer: Cambridge Glass Co., Cambridge, OH

Colors: Crystal, Amber, Dianthus Pink, Green, Heatherbloom, Mandarin Gold, Willow Blue

Notes: Some rare pieces are known in other Cambridge colors, notably Carmen (red). Prices given are for all pastel colors. Sometimes referred to as Rosalie.

L to R: Original Cataolg Illustrations:
No. 731 etchings on No. 3115 goblet and No. 955 jug

STEMWARE:
No. 3115

Cocktail, 3½ oz.	$24.00
Finger Bowl (2 styles)	28.00
Fruit Salad, 6 oz.	17.00
Goblet, 9 oz.	30.00
Plate, Finger Bowl	9.00
Sherbet, Low, 6 oz.	17.00
Sherbet, Tall, 6 oz.	20.00
Tumbler, Footed, 2½ oz.	42.00
Tumbler, Footed, 5 oz.	25.00
Tumbler, Footed, 8 oz. (water)	28.00
Tumbler, Footed, 10 oz. (water)	30.00
Tumbler, Footed, 12 oz. (iced tea)	32.00

ACCESSORIES:

Almond, Individual, 2½" (611)	$85.00
Bacon & Egg, 13" (covered dish) (950)	110.00
Basket, 7" (760)	35.00
Basket, 11" (977)	65.00
Bonbon, 5½" (758)	25.00
Bonbon, 6¼" (749)	28.00
Bowl, 5⅜" (1010)	35.00
Bowl, 10" (1013)	55.00
Bowl, 11" (shallow) (1117)	55.00
Bowl, 11½" (756)	85.00
Bowl, 11½" (turned-up rim) (1116)	85.00
Bowl, 2-handled, 8½" (deep) (971)	45.00
Bowl, 2-handled, 10" (984)	52.00
Bowl, 3-compartment, 10½" (959)	60.00
Bowl, Oval, 15" (turned-down rim) (839)	110.00
Bowl, Oval, 15½" (841)	125.00

Candlesticks, 1-light, 4", pr. (627)	75.00
Candlesticks, 3-light, (keyhole), pr. (638)	125.00
Candy Box & Cover, 3-compartment, 8½" (740)	125.00
Candy Box & Cover, 6" (864)	125.00
Celery & Relish, 2-compartment, 9" (1067)	45.00
Celery & Relish, 2-compartment, 11" (1067)	55.00
Celery Tray, 11" (1083 or 1183)	42.00
Cheese & Cover, 2-piece, 11" (822)	75.00
Comport, 5¾" (flared) (869)	38.00
Comport, 6" (812)	45.00
Comport, 6½" (532 or 808)	45.00
Comport, 6¾" (low) (1089)	55.00
Comport, Low, 6½" (608)	45.00
Cranberry Dish, 3½" (1101)	22.00
Cream & Sugar, pr. (1096)	44.00
Cup & Saucer (865)	45.00
Dish, 2-compartment, 10½" (rectangular) (962)	55.00
Dish, 4-compartment, 10½" (963)	55.00
Dish, Vegetable, 9" (round) (1085)	50.00
Dish, Vegetable, 10" or 11" (round) (1086)	50.00
Dish, Vegetable, Oval, 9½" (1087)	60.00
Dish, Vegetable, Oval, 10½" (1088)	65.00
Fruit, 5½" (1098)	20.00
Ice Bucket (847)	85.00
Ice Tub, 2-handled (1147)	88.00
Jug, 62 oz. (955)	265.00
Mayonnaise, 2-handled (Footed) (871)	58.00

Mayonnaise, 5" (981)	50.00
Mayonnaise, 5½" (Footed) (873)	50.00
Mayonnaise, Footed (818)	45.00
Mustard and Cover (838)	120.00
Pickle Tray, 9" (1082)	30.00
Plate, 7" (2-handled) (759)	18.00
Plate, 8⅜" (597)	18.00
Plate, Dinner (square) (1177)	75.00
Plate, Mayonnaise, 11" (818)	15.00
Plate, Salad (square) (1176)	15.00
Plate, Sandwich, 2-handled, 11" (972)	42.00
Plate, Service (square) (1178)	70.00
Plate, Soup, 8½" (bowl) (1012)	50.00
Platter, 11" or 12" (1077 or 1078)	65.00
Platter, 13" (1079)	95.00
Relish, Center-handled, 11" (keyhole) (861)	42.00
Salt & Pepper, pr. (716)	75.00
Salt Dip, 1½" (613)	85.00
Salver, 11" (707)	85.00
Server, Center-handled, 10½" (keyhole) (879)	45.00
Sugar Shaker	285.00
Sugar, Loaf (1018)	95.00
Syrup (matches sugar shaker)	180.00
Tray for Cream & Sugar	24.00
Tray for Sugar & Syrup	45.00
Tray, 13" (round) (1031)	85.00
Tray, Service, 13" (1084)	75.00
Tray, Wafer (1019)	125.00
Tumbler, Footed, 10 oz. (801)	30.00
Vase, 6" (1308)	75.00

DIAMONDS OR SQUARES *(continued)*

Original Catalog Illustration:
No. 10 Old English on
No. 1953 goblet

OLD ENGLISH, NO. 10

ROCK CRYSTAL ENGRAVING

Date: 1950s

Manufacturer: Cambridge Glass Co.,
Cambridge, OH

Colors: Crystal

STEMWARE:

NO. 1953
Cocktail. $15.00
Goblet. 20.00

Sherbet 10.00
Tumbler, Footed, 5 oz. 12.00
Tumbler, Footed, 12 oz. 18.00

ACCESSORIES:
Plate, Salad, 8" (556) $17.00

Original Catalog Illustration:
Old Master cutting on
No. 1953 goblet

OLD MASTER

ROCK CRYSTAL ENGRAVING

Date: 1950s

Manufacturer: Cambridge Glass Co.,
Cambridge, OH

Colors: Crystal

STEMWARE:

NO. 1953
Cocktail. $15.00
Goblet. 20.00

Sherbet 10.00
Tumbler, Footed, 5 oz. 12.00
Tumbler, Footed, 12 oz. 18.00

ACCESSORIES:
Plate, Salad, 8" (556) $17.00

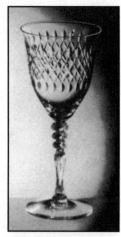

Original Catalog Illustration:
No. 683 Tiara cutting on
No. 5321 Trianon goblet

TIARA, NO. 683

ROCK CRYSTAL CUTTING

Date: 1940s

Manufacturer: Duncan & Miller Glass Co.,
Washington, PA

Colors: Crystal

STEMWARE:

NO. 5321 TRIANON
Claret, 5 oz., 6¾" tall. $30.00
Cocktail, Liquor, 3 oz., 5½" high 30.00
Cordial, 1 oz., 4½" tall 70.00
Finger Bowl, 4½" 15.00
Goblet, 10 oz., 7½" tall 45.00
Ice Cream, Footed, 6 oz.,
    3½" tall (sherbet) 17.00
Iced Tea, Footed, 13 oz., 6¼" tall 38.00
Oyster Cocktail, 4½ oz., 3½" tall 20.00
Saucer Champagne or Tall Sherbet,
    6 oz., 6" high 40.00
Wine, 3 oz., 6¼" tall 45.00

ACCESSORIES:
Bowl, Deep Salad, 9" (33) $55.00
Bowl, Flared, 12" (36) 68.00
Bowl, Low Foot, 13" (30). 68.00

Candlestick, Low, 3" pr. (115) 75.00
Candlesticks, 2-light, pr. (30) 115.00
Candy Box & Cover, 3-compartment,
    6½" (106) 85.00
Celery & Relish, Oblong, 2-handled,
    12" (30) 45.00
Comport, 6" (5317) 65.00
Comport, Tall, 7½" (8) 65.00
Cream & Sugar, pr. (38). 80.00
Iced Cocktail Set, 2-piece or
    3-piece (30) 85.00
Mayonnaise Set (8) 82.00
Nappy or Plate, 2-handled, 6" (30). 35.00
Plate, Bread & Butter, 6" (30½) 22.00
Plate, Dessert, 7½" (30½) 25.00
Plate, Salad, 8½" (30½). 25.00
Plate, Sandwich, 2-handled, 11" (30) . . . 65.00
Plate, Torte, 13" (33) 80.00
Relish, 2-handled, 2-compartment,
    6" (30) 35.00
Salad Dressing Set, 2-compartment,
    6", 2 piece (30). 55.00
Vase, 10" (506) 90.00
Vase, Flip, Flared 8" (30) 80.00

Chapter 20

FLORAL SPRAYS

This chapter contains floral etchings and cuttings which have distinct sprays or divisions as the primary motif as opposed to all-over floral etchings and cuttings listed in Flowers.

CAMELLIA

PLATE ETCHING

Date: 1952

Manufacturer: Fostoria Glass Co., Moundsville, WV

Colors: Crystal

STEMWARE:
No. 6036
Claret or Wine, 3¼ oz. $35.00
Cocktail, 3½ oz. 20.00
Cordial, 1 oz. 75.00
Goblet, 9½ oz. 25.00
High Sherbet or Saucer
    Champagne, 6 oz. 20.00
Iced Tea or Luncheon Goblet, 12 oz. . . . 20.00
Juice, Footed, 5 oz. 18.00
Oyster Cocktail, 4 oz. 15.00
Parfait, 5½ oz. 20.00
Sherbet, Low, 6 oz. 18.00

ACCESSORIES:
Basket, 10¼" (2630) $45.00
Bonbon, 3 Toed, 7½" (2630) 22.00
Bowl, Cereal, 6" (2630) 12.00
Bowl, Flared, 8" or 12" (2630) 35.00
Bowl, Footed, Rolled Edge or
    Flared (2630) 35.00
Bowl, Fruit, 5" (2630) 12.00
Bowl, Salad, 8½" or 10½" (2630) 45.00
Bowl, Snack (2630) 12.00
Bowl, Tricorn, 3 Toed, 7" (2630) 22.00
Bowl, Utility, Oval (2630) 20.00
Butter & Cover, Oblong, 7½" (2630). . . 35.00
Candlesticks, 4½", pr. (2630) 48.00
Candlesticks, Duo, pr. (2630). 70.00
Candlesticks, Trindle, pr. (2630) 90.00
Candy Jar & Cover, 7" (2630) 70.00
Cheese & Cracker (6036) 55.00
Comport, 4⅜" (2630) 14.00
Cream, Footed, 4¼" (2630) 20.00
Cream, Individual (2630) 18.00
Cup & Saucer (2630) 35.00
Dish, Serving, Handled (2630) 20.00

Dish, Vegetable, Oval, 9½" (2630) 24.00
Ice Bucket (2630) 60.00
Jug, Ice Lip, 3 Pint (2630-7) 85.00
Lily Pond, 9" or 11¼" (2630) 85.00
Mayonnaise, 2-part (2630) 22.00
Mayonnaise, 3½" (2630) 22.00
Mustard & Cover (2630) 30.00
Nappy, Handled, 4½" (2630) 12.00
Oil & Stopper, 5 oz. (2630) 50.00
Party Plate (2630) 20.00
Pickle, 8¾" (2630) 20.00
Pitcher, Cereal, 1 Pint (2630) 35.00
Plate, 6" or 7" (2630) 15.00
Plate, 8" or 9" (2630) 25.00
Plate, Cake, Handled (2630) 25.00
Plate, Dinner, 10½" 65.00
Plate, Mayonnaise (2630) 15.00
Plate, Torte, 14" or 16" (2630) 65.00
Platter, Oval, 12" (2630) 38.00
Preserve & Cover, Footed, 6" (2630). . . . 30.00
Relish, 2-part, 7⅜" (2630) 25.00
Relish, 3-part, 11⅛" (2630) 32.00
Salad, Crescent, 7½" (2630) 40.00
Salt & Pepper, pr. (2630) 55.00
Salver, Footed, 12¼" (2630) 55.00
Sugar, Footed (2630) 20.00
Sugar, Individual (2630) 18.00
Tid Bit, 2-tiered (1630) 50.00
Tid Bit, 3-toed, 8" (2630) 20.00
Tray for Sugar & Cream (2630) 100.00
Tray, Lunch, Center Handled,
    11¼" (2630) 40.00
Tray, Muffin, Handled (2630) 35.00
Tray, Snack, 10½" (2630) 25.00
Vase, 5½" (4121) 25.00
Vase, Bud, Footed (5092) 22.00
Vase, Bud, Footed, 6" (6021) 22.00
Vase, Flip, 8" (2660) 45.00
Vase, Footed, 10½" (2657) 40.00
Vase, Footed, 10" (2470) 40.00
Vase, Footed, 6" (4143) 25.00
Vase, Handled, 7½" (2630) 35.00
Vase, Oval, 8½" (2470) 40.00

Original Ad:
Camellia etching

FLORAL SPRAYS *(continued)*

Original Catalog Illustration:
Elaine etching on No. 1402/150
Tally Ho tall tumbler

Original Catalog Illustration:
Elaine etching on
No. 3104 Wine

Original Catalog Illustration:
Elaine etching on
footed Bonbon

ELAINE

PLATE ETCHING

Date: 1934

Manufacturer: Cambridge Glass Co.,
Cambridge, OH

Colors: Crystal

STEMWARE:

NO. 1402/150 TALLY HO

Claret, 5 oz.	$30.00
Cocktail, 3½ oz.	27.00
Cordial, 1 oz.	75.00
Finger Bowl	18.00
Plate, Finger Bowl	9.00
Sherbet, Low	17.00
Tumbler, Footed, or Tall Footed 12 oz.	30.00
Tumbler, Footed, 9 oz.	25.00
Wine, 3 oz.	30.00

NO. 3104

Brandy, ¾ oz.	$140.00
Claret, 4½ oz.	80.00
Cocktail, 3½ oz.	70.00
Cordial or Pousse Café, 1 oz.	140.00
Creme de Menthe, 2½ oz.	110.00
Finger Bowl	18.00
Goblet, 9 oz.	110.00
Hock, Tall, 5 oz.	78.00
Plate, Finger Bowl	9.00
Roemer, 5 oz.	100.00
Sherbet, Tall, 7 oz.	70.00
Sherry, 2 oz.	110.00
Wine, 3 oz.	95.00

NO. 3121

Café Parfait, 5 oz.	$40.00
Claret, 4½ oz.	45.00
Cocktail, 3 oz.	27.00
Cordial, 1 oz.	75.00
Goblet, 10 oz.	30.00
Iced Tea, Footed, 12 oz.	35.00
Oyster Cocktail, 4½ oz.	17.00
Sherbet, Low, 6 oz.	15.00
Sherbet, Tall, 6 oz.	24.00
Tumbler, Footed, 10 oz. (water)	30.00
Tumbler, Footed, 5 oz. (juice)	25.00
Wine, 3½ oz.	45.00

NO. 3500

Claret, 4½ oz.	$45.00
Cocktail, 3 oz.	27.00
Comport, Tall, 5⅜"	50.00
Cordial, 1 oz.	75.00
Goblet, 10 oz.	30.00
Iced Tea, Footed, 12 oz.	35.00
Oyster Cocktail, 4½ oz.	17.00
Parfait, 5 oz.	40.00
Sherbet, Low, 7 oz.	15.00
Sherbet, Tall, 7 oz.	22.00
Tumbler, Footed, 10 oz. (water)	30.00
Tumbler, Footed, 5 oz. (juice)	25.00
Wine, 2½ oz.	45.00

ACCESSORIES:

Basket, 2-handled, Footed, 6" (3500/55)	$24.00
Bonbon, 2-handled, 5¼" (3400/1180)	16.00
Bonbon, 2-handled, Footed, 6" (3500/54)	22.00
Bowl, 2-handled, 11" (3900/34)	50.00
Bowl, Flared, 4-footed, 12" (3900/62)	55.00
Bowl, Oval, 4-footed, 12" (3900/65)	60.00
Candlesticks, 1-light, 5", pr. (3900/67)	60.00
Candlesticks, 2-light, 6", pr. (3900/72)	85.00
Candlesticks, 3-light, 6", pr. (3900/74)	100.00
Candy Box & Cover (3900/165)	100.00
Celery & Relish, 3-part, or 5-part, 12" (3900/126 or 3900/120)	45.00
Cocktail Icer, 2 piece (968)	70.00
Comport, 5½" (3900/136)	38.00
Comport, Blown, 5⅜" (3121)	48.00
Cream & Sugar, pr. (3900/41)	40.00
Cream, Individual (3900/40 or 3500/15)	24.00
Cup & Saucer (3900/17)	32.00
Hurricane Lamp (1603 or 1617)	150.00
Ice Bucket (3900/671)	78.00
Mayonnaise (footed) (3900/19)	42.00
Mayonnaise, 2-compartment (3900/111)	40.00
Oil & Stopper, 6 oz. (3900/100)	110.00
Pickle, 9½" (477)	32.00
Plate, 2-handled, 6" (3400/1181)	20.00
Plate, 2-handled, Footed, 8" (3500/161)	22.00
Plate, 4-footed, 12" (3900/26)	42.00
Plate, Cake, 2-handled, 13½" (3900/35)	45.00
Plate, Dinner, 10½" (3900/24)	80.00
Plate, Rolled Edge, 14" (3900/166)	48.00
Plate, Salad, 8" (3900/22)	17.00
Plate, Torte, 4-footed, Rolled Edge, 13" (3900/32)	45.00
Relish or Pickle, 7" (3900/123)	28.00
Relish, 2-part, 6" (3400/90)	22.00
Relish, 2-part, 7" (3900/124)	28.00
Relish, 3-part, 6½" (3500/69)	22.00
Salt & Pepper, pr. (3900/1177)	50.00
Sugar, Individual (3900/40 or 3500/15)	24.00
Vase, "Flower Holder," Bud, 10" (274)	80.00
Vase, "Flower Holder," Footed, 8" (6004)	65.00
Vase, "Flower Holder," Footed, 9" (keyhole) (1237)	75.00
Vase, "Flower Holder," Footed, 11" (278 or 1299)	70.00
Vase, "Flower Holder," Footed, 12" (keyhole) (1238)	110.00
Vase, "Flower Holder," Footed, 13" (279)	85.00
Vase, "Flower Holder," Globe, 5" (1309)	60.00

JENNY

POLISHED CUTTING

Date: 1953

Manufacturer: Libbey Glass Co., Toledo, OH

Colors: Crystal

Notes: Designed by Freda Diamond.

Beverage, Footed (tumbler)	$9.00
Cocktail	10.00
Cordial	35.00
Goblet	15.00
Pilsner	18.00
Sherbet	9.00
Wine	15.00

Original Ad: Jenny cutting

LANGUAGE OF FLOWERS

ETCHING IN KATE GREENAWAY TRADITION

Date: 1940s

Manufacturer: Duncan & Miller Glass Co., Washington, PA

Colors: Crystal

Notes: Also called Apple Blossom according to old catalogs.

STEMWARE:

NO. 5331 VICTORY

Claret, 5 oz., 6" high	$35.00
Cocktail, Liquor, 3½ oz., 4½" high	35.00
Cordial, 1 oz., 4¼" tall	75.00
Finger Bowl, 4½"	20.00
Goblet, 10 oz., 7½" high	50.00
Ice Cream, Footed, 5 oz., 6¾" tall (sherbet)	20.00
Iced Tea, Footed, 13 oz., 7½" tall	45.00
Orange Juice, Footed, 5 oz., 5½" tall	27.00
Oyster Cocktail, 4½ oz., 4¾" tall	22.00
Saucer Champagne or Tall Sherbet, 6 oz., 4¾" high	45.00
Sherry, 2 oz., 4¾" tall	60.00
Tumbler, Footed, 10 oz., 7" tall	38.00
Wine, 3 oz., 5¾" high	50.00

ACCESSORIES:

Bowl, Oval, 10" x 7¼" (115)	$85.00
Candlesticks, 2-light, 6" tall, pr. (30)	130.00
Candlesticks, Low, 3", pr. (115)	95.00
Candy Box & Cover, 3-compartment, 8" (115)	95.00
Comport, Low, 6", 4¾" tall (115)	65.00
Cream & Sugar, 7 oz., 3¾" tall (115)	90.00
Cream, Individual, 2¾" tall (115)	40.00
Marmalade, Crimped, 4½" (115)	38.00
Plate, 14" (115)	90.00
Plate, 2-handled, 7½" (115)	35.00
Plate, 7½" or 8½" (30½)	25.00
Plate, Marmalade, 6" (115)	18.00
Relish, 3-handled, 3-compartment, 9" (115)	50.00
Relish, Oval, 2-handled, 2-compartment, 7" x 5¼" (115)	40.00
Sugar, Individual, 2½" tall (115)	40.00
Tray for Cream & Sugar, 8" x 4¾" (115)	30.00
Vase, Crimped, 5½" (115)	40.00

Original Catalog Illustration: Language of Flowers etching on 14" plate

Original Catalog Illustration: Language of Flowers etching on marmalade set

MEADOW ROSE, NO. 328

PLATE ETCHING

Date: 1937

Manufacturer: Fostoria Glass Co., Moundsville, WV

Colors: Crystal

Notes: No. 2496 indicates Baroque blanks. "An intricately etched design of primrose delicacy. It is perfectly executed on crystal with the softness and beauty of an art etching on paper."—From a Fostoria ad, 1937. At this time Fostoria was calling its plate etchings Master Etchings. Listings follow on next page.

Original Ad: Meadow Rose etching on assortment

FLORAL SPRAYS *(continued)*

Original Ad: Meadow Rose etching on footed jug

STEMWARE:

NO. 6016 WILMA

Brandy Inhaler, 15 oz., 5½" tall $60.00
Champagne, Continental, 5 oz., 8⅛" tall 35.00
Claret, 4 oz. or 4½ oz., 6" tall 35.00
Claret, Large, 6½ oz., 6¼" tall 37.00
Cocktail, 3½ oz., 5¼" tall 25.00
Cocktail/Sherry, 6 oz., 6³⁄₁₆" tall 30.00
Cordial, ¾ oz. or 1 oz., 3⅞" tall 75.00
Goblet, 9 oz. or 10 oz., 7⅝" tall 10.00
Oyster Cocktail, 4 oz., 3⅝" tall 30.00
Saucer Champagne, 5½ oz. or 6 oz., 5⅝" tall 32.00
Sherbet, Low, 5½ oz. or 6 oz., 4⅜" tall . . 25.00
Tumbler, Footed, 5 oz., 4⅝" tall (juice) . . 25.00
Tumbler, Footed, 10 oz., 5⅜" tall (water) 35.00
Tumbler, Footed, 13 oz., 5⅞" tall (iced tea) 35.00
Wine, 3 oz. or 3¼ oz., 5¼" tall 42.00

ACCESSORIES:

Bottle, Salad Dressing & Stopper, 7 oz., 6½" tall (2083) $85.00
Bowl, Flared, 12" (2496) 85.00
Bowl, Footed, Handled, 12" 85.00
Bowl, Handled, 10½" 70.00
Candlesticks, 4", pr. (2496) 70.00
Candlesticks, 5½", pr. (2496) 80.00
Comport, 5½" (2496) 40.00
Cream, 3½" (2496) 35.00
Cream, Individual, 3⅛" tall (2496) 32.00
Cup & Saucer, Footed (2496) 50.00
Dish, Sauce, Oblong, 6½" (2496) 25.00
Dish, Serving, 2 Handles, 8½" (2496) . . 60.00
Finger Bowl (869) 35.00
Floating Garden, 10" (2496) 70.00
Ice Bucket (2496) 165.00
Jelly & Cover, 7½" (2496) 100.00
Jug, Footed, 9¾" tall (5000) 175.00
Lunch Tray, Handled, 11" (2375) 55.00
Mayonnaise, 2 pt., 6½" (2496) 75.00
Mayonnaise, 5⅝" (2375) 70.00
Pickle, 8" (2496) 42.00
Plate, 6" or 7" (2496) 22.00
Plate, 8" (2496) 28.00
Plate, Cake, 2-handled, 10" (2496) 70.00
Plate, Mayonnaise, 7" (2375) 20.00
Plate, Torte, 14" (2496) 85.00
Relish, 3 pt., 10" (2496) 60.00
Relish, 5 pt., 13¼" (2419) 65.00
Relish, Square, 2 pt., 6" (2496) 35.00
Salt & Pepper, Footed, 3½", pr. (2375) . . 65.00
Sugar, 3½" (2496) 35.00
Sugar, Individual, 2⅞" tall (2496) 32.00
Sweetmeat, Square, 6" (2496) 25.00
Tray, Oblong, 8" (2496) 35.00
Vase, 5" 110.00
Vase, Footed, 10" 155.00

Original Catalog Illustration: No. 639 cutting on No. 3124 goblet

NO. 639

ROCK CRYSTAL ENGRAVING

Date: 1930s

Manufacturer: Cambridge Glass Company, Cambridge, OH

Colors: Crystal

STEMWARE:

NO. 3124

Claret, 4½ oz. $20.00
Cocktail, 3 oz. 15.00
Goblet, 10 oz. 20.00
Oyster Cocktail, 4½ oz. 12.00
Sherbet, Low, 7 oz. 12.00
Sherbet, Tall, 7 oz. 16.00
Wine, 3 oz. 20.00
Tumbler, Footed, 3 oz. 15.00
Tumbler, Footed, 5 oz. 15.00
Tumbler, Footed, 10 oz. 18.00
Tumbler, Footed, 12 oz. 18.00

Original Catalog Illustration: No. 641 rock crystal engraving on No. 3122 goblet

NO. 641

ROCK CRYSTAL ENGRAVING

Date: 1930s

Manufacturer: Cambridge Glass Company, Cambridge, OH

Colors: Crystal

STEMWARE:

NO. 3122

Claret, 4½ oz. $20.00
Cocktail, 3 oz. 15.00
Goblet, 10 oz. 20.00
Oyster Cocktail, 4½ oz. 12.00
Sherbet, Low, 7 oz. 12.00
Sherbet, Tall, 7 oz. 16.00
Wine, 3 oz. 20.00
Tumbler, Footed, 3 oz. 15.00
Tumbler, Footed, 5 oz. 15.00
Tumbler, Footed, 10 oz. 18.00
Tumbler, Footed, 12 oz. 18.00

(continued) # FLORAL SPRAYS

No. 655

ROCK CRYSTAL ENGRAVING

Date: 1930s

Manufacturer: Cambridge Glass Co.,
Cambridge, OH

Colors: Crystal

STEMWARE:

No. 3121
Claret, 4½ oz. $20.00
Cocktail, 3 oz. 16.00
Comport, Blown, 5⅜" 75.00

Cordial, 1 oz. 60.00
Goblet, 10 oz. 20.00
Iced Tea, Footed, 12 oz. 18.00
Oyster Cocktail, 4½ oz. 12.00
Sherbet, Low, 6 oz. 12.00
Sherbet, Tall, 6 oz. 16.00
Tumbler, Footed, 5 oz. 15.00
Tumbler, Footed, 10 oz. 18.00
Wine, 3½ oz. 20.00

Original Catalog Illustration:
No. 655 rock crystal engraving
on No. 3121 goblet

PASSION FLOWER

SILVER INTAGLIO ETCHING

Date: 1940s

Manufacturer: Duncan & Miller Glass Co.,
Washington, PA

Colors: Crystal

Bowl, Crimped, 10½" x 5" tall (115) . . $65.00
Bowl, Crimped, 9" (115) 60.00
Bowl, Floral, Flared, 12½" (30½) 70.00
Bowl, Oval, 10" (115) 60.00
Bowl, Oval, 11½" x 8¼" (115) 65.00
Bowl, Oval, 14" x 8" (126) 75.00
Bowl, Salad, 10½" x 4½" (30½) 58.00
Candleblocks, Square, 2", pr. (30) 55.00
Candy & Cover, 3-compartment,
    8" (115) 95.00

Candy & Cover, 6" or 8" (5200) 95.00
Candy & Knob Cover, Rectangular,
    2-compartment (30) 85.00
Candy & Knob Cover, Rectangular,
    8" (30) 85.00
Floating Garden, 12" x 7½" (30) 65.00
Lamp, Hurricane, 15" tall (1) 270.00
Plate, 14" (115) 60.00
Plate, Deviled Egg, 12" (30) 50.00
Urn, Square, 2-handled, 9½" (534) 85.00
Vase, 10" or 12" (506) 110.00
Vase, Cornucopia, 8" (117) 100.00
Vase, Flip, Flared, 8" (30) 80.00
Vase, Tall, 9" (115) 80.00

Passion Flower Silver Intaglio
etching on oval bowl

Passion Flower Silver Intaglio
etching on candy box and cover

RAMBLER, No. 323

PLATE ETCHING

Date: 1935

Manufacturer: Fostoria Glass Co.,
Moundsville, WV

Colors: Crystal

Notes: This etching when trimmed with gold
was given No. 615.

STEMWARE:

No. 6012 WESTCHESTER
Brandy, 1 oz., 4" tall. $35.00
Claret, 4½ oz., 5¾" tall 28.00
Cocktail, 3 oz., 4⅝" tall 25.00
Cordial, 1 oz., 3½" tall 35.00

Creme de Menthe, 2 oz., 4½" tall. 28.00
Goblet, 10 oz., 6⅞" tall 27.00
Oyster Cocktail, Footed, 4 oz., 3½" tall . 16.00
Rhine Wine, 4½" tall 28.00
Saucer Champagne, 5½ oz.,
    5" (high sherbet) 25.00
Sherbet, Low, 5½ oz., 4" tall 17.00
Sherry, 2 oz., 4½" tall 28.00
Wine, 3 oz., 5¼" tall 28.00
Tumbler, Footed, 5 oz., 4¼" tall (juice). . 15.00
Tumbler, Footed, 10 oz.,
    5⅜" tall (water) 17.00
Tumbler, Footed, 13 oz.,
    5¾" tall (iced tea) 21.00

Original Catalog Illustration:
No. 323 Rambler etching stems

109

FLORAL SPRAYS *(continued)*

ACCESSORIES:

Bonbon, Handled, 5" (2440)...... $15.00
Bowl, 10½" (2470½) 35.00
Bowl, Handled, 10" (2484)....... 38.00
Candlesticks, 5½", pr. (2470½).... 45.00
Candlesticks, Duo, pr. (2472) 60.00
Candlesticks, Trindle, pr.
  (2482 or 2496) 85.00
Candy Jar & Cover, Bubble (4117) .. 35.00
Champagne, Hollow Stem (798) 22.00
Cocktail Mixer (2524)........... 55.00
Cocktail Shaker, 42 oz. (2525)..... 75.00
Cream, Footed (2350½) 20.00

Cup & Saucer, Footed (2350) 35.00
Decanter (2525) 70.00
Decanter, Footed (6011) 80.00
Dish, Sauce, 6½" (2440)......... 18.00
Finger Bowl (1769)............. 12.00
Jug, Footed (6011) 75.00
Lemon, Handled, 5" (2440) 18.00
Mayonnaise, Oval, 2 pt. (2440) 25.00
Old Fashioned Cocktail,
  Sham (1184) 12.00
Plate, 6" or 7" (2337) 15.00
Plate, 8" (2337) 18.00
Plate, Torte, 13" (2440)......... 50.00

Relish, 4 pt. (2419).............. 35.00
Relish, 5 pt. (2419).............. 42.00
Relish, Handled, 2 pt. (2440) 28.00
Relish, Handled, 3 pt. (2440) 35.00
Relish, Square, 5 pt. (2514)....... 65.00
Salt & Pepper, pr. (2235) 85.00
Sugar, Footed (2350½)........... 20.00
Sweetmeat, Handled, 4½" (2440) ... 17.00
Tray, Oval, 8½" (2440).......... 40.00
Tumbler, Sham, 10 oz. or
  12 oz. (701)................ 15.00
Vase, 11½" (2470) 52.00
Whiskey, Sham, 1½ oz. (4122) 22.00

Original Catalog Illustration:
No. 998 Wedding Rose rock
crystal engraving on No. 3130

WEDDING ROSE, NO. 998

ROCK CRYSTAL ENGRAVING

Date: 1934

Manufacturer: Cambridge Glass Co.,
Cambridge, OH

Colors: Crystal

STEMWARE:

NO. 3130

Claret, 4½ oz. $25.00
Cocktail, 3 oz. 20.00
Cordial, 1 oz. 65.00
Fruit Salad, 6 oz. 15.00
Goblet, 8 oz. 25.00
Goblet, 9 oz. 25.00

Oyster Cocktail, 4½ oz............. 15.00
Sherbet, Low, 6 oz.. .... 15.00
Sherbet, Low, 7 oz.. .... 15.00
Sherbet, Tall, 6 oz. 20.00
Sherbet, Tall, 7 oz. 20.00
Tumbler, Footed with stem, 12 oz. 20.00
Tumbler, Footed, 2½ oz. (whiskey).... 28.00
Tumbler, Footed, 5 oz. (juice)....... 16.00
Tumbler, Footed, 8 oz. (water) 16.00
Tumbler, Footed, 10 oz. (water) 17.00
Tumbler, Footed, 12 oz. (iced tea)..... 18.00
Wine, 2½ oz.. .... 25.00

Original Catalog Illustration:
Wildflower rock crystal cutting
on D6 Eternal Life goblet

WILDFLOWER

ROCK CRYSTAL CUTTING

Date: 1950s

Manufacturer: Duncan & Miller Glass Co.,
Washington, PA

Colors: Crystal

Notes: Plates are from the Canterbury pattern.
It is likely other pieces may have been made.

STEMWARE:

NO. D6 ETERNAL LIFE

Cocktail, Liquor................. $30.00
Goblet......................... 45.00

Iced Tea, Footed................. 38.00
Juice, Footed 24.00
Saucer Champagne or Tall Sherbet 40.00
Seafood Cocktail 20.00
Wine or Claret.................. 45.00

ACCESSORIES:
Plate, 7½" (115) 12.00
Plate, 8½" (115) 15.00

Chapter 21
FLOWERS

Flowers are the most popular motif for decorations on glass, especially in etchings. Most etchings have flowers in them, but often they are not recognizable as specific types of flowers. Most flowers that we can identify as to type are listed in chapters of their own.

This category includes many almost all-over etchings either in a panel or a more all-over motif. The flowers and leaves are not easily distinguishable as to type. Cuttings can be highly stylized or naturalistic in appearance.

ACHILLES, No. 6998

ROCK CRYSTAL ENGRAVING

Date: 1930s

Manufacturer: Cambridge Glass Co., Cambridge, OH

Colors: Crystal

STEMWARE:
No. 3121
Claret, 4½ oz.	$30.00
Cocktail, 3 oz.	26.00
Comport, Blown, 5⅜"	75.00
Cordial, 1 oz.	60.00
Goblet, 10 oz.	30.00
Iced Tea, Footed, 12 oz.	24.00
Oyster Cocktail, 4½ oz.	15.00
Sherbet, Low, 6 oz.	18.00
Sherbet, Tall, 6 oz.	24.00
Tumbler, Footed, 5 oz.	18.00
Tumbler, Footed, 10 oz.	22.00
Wine, 3½ oz.	30.00

ACCESSORIES:
Bonbon, 2-handled, Footed, 7" (3900/130)	$27.00
Bowl, 4-footed, Flared, 12" (3900/62)	50.00
Candlesticks, 2-light, 6", pr. (3900/72)	65.00
Candy Box & Cover (3900/165)	55.00
Celery & Relish, 3-part, 12" (3900/126)	48.00
Celery & Relish, 3-part, 8" (3900/125)	42.00
Celery & Relish, 5-part, 12" (3900/120)	48.00
Cocktail Icer, 2 pc. (968)	75.00
Comport, 5½" (3900/136)	38.00
Cream (3900/41)	24.00
Mayonnaise (3900/129)	40.00
Mayonnaise, 2-compartment (3900/111)	38.00
Plate, Bonbon, 2-handled, Footed, 8" (3900/131)	24.00
Plate, Cake, 2-handled, 13½" (3900/35)	48.00
Plate, Mayonnaise (3900/129)	12.00
Plate, Rolled Edge, 14" (3900/166)	55.00
Plate, Salad, 7½" (3400/176 or 3900/22)	18.00
Plate, Salad, 8" (3900/22)	20.00
Sugar (3900/41)	24.00
Vase, Footed, 11" (278)	65.00

Original Catalog Illustration:
No. 6998 Achilles rock crystal engraving on No. 3121 stems

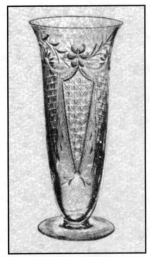

Original Catalog Illustration:
No. 6998 Achilles rock crystal engraving on No. 278 vase

FLOWERS *(continued)*

Original Catalog Illustration:
No. 720 Adonis rock crystal
engraving on No. 3500 Goblet

Original Catalog Illustration:
Adoration etching on No. 5321
Trianon stems

Adoration etching on
No. 5321 Trianon goblet and
Pall Mall salad plate

ADONIS, NO. 720

ROCK CRYSTAL ENGRAVING

Date: 1930s

Manufacturer: Cambridge Glass Co.,
Cambridge, OH

Colors: Crystal

STEMWARE:

NO. 3500 GADROON

Café Parfait, 5 oz..	$28.00
Claret, 4½ oz.	28.00
Cocktail, 3 oz.	28.00
Cordial, 1 oz..	60.00
Goblet, 10 oz.	28.00
Iced Tea, Footed, 12 oz.	24.00
Oyster Cocktail, 4½ oz.	15.00
Sherbet, Low, 7 oz..	18.00
Sherbet, Tall, 7 oz.	24.00
Tumbler, Footed, 5 oz. (juice)	20.00
Tumbler, Footed, 10 oz. (water)	22.00
Wine, 2½ oz..	28.00

ACCESSORIES:

Bonbon, 2-handled, Footed, 7" (3900/130).	$28.00
Bowl, Flared, 4-footed, 12" (3900/62)	55.00
Candlesticks, 2-light, 6" (3900/72)	75.00
Candy Box & Cover (3900/165)	60.00

Celery & Relish, 3-part, 12" (3900/126)	48.00
Celery & Relish, 3-part, 8" (3900/125)	42.00
Celery & Relish, 5-part, 12" (3900/120)	48.00
Cocktail Icer, 2 pc. (968)	75.00
Comport, 5½" (3900/136)	45.00
Comport, Blown, 5⅜" (3500/101)	55.00
Cream (3900/41)	22.00
Decanter, Footed, 28 oz. (1321)	190.00
Mayonnaise (3900/128)	35.00
Mayonnaise, 2-compartment (3900/111)	40.00
Plate, Bonbon, 2-handled, Footed, 8" (3900/131)	27.00
Plate, Cake, 2-handled, 13½" (3900/35)	50.00
Plate, Mayonnaise	15.00
Plate, Rolled Edge, 14" (3900/166)	58.00
Plate, Salad, 7½" (3500/167)	15.00
Plate, Salad, 8" (3900/22)	15.00
Plate, Salad, 8½" (3500/5)	15.00
Sherry, 2 oz. (7966)	27.00
Sugar (3900/41).	22.00
Vase, Footed, 10" (274)	50.00
Vase, Footed, 11" (278)	70.00

ADORATION

ETCHING

Date: 1940s

Manufacturer: Duncan & Miller Glass Co.,
Washington, PA

Colors: Crystal

Notes: Made to "harmonize with 1847 Rogers
Bros. 'Adoration' Silverplate." No. 30 refers to
Pall Mall pattern.

STEMWARE:

NO. 5321 TRIANON

Claret, 5 oz., 6¾" tall	$30.00
Cocktail, Liquor, 3 oz., 5½" high	30.00
Cordial, 1 oz., 4½" tall	70.00
Finger Bowl, 4½"	15.00
Goblet, 10 oz., 7½" tall	45.00
Ice Cream, Footed, 6 oz., 3½" tall (sherbet)	17.00
Iced Tea, Footed, 13 oz., 6¼" tall	38.00
Oyster Cocktail, 4½ oz., 3½" tall	20.00
Saucer Champagne or Tall Sherbet, 6 oz., 6" high	40.00
Wine, 3 oz., 6¼" tall	45.00

ACCESSORIES:

Bowl, Flower, 12", Straight or Crimped (8)	$70.00
Candlesticks, 2-light, 6", pr. (30)	120.00
Candy Box & Cover, 3-compartment, 7" (117)	90.00
Cream, 7 oz., 3½" tall (38)	45.00
Lamp, Hurricane, 1-light, 15" (1)	200.00
Mayonnaise, 6" (8)	70.00
Nappy, 2-handled, Flared, 6" (30)	35.00
Plate, 2-handled Sandwich, 11" (30)	70.00
Plate, 7½" Dessert or 8½" Salad (30½)	28.00
Plate, Bread & Butter, 6½" (30½)	24.00
Plate, Mayonnaise (8)	24.00
Relish, Flared, 3-handled, 9" (115)	45.00
Sugar, 8 oz., 2¾" tall (38)	45.00
Vase, Cornucopia, 8" (117)	80.00

(continued) **FLOWERS**

AIRDALE, NO. 175

CUTTING

Date: 1924

Manufacturer: Fostoria Glass Co.,
Moundsville, WV

Colors: Crystal

STEMWARE:

NO. 880

Ale, Tall	$11.00
Brandy (Pousse Café), ¾ or 1 oz.	14.00
Champagne, Hollow Stem	10.00
Champagne, Tall	9.00
Claret, 4½ oz. or 6½ oz.	10.00
Cocktail, 3 oz. or 3½ oz.	9.00
Cordial, ¾ or 1 oz.	25.00
Creme de Menthe	10.00
Goblet, 8, 9, 10 or 11 oz.	10.00
Grapefruit, Short	10.00

Grapefruit, Tall	10.00
Hot Whiskey	9.00
Rhine Wine	10.00
Saucer Champagne, 5½ oz. or 7 oz.	10.00
Sherbet	8.00
Sherry	10.00
Wine, 2½ or 3½ oz.	10.00

ACCESSORIES:

Bonbon (stemmed) (880)	$15.00
Finger Bowl (1769)	9.00
Jug (2040/3)	55.00
Nappy, 5" (footed) (803)	15.00
Plate, 6½" (2283)	6.00
Tumbler, 13 oz. (701)	14.00
Tumbler, Table (820)	14.00

Original Catalog Illustration:
No. 175 Airdale cutting on
No. 2040/3 jug

ALHAMBRA, NO. 607

ROCK CRYSTAL CUTTING

Date: 1930s

Manufacturer: Duncan & Miller Glass Co.,
Washington, PA

Colors: Crystal

STEMWARE:

NO. 504 GRANADA

Claret, 5 oz.	$30.00
Cocktail, Liquor, 3½ oz.	30.00
Cordial, 1 oz.	70.00
Goblet, 10 oz.	45.00
Ice Cream, Footed, 5 oz.	17.00
Iced Tea, Footed, 12 oz.	38.00
Orange Juice, Footed, 5 oz.	24.00
Oyster Cocktail, 4½ oz.	20.00
Saucer Champagne, 5 oz.	40.00
Sherry, 2 oz.	55.00
Tumbler, Ftd., 10 oz.	35.00
Whiskey, Ftd., 3 oz.	40.00
Wine, 3½ oz.	45.00

ACCESSORIES:

Bowl, Deep Salad, 9" (33)	$55.00
Bowl, Flared, 12" (36)	68.00
Bowl, Low Foot, 13" (30)	68.00
Candlesticks, Low, 3", pr. (115)	75.00

Candlesticks, 2-light, pr. (30)	115.00
Candy Box & Cover, 3-compartment, 6½" (106)	85.00
Celery & Relish, Oblong, 2-handled, 12" (30)	45.00
Comport, 6" (5317)	65.00
Comport, Tall, 7½" (8)	65.00
Cream (38)	40.00
Finger Bowl (30)	15.00
Iced Cocktail Set, 2 pc. or 3 pc. (30) . . .	85.00
Mayonnaise Set (8)	85.00
Nappy, 2-handled, 6" (30)	25.00
Plate, 2-handled., 6" (30)	35.00
Plate, Bread & Butter, 6" (30½)	22.00
Plate, Dessert, 7½" (30½)	25.00
Plate, Salad, 8½" (30½)	25.00
Plate, Sandwich, 2-handled., 11" (30) . . .	65.00
Plate, Torte, 13" (33)	80.00
Relish, 2-handled, 2-compartment, 6" (30)	35.00
Salad Dressing Set, 2-compartment, 6", 2-piece (30)	55.00
Sugar (38)	40.00
Vase, 10" (506)	90.00
Vase, Flip, Flared 8" (30)	80.00

Original Catalog Illustration:
No. 607 Alhambra cutting on
No. 504 Granada goblet

FLOWERS *(continued)*

Original Catalog Illustration:
No. 744 Apple Blossom etching on No. 3011 Cambridge
banquet goblet and table goblet

Original Catalog Illustration:
No. 744 Apple Blossom etching on No. 3025 stemware

Detail of No. 744 Apple Blossom etching

APPLE BLOSSOM, NO. 744

PLATE ETCHING

Date: 1930

Manufacturer: Cambridge Glass Co., Cambridge, OH

Colors: Crystal, Mandarin Gold, Green, Emerald Green, Amber, Blue

Notes: When this etching is found silver encrusted on Ebony, it is referred to as D971/S. "Dainty as apple blossoms and far less perishable are these lovely new examples of Cambridge glass, delicately etched, all wrought in the tender green of new foliage, the pink of early roses, the gold-krystol and amber of daffodils and the limpid blue of cloudless May skies."—Crockery & Glass Journal, May, 1930.

STEMWARE:	Crystal	Colors
NO. 3011 CAMBRIDGE NUDE		
Cocktail, 3½ oz.	$350.00	
Comport, Cupped or Flared, 7"	350.00	
Goblet, Banquet, 11 oz.	350.00	
Goblet, Table, 11 oz.	300.00	
Sherbet, Tall, 7 oz.	300.00	
NO. 3025		
Finger Bowl, Footed	$15.00	$20.00
Goblet, 10 oz.	22.00	30.00
Oyster Cocktail, 4½ oz.	15.00	24.00
Plate, Finger Bowl	12.00	18.00
Sherbet, Low, 7 oz.	14.00	20.00
Sherbet, Tall, 7 oz.	18.00	24.00
Tumbler, Footed, 4 oz.	15.00	22.00
Tumbler, Footed, 10 oz.	18.00	28.00
Tumbler, Footed, 12 oz.	22.00	45.00
NO. 3130		
Cocktail, 3 oz.	$18.00	$35.00
Finger Bowl	15.00	18.00
Goblet, 8 oz.	20.00	40.00
Plate, Finger Bowl	12.00	18.00
Sherbet, Low, 6 oz.	14.00	20.00
Sherbet, Tall, 6 oz.	14.00	24.00
Tumbler, Footed, 5 oz.	14.00	32.00
Tumbler, Footed, 8 oz.	16.00	32.00
Tumbler, Footed, 10 oz.	16.00	32.00
Tumbler, Footed, 12 oz.	18.00	30.00
NO. 3135		
Cocktail, 3 oz. (3135)	$17.00	$30.00
Goblet, 8 oz. (3135)	18.00	40.00
Sherbet, Low, 6" (3135)	14.00	20.00
Sherbet, Tall, 6 oz. (3135)	14.00	24.00
Tumbler, Footed, 5 oz. (3135)	14.00	32.00
Tumbler, Footed, 8 oz. (3135)	16.00	32.00
Tumbler, Footed, 10 oz. (3135)	15.00	30.00
Tumbler, Footed, 12 oz. (3135)	22.00	50.00
NO. 3400 STEMWARE		
Goblet, Lunch, 9 oz.	$17.00	$35.00
Sherbet, Footed, 6 oz.	12.00	20.00
Tumbler, Footed, 2½ oz. (whiskey)	25.00	70.00
Tumbler, Footed, 9 oz.	15.00	32.00
Tumbler, Footed, 12 oz.	22.00	50.00

(continued) **FLOWERS**

ACCESSORIES:	Crystal	Colors
Ashtray, 6"	$55.00	$180.00
Baker, 10" (3400/51)	42.00	80.00
Basket, 6" (2-handled) (3400/1182)	15.00	30.00
Bonbon, 5¼" (3400/1180 or 3400/1179)	15.00	30.00
Bowl, 10" (3400/1185)	45.00	90.00
Bowl, 12" (3400/4)	48.00	75.00
Bowl, 12½" (3400/2)	40.00	60.00
Bowl, 13" (3400/1)	40.00	60.00
Bowl, Fruit, 11" (3400/1188)	45.00	85.00
Bowl, Low, Footed, 11" (3400/3)	40.00	85.00
Bowl, Oval, 12" (3400/1240)	50.00	78.00
Butter & Cover, 5½" (3400/52)	145.00	295.00
Candelabra, 3-light, Keyhole, pr. (3400/638)	65.00	125.00
Candlesticks, 1-light, Keyhole, pr. (3400/646)	45.00	65.00
Candlesticks, 2-light, Keyhole, pr. (3400/647)	55.00	90.00
Candy Box & Cover, 7" (3400/9)	78.00	110.00
Celery & Relish, Service, 12" (3400/67)	40.00	60.00
Cereal, 6" (3400/53)	22.00	35.00
Cheese & Cracker, 2-piece, 11½" (3400/6)	50.00	65.00
Comport, 4" (3400/15)	15.00	22.00
Comport, Tall, 7" (3400/14)	42.00	65.00
Cream (3400/68)	18.00	48.00
Cream Soup (3400/55)	27.00	45.00
Cream, Footed, 6 oz. (3400/6)	18.00	40.00
Cup & Saucer (3400/54)	25.00	65.00
Finger Bowl (3135)	20.00	40.00
Fruit Saucer, 5½" (3400/56)	15.00	22.00
Jug, 8 oz. (3400/38)	150.00	325.00
Jug & Cover, Footed, 76 oz. (711)	200.00	400.00
Jug, 64 oz. (1205)	150.00	295.00
Jug, 64 oz. (935)	150.00	295.00
Jug, 67 oz. (3400/27)	145.00	350.00

	Crystal	Colors
Jug, Footed, 50 oz. (3400)	135.00	300.00
Mayonnaise (3400/11)	35.00	60.00
Pickle Tray, 9" (3400/59)	18.00	32.00
Plate, 6" (2-handled) (3400/1181)	15.00	30.00
Plate, 8½" (3400/62)	18.00	30.00
Plate, Bread & Butter (3400/1174)	9.00	18.00
Plate, Bread & Butter, 6" (3400/60)	9.00	18.00
Plate, Club Luncheon, Grill, 10" (3400/66)	38.00	70.00
Plate, Cream Soup (3400/55)	8.00	15.00
Plate, Dinner (3400/1177)	58.00	90.00
Plate, Dinner, Square (3400/1177)	58.00	90.00
Plate, Dinner, Round, 9½" (3400/63)	58.00	90.00
Plate, Mayonnaise (3400/11)	8.00	15.00
Plate, Salad (3400/1176)	18.00	30.00
Plate, Sandwich, 12½" (3400/1186)	30.00	40.00
Plate, Sandwich, 2-handled, 11½" (3400/8)	32.00	42.00
Plate, Service (3400/1178)	65.00	110.00
Plate, Tea, 7½" (round) (3400/61)	9.00	18.00
Platter, 11½" (3400/57)	45.00	90.00
Platter, 13½" (3400/58)	48.00	100.00
Salt & Pepper, pr. (3400/18)	48.00	85.00
Sugar (3400/68)	18.00	48.00
Sugar, Footed, 6 oz. (3400/6)	18.00	40.00
Tray, Sandwich, Center-handled, 11" (3400/10)	40.00	60.00
Tumbler, 12 oz. (3400/27)	20.00	50.00
Tumbler, 12 oz. (3400/38)	20.00	50.00
Tumbler, 12 oz. (498)	20.00	35.00
Vase, 10" (1301)	45.00	70.00
Vase, 12" (1296)	50.00	80.00
Vase, Keyhole Stem, 12" (1234)	54.00	250.00
Vase, 6" (1308)	40.00	85.00
Vase, 8" (1283 or 1300)	45.00	130.00

BURGUNDY, NO. 777

ROCK CRYSTAL CUTTING

Date: 1940s

Manufacturer: Duncan & Miller Glass Co., Washington, PA

Colors: Crystal

Notes: Probably matching pressed plates were made and possibly other items also, but we cannot document these.

STEMWARE:

NO. 5326 DEAUVILLE

Claret, 4½ oz., 6¾" high	$30.00
Cocktail, Liquor, 3½ oz., 5¼" high	30.00
Cordial, 1 oz., 5" high	70.00
Finger Bowl, 4½"	15.00
Goblet, 9 oz., 7¾" high	45.00
Goblet, Luncheon, 9 oz., 6" high	40.00
Ice Cream, 6 oz. (sherbet), 3¾" high	17.00
Iced Tea, Footed, 13 oz., 6¾" high	38.00
Orange Juice, Footed, 5 oz., 4¾" high	24.00
Oyster Cocktail, 4½ oz., 4¼" high	20.00
Plate, Finger Bowl, 6"	12.00
Saucer Champagne, 6 oz., 6" high	40.00
Wine, 3 oz., 6¼" high	45.00

Original Catalog Illustration: No. 777 Burgundy cutting on No. 5326 Deauville goblet

FLOWERS *(continued)*

Original Catalog Illustration:
No. 773 Chantilly cutting on
No. 5115 Canterbury goblet and
saucer champagne

Original Catalog Illustration:
Chantilly etching on
No. 3625 goblet

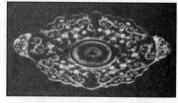

Original Brochure: Chantilly
etching on cake plate

CHANTILLY, NO. 773

ROCK CRYSTAL CUTTING

Date: 1940s

Manufacturer: Duncan & Miller Glass Co., Washington, PA

Colors: Crystal

STEMWARE

NO. 5115 CANTERBURY (BLOWN)

Claret, 5 oz., 6¾" tall. $30.00
Cocktail, Liquor, 3 oz., 5¼" tall 30.00
Cordial, 1 oz., 4¼" tall 70.00
Goblet, 10 oz., 7¼" tall 45.00
Ice Cream, Footed, 5 oz., 2¼" tall 17.00
Iced Tea, Footed, 12 oz., 5¾" tall 38.00
Orange Juice, Footed, 5 oz., 4¼" tall . . . 24.00
Oyster Cocktail, Footed,
     4 oz., 3¼" tall. 20.00
Saucer Champagne, 5 oz., 5½" tall 40.00
Tumbler, Footed, 10 oz., 4½" tall 35.00
Wine, 3½ oz., 6" tall 45.00

ACCESSORIES:

Bowl, Crimped, 10½" (115). $70.00
Bowl, Flared Flower, 12" (8). 70.00

Bowl, Flared, 12½" (30½) 70.00
Candlesticks, 2-light, pr. (41) 140.00
Celery & Relish Tray,
     5-compartment (31½) 70.00
Comport, High Foot, 7½" (8) 65.00
Cream, 7 oz. (115). 37.00
Mayonnaise Bowl, Flared, 5" (115). 65.00
Nappy, 2-handled, Round, (115) 45.00
Plate, 2-handled, 7½" (115) 30.00
Plate, 6" (115) 22.00
Plate, 7½" or 8½" (115) 30.00
Plate, Mayonnaise, 7½" (115) 18.00
Plate, Torte, 14" (115) 85.00
Plate, Torte, Rolled Edge, 14" (30½) . . . 80.00
Relish Tray, 2-compartment,
     Handled, 5" (115) 45.00
Relish Tray, 3-handled,
     3-compartment, 9" (115) 55.00
Sandwich Tray, 2-handled,
     10½" (115) 70.00
Sugar, 7 oz. (115). 37.00

CHANTILLY

PLATE ETCHING

Date: 1939

Manufacturer: Cambridge Glass Co., Cambridge, OH

Colors: Crystal

Notes: Called D/1061 when gold encrusted on Ebony.

STEMWARE:

NO. 3625

Claret $32.00
Cocktail 30.00
Cordial 75.00
Goblet. 37.00
Iced Tea, Footed. 35.00
Juice, Footed 30.00
Oyster Cocktail 28.00
Saucer Champagne. 30.00
Sherbet 28.00
Wine. 40.00

ACCESSORIES:

Basket, 2-handled, 6" (P55) $80.00
Bell, Dinner (3121) 175.00
Bonbon, 2-handled, 5¼" (3900/1180) . . 40.00
Bonbon, 2-handled, 6" (P54) 80.00
Bowl, 3-footed, 10" (3900/54) 78.00

Bowl, 4-footed, 11" (3400/48) 110.00
Bowl, 4-footed, 12" (3400/160) 110.00
Bowl, Crimped (3900/66) 65.00
Butter & Cover, ¼ lb. (3900/52) 325.00
Candlesticks, 2-light, 6" (3900/72) 55.00
Candlesticks, 3-light, 6" (1338) 85.00
Candlesticks, 3-light, 6" (3900/74) 65.00
Candlesticks, 5", pr. (3900/68) 70.00
Candlesticks, 5", pr.
     (Keyhole stem) (646) 40.00
Candlesticks, 6", pr.
     (Keyhole stem) (647) 50.00
Candy Box & Cover (3900/165) 130.00
Celery & Relish, 3 pt., 12" (3900/126). . 75.00
Celery & Relish, 3 pt., 9" (3900/125). . . 65.00
Celery & Relish, 5 pt., 12" (3900/120). . 80.00
Cheese & Cracker, 13½", 2 pc.
     (3900/135) 135.00
Cocktail Icer, 2 pc. (968) 90.00
Cocktail Shaker, 36 oz. (P101) 175.00
Cocktail, 4 oz. (7801) 45.00
Comport, 5⅜" (3121) 75.00
Comport, 5" (same as Cheese)
     (3900/135). 52.00
Comport, 5½" (3900/136). 62.00
Cream (3900/39). 25.00
Cream (3900/40). 25.00

Cream, Individual (3500/15) 35.00
Cream, Individual (3900/38) 25.00
Cup & Saucer (3900/17) 45.00
Decanter, Footed, 28 oz. (1321) 380.00
Hurricane Lamp, 10" (1603 or 1617) . . 275.00
Hurricane Lamp, 17" (1613) 400.00
Ice Bucket (3900/671) 270.00
Jug, 20 oz. (3900/117) 255.00
Jug, 32 oz. (3900/118) 320.00
Jug, 76 oz. (3900/115) 225.00
Jug, Martini, 32 oz. (3900/114) 425.00
Mayonnaise (1532) 65.00
Mayonnaise (3900/129) 75.00
Mayonnaise (3900/19) 60.00
Mayonnaise, 2-compartment
   (3900/111) 70.00
Oil & Stopper, 6 oz. (3900/100) 160.00
Pickle, 9½" (477) 50.00
Plate, 14" (3900/166 or 167) 85.00
Plate, 14" (3900/166) 75.00
Plate, 2-handled Bonbon,
   8" (3900/131) 48.00
Plate, 2-handled, 6" (3400/1181) 25.00
Plate, 2-handled, 8" (P56) 50.00
Plate, 3-footed, 12" (3900/26) 95.00
Plate, 3-footed, 13" (3900/33) 200.00
Plate, Bread & Butter, 6½" (3900/20) . . 18.00
Plate, Cake, 2-handled,
   13½" (3900/35) 80.00
Plate, Dinner, 10½" (3900/24) 160.00

Plate, Mayonnaise (1532) 18.00
Plate, Mayonnaise (3900/129) 18.00
Plate, Salad, 7½" (3400/176) 18.00
Plate, Salad, 7½" (555) 18.00
Plate, Salad, 8" (3900/22) 22.00
Plate, Salad, 8½" (3400/62) 25.00
Plate, Salad, 8½" (3900/5) 18.00
Relish & Pickle, 2 pt., 7" (3900/124) . . . 42.00
Relish & Pickle, 7" (3900/123) 40.00
Relish, 2 pt., 6" (3400/90) 40.00
Relish, 3 pt., 6½" (3500/69) 38.00
Relish, 3 pt., 8" (3400/91) 42.00
Salt & Pepper, pr. (1956/105) 75.00
Salt & Pepper, pr. (3900/1177) 55.00
Salt & Pepper, pr. (P360) 75.00
Sherry, 2 oz. (trumpet shape) (7966) 60.00
Sugar (3900/39) 25.00
Sugar (3900/40) 25.00
Sugar, Individual (3500/15) 35.00
Sugar, Individual (3900/38) 25.00
Tray for Cream & Sugar (3900/37) 30.00
Tumbler, 13 oz. (3900/115) 50.00
Tumbler, 14 oz. (498) 65.00
Vase, 12" (Keyhole stem) (1238) 175.00
Vase, 6" (6004) 70.00
Vase, 9" (Keyhole stem) (1237) 140.00
Vase, Bud, 10" (274) 90.00
Vase, Footed (278) 120.00
Vase, Footed, 8" (6004) 70.00

Original Brochure: Chantilly
etching on ice bucket

CHATTERIS, No. 197

CUTTING

Date: 1927

Manufacturer: Fostoria Glass Co., Moundsville, WV

Colors: Crystal

STEMWARE:
No. 877
Claret, 4 oz. $18.00
Cocktail, 3½ oz. 15.00
Cordial, ¾ oz. 35.00
Goblet, 10 oz., 7⅞" tall 20.00
Oyster Cocktail, 4½ oz., 3¾" tall 12.00
Parfait 18.00
Sherbet, High, 6 oz., 6⅛" tall 18.00
Sherbet, Low, 6 oz., 4" tall 12.00
Tumbler, Footed, 5 oz. (juice) 12.00
Tumbler, Footed, 9 oz. (water) 12.00
Tumbler, Footed, 12 oz. (iced tea) 18.00
Whiskey, Footed, 2½ oz. 13.00
Wine, 2¾ oz. 18.00

ACCESSORIES:
Bowl, 12" (2394) $35.00
Candlesticks, 2", pr. (2394) 40.00
Comport, 6" (2400) 22.00
Cream, Footed (2350½) 18.00
Sugar, Footed (2350½) 18.00

Original Catalog Illustration: No. 197 Chatteris cutting
on No. 877 low sherbet

Original Catalog Illustration: No. 197 Chatteris cutting
on pressed bowl

FLOWERS *(continued)*

Original Catalog Illustration:
Chinese Garden rock crystal cutting
on No. D1 Mandarin goblet

Original Catalog Illustration:
No. 338 Chintz etching on plate

Original Catalog Illustration:
No. 338 Chintz etching on
footed jug

CHINESE GARDEN

ROCK CRYSTAL CUTTING

Date: 1950s

Manufacturer: Duncan & Miller Glass Co.,
Washington, PA

Colors: Crystal

STEMWARE

NO. D1 MANDARIN

Cocktail, Liquor, 3½ oz. $25.00
Goblet, 11 oz. 40.00
Iced Tea, Footed, 14 oz. 35.00
Orange Juice, Footed, 5 oz. 22.00
Oyster Cocktail, Footed, 4½ oz. 18.00
Saucer Champagne or
    Tall Sherbet, 5 oz. 30.00
Wine or Claret, 4 oz. 35.00

ACCESSORIES:

Bowl, Flared Flower, 12" (8) $50.00
Bowl, Flared Flower, 12½" (30½) 50.00
Bowl, Salad, 10½" (30½) 25.00

Candlesticks, 2-light, pr. (41) 95.00
Candy Box & Cover (5200) 75.00
Candy Jar & Cover (25) 70.00
Celery & Relish, 2-handled, 3 Compt.,
    Oblong, 12" (30) 40.00
Celery & Relish, 5-compartment,
    12" (31½) 40.00
Celery Tray, 11" (91) 40.00
Cheese & Cracker, 11" (30) 50.00
Comport, High Foot, 7½" (8) 60.00
Cream (38) 35.00
Mayonnaise (30) 40.00
Plate, 6" (30½) 20.00
Plate, 7½" (30½) 22.00
Plate, 8½" (30½) 22.00
Plate, Mayonnaise (30) 12.00
Plate, Torte, 14" (30½) 72.00
Relish, 5-compartment, 10" (31½) 50.00
Sandwich Tray, 2-handled, 11" (30) 60.00
Sugar (38) 35.00
Vase, Flip, 8" (30) 65.00

CHINTZ, NO. 338

PLATE ETCHING

Date: 1940

Manufacturer: Fostoria Glass Co.,
Moundsville, WV

Colors: Crystal

Notes: No. 2496 refers to Baroque blanks.

STEMWARE

NO. 6026 GREENBRIAR

Claret-Wine, 4½ oz., 5⅜" tall $55.00
Cocktail, 4 oz., 5" tall 30.00
Cocktail, Footed, 4 oz., 3⅝" tall 25.00
Cordial, 1 oz., 3⅞" tall 70.00
Goblet, 9 oz., 7⅝" tall 37.00
Goblet, Low, 9 oz., 6⅞" tall 30.00
Oyster Cocktail, 4 oz., 3⅝" tall 18.00
Saucer Champagne, 6 oz., 5½" tall 35.00
Sherbet, Low, 6 oz., 4⅜" tall 24.00
Tumbler, Footed, 5 oz.,
    4¾" tall (juice) 30.00
Tumbler, Footed, 13 oz.,
    6" tall (iced tea) 40.00

ACCESSORIES:

Bonbon, 7" $45.00
Bottle & Stopper,
    Salad Dressing, 7 oz. 85.00
Bowl, Footed, Handled, 5" 40.00
Bowl, Flared, Handled, 12" 130.00
Bowl, Handled, 10½" 95.00
Candlesticks, 2-light, pr. 90.00

Candlesticks, 3-light, pr. 145.00
Candlesticks, 4" or 5½", pr. 75.00
Candy Box & Cover,
    3-compartment 165.00
Celery, 11" (2496) 50.00
Compote, 5" 55.00
Cream Soup (2496) 32.00
Cream, Footed, 3¾" (2496) 32.00
Cream, Individual, 3⅛" tall (2496) 30.00
Cup & Saucer, Footed (2496) 50.00
Dish, Vegetable, 9½" (2496) 90.00
Finger Bowl, 4½" (869) 55.00
Fruit, 5" (2496) 40.00
Jug, Footed, 3 pt., 9⅜" tall (5000) 150.00
Mayonnaise, 3½" tall (2496½) 50.00
Oil & Stopper, 3½ oz. (2496) 85.00
Pickle, 8" (2496) 38.00
Plate, 6" or 7" (2496) 20.00
Plate, 8" (2496) 30.00
Plate, Cake, Handled, 10" 85.00
Plate, Cream Soup (2496) 18.00
Plate, Dinner, 9½" 65.00
Plate, Mayonnaise (2496½) 18.00
Plate, Torte, 16" 140.00
Platter, Oval, 12" (2496) 120.00
Salt & Pepper, 2¾", pr. (2496) 70.00
Sugar, Footed, 3½" (2496) 32.00
Sugar, Individual, 2⅞" tall (2496) 30.00
Tray for Sugar & Cream
    (Individual) (2496) 35.00
Tray, Center-handled, 11½" 65.00

CORDELIA, NO. 812

ROCK CRYSTAL ENGRAVING

Date: 1940s

Manufacturer: Cambridge Glass Co., Cambridge, OH

Colors: Crystal

STEMWARE:

NO. 3130
Claret, 4½"	$22.00
Cocktail, 3 oz.	15.00
Cordial, 1 oz.	55.00
Goblet, 9 oz.	22.00
Iced Tea, Footed, 12 oz.	18.00

Oyster Cocktail, 4½ oz.	12.00
Sherbet, Low, 7 oz.	11.00
Sherbet, Tall, 7 oz.	14.00
Tumbler, Footed, 5 oz. (juice)	14.00
Tumbler, Footed, 10 oz. (water)	15.00
Wine, 2½ oz.	22.00

ACCESSORIES:
Cocktail Icer, 2-piece (968)	$55.00
Plate, Salad, 7½"	11.00
Plate, Salad, 8½" (3400/62)	11.00

Catalog Illustration: No. 812
Cordelia rock crystal engraving
on No. 3130 stem

DIANE, NO. 752

PLATE ETCHING

Date: Ca. 1934

Manufacturer: Cambridge Glass Co., Cambridge, OH

Colors: Crystal, Amber, Crown Tuscan, Dianthus Pink, Emerald Green, Heatherbloom, Mandarin Gold, Moonlight Blue

Notes: Made for a long period of time, resulting in a great variety of pieces. Not all pieces were made in all colors. For pieces in Crown Tuscan, add 200+%. For other colors, add 100%.

STEMWARE:

NO. 1066 AURORA
Claret, 4½ oz.	$38.00
Cocktail, Low, 3 oz.	20.00
Cocktail, Tall, 3½ oz.	22.00
Cordial, 1 oz.	65.00
Goblet, 11 oz.	32.00
Oyster Cocktail, 5 oz.	17.00
Sherbet, Low, 7 oz.	18.00
Sherbet, Tall, 7 oz.	20.00
Tumbler, Footed, 3 oz. (whiskey)	30.00
Tumbler, Footed, 5 oz. (juice)	18.00
Tumbler, Footed, 9 oz. (water)	20.00
Tumbler, Footed, 12 oz. (Iced Tea)	25.00
Tumbler, Sham Bottom, 2½ oz.	40.00
Tumbler, Sham Bottom, 5 oz.	30.00
Tumbler, Sham Bottom, 7 oz.	35.00
Tumbler, Sham Bottom, 10 oz.	35.00
Tumbler, Sham Bottom, 12 oz.	38.00
Tumbler, Sham Bottom, 14 oz.	50.00
Wine, 3 oz.	35.00

NO. 3106
Brandy	$60.00
Claret, 4½ oz.	45.00
Cocktail, 3 oz.	20.00
Créme de Menthe, 2½ oz.	30.00
Finger Bowl	15.00
Goblet, Low Bowl, 10 oz.	30.00
Goblet, Tall Bowl, 9 oz.	35.00
Oyster Cocktail, 5 oz.	18.00
Plate, Finger Bowl	12.00
Pousse Café, 1 oz.	60.00

Sherbet, Low, 7 oz.	15.00
Sherbet, Tall, 7 oz.	18.00
Sherry, 2 oz.	70.00
Tumbler, Footed, 3 oz. (whiskey)	40.00
Tumbler, Footed, 5 oz. (juice)	20.00
Tumbler, Footed, 9 oz. (water)	22.00
Tumbler, Footed, 12 oz. (iced tea)	25.00
Wine, 2½ oz.	40.00

NO. 3122 (CRYSTAL ONLY)
Claret, 4½ oz.	$45.00
Cocktail, 3 oz.	20.00
Cordial, 1 oz.	65.00
Finger Bowl	15.00
Goblet, 9 oz.	30.00
Oyster Cocktail, 4½ oz.	18.00
Plate, Finger Bowl	12.00
Sherbet, Low, 7 oz.	17.00
Sherbet, Tall, 7 oz.	22.00
Tumbler, Footed, 2½ oz. (whiskey)	40.00
Tumbler, Footed, 5 oz. (juice)	18.00
Tumbler, Footed, 9 oz. (water)	20.00
Tumbler, Footed, 12 oz. (iced tea)	25.00
Wine, 2½ oz.	40.00

ACCESSORIES:
Baker, 10" (3500/51)	$52.00
Bowl, 4-toed, 11" (2400/45)	55.00
Bowl, Oval, 4-toed, 12" (3440/1240)	55.00
Candelabra, 3-light, Keyhole Stem, pr. (3400/638)	85.00
Candlesticks, 1-light, Keyhole Stem, pr. (3400/646)	55.00
Candlesticks, 2-light, Keyhole Stem, pr. (3400/647)	70.00
Cereal, 6" (3400/53)	32.00
Cream (3400/68)	18.00
Cream Soup (3400/55)	30.00
Cup & Saucer (3400/54)	30.00
Plate, 8½" (3400/62)	15.00
Plate, Bread & Butter, Square, 6" (3400/1174)	9.00
Platter, 2-handled, 13½" (3400/58)	85.00
Salt & Pepper, pr. (3400/77)	55.00
Sugar (3400/68)	18.00
Vase, 18" (1336)	85.00

Catalog Illustration: No. 752
Diane etching on No. 1066
Aurora goblet

Catalog Illustration: No. 752
Diane etching on creamer

119

FLOWERS *(continued)*

Catalog Illustration: No. 406
Double Columbine cutting on
glass and jug with cover

DOUBLE COLUMBINE, NO. 406

CUTTING

Date: Ca. 1930

Manufacturer: U.S. Glass Co., Tiffin, OH

Colors: Crystal, Crystal with Amber trim

STEMWARE
No. 15037

Café Parfait	$20.00
Claret	25.00
Cocktail	20.00
Cordial	55.00
Goblet	25.00
Saucer Champagne	20.00

Sundae (sherbet)	15.00
Table (tumbler)	20.00
Wine	25.00

ACCESSORIES:

Candleholders, pr. (9758)	$60.00
Cream (185)	20.00
Decanter & Stopper, Footed (185)	85.00
Finger Bowl (002)	15.00
Grapefruit (251)	25.00
Jug & Cover (194)	155.00
Sugar (185)	20.00

FAIRFAX, NO. 167

CUTTING

Date: 1922

Manufacturer: Fostoria Glass Co., Moundsville, WV

Colors: Crystal

Notes: Do not confuse this cutting with the pressed tableware pattern also called Fairfax and also made by Fostoria.

STEMWARE
No. 863

Brandy (Pousse Café)	$15.00
Café Parfait	13.00
Champagne, Hollow Stem (cut flutes)	13.00
Champagne, Tall	13.00
Claret	13.00
Cocktail, 3 oz. or 3½ oz.	15.00
Cordial	18.00
Creme de Menthe	12.00
Fruit	11.00
Goblet, 5 oz.or 10½ oz.	12.00

Goblet, Long Stem, 7 oz.	12.00
Goblet, Short Stem, 9 oz.	12.00
Rhine Wine	12.00
Roemer, 4½ oz. or 5½ oz.	15.00
Saucer Champagne	11.00
Sherry	12.00
Wine	12.00

ACCESSORIES:

Bonbon, 5½" (880)	$15.00
Finger Bowl (1769)	9.00
Iced Tea, 12 oz. (701)	12.00
Iced Tea, Handled, 12 oz. (4011)	15.00
Jug & Cover, No. 7, 60 oz. (2230)	85.00
Jug (303 or 2982)	70.00
Oyster Cocktail (837)	10.00
Parfait, 5½ oz. (661)	12.00
Plate, Finger Bowl, 6"	8.00
Salt, Individual, Footed (880)	18.00
Tumbler (701, 820 or 4011)	10.00

Catalog Illustration:
No. 167 Fairfax cutting on
finger bowl and plate

First Love etching on No. 5111½ Terrace stems

FIRST LOVE

PLATE ETCHING

Date: 1940s

Manufacturer: Duncan & Miller Glass Co., Washington, PA

Colors: Crystal

Notes: Made to harmonize with 1847 Rogers Bros. "First Love" Silverplate. This is Duncan's most popular etching, made in a wide variety of pieces. Note the small fan-shaped design between the floral sprays. No. 111 refers to Terrace blanks, No. 115 to Canterbury, No. 41 to Early American Sandwich, and No. 117 to Three Feathers. Price listings follow on the next page.

(continued) # FLOWERS

STEMWARE:

NO. 5111½ TERRACE

Claret, Tall Stem, 4½ oz., 6" tall $45.00
Cocktail, Liquor, 3½ oz., 4½" tall 45.00
Cordial, 1 oz., 3¾" tall 85.00
Finger Bowl, 4" 25.00
Goblet, Luncheon, Low, 10 oz.,
　5¾" tall 45.00
Goblet, Tall Stem, 10 oz. 6¾" tall 50.00
Ice Cream, Short Stem,
　Footed (sherbet), 5 oz., 4" tall 25.00
Iced Tea, Footed, 12 oz., 6½" tall 40.00
Iced Tea, Footed, 14 oz., 6¾" tall 45.00
Orange Juice, Footed, 5 oz.,
　5¼" tall 42.00
Oyster Cocktail, 4 oz., 3¾" tall 30.00
Pousse Café, 1 oz., 3¾" tall 75.00
Saucer Champagne, Tall Stem, 5 oz.,
　5" tall. 45.00
Whiskey, Footed, 3 oz., 4½" tall. 60.00
Wine, 3 oz., 5¼" tall 70.00

ACCESSORIES:

Ashtray, Club, 4" or 5" (12) $45.00
Ashtray, Rectangular, 3½" x 2½" (30). . . 35.00
Ashtray, Rectangular, 5" x 3¼" (30) 45.00
Ashtray, Rectangular, 6½" x 4¼" (30). . . 45.00
Basket, Oval, Handled, 10" (115) 195.00
Bowl, Crimped, 10½" (115). 85.00
Bowl, Deep Salad, 9" (111) 75.00
Bowl, Flared, 11" (111) 95.00
Bowl, Flared, 12" (115) 110.00
Bowl, Flared, Footed, 12" (111) 110.00
Bowl, Flower, Flared (6) 80.00
Bowl, Flower, Flared, 12" (6) 100.00
Bowl, Oval Flared, 13" (115) 120.00
Bowl, Oval Flower, 12" (117). 90.00
Bowl, Oval, 11½" (126). 110.00
Bowl, Salad Dressing, 2-compartment,
　5½" (30) 40.00
Bowl, Salad Dressing,
　2-compartment, 6" (111 or 115) 45.00
Bowl, Salad, Shallow, 11" (111) 65.00
Bowl, Scalloped, Footed, 10" (126). 80.00
Breakfast Set: 3 Pc. (Sugar, Cream,
　Individual Butter) (28) 95.00
Candelabra, 2-light, 6", pr. (30) 110.00
Candlesticks or Vase, 4", pr. (117) 85.00
Candlesticks, 2-light, 5", pr. (41) 170.00
Candlesticks, 2-light, 6", pr. (41) 85.00
Candlesticks, 3-light, 5", pr. (41) 175.00
Candlesticks, Low, 3", pr. (115) 70.00
Candlesticks, Low, 4" (111) 85.00
Candy Box & Cover,
　3-compartment, 6" (106) 80.00
Candy Box & Cover, 3-handled,
　8" (115) 85.00
Candy Jar & Cover, 7¼" (25) 80.00
Celery & Relish Tray, 2-handled
　Oblong, 12" (30) 75.00
Celery & Relish, 2-handled,
　3-compartment, 10½" (115) 75.00

Celery & Relish, 2-handled, 5
　Compartment, 10½" (111) 75.00
Celery Tray, 11" (91) 55.00
Celery Tray, 2-handled, 8" (111) 50.00
Celery, Oblong, 2-handled, 12" (30) 55.00
Cheese & Cracker, 2-piece, 11"
　(111 or 115) 110.00
Cigarette Box & Cover, Rectangular,
　4½" x 3½" (30) 90.00
Cocktail Shaker, 14 oz. or
　18 oz. (5200) 145.00
Cocktail Shaker, 32 oz., 9" (5200) 160.00
Cocktail Tumbler, 3½ oz.,
　3" tall (5200) 35.00
Cocktail Tumbler, Sham,
　3½ oz. (5200) 35.00
Comport, High Foot, 5½" (115) 65.00
Comport, Low, 4¾" tall (115) 50.00
Cream & Sugar, pr. (111 or 115) 100.00
Cream, Individual, 2½" tall (115). 40.00
Cup, Tea and Saucer (115) 55.00
Ice Bucket, 6" (30). 200.00
Jug, Ice Lip, 80 oz. (5202) 220.00
Lamp, Hurricane, l-light with
　Chimney, 15" each 225.00
Mayonnaise Bowl, Footed, Handled,
　5½" (111) 38.00
Mayonnaise, Crimped, 5½" (115) 40.00
Nappy, 1 Handled, Round, 5" (115). . . . 35.00
Nappy, 2-handled, Round, 6" (115) 38.00
Nappy, 2-handled, 6" (111) 38.00
Nappy, 2-handled, 10" (111) 65.00
Nappy, Basket Shape, 2-handled,
　6" (111) 110.00
Nappy, Square, 5½" or 7" (111) 45.00
Olive, 2-handled, Oval, 6" (115) 38.00
Pickle & Olive, 2-compartment,
　9" (115) 65.00
Plate with Ring, 7½" (30) 22.00
Plate, 14" (115) 95.00
Plate, 2-handled Lemon, 6" (111). 25.00
Plate, 2-handled Sandwich,
　11" (111 or 115) 75.00
Plate, Mayonnaise, 2-handled,
　7½" (115) 25.00
Plate, Bread & Butter, 6" (115) 25.00
Plate, Dessert, 7½" or 8½" Salad (115) . . 35.00
Plate, Deviled Egg, 12" (30) 85.00
Plate, Round, 6" or 7" (111) 45.00
Plate, Salad, Round, 8½" (111) 48.00
Plate, Salad, Square, 6" or 7½" (111) . . . 45.00
Plate, Sandwich, 2-handled,
　11" (111) 70.00
Plate, Torte, Flat or Rolled Edge,
　13" (111) 85.00
Relish, 2-handled, 2-compartment,
　Round, 6" (111 or 115) 45.00
Relish, 2-handled, 2-compartment,
　9" (111) 55.00
Relish, 2-handled, 3-compartment,
　9" (115) 60.00
Relish, 2-handled, 4-compartment.
　9" (111) 65.00

Catalog Illustration: First Love
etching on low candlestick

Catalog Illustration:
First Love etching on
hurricane lamp

Catalog Illustration: First Love
etching on torte plate

FLOWERS *(continued)*

Catalog Illustration:
First Love etching on 10" vase

Gold Lace etching on No. 2496
Baroque sugar

Gold Lace etching on
2-light candlestick

Catalog Illustration: Lily of the
Valley cutting on No. D4 goblet

Relish, Diamond Shape, 2-handled,
2-compartment, 7" (111) 60.00
Relish, 2-handled, 2-compartment,
6" (111) 45.00
Salad Dressing, 2-compartment,
4¾" tall (30) 38.00
Salt & Pepper, 3", pr. (30) 90.00
Sugar, Individual (115) 45.00
Tray for Sugar & Cream, 8" (115) 30.00
Tumbler, Sham, 5 oz. or 7 oz. (5200) 25.00
Tumbler, Sham, 10 oz. (5200) 37.00
Tumbler, Sham, 12 oz. or 14 oz. (5200) . . 40.00
Tumbler, Sham, 16 oz. or 18 oz. (5200) . . 45.00
Vase or Urn, 5" (525) 60.00
Vase or Urn, 7" (529) 75.00

Vase, 7" or 8" (5200 . . . . 95.00
Vase, 10" (5200) 120.00
Vase, Bud, 9" (506, 590 or 510) 125.00
Vase, Cornucopia, 4" (117) 50.00
Vase, Cornucopia, 8" (117) 75.00
Vase, Crimped, 5" (115) 45.00
Vase, Flared, 12" (115) 95.00
Vase, Footed, 6" or 8" (507) 60.00
Vase, Footed, 8" (505 or 506) 70.00
Vase, Footed, 10" (111) 75.00
Vase, Footed, 10" or 12"
(505, 506 or 507) 85.00
Vase, Square Shape, Footed, 11" (126) . . 95.00
Whiskey or Cordial Tumbler,
1½ oz., 2" tall (5200) 60.00

GOLD LACE, NO. 514

PLATE ETCHING

Date: 1938

Manufacturer: Fostoria Glass Co.,
Moundsville, WV

Colors: Crystal

Notes: When decorated with a gold edge it is
called No. 514 Italian Lace. No. 2496 refers to
Baroque blanks.

Candlesticks, 2-light, pr. $75.00
Candy Box & Cover, 3 pt., 7¼" (2496) . . 90.00
Celery, 11" (2496) 38.00
Cheese & Cracker, 2 pc., 11" (2496) . . . 45.00
Comport, 5½" (2496) 25.00
Cream, Footed (2496) 22.00

Dish, Oblong Sauce, 6½" (2496) 20.00
Mayonnaise, 2 pt., 6½" (2496) 30.00
Mayonnaise (2496½) 25.00
Nappy, Handled, 3-corner,
Flared or Square , 4⅝" (2496) 20.00
Pickle, 8" (2496) 22.00
Plate, Cake, 2-handled, 10" (12496) 35.00
Plate, Mayonnaise (2496½) 15.00
Plate, Torte, 14" (2496) 45.00
Relish, 3-part, 10" (2496) 35.00
Relish, Square, 2-part, 6" (2496) 22.00
Sugar, Footed (2496) 22.00
Sweetmeat, Square, 6" (2496) 22.00
Tray, Oblong, 8" (2496) 25.00

LILY OF THE VALLEY

CUTTING

Date: 1950s

Manufacturer: Duncan & Miller Glass Co.,
Washington, PA

Colors: Crystal

Notes: Designed by Robert A. May. Usually
found with satin finish on flowers of stem.
No. 115 indicates Canterbury blanks while
No. 30 refers to Pall Mall.

STEMWARE:

NO. D4 LILY OF THE VALLEY

Cocktail, Liquor, 3½ oz. $35.00
Goblet, 10 oz. 50.00
Iced Tea, Footed, 14 oz. 42.00
Orange Juice, Footed, 5 oz. 28.00
Oyster Cocktail, 4½ oz. 25.00
Saucer Champagne or
Tall Sherbet, 5 oz. 42.00
Wine or Claret, 4 oz. 50.00

ACCESSORIES:

Bowl, Flared (115) $70.00
Bowl, Flared Flower, 12" (8 or 30½) 78.00
Bowl, Salad, 10½" (30½) 72.00
Candlesticks, 2-light, pr. (41) 125.00
Candy Box & Cover (5200) 95.00
Candy Jar & Cover (25) 110.00
Celery & Relish, 2-handled,
3-compartment, Oblong, 12" (30) . . . 65.00
Celery & Relish, 5-compartment,
12" (31½) 75.00
Celery Tray, 11" (91) 55.00
Cheese & Cracker, 11" (30) 75.00
Comport, High Foot, 7½" (8) 65.00
Cream & Sugar, pr. (38) 90.00
Mayonnaise (30) 75.00
Plate, 6" (115) 27.00
Plate, 7½" or 8½" (115) 32.00
Plate, Mayonnaise (30) 20.00
Relish, 5-compartment, 10" (31½) 75.00
Sandwich Tray, 2-handled, 11" (30) 75.00
Vase, Flip, 8" (30) 100.00

LILY OF THE VALLEY, NO. 1069

ROCK CRYSTAL ENGRAVING

Date: 1940s
Manufacturer: Cambridge Glass Co., Cambridge, OH
Colors: Crystal

STEMWARE:

NO. 3790

Claret	$20.00
Cocktail	17.00
Cordial	55.00
Goblet	20.00
Iced Tea, Footed, 12 oz.	17.00
Oyster Cocktail or Sherbet, Low	11.00
Sherbet, Low	11.00
Tumbler, Footed, 5 oz. (juice)	14.00
Wine	20.00

Catalog Illustration:
No. 1069 Lily of the Valley on No. 3790 goblet

LORNA, NO. 748

PLATE ETCHING

Date: 1930

Manufacturer: Cambridge Glass Co., Cambridge, OH

Colors: Crystal, Amber, Emerald Green, Gold Krystol, Moonlight Blue, Peach Blo

Notes: most pressed pieces are from the Decagon line.

Catalog Illustration: No. 748 Lorna etching on bonbon

STEMWARE:

NO. 3015	Crystal	Colors
Cocktail, 2½ oz.	$10.00	$17.00
Finger Bowl	7.00	10.00
Fruit Salad, 6 oz.	7.00	10.00
Goblet, 9 oz.	15.00	25.00
Plate, Finger Bowl	8.00	10.00
Sherbet, Low, 6 oz.	7.00	10.00
Sherbet, Tall, 6 oz.	8.00	12.00
Tumbler, Footed, 5 oz.	8.00	14.00
Tumbler, Footed, 10 or 12 oz.	9.00	16.00
Wine, 2½ oz.	15.00	22.00

ACCESSORIES:

	Crystal	Colors
Bonbon, 2-handled, 6¼" (749)	$10.00	$18.00
Bowl, 12½" (4-toed) (993)	35.00	50.00
Bowl, 2-handled, 9" (1225)	25.00	42.00
Candy Box & Cover (864)	55.00	85.00
Celery, 2-handled, 11" (3400/87)	22.00	40.00
Comport, 7" (keyhole stem) (3400/28)	45.00	70.00
Cream & Sugar, pr. (867)	15.00	28.00
Cream & Sugar, pr. (1076)	36.00	56.00

	Crystal	Colors
Cream Soup (1075)	10.00	17.00
Cup & Saucer (865)	15.00	22.00
Fruit, 5½" (1098)	6.00	10.00
Globe Jar (vase), 5" (3400/102)	30.00	65.00
Ice Pail (851)	55.00	85.00
Jug, 64 oz. (935)	65.00	125.00
Jug, 67 oz. (3400/27)	75.00	150.00
Jug, 80 oz. (ball) (3400/38)	80.00	160.00
Plate, Salad, 8⅜" (597)	9.00	17.00
Plate, Sandwich 2-handled, 10" (1226)	22.00	35.00
Relish, 2-compartment, 2-handled, 8¾" (3400/88)	20.00	32.00
Relish, 2-part, 11" (1068)	18.00	25.00
Relish, Center Handle, 6" (1093)	25.00	38.00
Tumbler, 12 oz. (3400/27 or /38)	17.00	25.00
Vase, 7" (1303)	35.00	60.00
Vase, 9" or 9½" (1237 or 1233)	30.00	45.00
Vase, 10" (1284 or 1295)	30.00	45.00
Vegetable, Oval, 9½" (1087)	20.00	28.00

FLOWERS *(continued)*

Catalog Illustration: No. 168
Louisa cutting on jelly and cover

Catalog Illustration: No. 652
Lucerne cutting on No. 5317
Cathay goblet

Catalog Illustration:
No. 824 Lucia rock crystal
engraving on No. 3116 goblet

LOUISA, No. 168

CUTTING

Date: 1922

Manufacturer: Fostoria Glass Co.,
Moundsville, WV

Colors: Crystal

STEMWARE:

No. 661

Cocktail, 3 oz.	$8.00
Fruit, 6 oz., 3½" tall (low sherbet)	8.00
Goblet, 9 oz., 7" tall.	12.00
Parfait, 5½", 6" tall	9.00
Saucer Champagne, 6 oz., 4⅞" tall	9.00
Wine, 2 oz., 4¾" tall	9.00

ACCESSORIES:

Finger Bowl, Optic (1769)	$10.00
Grapefruit (945½)	15.00
Jelly & Cover, Optic, 7" (825)	25.00
Jug (303 or 317½)	75.00
Marmalade & Cover, Optic, 4½" (4087)	25.00
Plate, 8¼" (2283)	12.00
Plate, 11" (2283)	20.00
Plate, Finger Bowl (1736).	8.00
Salt & Pepper, pr. (2235)	25.00
Salt, Individual (2263)	15.00
Tumbler (4011 or 4085).	10.00

LUCERNE, No. 652

ROCK CRYSTAL CUTTING

Date: 1940s

Manufacturer: Duncan & Miller Glass Co.,
Washington, PA

Colors: Crystal

STEMWARE:

No. 5317 CATHAY

Claret, 5 oz., 5¾" tall	$30.00
Cocktail, Liquor, 3½ oz., 4" tall	30.00
Cordial, 1 oz., 3½" tall	70.00
Finger Bowl, 4½"	10.00
Goblet, 10 oz., 6¼" tall	45.00
Iced Tea, Footed, 12 oz., 7½" tall	38.00
Juice, Orange, Footed, 5 oz., 4¾" tall	24.00
Oyster Cocktail, 4½ oz., 3½" tall	20.00
Saucer Champagne, 5 oz., 4½" tall	40.00
Sherbet, Footed, 5 oz. 3½" tall	17.00
Tumbler, Footed, 9 oz., 5½" tall	32.00
Wine, 3 oz., 5" tall	45.00

ACCESSORIES:

Bowl, Deep Salad, 9" (33)	$55.00
Bowl, Flared, 12" (36)	68.00

Bowl, Low Foot, 13" (30)	68.00
Candlesticks, Low, 3" pr. (115)	75.00
Candlesticks, 2-light, pr. (30)	115.00
Candy Box & Cover, 3-compartment, 6½" (106)	85.00
Celery & Relish, Oblong, 2-handled, 12" (30)	45.00
Comport, Tall, 7½" or 6" (8 or 5317)	65.00
Cream & Sugar, pr. (38)	80.00
Finger Bowl (30)	15.00
Iced Cocktail Set, 2-piece or 3-piece (30)	85.00
Mayonnaise Set (8)	85.00
Plate, or Nappy, 2-handled, 6" (30)	35.00
Plate, Bread & Butter, 6" (30)	22.00
Plate, Dessert, 7½" or Salad, 8½" (30½)	25.00
Plate, Sandwich, 2-handled, 11" (30)	65.00
Plate, Torte, 13" (33)	80.00
Relish, 2-handled, 2-compartment, 6" (30)	35.00
Salad Dressing Set, 2-compartment, 6", 2-piece (30)	55.00
Vase, 10" (506)	90.00
Vase, Flip, Flared, 8" (30)	80.00

LUCIA, No. 824

ROCK CRYSTAL ENGRAVING

Date: 1940s

Manufacturer: Cambridge Glass Co.,
Cambridge, OH

Colors: Crystal

STEMWARE:

No. 3116

Cocktail, 3 oz.	$15.00
Goblet, 10 oz.	20.00
Iced Tea, Footed, 12 oz.	17.00
Oyster Cocktail, 4½ oz.	10.00
Sherbet, Low, 6 oz..	10.00
Sherbet, Tall, 6 oz.	17.00
Tumbler, Footed, 5 oz. (juice)	15.00

Tumbler, Footed, 10 oz. (water)	16.00
Wine, 3 oz.	20.00

ACCESSORIES:

Bowl, 4-footed, Flared, 12" (3900/62)	$45.00
Candlesticks, 2-light, 6", pr. (3900/72)	65.00
Celery & Relish, 3-part, 12" (3900/126)	45.00
Celery & Relish, 3-part, 8" (3900/125)	40.00
Celery & Relish, 5-part, 12" (3900/120)	45.00
Comport, Blown, 5⅜" (3121)	50.00
Cream & Sugar, pr. (3900/41)	40.00
Mayonnaise & Plate, pr. (3900/111)	37.00
Plate, Rolled Edge, 14" (3900/166)	45.00
Plate, Salad, 8" (3900/22)	12.00

(continued) **FLOWERS**

MAYTIME, NO. 698

ROCK CRYSTAL CUTTING

Date: 1940s

Manufacturer: Duncan & Miller Glass Co.,
Washington, PA

Colors: Crystal

Notes: No. 115 refers to pressed Canterbury.

STEMWARE:

NO. 5115 CANTERBURY (BLOWN)
Claret, 5 oz., 6¾" tall $30.00
Cocktail, Liquor, 3 oz., 5¼" tall 30.00
Cordial, 1 oz., 4¼" tall 70.00
Goblet, 10 oz., 7¼" tall 45.00

Iced Tea, Footed, 12 oz., 5¾" tall 38.00
Orange Juice, Footed, 5 oz., 4¼" tall . . . 24.00
Oyster Cocktail, Footed, 4 oz.,
   3¼" tall 20.00
Saucer Champagne, 5 oz., 5½" tall 35.00
Sherbet, Footed, 5 oz., 2¼" tall 17.00
Tumbler, Footed, 10 oz., 4½" tall 32.00
Wine, 3½ oz., 6" tall 45.00

ACCESSORIES:
Plate, 6" (115) $22.00
Plate, 7½" or 8½" (115) 25.00

Catalog Illustration:
No. 698 Maytime cutting on
No. 5115 Canterbury goblet and
saucer champagne

MILLEFLEUR, NO. 195

CUTTING

Date: 1929

Manufacturer: Fostoria Glass Co.,
Moundsville, WV

Colors: Crystal

Notes: Available on No. 2419 Mayfair and
No. 2350 Pioneer dinner services.

STEMWARE:

NO. 4020
Claret, 4 oz. $30.00
Cocktail, 4 oz., 3⅝" tall 18.00
Goblet, 11 oz., 5¾" tall 30.00
Iced Tea, Footed, 16 oz., 6" tall 25.00
Juice, Footed, 5 oz., 4⅛" tall 24.00
Sherbet, Low, 5 oz., 2⅞" tall 22.00

Sherbet, Low, 6 oz., 3" tall 22.00
Sherbet, Tall, 7 oz., 4⅜" tall 30.00
Tumbler, Footed, 10 oz., 5" tall 22.00
Tumbler, Footed, 13 oz., 5" tall 28.00
Whiskey, 2 oz., 2⅛" tall 30.00
Wine, 3 oz. 30.00

ACCESSORIES:
Cream & Sugar, pr. (4020) $50.00
Cream Soup (2350) 25.00
Cup & Saucer, After Dinner (2350) 38.00
Cup & Saucer, Footed (2350½) 30.00
Finger Bowl (4021 or 4121) 14.00
Jug, Footed (4020) 95.00
Plate, 9" (2350) 22.00

Catalog Illustration:
No. 195 Millefleur cutting on
after dinner cup & saucer

MONTROSE, NO. 1004

ROCK CRYSTAL ENGRAVING

Date: 1940s

Manufacturer: Cambridge Glass Co.,
Cambridge, OH

Colors: Crystal

STEMWARE:

NO. 3700
Claret, 4½ oz. $30.00
Cocktail, 3 oz. 15.00
Cordial, 1 oz. 55.00
Goblet, 9 oz. 20.00

Iced Tea, Footed, 12 oz. 17.00
Oyster Cocktail, 4½ oz. 10.00
Sherbet, Low, 6 oz.. . . . . 11.00
Sherbet, Tall, 6 oz. 15.00
Tumbler, Footed, 5 oz. (juice) 13.00
Tumbler, Footed, 10 oz. (water) 16.00
Wine, 2½ oz.. 20.00

ACCESSORIES:
Plate, Salad, 7½" (555) $12.00

Catalog Illustration:
No. 1004 Montrose rock crystal
engraving on No. 3700 goblet

FLOWERS (continued)

Original Company Brochure:
Moonstone cutting on
No. 17684 goblet

Original Brochure:
No. 965 Narcissus cutting on
No. 3408 Jamestown goblet

MOONSTONE

CUTTING

Date: 1950s

Manufacturer: U.S. Glass Co., Tiffin, OH

Colors: Crystal

Notes: "Star-traced fantasy in this dainty yet most luxurious Tiffin cutting"—original Tiffin brochure.

STEMWARE:
No. 17684
Champagne/Sherbet $30.00
Claret 35.00

Cocktail 30.00
Cordial 70.00
Goblet 35.00
Iced Tea 30.00
Juice 20.00

ACCESSORIES:
Finger Bowl $15.00
Nappy, Dessert 15.00
Plate, Salad, 8" 18.00

NARCISSUS, No. 965

ROCK CRYSTAL CUTTING

Date: 1941

Manufacturer: A.H. Heisey & Co., Newark, OH

Colors: Crystal

Notes: Many tableware items were made in No. 1519 Waverly pressed tableware. "Spring or no, a young woman's fancy turns to thoughts of love...and to NARCISSUS, the exquisite Heisey rock crystal cutting." —Heisey pattern folder.

STEMWARE:
No. 3408 JAMESTOWN
Bell, Dinner $215.00
Claret, 4½ oz. 65.00
Cocktail, 3 oz. 50.00
Cordial, 1 oz. 120.00
Finger Bowl 25.00
Goblet, 9 oz. 65.00
Iced Tea, Footed, 12 oz. 52.00
Oyster Cocktail, 4½ oz. 25.00
Parfait, 5 oz. 50.00
Saucer Champagne, 6 oz. 52.00
Sherbet, 6 oz. 25.00
Sherry, 1½ oz. 120.00
Soda, Footed, 5 oz. (also 3408½) 45.00
Soda, Footed, 13 oz. 52.00
Tumbler, Footed, 9 oz. 45.00
Wine, 2 oz. 65.00

ACCESSORIES:
Bar, 2 oz. (2401) $38.00
Bottle, French Dressing, 8 oz. (5031) . . 125.00
Bowl, Combination Dressing,
 6½" or 8" (1519) 50.00
Bowl, Floral, Crimped (1519) 95.00
Bowl, Gardenia, 13" (1519) 95.00
Bowl, Salad, 9" (1519) 95.00
Box, Trinket & Cover, 6½",
 Lion finial (1519) 475.00
Butter & Cover (1519) 170.00

Candelabra, 1-light, 7½", pr. (1509) . . . 185.00
Candlesticks, 1-light, pr. (112) 70.00
Candlesticks, 2-light, pr. (134 or 1519) . . . 95.00
Candlesticks, 3-light, pr. (142 or 1519) . . 135.00
Candy Box & Cover, 5" (1519) 110.00
Celery, 12" or 13" (1519) 45.00
Champagne, Hollow Stem, 6 oz. (3304) . . 50.00
Cocktail Icer & Liner (3304) 75.00
Comport, Low, Footed, 6" (1519) 60.00
Comport, Oval, Footed, 6" (1519) 70.00
Cream, Footed (1519 or 1951) 50.00
Cream, Individual (1519) 60.00
Cup & Saucer (1509 or 1519) 70.00
Decanter & Stopper, 1 pt. (4036) 90.00
Dish, Honey or Cheese, 6½" (1519) 60.00
Iced Tea, 12 oz. (2351) 30.00
Jelly, Footed, Handled, 6" (1509) 35.00
Jug, ½ gal. (3484) 195.00
Jug, Ice, 73 oz. (4164) 195.00
Mayonnaise, Footed (1519) 50.00
Mint, Footed, 6" (1509) 40.00
Oil & Stopper, 3 oz. (1519) 150.00
Plate, 10½" (1519) 145.00
Plate, Mayonnaise (1519) 18.00
Plate, Salad (1184 or 1519) 22.00
Plate, Sandwich, 14" (1519) 65.00
Plate, Torte, 11" (1519) 55.00
Plate, Torte, 14" (1519) 90.00
Relish, 3-compartment, 11" (1519) 60.00
Relish, 4-compartment, Round,
 9" (1519) 60.00
Salt & Pepper, pr. (57 or 1519) 125.00
Sandwich, Center-handled,
 12" (1509 or 1519) 58.00
Salver, Footed, 12" (1519) 145.00
Sugar, Footed (1519 or 1951) 50.00
Sugar, Individual (1519) 60.00
Tray, Social Hour, 15" (1509) 110.00
Vase, Bud, 6" (4191) 60.00
Vase, Footed, 7" (1519) 85.00
Vase, Footed, 9" (4192½) 90.00
Vase, Tall (4192) 90.00

NAVARRE, NO. 327

PLATE ETCHING

Date: 1937

Manufacturer: Fostoria Glass Co., Moundsville, WV

Colors: Crystal, Azure, Pink

Notes: No. 2496 refers to Baroque blanks. "Henry the Fourth of Navarre and France founded the Bourbon dynasty which inspired this lovely design: an unusually fine Master-Etching of aristocratic charm." —From a Fostoria ad, 1937. Prices are for Crystal. For colors add 50% to 75%.

STEMWARE:

NO. 6016 WILMA

Brandy Inhaler, 15 oz., 5½" $65.00
Champagne, Continental, 5 oz., 8⅛" tall 65.00
Claret, 4 oz. or 4½ oz., 6" tall 45.00
Claret, Large, 6½ oz., 6¼" tall 50.00
Cocktail, 3½ oz., 5¼" tall 32.00
Cocktail/Sherry, 6 oz., 6³⁄₁₆" tall 65.00
Cordial, ¾ oz. or 1 oz., 3⅞" tall 85.00
Goblet, 9 oz. or 10 oz., 7⅝" tall 60.00
Oyster Cocktail, 4 oz., 3⅝" tall 30.00
Saucer Champagne, 5½" oz. or 6 oz., 5⅝" tall 32.00
Sherbet, Low, 5½ oz. or 6 oz., 4⅜" tall .. 30.00
Tumbler, Footed, 5 oz., 4⅝" tall (juice) .. 35.00
Tumbler, Footed, 10 oz., 5⅜" tall (water) 37.00
Tumbler, Footed, 13 oz., 5⅞" tall (iced tea) 55.00
Wine, 3 oz. or 3¼ oz., 5¼" tall 60.00

ACCESSORIES:

Bell, Dinner $70.00
Bonbon, 3-toed, 7⅜" (2496) 32.00
Bottle, Salad Dressing, 7 oz., 6½" tall (2083) 450.00
Bowl, 10½" (2470½) 68.00
Bowl, Handled, 10½" (2946) 75.00
Bowl, Nut, Cupped, 3-toed, 6¼" (2496) 24.00
Candlesticks, 5½", pr. (2496) 90.00
Candlesticks, Duo, 4½". pr. (2496) 90.00
Candlesticks, Duo, 5", pr. (2472) 120.00
Candlesticks, Trindle, 6", pr. (2496) ... 125.00
Candlesticks, Trindle, 6¾", pr. (2482) . 145.00
Candy Box & Cover, 3 pt., 6¼" (2496) .. 145.00
Celery, 11" (2496) 55.00
Cheese & Cracker, 11" (2496) 75.00
Comport, 5½" (2496) 38.00
Cream, Footed, 4¼" (2440) 24.00
Cream, Individual, 3⅛" (2496) 22.00
Cup & Saucer (2440) 30.00
Finger Bowl (869) 55.00
Floating Garden, 10" (2496) 65.00
Ice Bucket, 4⅜" x 6½" (2496) (2 styles) 165.00
Jug, Footed, 9¾" tall (5000) 420.00
Luster, "Flame", 7½", pr. (2545) 165.00
Nappy, Handled, 3 Corner, 4⅝" (2496) .. 18.00
Nappy, Handled, Flared, 5" (2496) 18.00
Nappy, Handled, Regular, 4⅜" (2496) .. 18.00
Nappy, Handled, Square, 4" (2496) 18.00
Pickle (2 styles) 35.00
Plate, 6" (2364) 13.00
Plate, 6" or 7" (2440) 18.00
Plate, 8" (2440) 27.00
Plate, Cake, 2-handled (2496) 60.00
Relish, 2-part, Square, 6" (2496) 40.00
Relish, 3-part, 10" (2496) 55.00
Relish, 4-part, 10" (2496) 60.00
Relish, 5-part, 13¼" (2419) 100.00
Salt & Pepper, Footed, 3½", pr. (2375) .. 150.00
Salt & Pepper, pr. (2364) 140.00
Sugar, Footed, 3½" (2440) 22.00
Sugar, Individual, 2⅞" (2496) 20.00
Syrup (2586) 450.00
Tid Bit, 3-toed, 8¼" (2496) 28.00
Vase, 5" (3 styles) 120.00
Vase, 10" (2470) 185.00

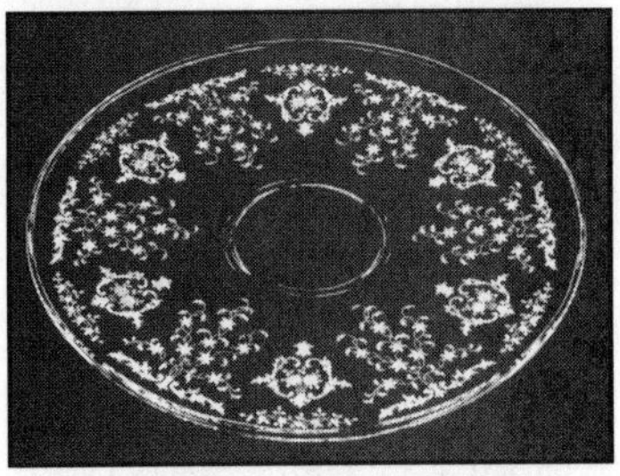

Navarre design on plate

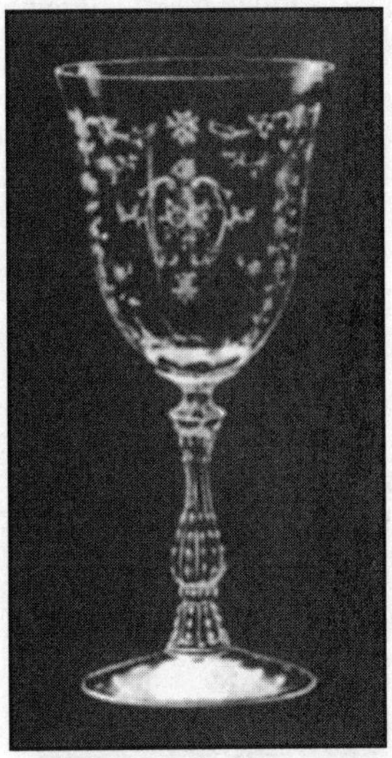

Navarre design on No. 6016 Wilma goblet

NO. 279

CUTTING

Date: 1940s

Manufacturer: Imperial Glass Corporation, Bellaire, OH

Colors: Crystal

Notes: It is likely that more items in Candlewick were cut with this design.

STEMWARE:

NO. 3400 CANDLEWICK

Claret $65.00
Cocktail, Stem 24.00
Goblet 32.00
Sherbet, Tall 22.00
Tumbler, Footed, 12 oz. 21.00

ACCESSORIES:

Bowl, Salad (400/75B) $40.00
Cream & Sugar, Footed, pr. (400/31) ... 48.00
Finger Bowl (3400) 18.00
Mayonnaise (400/52) 20.00
Oil or Vinegar & Stopper (400/119) 60.00
Plate, Dinner, 10½" (400/10D) 50.00
Plate, for Salad Set (400/65B) 14.00
Plate, Mayonnaise (400) 14.00
Salt & Pepper, pr. (400/96) 18.00
Vase, Fan, 8" (400/87F) 37.00

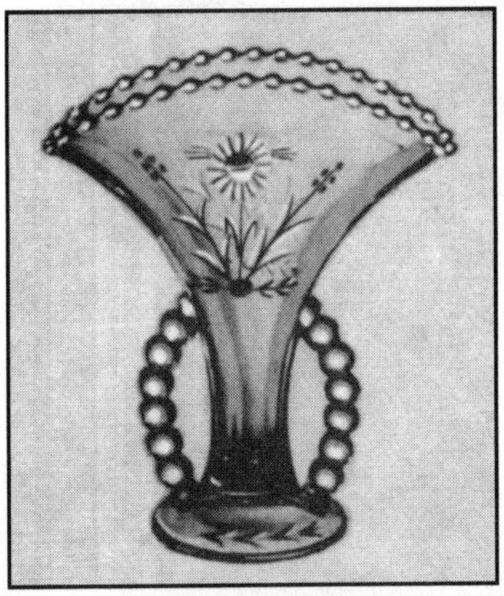

Catalog Illustration:
No. 279 cutting on No. 3400 Candlewick fan vase

FLOWERS *(continued)*

Catalog Illustration:
No. 603 rock crystal engraving
on No. 3122 goblet

NO. 603

ROCK CRYSTAL ENGRAVING

Date: 1930s

Manufacturer: Cambridge Glass Co.,
Cambridge, OH

Colors: Crystal

STEMWARE:

No. 3122

Claret, 4½ oz.	$20.00
Cocktail, 3 oz.	15.00
Cordial, 1 oz.	50.00

Fruit Salad, 7 oz.	12.00
Goblet, 9 oz.	20.00
Oyster Cocktail, 4½ oz.	12.00
Sherbet, Low, 7 oz.	12.00
Sherbet, Tall, 7 oz.	16.00
Wine, 2½ oz.	20.00
Tumbler, Footed, 2½ oz.	15.00
Tumbler, Footed, 5 oz.	15.00
Tumbler, Footed, 7 oz.	18.00
Tumbler, Footed, 9 oz.	18.00
Tumbler, Footed, 12 oz.	20.00

Original Catalog Illustration:
No. 611 rock crystal engraving
on No. 3124 goblet

NO. 611

ROCK CRYSTAL ENGRAVING

Date: 1930s

Manufacturer: Cambridge Glass Co.,
Cambridge, OH

Colors: Crystal

STEMWARE:

No. 3124

Claret, 4½ oz.	$20.00
Cocktail, 3 oz.	15.00

Goblet, 10 oz.	20.00
Oyster Cocktail, 4½ oz.	12.00
Sherbet, Low, 7 oz.	12.00
Sherbet, Tall, 7 oz.	16.00
Wine, 3 oz.	20.00
Tumbler, Footed, 3 oz.	15.00
Tumbler, Footed, 5 oz.	15.00
Tumbler, Footed, 10 oz.	18.00
Tumbler, Footed, 12 oz.	18.00

Original Catalog Illustration:
No. 613 rock crystal engraving
on No. 3035 goblet

NO. 613

ROCK CRYSTAL ENGRAVING

Date: 1930s

Manufacturer: Cambridge Glass Co.,
Cambridge, OH

Colors: Crystal

STEMWARE:

No. 3035

Claret, 4½ oz.	$20.00
Cocktail, 3 oz.	16.00
Cordial, 1 oz.	50.00

Fruit Salad, 6 oz.	14.00
Goblet, 9 oz.	18.00
Oyster Cocktail, 4½ oz.	14.00
Sherbet, Low, 6 oz.	9.00
Sherbet, Tall, 6 oz.	11.00
Tumbler, Footed, 2½ oz.	15.00
Tumbler, Footed, 5 oz.	11.00
Tumbler, Footed, 8 oz.	11.00
Tumbler, Footed 10 oz.	12.00
Tumbler, Footed, 12 oz.	12.00
Wine, 2½ oz.	15.00

(continued) # FLOWERS

No. 614

ROCK CRYSTAL ENGRAVING

Date: 1930s

Manufacturer: Cambridge Glass Co., Cambridge, OH

Colors: Crystal

STEMWARE:
No. 3035
Claret, 4½ oz. $20.00
Cocktail, 3 oz. 15.00
Cordial, 1 oz. 50.00

Fruit Salad, 6 oz. 12.00
Goblet, 9 oz. 20.00
Oyster Cocktail, 4½ oz. 12.00
Sherbet, Low, 6 oz. 12.00
Sherbet, Tall, 6 oz. 16.00
Tumbler, Footed, 2½ oz. (whiskey) 20.00
Tumbler, Footed, 5 oz. (juice) 16.00
Tumbler, Footed, 8 oz. (water) 16.00
Tumbler Footed, 10 oz. (water). 16.00
Tumbler, Footed, 12 oz. (iced tea). 18.00
Wine, 2½ oz.. 25.00

Original Catalog Illustration:
No. 614 rock crystal engraving
on No. 3035 goblet

No. 661

ROCK CRYSTAL ENGRAVING

Date: 1930s

Manufacturer: Cambridge Glass Co., Cambridge, OH

Colors: Crystal

STEMWARE:
No. 3122
Claret, 4½ oz. $20.00
Cocktail, 3 oz. 15.00

Cordial, 1 oz. 50.00
Fruit Salad, 7 oz. 12.00
Goblet, 9 oz. 20.00
Oyster Cocktail, 4½ oz. 12.00
Sherbet, Low, 7 oz.. . . . . 12.00
Sherbet, Tall, 7 oz. 16.00
Tumbler, 5 oz. or 7 oz. 15.00
Tumbler, Footed, 9 oz. or 12 oz. 18.00
Wine, 2½ oz.. 20.00

Catalog Illustration: No. 661
rock crystal engraving on
No. 3122 goblet

PRELUDE

PLATE ETCHING

Date: Ca. 1947

Manufacturer: Viking Glass Co., New Martinsville, WV

Colors: Crystal

Notes: Author James Measell attributes this etching exclusively to the Viking Glass Co. beginning in 1947-1948. Since Viking was the successor to the New Martinsville Glass Co., many of the pieces on which Prelude is etched are from original New Martinsville molds. There appear to be two styles of stemware: one with a plain stem, the other with a ball-shaped knop. The following list is incomplete, but gives representative pieces and values.

Bonbon (1009) $17.00
Bowl, 13" (5201) 42.00
Bowl, Crimped, 10" (1003) 38.00

Candlesticks, 2-light, pr.. . . . . 70.00
Cocktail Shaker 120.00
Cream & Sugar, pr. (5247) 30.00
Goblet (ball knop) 25.00
Iced Tea, Footed. 22.00
Jug 200.00
Plate, 2-handled, 13" 32.00
Plate, 14" (5217) 32.00
Plate, 3-toed (1091) 30.00
Plate, Lemon (1010) 20.00
Relish, 3-part, 10" (5238). 32.00
Relish, 5-part, 13" (5287). 38.00
Salt & Pepper, pr. (13) 45.00
Salver, Cake, 11" (5226). 48.00
Sandwich Tray, Center Harp
   Handle, 11" 38.00
Sherbet 12.00
Vase, 8" (7539) 35.00

Prelude etching on sherbet

Detail of Prelude etching

FLOWERS *(continued)*

Catalog Illustration: No. 651
Rhapsody cutting on No. 5317
Cathay goblet

RHAPSODY, NO. 651

ROCK CRYSTAL CUTTING

Date: 1940s

Manufacturer: Duncan & Miller Glass Co., Washington, PA

Colors: Crystal

Notes: Nos. 30 and 30½ refer to the Pall Mall line.

STEMWARE:
NO. 5317 CATHAY
Claret, 5 oz., 5¾" tall	$30.00
Cocktail, Liquor, 3½ oz., 4" tall	30.00
Cordial, 1 oz., 3½" tall	70.00
Finger Bowl, 4½"	15.00
Goblet, 10 oz., 6¼" tall	45.00
Ice Cream, Footed (sherbet), 5 oz., 3½" tall	17.00
Iced Tea, Footed, 12 oz., 6½" tall	38.00
Juice, Orange, Footed, 5 oz., 4¾" tall	24.00
Oyster Cocktail, 4½ oz., 3½" tall	20.00
Saucer Champagne, 5 oz., 4½" tall	40.00
Tumbler, Footed, 9 oz., 5½" tall	22.00
Wine, 3 oz., 5" tall	45.00

ACCESSORIES:
Bowl, Deep Salad, 9" (33)	$55.00
Bowl, Flared, 12" (36)	68.00
Bowl, Low Foot, 13" (30)	68.00
Candlesticks, Low, 3" pr. (115)	75.00
Candlesticks, 2-light, pr. (30)	115.00
Candy Box & Cover, 3-compartment, 6½" (106)	85.00
Celery & Relish, Oblong, 2-handled, 12" (30)	45.00
Comport, 6" (5317)	65.00
Comport, Tall, 7½" (8)	65.00
Cream (38)	40.00
Finger Bowl (30)	15.00
Iced Cocktail Set, 2-piece or 3-piece (30)	85.00
Mayonnaise Set (8)	85.00
Nappy, 2-handled, 6" (30)	25.00
Plate, 2-handled, 6" (30)	30.00
Plate, Bread & Butter, 6" (30½)	22.00
Plate, Dessert, 7½" (30½)	25.00
Plate, Salad, 8½" (30½)	25.00
Plate, Sandwich, 2-handled, 11" (30)	65.00
Plate, Torte, 13" (33)	80.00
Relish, 2-handled, 2-compartment, 6" (30)	35.00
Salad Dressing Set, 2-compartment, 2-piece, 6" (30)	35.00
Sugar (38)	40.00
Vase, 10" (506)	90.00
Vase, Flip, Flared, 8" (30)	80.00

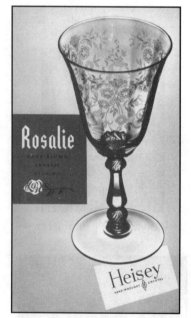

Company Brochure: No. 497
Rosalie etching on No. 3408
Jamestown goblet

ROSALIE, NO. 497

PLATE ETCHING

Date: 1937

Manufacturer: A.H. Heisey & Co., Newark, OH

Colors: Crystal

Notes: No. 1401 refers to Empress tableware. No. 1509 refers to Queen Ann tableware. The difference in these patterns is as follows: 1. Empress comes in many colors, 2. Empress has no optic but Queen Ann has a thick, undulating optic on most pieces. No. 1495 refers to Fern accessories. Note the small cornucopia in the midst of the flowers—making identification easy. "This is ROSALIE...Heisey's floral pattern that's delicately etched with rose petals and leaves. Reminiscent of the charm and fragrance of a formal garden, ROSALIE'S complete line of stemware and table accessories wins lasting envious admiration for the hostess whose table it graces."—Heisey pattern folder.

STEMWARE:
NO. 3408 JAMESTOWN
Bell, Dinner	$195.00
Claret, 4½ oz.	28.00
Cocktail, 3 oz.	20.00
Cordial, 1 oz.	75.00
Goblet, 9 oz.	30.00
Iced Tea, Footed, 12 oz. (3408½)	16.00
Juice, Footed, 5 oz. (3408½)	15.00
Oyster Cocktail, 4 oz.	15.00
Saucer Champagne, 6 oz.	22.00
Sherbet, 6 oz.	15.00
Sherry, 1½ oz.	75.00
Soda, Footed, 13 oz. (Iced Tea)	16.00
Tumbler, Footed, 9 oz. (water)	16.00
Wine, 2 oz.	30.00

NO. 4091 KIMBERLY
Claret, 4½ oz.	$35.00
Cocktail, 3 oz.	30.00
Cordial, 1 oz.	95.00

(continued) # FLOWERS

Finger Bowl (3335) 15.00
Goblet, 10 oz. 35.00
Oyster Cocktail, 4½ oz. (3542) 15.00
Rhine Wine, 6 oz. 50.00
Saucer Champagne, 5½ oz. 28.00
Sherbet, 5½ oz. 20.00
Soda, Footed, 5 oz. (4091½) 18.00
Soda, Footed, 12 oz. (4091½) 22.00
Wine, 2 oz. 50.00

No. 4092 Kenilworth
Brandy, Tall Stem, ¾ oz. $85.00
Claret, 4½ oz. 40.00
Cocktail, 3 oz. 30.00
Compote 80.00
Cordial, Tall Stem, 1 oz. 85.00
Finger Bowl (3333) 20.00
Goblet, 10 oz. 40.00
Oyster Cocktail, 3 oz. 15.00
Saucer Champagne, 5½ oz. 25.00
Sherbet, 5½ oz. 15.00
Sherry, Tall Stem, 1½ oz. 85.00
Soda, Footed, 12 oz.
 (iced tea) (4092½) 28.00
Soda, Footed, 5 oz. (juice) (4092½) 25.00
Wine, 2 oz. 40.00

No. 5009 Queen Ann
Cocktail, 3½ oz. $32.00
Finger Bowl (3309) 20.00
Goblet, 10 oz. 45.00
Oyster Cocktail, 4 oz. 20.00
Saucer Champagne, 6 oz. 38.00
Soda or Iced Tea, Footed, 12 oz. 28.00
Soda, Footed, 5 oz. (juice) 25.00
Wine, 2½ oz. 45.00

Accessories:
Bonbon, Handled (1495) $20.00
Bowl, Floral, 11" (1401 or 1509) 100.00
Bowl, Floral, 2-handled, Footed,
 8½" (1509) 45.00
Bowl, Fruit, Handled, 13" (1495) 65.00
Bowl, Oval Floral, Handled,
 11" (1495) 55.00
Bowl, Salad, Handled, 11" (1495) 65.00
Bowl, Sauce, Handled (1495) 25.00
Candlesticks, 2-light, 5", pr. (134) 75.00
Candlesticks, 2-light, pr. (1495) 140.00
Celery Tray, 11" (1509) 25.00
Celery Tray, 13" (1509) 30.00
Champagne, Hollow Stem,
 6 oz. (3304) 45.00
Cheese & Cracker & Cover,
 15" (1495) 100.00

Cheese & Cracker, 2-piece,
 12" (1509/1447) 75.00
Cheese, Handled, 6" (1495) 20.00
Combination Dressing, 6½" (1509) . . . 45.00
Comport, High Footed, 7" (3368) 95.00
Comport, Oval, 7" (1509) 55.00
Cream (1401 or 1509) 55.00
Cream (1495) 32.00
Cream, Individual (1401 or 1509) 35.00
Cream, Individual (1495) 45.00
Cup & Saucer (1401 or 1509) 45.00
Dish, Jello, Handled & Footed (1495) . . 60.00
Ice Bucket (1401 or 1509) 100.00
Jelly, 2-handled, Footed,
 6" (1401 or 1509) 24.00
Jelly, Handled, 6" (1495) 20.00
Lemon & Cover, 6½" (1401 or 1509) . . 60.00
Mayonnaise, 5½" (1401 or 1509) 40.00
Mayonnaise, Twin, Handled, 6" (1495) . . 30.00
Mint, Footed, 6" (1401 or 1509) 22.00
Mint, Handled, 6" (1495) 20.00
Nappy, Footed, 7½" (1401 or 1509) 45.00
Nappy, Handled, 4½" (1495) 20.00
Old Fashioned, 8 oz. (2401) 18.00
Pickle & Olive Tray, 11" (1509) 25.00
Pickle & Olive Tray, 13" (1509) 30.00
Plate, 15" (1495) 60.00
Plate, Buffet, 16" (1184) 75.00
Plate, Buffet, 16" (1401) 75.00
Plate, Mayonnaise, 8" (1495) 12.00
Plate, Mayonnaise, Round,
 6" (1401 or 1509) 15.00
Plate, Round or Square,
 7" (1401 or 1509) 18.00
Plate, Round or Square, 8" (1401) 30.00
Plate, Sandwich, 13" (1495) 40.00
Plate, Sandwich, 2-handled, Round,
 12" (1401 or 1509) 42.00
Plate, Torte, Handled, 13" or
 14" (1495) 65.00
Relish, 3-compartment,
 Handled & Footed, 10½" (1495) . . . 60.00
Relish, Triplex, 7" (1401 or 1509) 30.00
Sugar (1401 or 1509) 55.00
Sugar (1495) 32.00
Sugar, Individual (1401 or 1509) 35.00
Sugar, Individual (1495) 45.00
Tid Bit, Handled, 6" (1495) 20.00
Tray for Cream & Sugar,
 8" (1401 or 1509) 60.00
Tray, Social Hour, 15" (1509) 65.00
Whipped Cream or Mayonnaise,
 6" (1495) 32.00

Company Brochure: No. 497
Rosalie etching on assorted pieces

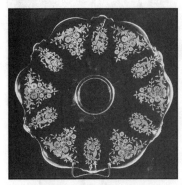

Rosalie etching on No. 1509
Queen Ann torte plate

Detail of Rosalie etching

FLOWERS *(continued)*

Original Catalog Illustration:
Rose Point etching on No. 3121
footed iced tea

Rose Point etching on
No. 3900/671 ice bucket

Original Catalog Illustration:
Rose Point etching on
cocktail shaker

ROSE POINT

PLATE ETCHING

Date: 1935

Manufacturer: Cambridge Glass Co., Cambridge, OH

Colors: Crystal. Some pieces in Crown Tuscan and Ebony

Notes: Some pieces have gold encrustation. Called D/1041 when gold encrusted on Ebony. The following is a portion of the items made. Rose Point maintained its popularity for many years, and is generally recognized as the most popular etching made. It was continued by the Imperial Glass Corporation after they purchased the Cambridge Glass Co.

STEMWARE:

NO. 3121
Champagne	$35.00
Cocktail	35.00
Goblet	55.00
Iced Tea	45.00
Parfait	100.00
Sherbet	27.00
Tumbler, Footed	35.00

No. 3500
Claret, 4½ oz.	$100.00
Cocktail	40.00
Cordial, 1 oz.	140.00
Finger Bowl	25.00
Finger Bowl, Footed	28.00
Goblet, Long Bowl	65.00
Goblet, Short Bowl	55.00
Oyster Cocktail	22.00
Parfait, Café, 5 oz.	100.00
Sherbet, Low, 7 oz.	27.00
Sherbet, Tall, 7 oz.	30.00
Tumbler, 2½ oz.	40.00
Tumbler, Footed, 5 oz. or 10 oz.	35.00
Tumbler, Footed, 13 oz.	40.00
Wine, 2½ oz.	75.00
Wine, Low, 2½ oz.	45.00

ACCESSORIES:
Basket, 2-handled, 6" (P55)	$80.00
Bell, Dinner (3121)	175.00
Bonbon, 2-handled, 5¼" (3900/1180)	40.00
Bonbon, 2-handled, 6" (P54)	80.00
Bowl, 3-footed, 10" (3900/54)	78.00
Bowl, 4-footed, 11" (3400/48) or 12" (3400/160)	110.00
Bowl, Crimped (3900/66)	85.00
Butter & Cover, ¼ lb. (3900/52)	325.00
Candlesticks, 2-light, 6", pr. (3900/72)	55.00
Candlesticks, 3-light, 6", pr. (1338)	85.00
Candlesticks, 3-light, 6", pr. (3900/74)	65.00
Candlesticks, 5" pr. (3900/68)	70.00
Candlesticks, 5", pr. (keyhole stem) (646)	40.00
Candlesticks, 6", pr. (keyhole stem) (647)	50.00

Candy Box & Cover (3900/165)	130.00
Celery & Relish, 3-part, 9" (3900/125)	65.00
Celery & Relish, 3-part, 12" (3900/126)	75.00
Celery & Relish, 5-part, 12" (3900/120)	80.00
Cheese & Cracker, 2-piece, 13½" (3900/135)	135.00
Cocktail Icer, 2 piece (968)	90.00
Cocktail Shaker, 36 oz. (P101)	175.00
Cocktail, 4 oz. (7801)	45.00
Comport, 5⅜" (3121)	75.00
Comport, 5" (same as Cheese) (3900/135)	52.00
Comport, 5½" (3900/136)	62.00
Cream & Sugar, pr. (3900/39 or /40)	50.00
Cream, Individual (3900/15)	35.00
Cream, Individual (3900/38)	25.00
Cup & Saucer (3900/17)	45.00
Decanter, Footed, 28 oz. (1321)	380.00
Hurricane Lamp, 10" (1603 or 1617)	275.00
Hurricane Lamp, 17" (1613)	400.00
Ice Bucket (3900/671)	270.00
Jug, 20 oz. (3900/117)	255.00
Jug, 32 oz. (3900/118)	320.00
Jug, 76 oz. (3900/115)	225.00
Jug, Martini, 32 oz. (3900/114)	425.00
Mayonnaise (1532, 3900/129, or 3900/19)	68.00
Oil & Stopper, 6 oz. (3900/100)	160.00
Pickle, 9½" (477)	50.00
Plate, 14" (3900/166 or 167)	85.00
Plate, 2-handled Bonbon, 8" (3900/131)	48.00
Plate, 2-handled, 6" (3400/1181)	25.00
Plate, 2-handled, 8" (P56)	50.00
Plate, 3-footed, 12" (3900/26)	95.00
Plate, 3-footed, 13" (3900/33)	190.00
Plate, Bread & Butter, 6½" (3900/20)	18.00
Plate, Cake, 2-handled, 13½" (3900/35)	80.00
Plate, Dinner, 10½" (3900/24)	160.00
Plate, Mayonnaise (1532 or 3900/129)	18.00
Plate, Salad, 7½" (555 or 3400/176)	18.00
Plate, Salad, 8" (3900/22)	22.00
Plate, Salad, 8½" (3400/62 or 3900/5)	22.00
Relish & Pickle, 7" (3900/124 or 125)	40.00
Relish, 2-part, 6" (3400/90)	40.00
Relish, 3-part, 6½" (3500/69)	38.00
Relish, 3-part, 8" (3400/91)	42.00
Salt & Pepper, pr. (P360 or 1956/105)	60.00
Salt & Pepper, pr. (3900/1177)	70.00
Sherry, 2 oz. (trumpet shape) (7966)	60.00
Sugar, Individual (3500/15)	35.00
Sugar, Individual (3900/38)	25.00
Tray for Cream & Sugar (3900/37)	30.00
Tumbler, 13 oz. (3900/115)	50.00
Tumbler, 14 oz. (498)	65.00
Vase, 6" (6004)	70.00
Vase, Keyhole Stem, 9" (1237)	140.00
Vase, Keyhole Stem, 12" (1238)	175.00
Vase, Bud, 10" (274)	90.00
Vase, Footed (278)	75.00
Vase, Footed (6004)	70.00

SPRING BEAUTY

ROCK CRYSTAL CUTTING

Date: 1950s

Manufacturer: Duncan & Miller Glass Co., Washington, PA

Colors: Crystal

Notes: No. 30½ refers to Pall Mall pattern.

STEMWARE:

NO. D5 DUNCAN SCROLL
Cocktail, Liquor. $30.00
Goblet. 45.00

Iced Tea, Footed. 38.00
Juice, Footed 24.00
Saucer Champagne or Tall Sherbet 40.00
Seafood Cocktail 20.00
Wine or Claret. 45.00

ACCESSORIES:
Plate, 7½" or 8½" (30½) $15.00

Catalog Illustration:
Spring Beauty cutting on
No. D5 Duncan Scroll goblet

SPRING GLORY

ROCK CRYSTAL CUTTING

Date: 1950s

Manufacturer: Duncan & Miller Glass Co., Washington, PA

Colors: Crystal

Notes: No. 30½ refers to Pall Mall pattern.

STEMWARE:

NO. D1 MANDARIN
Cocktail, Liquor, 3½ oz. $30.00
Goblet, 11 oz. 45.00

Iced Tea, Footed, 14 oz. 38.00
Orange Juice, Footed, 5 oz. 24.00
Oyster Cocktail, Footed, 4½ oz. 20.00
Saucer Champagne or
      Tall Sherbet, 5 oz. 40.00
Wine or Claret, 4 oz. 45.00

ACCESSORIES:
Plate, 6" (30½) $12.00
Plate, 7½" or 8½" (30½). 15.00

Catalog Illustration:
Spring Glory cutting on
No. D1 Mandarin goblet

STARBURST, NO. 4P

ROCK CRYSTAL ENGRAVING

Date: 1950

Manufacturer: Cambridge Glass Co., Cambridge, OH

Colors: Crystal

STEMWARE:

NO. 3790 SIMPLICITY
Claret $25.00
Cocktail. 20.00
Cordial 65.00
Goblet. 25.00
Iced Tea, Footed, 12 oz. 22.00
Oyster Cocktail 15.00

Sherbet, Low 15.00
Tumbler, Footed, 5 oz. (juice). 15.00
Wine. 25.00

ACCESSORIES:
Bell, Dinner (3750) $75.00
Decanter & Stopper (1429) 95.00
Plate, Salad, 8" (556) 10.00
Vase (1528) 45.00
Vase, 6" (1517) 40.00
Vase, 8" (1518) 50.00
Vase, 10" (1519) 75.00

Catalog Illustration: No. 4P
Starburst rock crystal engraving
on No. 3790 Simplicity goblet

133

FLOWERS *(continued)*

Catalog Illustration: No. 10P
Starlite rock crystal engraving on
No. 3790 Simplicity goblet

STARLITE, NO. 10P

ROCK CRYSTAL ENGRAVING

Date: 1950

Manufacturer: Cambridge Glass Co.,
Cambridge, OH

Colors: Crystal

STEMWARE:
NO. 3790 SIMPLICITY

Claret	$25.00
Cocktail	20.00
Cordial	65.00
Goblet	25.00
Iced Tea, Footed, 12 oz.	22.00
Oyster Cocktail	15.00
Sherbet, Low	15.00
Tumbler, Footed, 5 oz. (juice)	15.00
Wine	25.00

ACCESSORIES:

Bell, Dinner (3750)	$75.00
Decanter & Stopper (1429)	95.00
Plate, Salad, 8" (556)	10.00
Vase (1528)	45.00
Vase, 6" (1517)	40.00
Vase, 8" (1518)	50.00
Vase, 10" (1519)	75.00

Catalog Illustration:
No. 277 Vernon etching on
handled lunch tray

Catalog Illustration:
No. 277 Vernon etching on
footed jug

VERNON, NO. 277

PLATE ETCHING

Date: 1927

Manufacturer: Fostoria Glass Co.,
Moundsville, WV

Colors: Crystal, Amber, Azure, Green, Orchid

Notes: No. 2375 refers to Fairfax dinnerware pattern.

STEMWARE:
NO. 877

Claret, 4 oz.	$30.00
Cocktail, 3½ oz.	22.00
Cordial, ¾ oz.	70.00
Goblet, 10 oz.	25.00
Oyster Cocktail, 4½ oz.	15.00
Parfait	22.00
Sherbet, High, 6 oz.	20.00
Sherbet, Low, 6 oz.	15.00
Tumbler, Footed, 5 oz. (juice)	15.00
Tumbler, Footed, 9 oz. (water)	17.00
Tumbler, Footed, 12 oz. (iced tea)	20.00
Whiskey, Footed, 2½ oz.	30.00
Wine, 3¾ oz.	30.00

ACCESSORIES:

Baker, 9" 2375)	$32.00
Bouillon, Footed (2375)	22.00
Bowl, 12" (2375)	40.00
Candlesticks (low), 1-light, pr. (2375½)	60.00
Candlesticks, 3", 1-light, pr. (2375)	60.00
Candy Box & Cover (2331)	75.00
Centerpiece, Oval, 13" (2375½)	50.00
Cereal, 6" (2350)	20.00
Cheese & Cracker, 2-piece, 11"	38.00
Comport, 7" (2375)	45.00
Cream Soup, Footed (2375)	20.00
Cream, Footed (2375½)	20.00
Cup & Saucer (2375)	25.00
Fruit, 5" (2375)	15.00
Ice Bucket (2378)	75.00
Jug, Footed, No. 7 (5000)	110.00
Lunch Tray, Handled, 11" (2375)	30.00
Mayonnaise, Footed (2375)	25.00
Plate, 7" (2375)	15.00
Plate, Cream Soup (2375)	15.00
Plate, Mayonnaise (2375)	15.00
Platter, 12" (2375)	45.00
Relish, 8½" (2375)	28.00
Soup, 7" (2375)	28.00
Sugar, Footed (2375)	20.00

VESPER, NO. 275

PLATE ETCHING

Date: 1926

Manufacturer: Fostoria Glass Co., Moundsville, WV

Colors: Crystal, Amber, Blue, Green

Notes: Patented: No. 70356 and 70357. Prices given are for Amber or Green. For Crystal deduct 20%. For Blue, add 40%.

STEMWARE:
No. 5093
Claret, 4½ oz.	$35.00
Cocktail, 3 oz.	20.00
Cordial, ¾ oz.	85.00
Goblet, 9 oz.	28.00
Parfait	28.00
Sherbet, High, 6 oz.	25.00
Sherbet, Low, 6 oz.	18.00
Wine, 2¾ oz.	35.00

ACCESSORIES:
Celery (2350)	$28.00
Cheese & Cracker, 2 piece (2368)	50.00
Cream Soup (2350)	20.00
Cup & Saucer (2350)	25.00
Finger Bowl (869)	15.00
Grapefruit & Liner (both etched) (5082½/945½)	45.00
Oyster Cocktail (5000)	16.00
Plate, 6" (2283)	9.00
Plate, 7" (2350)	12.00
Tumbler, Footed, 5 oz. (juice) (5000)	20.00
Tumbler, Footed, 9 oz. (water) (5000)	18.00
Tumbler, Footed, 12 oz. (iced tea) (5000)	25.00

Catalog Illustration: No. 275 Vesper etching on footed tumbler

WILD ROSE

ROCK CRYSTAL CUTTING

Date: 1949

Manufacturer: Duncan & Miller Glass Co., Washington, PA

Colors: Crystal

STEMWARE:
NO. D3 DUNCAN-PHYFE
Cocktail, Liquor, 3½ oz.	$30.00
Goblet, 10 oz.	45.00
Iced Tea, Footed, 14 oz.	38.00
Orange Juice, Footed, 5 oz.	24.00
Oyster Cocktail, Footed, 4½ oz.	20.00
Saucer Champagne or Tall Sherbet, 5 oz.	40.00
Wine or Claret, 4 oz.	45.00

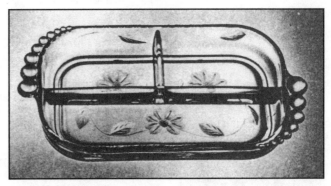

Catalog Illustration: Wild Rose cutting on celery and relish

ACCESSORIES:
Bowl, Flared Flower, 12" (8)	$70.00
Bowl, Flared Flower, 12½" (30½)	65.00
Bowl, Salad, 10½ " (30½)	40.00
Candlesticks, 2-light, pr. (41)	95.00
Candy Box & Cover (5200)	75.00
Candy Jar & Cover (25)	80.00
Celery & Relish, 2-handled, 3-compartment, Oblong, 12" (30)	40.00
Celery & Relish, 5-compartment, 12" (31½)	50.00
Celery Tray, 11" (91)	45.00
Cheese & Cracker, 11" (30)	75.00
Comport, High Foot, 7½ " (8)	55.00
Cream & Sugar, pr. (38)	56.00
Mayonnaise (30)	55.00
Plate, Mayonnaise (30)	17.00
Plate, Torte, 14" (30½)	75.00
Relish, 5-compartment, 10" (31½)	50.00
Sandwich Tray, 2-handled, 11" (30)	58.00
Vase, Flip (30)	75.00

Catalog Illustration: Wild Rose cutting on serving tray

FLOWERS *(continued)*

Catalog Illustration: Wildflower etching on No. 3121 tall sherbet

Catalog Illustration: Wildflower etching on No. 3121 parfait

WILDFLOWER

PLATE ETCHING

Date: Ca. 1940

Manufacturer: Cambridge Glass Co., Cambridge, OH

Colors: Crystal, Ebony

Notes: Some items are gold encrusted. Called D/1047 when gold encrusted on Ebony.

STEMWARE:

No. 3121
Champagne $35.00
Claret 50.00
Cocktail. 35.00
Cordial 70.00
Goblet. 50.00
Iced Tea. 37.00
Juice 35.00
Oyster Cocktail 32.00
Parfait 58.00
Sherbet 30.00
Tumbler, Footed 35.00

ACCESSORIES:
Basket, 2-handled, 6" (P55) $80.00
Bell, Dinner (3121) 125.00
Bonbon, 2-handled,
    5¼" (3900/1180) 45.00
Bonbon, 2-handled, 6" (P54) 60.00
Bowl, 3-footed, 10" (3900/54) 65.00
Bowl, 4-footed, 11" (3400/48) 80.00
Bowl, 4-footed, 12" (3400/160) 90.00
Bowl, Crimped (3900/66) 70.00
Butter & Cover, ¼ lb. (3900/52) 220.00
Candlesticks, 2-light,
    6", pr. (3900/72) 55.00
Candlesticks, 3-light, pr. (1338) 85.00
Candlesticks, 3-light, pr. (3000/74). . . . 65.00
Candlesticks, 5", pr. (3900/68) 70.00
Candlesticks, 5", pr.
    (keyhole stem) (646) 40.00
Candlesticks, 6", pr.
    (keyhole stem) (647) 50.00
Candy Box & Cover (3900/165) 80.00
Celery & Relish, 3-part, 9" (3900/125). . 62.00
Celery & Relish, 3-part,
    12" (3900/126). 68.00
Celery & Relish, 5-part,
    12" (3900/120). 80.00
Cheese & Cracker, 2-piece,
    13½" (3900/135) 110.00
Cocktail Icer, 2 piece (968). 100.00
Cocktail Shaker, 36 oz. (P101) 175.00
Cocktail, 4 oz. (7801) 45.00
Comport, 5" (same as cheese)
    (3900/135) 45.00
Comport, 5⅜" (3121) 65.00

Comport, 5½ " (3900/136) 60.00
Cream (3900/39 or 3900/40) 45.00
Cream, Individual
    (3500/15 or 3900/38) 40.00
Cup & Saucer (3900/17) 45.00
Decanter, Footed, 28 oz. (1321) 295.00
Hurricane Lamp, 10" (1603 or 1617) . . 250.00
Hurricane Lamp, 17" (1613) 325.00
Ice Bucket (3900/671) 175.00
Jug, 20 oz. (3900/117) 170.00
Jug, 32 oz. (3900/118) 190.00
Jug, 76 oz. (3900/115) 170.00
Jug, Martini, 32 oz. (3900/114) 250.00
Mayonnaise (1532) 55.00
Mayonnaise (3900/19 or 3900/129) 60.00
Mayonnaise, 2-compartment
    (3900/111) 60.00
Oil & Stopper, 6 oz. (3900/100) 110.00
Pickle, 9½ " (477) 50.00
Plate, 2-handled Bonbon,
    8" (3900/131) 35.00
Plate, 2-handled, 6" (3400/1181) 25.00
Plate, 2-handled, 8" (P56) 55.00
Plate, 3-footed, 12" (3900/26) 70.00
Plate, 3-footed, 13" (3900/33) 90.00
Plate, 14" (3900/166 or 167) 85.00
Plate, Bread & Butter, 6½ " (3900/20) . . 22.00
Plate, Cake, 2-handled,
    13½ " (3900/35) 80.00
Plate, Dinner, 10½" (3900/24). 90.00
Plate, Mayonnaise (1532 or 3900/129) . . 18.00
Plate, Salad, 7½" (555 or 3400/176) . . . 24.00
Plate, Salad, 8" (3900/22) 22.00
Plate, Salad, 8½"
    (3400/62 or 3900/5). 27.00
Relish & Pickle, 2-part, 7" (3900/124) . . 50.00
Relish & Pickle, 7" (3900/123) 50.00
Relish, 2-part, 6" (3400/90) 50.00
Relish, 3-part, 6½" (3500/69) 50.00
Relish, 3-part, 8" (3400/91) 65.00
Salt & Pepper, pr. (1956/105). 80.00
Salt & Pepper, pr. (3900/1177). 80.00
Salt & Pepper, pr. (P360) 80.00
Sherry, Trumpet-shape, 2 oz. (7966) . . . 60.00
Sugar (3900/39 or 3900/40) 37.00
Sugar, Individual
    (3500/15 or 2900/38) 40.00
Tray for Cream & Sugar (3900/37) 55.00
Tumbler, 13 oz. (3900/115) 60.00
Tumbler, 14 oz. (498) 60.00
Vase, 6" (6004) 80.00
Vase, Keyhole Stem, 9" (1237) 120.00
Vase, Keyhole Stem, 12" (1238) 165.00
Vase, Bud, 10" (274) 175.00
Vase, Footed (278) 90.00
Vase, Footed, 8" (6004) 100.00

Chapter 22
FUCHSIAS

FUCHSIA, NO. 310

PLATE ETCHING

Date: 1931

Manufacturer: Fostoria Glass Co., Moundsville, WV

Colors: Crystal, Wisteria

Notes: Tableware blanks are mostly from the No. 2440 Lafayette pattern. For Wisteria, add 100%+.

STEMWARE:
No. 6004
Claret, 4 oz.	$35.00
Cocktail, 3 oz.	25.00
Cordial, ¾ oz.	70.00
Goblet, 9 oz.	30.00
Oyster Cocktail, 4½ oz.	15.00
Parfait, 5½ oz.	30.00
Saucer Champagne, 5½ oz.	27.00
Sherbet, Low, 5½ oz.	18.00
Wine, 2½ oz.	40.00
Tumbler, Footed, 2½ oz. (bar or whiskey)	38.00
Tumbler, Footed, 5 oz. (juice)	18.00
Tumbler, Footed, 9 oz. (water)	20.00
Tumbler, Footed, 12 oz. (iced tea)	27.00

ACCESSORIES:
Bonbon (2470)	$15.00
Bowl, "B", 10½" (2440)	35.00
Bowl, 10" (2395)	35.00
Bowl, 10½" (2470½)	35.00
Bowl, 12" (2470)	45.00
Candlesticks, 3", pr. (2375)	45.00
Candlesticks, 5", pr. (2395½)	60.00
Candlesticks, 5½", pr. (2470½)	60.00
Candlesticks, 5½", pr. (2470)	60.00
Comport, Low, 6" (2470)	24.00
Cream, Footed (2440)	18.00
Cup & Saucer (2440)	20.00
Dish, Lemon (2470)	24.00
Finger Bowl (869)	12.00
Plate, Bread & Butter, 6" (2440)	8.00
Plate, Cake, 10" (2470)	32.00
Plate, Dinner, 9" (2440)	35.00
Plate, Luncheon, 8" (2440)	12.00
Plate, Salad, 7" (2440)	10.00
Sugar, Footed (2440)	18.00
Sweetmeat (2470)	18.00
Tumbler, 2 oz. (833)	15.00
Tumbler, 5 oz. (833)	15.00
Tumbler, 8 oz. (833)	20.00
Tumbler, 12 oz. (833)	22.00

Original Catalog Illustration: No. 310 Fuchsia etching

Detail of No. 310 Fuchsia etching

FUCHSIAS *(continued)*

Fuchsia plate etching

FUCHSIA

PLATE ETCHING

Date: 1938

Manufacturer: U.S. Glass Co., Tiffin, OH

Colors: Crystal

Notes: Made on a wide variety of U.S. Glass/Tiffin items. One of the most popular Tiffin etchings with collectors today.

STEMWARE:
No. 15083, No. 17449, No. 17453, OR No. 17454

Claret	$45.00
Cocktail	28.00
Cordial	120.00
Goblet	45.00
Parfait	40.00
Saucer Champagne	35.00
Sherbet	20.00
Wine	45.00

ACCESSORIES:

Bowl, Large (526)	$65.00
Bowl, Medium (526)	50.00
Bowl, Nut, 6" (5902)	45.00
Bowl, Salad, 10" (5902)	75.00
Bowl, Small (526)	40.00
Candlesticks, 2-light, pr. (5902)	85.00
Celery Tray (5902)	40.00
Centerpiece, Cone-shape, 12½" (5902)	110.00
Centerpiece, Crimped, 12" (5902)	110.00
Centerpiece, Shallow, 13" (5902)	100.00
Comport, Tall (15082)	65.00
Cream (5902)	30.00
Cup & Saucer	85.00
Jug (14194)	300.00
Jug, 60 oz. (5959)	320.00
Mayonnaise (5902)	40.00
Nappy, 7" (5902)	35.00
Plate, Cake, Center-handled (5909)	55.00
Plate, Handled Cake (5902)	65.00
Plate, Lily or Floater (5902)	85.00
Plate, Mayonnaise, 6" (5902)	20.00
Plate, Salad, 8" (5902)	20.00
Plate, Sandwich, 14" (5902)	55.00
Relish, 3-part, large (5902)	65.00
Relish, 3-part, small (5902)	40.00
Salt & Pepper, pr. (2)	120.00
Seafood Cocktail Set (6021)	150.00
Vase, Bud, 6" (14185)	35.00
Vase, Bud, 8" (14185)	45.00
Vase, Bud, 10" (14185)	55.00
Vase, Bud, 11" (15082)	55.00

Original Catalog Illustration:
Marjorie etching on
No. 7606 goblet

MARJORIE

PLATE ETCHING

Date: 1922

Manufacturer: Cambridge Glass Co., Cambridge, OH

Colors: Crystal

Notes: Made during the trademark era of "Near Cut."

STEMWARE:
No. 7606

Café Parfait, 5½ oz.	$25.00
Claret, 5½ oz.	25.00
Cocktail, 3 oz.	20.00
Cordial, ⅞ oz.	65.00
Creme de Menthe, 2 oz.	35.00
Decanter, 28 oz.	120.00
Finger Bowl	12.00
Goblet, 10 oz.	25.00
Plate, Finger Bowl	10.00
Sherbet, Low, 6 oz.	15.00
Sherbet, Tall, 6 oz.	18.00
Tumbler, 1½ oz.	32.00
Tumbler 5 oz.	17.00
Tumbler, 8 oz.	22.00
Tumbler, 12 oz.	22.00
Tumbler, Table, 10 oz.	22.00
Wine, 2½ oz.	38.00

ACCESSORIES:

Comport, Tall stem, 5" (4004)	$40.00
Comport, Low, Jelly, 5" (2090)	30.00
Cream (1917/10)	35.00
Cream (1917/18)	35.00
Jug & Cover, 30 oz. (106)	155.00
Jug & Cover, 66 oz. (106)	175.00
Jug, 3 pt. (93)	100.00
Jug, 3½ pt. (108)	125.00
Jug, 3½ pt. (111)	110.00
Jug, 4 pt. (110)	125.00
Marmalade & Cover (145)	55.00
Oil & Stopper (32)	85.00
Plate, Salad or Finger Bowl, 7" (7606)	14.00
Sugar (1917/10)	35.00
Sugar (1917/18)	35.00
Syrup & Cover, 8 oz. (106)	75.00
Tumbler, Juice, 5 oz. (8858)	17.00
Tumbler, 12 oz. (8858)	22.00
Tumbler, Handled & Footed, 10 oz. (7606 or 8023)	35.00
Tumbler, Handled, 12 oz. (8858)	35.00
Tumbler, Table, 9 oz. (8858)	22.00

So proudly we Hail

THE CHARMING AMERICAN LADY

You'll want this bewitching stemware, in luminous
amethyst for your table drama. Or you may prefer
the cool tranquility of clear crystal. Whichever
your choice, *American Lady* stemware will
match the solid splendor of Fostoria's table
accessories in the *American* pattern . . .
all handmade by American craftsmen
. . . all inexpensively priced at
the better stores everywhere.

PHOTO BY
VICTOR KEPPLER

Fostoria
MADE IN U.S.A.

FOSTORIA GLASS COMPANY · · MOUNDSVILLE · WEST VIRGINIA

Original Advertisement for Fostoria's American Lady stemware line

Top left: Tiffin Glass Co. No. 17578 stems with Wistaria bowls

Middle left: U.S. Glass Co. No. 10 Candlesticks, handpainted floral decoration, green

Bottom left: Tiffin Art Glass Co. Empress Floral bowl, ruby and crystal

Bottom Right: Consolidated Lamp and Glass Co. Vase, Sunset

Top right: Fostoria Glass Co. No. 289 Paradise brocade etching on floral bowl, green

Middle left: Consolidated Lamp and Glass Co. compote, Sunset

Middle right: Consolidated Lamp and Glass Co. Love Birds banana boat shaped vase in metal filigree frame, crystal with red stain

Bottom: Morgantown's Filament stems, No. 7620 Fontanne, No. 7701 Fischer, No 7880 Carlos, No. 7659Z\x Lenox with Amber filaments

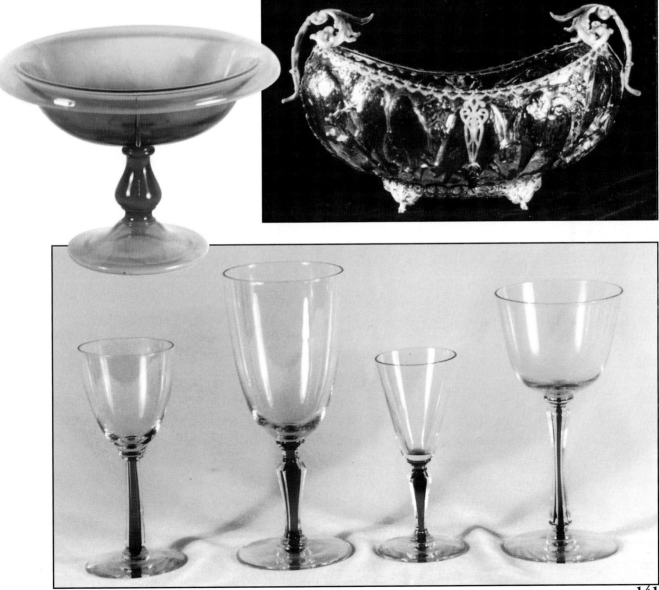

Heisey Rose... **enchantment in crystal**

*Sparkling and gay, this new Heisey etching
will contribute more than its share to love and life and laughter
'round your table. You'll want this sentimental pattern
in lovely hand-blown stemware for yourself. As a romantic gift,
send one dozen roses . . . by Heisey. Request the new Heisey Rose folder
to help you choose matching table accessories.*
Write A. H. Heisey & Co., Dept. H-6, Newark, Ohio.

Original Advertisement for A.H. Heisey & Co. Heisey Rose etching

Top right: U.S. Glass Co. Flower Garden &
     Butterflies dresser set, pink

Middle left: U.S. Glass Co. console bowl,
     orange Carrera

Middle center: U.S. Glass Co./Tiffin
        No. 15028 goblet, green

Middle right: U.S. Glass Co./Tiffin
        No. 14196 goblet with Char-
        mian etching with gold inlay,
        amber

Bottom: L to R: Offhand whale, green;
     mouse, amber; snail, green by
     Pilgrim Glass Co.

Top left: U.S. Glass Co. open-work compote/vase, amberina

Middle left: Imperial Glass Co. Hobnail powder box, green opalscent

Middle right: Rabbit family by Viking from Heisey molds, ruby

Bottom left: Duncan & Miller No. 5111Z\x Terrace stems with First Love etching

Bottom right: U.S. Glass Co./Tiffin No. 9557 covered candy, blue with canary foot

Top right: Morgantown's No. 7720 Palazzo stems with green filaments

Middle left: U.S. Glass Co. No. 75 Satin amberina candlesticks

Middle right: Fostoria Baroque sugar with No. 514 Gold Lace etching

Bottom: Morgantown Patrick baskets, amber, cobalt, ruby

Handmade Gifts of Authentic Westmoreland

A gift should appropriately suit the occasion; it should expressively convey the sentiments of the donor, and should possess in combination both utility and beauty. Regardless of its cost, its worth should increase through the years with use and cherished association.

Westmoreland authentic handmade reproductions in milk glass, black glass, antique blue glass, crystal and crystal-with-ruby, meet the requisites of those who are meticulous in their gift selections.

GET YOUR COPY OF THIS BEAUTIFUL BOOK

Informal Table Settings

Send twenty-five cents in coin for your copy

Handmade Glassware of Quality

WESTMORELAND GLASS COMPANY

GRAPEVILLE, PENNSYLVANIA

Original Advertisement with assortment of Westmoreland decorative items

Chapter 23
GRAPES

BACCHUS

PLATE ETCHING

Date: 1934

Manufacturer: Cambridge Glass Co., Cambridge, OH

Colors: Crystal

STEMWARE:
NO. 7966

Champagne, Hollow Stem, 6 oz...... $20.00
Champagne, Tall, 5 oz............. 11.00
Claret, 4 oz...................... 15.00

Cocktail, 3 oz.................... 14.00
Cocktail, 3½ oz. 14.00
Cordial, 1 oz..................... 48.00
Finger Bowl...................... 15.00
Goblet, 9 oz..................... 15.00
Plate, Finger Bowl................ 8.00
Saucer Champagne................. 11.00
Sherry, 1½ oz. 18.00
Sherry, 2 oz...................... 18.00
Wine, 3 oz. 17.00

Original Catalog Illustration:
Bacchus etching on
No. 7966 stemware

CATAWBA

ETCHING

Date: 1930s

Manufacturer: Cambridge Glass Co., Cambridge,OH

Colors: Crystal

Notes: It is most likely that a full line of stemware was made with this etching.

Goblet, 14 oz. (1402/2-Tally Ho) $30.00

Original Catalog Illustration:
Catawba etching on No. 1402
Tally Ho goblet

GRAPE, NO. 6

GRAY CUTTING

Date: Late 1920s

Manufacturer: Standard Glass Mfg. Co., Lancaster, OH

Colors: Crystal, Green, Pink, Topaz

Notes: For colors, add 25%.

Cocktail (32) $10.00
Cream (53) 15.00
Cup (179) & Saucer (729) 25.00
Goblet (42) 15.00
Iced Tea (33) 12.00
Iced Tea, 12 oz. (308 or 3306) 12.00
Iced Tea, Footed (88) 12.00
Jug & Cover (55)................. 40.00
Jug (64) 35.00
Jug, 57 oz. (54) 35.00
Juice, Fruit, Footed (80) 9.00
Night Set (tumble up) (125)........ 55.00
Plate, 8" (740) 7.00

Plate, Sherbet, 6" (131) 5.00
Plate, Sherbet, 6" (729) 5.00
Salt & Pepper, pr. (23) 40.00
Salt & Pepper, pr. (24) 40.00
Sherbet (33)..................... 9.00
Sherbet, Footed (22) 9.00
Sherbet, High (134)............... 12.00
Sugar (53) 15.00
Sundae, Tall sherbet or Champagne (34) .. 12.00
Tumbler (115) 12.00
Tumbler, 2½ oz. (3305)........... 15.00
Tumbler, 3 oz. (65 or 303) 15.00
Tumbler, 5 oz. (33 or 3303) 12.00
Tumbler, 8 oz. (34) 12.00
Tumbler, 9 oz. (3301) 12.00
Tumbler, 10 oz. (36 or 306) 12.00
Tumbler, Barrel, 10 oz. (112) 12.00
Tumbler, Footed (81) 12.00
Tumbler, Footed, 10 oz. (161) 12.00

Original Catalog Illustration:
No. 6 Grape cutting

GRAPES *(continued)*

Original Catalog Illustration:
Modern Vintage parfait
and goblet

MODERN VINTAGE

ETCHING

Date: Ca. 1920

Manufacturer: Fostoria Glass Co., Moundsville, WV

Colors: Crystal

STEMWARE:
No. 766

Cocktail $12.00
Cordial 28.00
Finger Bowl, 4½" wide 8.00
Fruit, 4½ oz. (sherbet), 3¼" tall 10.00
Goblet, 9 oz., 7" tall. 15.00
Parfait, 6 oz., 5¾" tall 12.00

Saucer Champagne, 5 oz., 4⅜" tall 12.00
Tumbler, Handled & Footed,
    12 oz., 5¼" tall. 15.00

ACCESSORIES:
Bowl & Cover, 6" (896) $25.00
Nappy, Footed, 5 oz., 3" tall 22.00
Oyster Cocktail, 4½ oz., 3¼" tall (837) . . 7.00
Plate, 6" (1736) 6.00
Tankard, No. 7 (300) 75.00
Tumbler, 12 oz., 5⅜" tall (4011) 15.00
Tumbler, Table, 4" tall (4011½) 8.00

NECTAR, NO. 322

PLATE ETCHING

Date: 1934

Manufacturer: Fostoria Glass Co., Moundsville, WV

Colors: Crystal

Original Catalog Illustration:
No. 322 Nectar etching on No. 6011 Neo Classic stems

STEMWARE:
No. 6011 NEO CLASSIC

Brandy, 1 oz., 4" tall $28.00
Claret, 4½ oz., 5⅝" tall 20.00
Cocktail, 3 oz., 4⅝" tall 17.00
Cordial, 1 oz., 3¼" tall 25.00
Creme de Menthe, 2 oz., 4½" tall. 18.00
Decanter or Jug, Footed 80.00
Goblet, 10 oz., 6⅜" tall 20.00
Oyster Cocktail, 4 oz., 3¼" tall 10.00
Rhine Wine, 4½ oz., 6" tall 22.00
Saucer Champagne, 5½ oz., 4¾" tall 17.00
Sherbet, Low, 5½ oz., 3¼" tall. 10.00
Sherry, 2 oz., 4⅝" tall 25.00
Tumbler, Footed, 2 oz., 2¾" tall (whiskey or bar). . 22.00
Tumbler, Footed, 5 oz., 3⅞" tall (juice). 15.00
Tumbler, Footed, 10 oz., 4½" tall (water) 15.00
Tumbler, Footed, 13 oz., 5⅜" tall (iced tea) 18.00
Wine, 3 oz., 5" tall. 22.00

ACCESSORIES:
Bowl, Footed, 10½" (4024) $22.00
Brandy Inhaler (906) 25.00
Candlesticks, 6", pr. (4024) 50.00
Champagne, Hollow Stem, 5½ oz. (795) 10.00
Comport, 5" (4024) 15.00
Cream & Sugar, Footed, pr. (2350½) 40.00
Cup & Saucer, After Dinner (2350) 25.00
Cup & Saucer, Footed (2350) 20.00
Finger Bowl (1769) 9.00
Old Fashioned Cocktail, Sham (1184) 8.00
Plate, 6" or 7" (2337) 9.00
Plate, 8" (2337) 10.00
Plate, 11" (2337) 20.00
Plate, Torte, 13" (2440) 18.00
Salt & Pepper, pr. (2235) 40.00
Tumbler, Sham, 10 oz. or 12 oz. (701) 9.00
Whiskey, Sham, 1½ oz. (4122). 15.00

NEW VINTAGE, NO. 227

PLATE ETCHING

Date: 1913

Manufacturer: Fostoria Glass Co., Moundsville, WV

Colors: Crystal

Notes: Although earlier than the scope of this book, it will be helpful to have all grape designs together. The etching did continue until about 1927.

STEMWARE:

NO. 858

Ale	$18.00
Brandy	12.00
Champagne, Hollow Stem	10.00
Champagne, Long Stem	18.00
Champagne, Tall	10.00
Claret, 4½ oz.	12.00
Claret, 6½ oz.	12.00
Cocktail	10.00
Comport, Short Cake (footed)	9.00
Cordial	17.00
Creme de Menthe	10.00
Fruit Salad (footed)	9.00
Goblet, 7 oz.	10.00
Goblet, 9 oz.	10.00
Goblet, 10½ oz.	12.00
Hot Whiskey	12.00
Oyster Cocktail	7.00
Parfait	10.00
Saucer Champagne, 5½ oz.	9.00
Saucer Champagne, 7 oz.	9.00
Sherbet	9.00
Sherry	12.00
Sweetmeat	15.00
Tumbler, 3½ oz. *	10.00
Tumbler, 5 oz. *	8.00
Tumbler, 6½ oz. *	8.00
Tumbler, 8 oz. *	10.00
Tumbler, 10 oz. *	10.00
Tumbler, 12 oz. *	12.00
Tumbler, 16 oz. *	16.00
Tumbler, Table *	10.00
Wine, 2¾ oz.	12.00
Wine, 3½ oz.	12.00

* these tumblers have cut flutes

NO. 863

Brandy (pousse café)	$11.00
Café Parfait	11.00
Champagne, Hollow Stem (cut flutes)	11.00
Champagne, Tall	11.00
Claret	11.00
Cocktail, 3 oz.	10.00
Cocktail, 3½ oz.	10.00
Cordial	11.00
Creme de Menthe	11.00
Fruit	9.00

Goblet, 5½ oz.	11.00
Goblet, 10½ oz.	11.00
Goblet, Long Stem, 7 oz.	11.00
Goblet, Short Stem, 9 oz.	11.00
Rhine Wine	11.00
Roemer (tall cocktail), 4½ oz.	12.00
Roemer (tall cocktail), 5½ oz.	12.00
Saucer Champagne	9.00
Sherry	11.00
Wine	11.00

NO. 880

Ale, Tall	$9.00
Brandy (pousse café), ¾ or 1 oz.	11.00
Champagne, Hollow Stem	9.00
Champagne, Tall	8.00
Claret, 4½ oz. or 6½ oz.	9.00
Cocktail, 3 oz. or 3½ oz.	8.00
Cordial, ¾ or 1 oz.	15.00
Creme de Menthe	9.00
Goblet, 8, 9, 10 or 11 oz.	9.00
Grapefruit, Short	9.00
Grapefruit, Tall	9.00
Hot Whiskey	8.00
Rhine Wine	9.00
Saucer Champagne, 5½ oz. or 7 oz.	9.00
Sherbet	7.00
Sherry	9.00
Wine, 2½ or 3½ oz.	9.00

ACCESSORIES

Almond, Individual (863)	$20.00
Comport, 5" (803)	15.00
Cream (1478)	20.00
Custard (punch cup) (481-blown or 868-pressed)	9.00
Decanter & Stopper, cut flutes (1491)	75.00
Grapefruit (945½)	10.00
Iced Tea, Footed & Handled (766)	15.00
Jug (300, 303, 318 or 1236)	75.00
Jug & Cover (317)	90.00
Lemonade, Handled (4061)	12.00
Nappy, 8" (1227)	12.00
Nappy, Deep, 4½" (footed) (803)	9.00
Nappy, Deep, 6" (footed) (803)	12.00
Nappy, Shallow, 5" (footed) (803)	9.00
Oil & Stopper (312 or 1465)	35.00
Oyster Cocktail (5039)	9.00
Parfait (822, 5036 or 5054)	10.00
Plate, Sherbet	7.00
Sherbet (840)	9.00
Sugar (1478)	20.00
Tankard (300, 724 or 1743)	75.00
Tumbler, 3 oz. (887)	9.00
Tumbler, 5 oz. (889)	7.00
Tumbler, 8 oz. (833)	9.00
Tumbler (701, 833, 858, or 4011)	9.00
Water Bottle, cut flutes (1558)	35.00

Original Catalog Illustration:
No. 227 New Vintage etching on
No. 863 stems

Original Catalog Illustration:
No. 227 New Vintage etching on
cut flute tumblers

Original Catalog Illustration:
No. 227 New Vintage etching on
cut flute water bottle

GRAPES *(continued)*

Original Catalog Illustration:
No. 401 Old Fashioned
Grape tumbler

OLD FASHIONED GRAPE, NO. 401

PLATE ETCHING

Date: Ca. 1930s

Manufacturer: Cambridge Glass Co., Cambridge, OH

Colors: Crystal

STEMWARE:

No. 1401

Claret, 4½ oz.	$12.00
Cocktail, 3 oz.	9.00
Cordial, 1 oz.	45.00
Finger Bowl	8.00
Goblet, 10 oz. (1400)	12.00
Goblet, 10 oz.	12.00
Sherbet, Tall, 6 oz.	9.00

Tumbler, Footed, 5 oz. (juice)	9.00
Tumbler, Footed, 10 oz. (water)	9.00
Wine, 3 oz.	12.00

ACCESSORIES
No. 1203

Juice, Orange or Tomato, 5 oz.	$8.00
Old Fashioned Cocktail, 7 oz.	8.00
Tumbler, 2½ oz.	12.00
Tumbler, 8 oz.	8.00
Tumbler, 10 oz.	8.00
Tumbler, 12 oz.	8.00
Tumbler, 14 oz. (1204)	8.00
Tumbler, 14 oz.	8.00

Original Catalog Illustration:
No. 204 Vintage etching on
No. 858 sherry and wine

VINTAGE, NO. 204

PLATE ETCHING

Date: 1904

Manufacturer: Fostoria Glass Co., Moundsville, WV

Colors: Crystal

Notes: Although earlier than the scope of this book, it will be helpful to have all grape designs together. The etching did continue until about 1928.

STEMWARE
No. 858

Ale	$18.00
Brandy	12.00
Champagne, Hollow Stem	10.00
Champagne, Long Stem	18.00
Champagne, Tall	10.00
Claret, 4½ oz.	12.00
Claret, 6½ oz.	12.00
Cocktail	10.00
Cordial	17.00
Creme de Menthe	10.00
Fruit	9.00
Goblet, 8 oz.	10.00
Goblet, 9 oz.	10.00
Goblet, 10 oz.	12.00
Goblet, 11 oz.	12.00
Hot Whiskey	12.00
Oyster Cocktail	7.00
Parfait	10.00
Saucer Champagne, 5½ oz.	9.00
Saucer Champagne, 7 oz.	9.00
Sherbet	9.00
Sherry	12.00
Wine, 2¾ oz.	12.00
Wine, 3½ oz.	12.00

No. 863

Brandy (pousse café)	$11.00
Café Parfait	11.00
Champagne, Hollow Stem (cut flutes)	11.00
Champagne, Tall	11.00
Claret	11.00
Cocktail, 3 oz.	10.00
Cocktail, 3½ oz.	10.00
Cordial	11.00
Creme de Menthe	11.00
Fruit	9.00
Goblet, 5½ oz.	11.00
Goblet, 10½ oz.	11.00
Goblet, Long Stem, 7 oz.	11.00
Goblet, Short Stem, 9 oz.	11.00
Rhine Wine	11.00
Roemer (tall cocktail), 4½ oz.	12.00
Roemer (tall cocktail), 5½ oz.	12.00
Saucer Champagne	9.00
Sherry	11.00
Wine	11.00

ACCESSORIES

Café Parfait (822)	10.00
Cracker Jar & Cover (1061)	110.00
Cream & Sugar, pr. (1480 or 1478)	40.00
Cream & Sugar, cut beaded top, pr. (1480)	50.00
Custard, Punch cup (481-blown or 858-pressed)	9.00
Decanter, 18 oz., cut flutes (1464)	75.00
Decanter, Optic, cut flutes (1491)	75.00
Decanter, qt., cut flutes (300)	75.00
Finger Bowl (315, 858 or 1499)	7.00
Grapefruit (945½)	14.00
Horseradish and Stopper (1132)	35.00

Original Catalog Illustration:
No. 204 Vintage etching on
blown cracker jar

(continued) # GRAPES

Iced Tea, Footed & Handled (766) 12.00	Parfait (863 or 5054) 10.00
Jug (300) 75.00	Punch Bowl & Foot,
Jug (303-7) 75.00	cut beaded top (1227) . . . . 500.00+
Jug, Optic (318-7) 75.00	Salt & Pepper, pr. (1165) 35.00
Jug (724) 75.00	Sherbet (840) 9.00
Jug (1236) 75.00	Tankard (300-3½) 50.00
Jug (1852) 75.00	Tankard (300-7) 75.00
Jug & Cover (317½) 90.00	Tankard (724-7) 75.00
Nappy, 4½" (315 or 1227) 7.00	Tankard (1743) 75.00
Nappy, 8" (315 or 1227) 12.00	Tankard, Claret (300) 85.00
Oil & Stopper, cut flutes (1465) 35.00	Tumbler (701, 820, 833, 858,
Oil & Stopper, Large (300) 35.00	887, 889, 4011) 9.00
Oyster Cocktail (1389 or 5039) 7.00	Water Bottle, cut flutes (160½) 35.00

Original Catalog Illustration:
No. 204 Vintage etching on
optic jug

VINTAGE

PLATE ETCHING

Date: Ca. 1934

Manufacturer: Cambridge Glass Co., Cambridge, OH

Colors: Crystal

Notes: The champagne and burgundy with hollow stems were also
made with cut flutes on the stem which adds to the value.

STEMWARE:
No. 3109

Ale, Tall, 6 oz. $14.00
Café Parfait, 5 oz. 20.00
Champagne, Hollow Stem, 6 oz. 15.00
Champagne, Tall, 5 oz. 12.00
Champagne, Tall, 5½ oz. 12.00
Claret, 4 oz. 15.00
Cocktail, 3 oz. 12.00
Cocktail, 3½ oz. 12.00
Cocktail, 4 oz. 12.00
Cordial, 1 oz. 45.00
Creme de Menthe, 2½ oz. 15.00
Finger Bowl 15.00
Fruit Salad, 6 oz. 8.00
Goblet, 9 oz. 15.00
Oyster Cocktail, 4½ oz. 7.00
Plate, Finger Bowl 8.00
Pousse Café, 1 oz. 45.00
Saucer Champagne, 6 oz. 10.00
Sherbet, Low, 6 oz. 9.00
Sherbet, Tall Bowl, 5 oz. 9.00
Sparkling Burgundy, Hollow Stem, 5 oz. 15.00
Tumbler, 1 oz. 22.00
Tumbler, 2 oz. 18.00
Tumbler, 3 oz. 18.00
Tumbler, 5 oz. 8.00
Tumbler, 8 oz. 8.00
Tumbler, 9 oz. 8.00
Tumbler, 10 oz. 9.00
Tumbler, 12 oz. 9.00
Tumbler, 14 oz. 9.00
Tumbler, Footed, 3 oz. 7.00
Tumbler, Footed, 5 oz. 7.00
Tumbler, Footed, 10 oz. 9.00
Tumbler, Footed, 12 oz. 9.00
Wine, 2 oz. 17.00
Wine, 3 oz. 15.00

Original Catalog Illustration:
Vintage etching on sparkling burgundy and tall champagne

Original Catalog Illustration:
Vintage etching on finger bowl and plate

Chapter 24
HALF FLOWERS

Half flowers contains in profile flower motifs, usually stylized and often in cuttings.

1925 Huntington ad
for Avon pattern

AVON

GRAY CUTTING

Date: 1930

Manufacturer: Huntington Tumbler Co.,
Huntington, WV

Colors: Crystal, Green

Notes: Huntington Tumbler made many
colored stems, but it is uncertain whether this
line came in colors. However, a wholesale
catalog indicates that the stemware was available
in "green bell shaped iridescent glass with cut
band at the top broken by two medallions."

Two types of goblets are known, so the
cutting must have been done on at least two
lines. One of the stems shown has a narrow
optic. Probably many items were made with
this decoration. Name given by Hazel
Marie Weatherman.

Cocktail	$10.00
Comport, Tall Stem	15.00
Goblet	12.00
Iced Tea	8.00
Sherbet, High	10.00

NO. 404

CUTTING

Date: 1920s

Manufacturer: U.S. Glass Co., Tiffin, OH

Colors: Crystal

Notes: Compare this with Huntington Tumbler's Avon cutting above.
This cutting appears on stemware with a pressed stem, while
Huntington's is on a pulled stem.

STEMWARE:

NO. 14187

Café Parfait	$20.00
Cocktail, 3 oz.	20.00
Goblet, 9 oz.	25.00
Saucer Champagne	22.00
Sundae (sherbet)	10.00
Wine, 2½ oz.	25.00

ACCESSORIES:

Finger Bowl (14184)	$12.00
Iced Tea, 12 oz. (517)	18.00
Iced Tea, Handled, 12 oz. (517)	28.00
Jug, 3 Pint (114)	85.00
Oil & Stopper (14194)	75.00
Oyster Cocktail (14185)	10.00
Plate, Finger Bowl (8814)	8.00
Plate, Salad, 8" (8833)	12.00
Table, 10 oz. (water tumbler) (580)	15.00
Tumbler, 4½ oz. (520)	12.00
Vase, Bud (14185)	25.00

Original Catalog Illustration: No. 404 cutting
on goblet and champagne

(continued) # HALF FLOWERS

NO. 616

ROCK CRYSTAL ENGRAVING

Date: 1930s

Manufacturer: Cambridge Glass Co., Cambridge, OH

Colors: Crystal

STEMWARE:
NO. 3035

Claret, 4½ oz.. . . . . $25.00
Cocktail, 3 oz. 16.00
Cordial, 1 oz. 50.00
Fruit Salad, 6 oz.. . . . . 14.00

Goblet, 9 oz.. . . . . 18.00
Oyster Cocktail, 4½ oz. 14.00
Sherbet, Low, 6 oz. 15.00
Sherbet, Tall, 6 oz. 16.00
Tumbler, Footed, 2½ oz.. . . . . 11.00
Tumbler, Footed, 5 oz. 14.00
Tumbler, Footed, 8 oz. 14.00
Tumbler, Footed, 10 oz. 16.00
Tumbler, Footed, 12 oz. 16.00
Wine, 2½ oz. 25.00

No. 616 rock crystal engraving
on No. 3035 goblet

ROXBURY, NO. 1030

ROCK CRYSTAL ENGRAVING

Date: 1940s

Manufacturer: Cambridge Glass Co., Cambridge, OH

Colors: Crystal

STEMWARE:
NO. 3775
Claret, 4½ oz.. . . . . $18.00
Cocktail, 3 oz. 17.00
Cordial, 1 oz. 55.00
Goblet, 9 oz. 18.00

Iced Tea, Footed, 12 oz. 17.00
Oyster Cocktail, 4½ oz. 10.00
Sherbet, Low, 6 oz. 10.00
Sherbet, Tall, 6 oz. 15.00
Tumbler, Footed, 5 oz. (juice) 14.00
Wine, 2½ oz. 18.00

ACCESSORIES:
Cocktail Icer, 2-piece (98) $75.00
Plate, Salad, 7½" (555). 12.00

Original Company Brochure:
No. 1030 Roxbury rock crystal
engraving on No. 3775 goblet

TEMPO, NO. 1029

ROCK CRYSTAL ENGRAVING

Date: 1940s

Manufacturer: Cambridge Glass Co., Cambridge, OH

Colors: Crystal

STEMWARE:
NO. 3770
Claret, 4½ oz.. . . . . $20.00
Cocktail, 3 oz. 17.00
Cordial, 1 oz. 60.00
Goblet, 9 oz.. . . . . 20.00

Iced Tea, Footed, 12 oz. 17.00
Oyster Cocktail, 4½ oz. 11.00
Sherbet, Tall, 6 oz. 17.00
Sherbet, Low, 6 oz. 11.00
Tumbler, Footed, 5 oz. (juice) 15.00
Wine, 2½ oz. 20.00

ACCESSORIES:
Cocktail Icer, 2-piece (968) 75.00
Plate, Salad, 7½" (555) 12.00

Original Catalog Illustration:
No. 1029 Tempo rock crystal
engraving on No. 3700
tall sherbet

Chapter 25
HUMANS, FAIRIES & ANIMALS

Aurora etching on No. 20069 Melon jug

Original Catalog Illustration:
Black Forest Assortment

Detail of Black Forest Etching

AURORA

ETCHING

Date: 1930s

Manufacturer: Morgantown Glass Co., Morgantown, WV

Colors: Crystal with Ebony

Melon Jug, Crystal Satin. $2000.00

BLACK FOREST

DEEP PLATE ETCHING

Date: 1930

Manufacturer: Probably various companies, but distributed exclusively by Van Deman & Son, New York.

Colors: Crystal, Amber, Black, Blue, Deep Blue, Green, Pink, Red

Notes: "The popularity of deep plate etched 'Black Forest' glassware...has prompted this company to add a matching line of 'Black Forest' stemware to complete the ensemble. The forest-etched black glassware which is available in luncheon sets and fancy pieces gives the dealer a profitable line to feature for fall and with the addition of matching stemware of crystal and black combination, the shopper can now buy an entire table service in this interesting design. Included is a low footed line and tall footed line."—Trade Report, August 1930. Black Forest depicts moose in a forest. Compare this with Deerwood in this chapter and Call of the Wild in Chapter 45 Lotus Decorating. Pieces listed below are only a sample of what can be collected in this pattern. Not all pieces were made in all colors. Prices given are for Crystal pieces. For Black, add 50%. For other colors add 25%.

Bowl, Floral, 11" $55.00
Candlesticks, 1-light, pr. 90.00
Candy Jar and Cover 65.00
Cup & Saucer 95.00
Mayonnaise 55.00
Night Set, Handled (tumble up) 450.00
Plate, Bread & Butter, 6" 25.00
Plate, Luncheon, 8" 28.00
Plate, Mayonnaise 15.00
Plate, Sandwich, 2-handled. 50.00
Vase, 10" 90.00

(continued) HUMANS, FAIRIES & ANIMALS

BO-PEEP, NO. 854

DOUBLE ETCHING

Date: Ca. 1927

Manufacturer: Monongah Glass Co., Fairmont, WV

Colors: Rose. Crystal with Green Trim. Crystal stem with Topaz bowl and foot

Notes: Made with optic.

STEMWARE:

No. 6102
Cocktail............................$35.00
Finger Bowl, Footed................22.00
Goblet.............................45.00

Parfait.............................38.00
Sherbet, High.......................35.00
Sherbet, Low........................22.00
Wine................................45.00

ACCESSORIES:
Iced Tea, Footed...................$28.00
Jug & Cover, Footed (20)...........195.00
Jug, Footed (20)...................175.00
Plate, Salad, 7½" (10310)..........35.00
Seltzer, Footed (juice)............22.00
Table, Footed (water tumbler)......25.00
Vase, 9" (0713)....................75.00

Detail of Bo-Peep etching

CLASSIC

ETCHING

Date: 1922

Manufacturer: U.S. Glass Co., Tiffin, OH

Colors: Crystal, Rose

Notes: It is very probable that many other pieces may be found with this etching as it was made for several years. For pieces in Rose, add 75% to Crystal prices.

STEMWARE:

No. 14185, No. 17024
Claret.............................$55.00
Cocktail...........................45.00
Goblet.............................35.00

Parfait.............................40.00
Saucer Champagne....................25.00
Sundae (sherbet)....................18.00
Wine................................38.00

ACCESSORIES:
Cream (6)..........................$40.00
Finger Bowl (185)..................20.00
Iced Tea (185).....................32.00
Jug & Cover (194)..................360.00
Plate, 8" (8833)...................17.00
Sugar (6)..........................40.00
Vase, Bud, 10½"....................55.00
Vase, Bud, 6½".....................32.00

Classic etching jug & cover

DEERWOOD

ETCHING

Date: 1929

Manufacturer: U.S. Glass Co., Tiffin for stems, Glassport for pressed ware.

Colors: Crystal, Green, Pink, Amber. Some tableware items in Black. Black items found with Gold encrustation.

Notes: Decorated at Glassport, PA. Prices are for Crystal pieces. For items in Green, Pink or Amber, add 50%. For black pieces, add 100%.

Original Catalog Illustration: Deerwood etching

STEMWARE:

No. 2809
Cocktail...........................$55.00
Goblet.............................60.00
Saucer Champagne...................48.00
Wine...............................70.00

ACCESSORIES:
Bowl, Centerpiece, 12" (8177)....$50.00
Bowl, Salad, Straight Edge (8105)...45.00

Cake Plate, Center-handled,
  10" (330).......................40.00
Candleholders, Low, pr. (101)......50.00
Candy Jar & Cover, Conic (330)....70.00
Celery Tray (151)..................38.00
Cheese & Cracker, 2-piece (330)....65.00
Comport, Low Foot, Flared
  (330-102)........................38.00
Cream (179)........................32.00
Cup & Saucer (9395)................50.00
Dish, Breakfast (8133).............30.00

Plate, Dinner, 10" (8859).........50.00
Plate, Salad, 7½" (8836)..........18.00
Salver, Low Foot, 10" (330)
  (cake stand).....................40.00
Sugar (179)........................32.00
Tumbler, Iced Tea (2808)...........30.00
Tumbler, Table (2808)..............30.00
Vase, 10" (6471)...................60.00
Vase, Sweet Pea, Rolled Edge,
  7" (151).........................50.00
Whipped Cream & Ladle (330)........32.00

155

HUMANS, FAIRIES, & ANIMALS *(continued)*

L to R: Diana etching with bow, a stag, a dog.

DIANA, NO. 442

DOUBLE PLATE ETCHING

Date: 1925

Manufacturer: A.H. Heisey & Co., Newark, OH

Colors: Crystal, Flamingo. Crystal bowl with Moongleam stem and foot.

Notes: The medallions of Diana etching are Diana with her bow, a stag, and a dog. Larger pieces may have another medallion of a different dog.

Original Catalog Illustration:
Faun decoration on No. 7640 Art Moderne goblet

STEMWARE:

NO. 3357 KING ARTHUR

Cocktail, 4 oz.	$28.00
Cordial, 1 oz.	90.00
Finger Bowl	20.00
Goblet, 10 oz.	30.00
Goblet, Luncheon, 10 oz.	30.00
Iced Tea, Footed, 12 oz.	28.00
Oyster Cocktail, 3¾ oz.	16.00
Parfait, 5 oz.	30.00
Saucer Champagne, 6½ oz.	28.00
Sherbet, 6½ oz.	18.00
Wine, 2½ oz.	42.00

ACCESSORIES:

Iced Tea, Footed, 12 oz. (3481)	$35.00
Jug (3355)	195.00
Jug, 3 pt. (3480)	175.00
Jug, 73 oz. (4164)	175.00
Plate, 6" (3350)	15.00
Plate, 8" (4182)	22.00
Soda, 5½ oz. (2401)	20.00
Soda, 8 oz. (2351)	25.00
Soda, 12 oz. (2351)	25.00
Soda, Footed, 12 oz. (3480)	25.00
Tumbler, 10 oz. (2930)	25.00
Tumbler, 8½ oz. (3481)	25.00

FAUN

Date: 1932

Manufacturer: Morgantown Glass Works, Morgantown, WV

Colors: Crystal; Crystal bowl with Ebony stem

Notes: Made with antique gold band. Certainly made on many more items.

STEMWARE:

NO. 7640 ART MODERNE

Goblet	$150.00
Saucer Champagne	120.00
Wine	150.00

Assortment of Novelty Cuttings

FISH, SAILFISH, SEA HORSE, OWL, ROOSTER, WAIKIKI

NOVELTY CUTTINGS-GRAY CUTTING

Date: 1930s

Manufacturer: Duncan & Miller Glass Co., Washington, PA

Colors: Crystal. Available with Crystal bowl and Green, Amber, Royal Blue (cobalt), Sapphire Blue, or Ruby bases.

Notes: Any of the above listed cuttings were available on the following list of pieces. This is basically a barware set rather than tableware. Designed by Lou Rice who also designed many of Duncan's rock crystal cuttings.

Cocktail Shaker, Footed, 30 oz. (500)	$135.00	High Ball, Footed, 8 oz. (502)	27.00	Orange Juice, Footed, 3½ oz. (500)	32.00
Cocktail, 3 oz. (501)	32.00	High Ball, Footed, 10 oz. (502)	30.00	Orange Juice, Footed, 5 oz. (500)	27.00
Cocktail, 4 oz. (501)	35.00	High Ball, Footed, 12 oz. (502)	32.00	Orange Juice, Footed, 5 oz. (502)	30.00
High Ball, 8 oz. (500)	27.00	High Ball, Footed, 14 oz. (502)	35.00	Plate, Coupe, 8" (9)	18.00
High Ball, 12 oz. (500)	32.00	Martini Mixer, Footed (500)	120.00	Tumbler, 9 oz. (500)	30.00
High Ball, 14 oz. (500)	35.00	Old Fashioned, 6 oz. (500)	22.00	Whiskey, 2 oz. (500)	40.00
		Old Fashioned, Footed, 7 oz. (502)	22.00	Whiskey, Footed, 2 oz. (502)	40.00

(continued) HUMANS, FAIRIES, & ANIMALS

FONTINELLE

DOUBLE PLATE ETCHING

Date: 1930

Manufacturer: Morgantown Glass Works, Morgantown, WV

Colors: Crystal. Crystal bowl with Black stem. Some items with various colored accents.

Notes: Precise catalog information is not available, but certainly a complete line was made. "A charming pattern that creates a style all its own is "Fontinelle." Combining a duo-tone silvery etching with an artistic touch of Black encased in Crystal stems, it fits admirably with any color scheme."—Catalog description.

STEMWARE:

NO. 7620
Goblet $140.00
Saucer Champagne (tall sherbet) 100.00

ACCESSORIES:
Bowl, 13" (4355) $425.00
Candlesticks, 4¾", Ebony filament
   (7620), pr. 325.00
Compote (7620) 425.00
Finger Bowl, Footed (2940) 65.00
Iced Tea (7639½) 85.00
Plate, Salad, 7¼" (1500) 65.00

Fontinelle etching on
No. 7620 goblet

HARDING

PLATE ETCHING

Date: Ca. 1921

Manufacturer: Central Glass Co., Wheeling, WV

Colors: Crystal

Notes: President Warren G. Harding and Mrs. Harding used this tableware as their private dinner service. Many more items were made than those listed.

Cocktail $30.00
Goblet 40.00
Saucer Champagne 32.00
Wine 40.00

Detail of Harding etching

IMPERIAL HUNT

PLATE ETCHING

Date: 1932

Manufacturer: Cambridge Glass Co., Cambridge, OH

Colors: Crystal, Amber, Dianthus Pink, Green, Willow Blue. Limited items in Emerald Green and Ebony.

Notes: Some pieces are known with gold encrusted etching. Prices for Ebony and Emerald Green, add 125% to Crystal values.

STEMWARE:

NO. 1402 TALLY HO (CRYSTAL ONLY)
Claret, 4½ oz. $55.00
Cocktail or Oyster Cocktail,
   Low Stem, 4 oz. 35.00
Cocktail, 3 oz. 45.00
Cordial, 1 oz. 200.00
Finger Bowl 40.00
Goblet, 10 oz. 48.00
Goblet, 14 oz. 60.00
Goblet, 18 oz. 75.00
Goblet, Lunch, 10 oz. (low foot) 40.00
Juice, Tomato or Orange,
   Low Stem, 5 oz. 35.00

Juice, Tomato or Orange,
   Tall Stem, 6 oz. 40.00
Plate, Finger Bowl 15.00
Sherbet, Low, 6½ oz. 30.00
Sherbet, Tall, 7½ oz. 35.00
Wine, 2½ oz. 65.00

NO. 3085
Café Parfait, 5½ oz. $70.00
Claret, 4½ oz. 75.00
Cocktail, 2½ oz. 50.00
Comport, 5½" 50.00
Cordial, 1 oz. 200.00
Finger Bowl 40.00
Fruit Salad, 6½" 35.00
Goblet, 9 oz. 50.00
Iced Tea or Footed Iced Tea, 12 oz. . . . 48.00
Plate, Finger Bowl 15.00
Sherbet, 6 oz. 27.00
Tumbler, 2 oz. (whiskey) 60.00
Tumbler, 5 oz. (juice) 40.00
Tumbler, 10 oz. (water) 42.00
Tumbler, Footed, 2½ oz. (whiskey) 60.00
Tumbler, Footed, 5 oz. (juice) 40.00
Tumbler, Footed, 10 oz. (water) 42.00
Wine, 2½ oz. 75.00

Original Catalog Illustration:
Imperial Hunt etching on
No. 1402 Tally Ho goblet

HUMANS, FAIRIES, & ANIMALS *(continued)*

ACCESSORIES:	Crystal	Colors
Candlesticks, 2-light, pr. (keyhole stem)	$55.00	$100.00
Candlesticks, 3-light, pr. (keyhole stem)	70.00	150.00
Cup & Saucer (1402)	50.00	90.00
Decanter & Stopper.	—	250.00
Humidor, Cigar (1025)	—	425.00

	Crystal	Colors
Ice Tub (847)	50.00	95.00
Jug & Cover, 76 oz. (711 or 712).	195.00	325.00
Plate, 8"	18.00	30.00
Plate, Sandwich, 2-handled	35.00	65.00
Tumbler (881).	18.00	40.00

Original Catalog Illustration:
Luciana etching on jug and cover

LUCIANA

PLATE ETCHING

Date: Ca. 1925

Manufacturer: U.S. Glass Co., Tiffin, OH

Colors: Crystal with Black Trim, Crystal with Amber Trim, Crystal with Nile Green Trim

Notes: The medallions contain the Three Graces, or at least three women, dancing with ribbons or shawls. Difficult to find in No. 15037 stems with Ebony stem and foot.

STEMWARE:

No. 15016

Claret	$52.00
Cocktail, 3 oz.	40.00
Goblet, 11 oz.	52.00
Parfait	45.00

Saucer Champagne.	45.00
Sundae (sherbet)	22.00
Wine, 2½ oz..	52.00

ACCESSORIES:

Bonbon, 5½" High (004).	$50.00
Candy Jar & Cover (9557)	135.00
Cream & Sugar, pr. (6).	160.00
Decanter & Cut Stopper (185).	195.00
Finger Bowl (002 or 185).	22.00
Iced Tea (194)	28.00
Jug & Cover (194).	400.00
Oyster Cocktail (196)	20.00
Plate, 7½" (8814) or 8" (8833)	18.00
Vase, Bud, 10½" (004).	140.00

Original Catalog Illustration:
No. 503 Minuet double plate
etching on No. 5010
Symphone goblet

MINUET, NO. 503

DOUBLE PLATE ETCHING

Date: 1939

Manufacturer: A.H. Heisey & Co., Newark, OH

Colors: Crystal

Notes: "A pattern inspired by history's gracious days of curtsies and Beethoven, light music and light laughter. Chic...Charming...Enchanting, Minuet's loveliness has made it an outstanding favorite with hostesses everywhere."—Heisey ad. Medallions show different motifs: lady in old fancy dress, man in old fancy dress, cello player, and lady reading dance card. No. 1509 refers to Queen Ann pattern; No. 1511 to Toujours pattern. No. 1509 items with an asterisk (*) indicate pieces with dolphin feet.

STEMWARE:

No. 5010 SYMPHONE

Claret, 4 oz..	$60.00
Cocktail, 3½ oz.	40.00
Comport, 5½".	95.00
Cordial, 1 oz..	165.00
Finger Bowl	24.00
Goblet, 9 oz..	45.00
Goblet, Low Foot, 9 oz.	40.00

Oyster Cocktail, 4½ oz.	40.00
Saucer Champagne, 6 oz.	45.00
Sherbet, 6 oz..	40.00
Soda, Footed, 5 oz. (juice)	45.00
Soda, Footed, 12 oz. (iced tea)	55.00
Wine, 2½ oz..	80.00

ACCESSORIES:

Bell, Dinner (3408)	$195.00
Bowl, Combination Dressing, 6½" (1509)	60.00
Bowl, Floral, 13" (1511).	75.00
Bowl, Floral, Footed, 11" * (1509)	125.00
Bowl, Floral, Oval, 12" (1511)	90.00
Bowl, Oval, 3-compartment, 12" (1514)	85.00
Bowl, Salad, 10" (1511)	65.00
Bowl, Salad, Shallow, 13½" (1509). . . .	95.00
Bowl, Sauce, Footed, 7½" * (1509). . . .	75.00
Candelabra & Prisms, 1-light, pr. (1509)	300.00
Candelabra, Bobeches & Prisms, 2-light, pr. (1511)	350.00
Candlesticks, 1-light, pr. (112)	80.00
Candlesticks, 2-light, pr. (134)	150.00

(continued) HUMANS, FAIRIES, & ANIMALS

Candlesticks, 3-light, pr. (142). 180.00
Celery, 12" (1511) 60.00
Centerpiece, Vase & Prisms,
    pr. (1511) 700.00
Cocktail Icer & Liner (3304). 250.00
Comport, 7½" (1511) 85.00
Cream & Sugar, pr. (1511) 130.00
Cream & Sugar, pr. * (1509) 110.00
Cream, Individual (1509) 45.00
Cream, Individual (1511) 65.00
Cup & Saucer (1509) 100.00
Ice Cube Bucket * (1509) 195.00
Jelly, 2 Handled, Footed, 6" (1509) . . 30.00
Jug, 73 oz. (4164). 325.00
Marmalade & Cover (apple) (1511). . 160.00
Mayonnaise, 5½" * (1509) 60.00
Mayonnaise, Footed (1511). 90.00

Mint, Footed, 6" * (1509) 30.00
Pickle & Olive, 13" (1509) 50.00
Plate & Center, Snack Rack,
    16" (1509/1447) 100.00
Plate, 7" (1509 or 1511) 22.00
Plate, 8" (1509 or 1511) 28.00
Plate, 10½" (dinner) (1509) 190.00
Plate, Mayonnaise, 7" (1509) 20.00
Plate, Sandwich, 15" (1511) 110.00
Plate, Sandwich, 2-handled,
    Round, 12" (1509) 65.00
Plate, Torte, 14" (1511). 65.00
Plateau, Floral, 13" (1511) 75.00
Relish, 5 O'clock, 3-compartment,
    11" (1509) 90.00
Relish, 5 O'clock, 3-compartment,
    9½" (1509) 75.00

Relish, Oval, 12" (1514) 75.00
Relish, Triplex, 7" (1509) 50.00
Salt & Pepper, pr. (10) 100.00
Soda, 12 oz. (2351). 50.00
Sugar, Individual (1509) 45.00
Sugar, Individual (1511) 65.00
Tray for Individual Cream &
    Sugar (1509) 50.00
Tray, Social Hour, 15" (1509) 95.00
Vase, 5" (5013). 75.00
Vase, 6" (5012) 90.00
Vase, 7½" (5012) 120.00
Vase, 8" (4196). 100.00
Vase, 9" (5012) 150.00
Vase, 10" (4192) 120.00
Vase, 10", Saturn Optic (4191) 138.00
Vase, Footed, 5½" (1511) 65.00

MORGAN

PLATE ETCHING

Date: 1922

Manufacturer: Central Glass Works,
Wheeling, WV

Colors: Crystal, Lilac, Black, Blue, Green, Pink

Notes: Used in the West Virginia Governor's
Mansion by Governor Morgan, thus the name.
Few or no original catalogs have been found to
supply accurate information about this etching.
Expect to find other pieces than those listed
below. There are at least two styles of stemware.
Some pieces in black are known with gold
encrustation in the etching. Prices given are for
all colors. Crystal is valued at 25% less. Some
of the more difficult to find colors including
Black, Lilac and Blue are valued about 25-30%
higher than other colors.

STEMWARE:

Cocktail. $38.00
Goblet. 50.00
Iced Tea, Footed. 35.00
Juice, Footed 30.00
Oyster Cocktail 20.00
Saucer Champagne or High Sherbet 42.00
Sherbet 30.00
Tumbler, Footed 30.00
Wine. 50.00

ACCESSORIES:

Bonbon, 2-handled, 6" $40.00
Bowl, 10" 65.00
Bowl, 13" 80.00
Bowl, Footed, 4" 32.00
Candlesticks, pr. 95.00

Candy & Cover, Footed 120.00
Comport, 5" or 6" 50.00
Cream, Footed. 45.00
Cup & Saucer 75.00
Decanter with Stopper 200.00
Ice Bucket 110.00
Jug 185.00
Mayonnaise 50.00
Oil & Stopper 80.00
Plate, 6½" 12.00
Plate, 7¼" 18.00
Plate, 8½" 25.00
Plate, 9¼" 40.00
Plate, Mayonnaise 17.00
Sandwich Tray, Center-handled
    (flat or cupped). 80.00
Sugar, Footed. 45.00
Tumbler 30.00
Vase, 8" 85.00
Vase, 10", Cylinder with Flared Top . . . 150.00
Vase, Bud, 10" 115.00
Whiskey 40.00

Original Company Ad: Morgan
etching, 1922 ad

Detail of Morgan etching

HUMANS, FAIRIES, & ANIMALS *(continued)*

Original Catalog Illustration:
No. 439 Pied Piper double plate
etching on No. 3350 Wabash jug

Original Catalog Illustration:
Plymouth etching on
No. 6025 Iced Tea

Original Catalog Illustration:
Plymouth etching on footed jug

PIED PIPER, NO. 439

DOUBLE PLATE ETCHING

Date 1922

Manufacturer: A.H. Heisey & Co.,
Newark, OH

Colors: Crystal only

Notes: Designed by Josef Balda for Heisey.
Patented February 10, 1925. There are three
different cameos: two dancing girls with shawls
and a Pan figure playing a pipe. The 4026
decanter and the 4164 jug were available both
plain and with cut flutes on the neck.

STEMWARE:

NO. 3350 WABASH

Claret, 4 oz.	$40.00
Cocktail, 3 oz.	27.00
Comport & Cover, 6"	95.00
Cordial, 1 oz.	90.00
Finger Bowl (2 styles)	18.00
Goblet, 10 oz.	40.00
Grapefruit, Footed	40.00
Iced Tea, Footed & Handled, 12 oz.	40.00

Iced Tea, Footed, 12 oz.	30.00
Jug, Squat, 3 pt.	225.00
Oyster Cocktail, 4 oz.	18.00
Parfait, 5 oz.	40.00
Plate, 6" (pressed)	10.00
Saucer Champagne, 6 oz.	30.00
Sherbet, 6 oz.	20.00
Tankard, 3 pt.	225.00
Tumbler, Footed, 10 oz.	30.00
Wine, 2½ oz.	45.00

ACCESSORIES:

Bar, 2 oz. (whiskey) (2052)	$40.00
Decanter, 16 oz. (4026)	135.00
Jug, 73 oz. (4164)	135.00
Plate, 6", 7" or 8" (4182)	10.00–18.00
Soda, 5 oz. (2401)	20.00
Soda, 8 oz. or 10 oz. (2351)	24.00
Soda, 12 oz. (2351)	22.00
Tankard, 54 oz. (4163)	155.00
Tumbler, 10 oz. (2930)	24.00

PLYMOUTH, NO. 336

PLATE ETCHING

Date: 1933

Manufacturer: Fostoria Glass Co.,
Moundsville, WV

Colors: Crystal

STEMWARE:

NO. 6025 CABOT

Claret-Wine, 4 oz., 4" tall	$22.00
Cocktail, 3½ oz., 3½" tall	17.00
Cordial, 1 oz., 2⅞" tall	42.00
Goblet, 10 oz., 5½" tall	24.00
Oyster Cocktail, 4 oz., 3½" tall	12.00
Sherbet, 6 oz., 3¾" tall	17.00
Tumbler, Footed, 5 oz., 4¼" tall (juice)	13.00
Tumbler, Footed, 12 oz., 5⅝" tall (water or iced tea)	20.00

ACCESSORIES:

Bonbon, 5" (2574)	18.00
Celery, 10½" (2574)	20.00

Comport, Blown, 5", 4¾" tall (6023)	22.00
Cream, Footed (2574)	20.00
Cream, Individual (2574)	25.00
Cup, Footed, & Saucer (2574)	25.00
Dish, Serving, 8½" (2574)	35.00
Finger Bowl (766)	12.00
Jug, Footed, 53 oz. (6011)	95.00
Lemon, 2-handled, 6½" (2574)	15.00
Oil & Stopper, 4¾ oz. (2574)	55.00
Olive, 6" (2574)	15.00
Pickle, 8" (2574)	18.00
Plate (various sizes) (2574)	15.00
Plate, Sandwich (2574)	25.00
Relish, 3-part, 10" (2574)	30.00
Salt & Pepper, pr. (2574)	42.00
Sugar, Footed (2574)	20.00
Sugar, Individual (2574)	25.00
Sweetmeat, 5¼" (2574)	18.00
Whipped Cream, 5" (2574)	18.00

(continued) HUMANS, FAIRIES, & ANIMALS

PSYCHE

PLATE ETCHING

Date: 1926

Manufacturer: U.S. Glass Co., Tiffin, OH

Colors: Crystal with Green Trim

Notes: U.S. Glass applied for a patent on this decoration. The pattern is of a woman dancing with her shawl swirling wildly about her.

STEMWARE:

NO. 15003, 15016 OR 15039

Claret	$80.00
Cocktail.	65.00
Finger Bowl.	30.00
Goblet.	90.00
Parfait, Café.	65.00
Saucer Champagne.	75.00
Sundae (sherbet)	30.00
Wine.	90.00

ACCESSORIES:

Bonbon	$50.00
Bowl, Centerpiece, 13" (8153)	120.00
Candleholders, pr. (1-light, low) (9758). .	125.00
Cream (039)	50.00
Cup & Saucer (8869).	60.00
Grapefruit (251)	45.00
Iced Tea.	45.00
Jug & Cover (039)	210.00
Oyster Cocktail	35.00
Plate, 6"	20.00
Plate, 8"	25.00
Plate, 10".	135.00
Seltzer (Juice) (039)	35.00
Sugar (039)	50.00
Tumbler, Table (039)	45.00
Vase, Bud	95.00

Original Catalog Illustration:
Detail of Psyche etching

RENAISSANCE, NO. 413

DOUBLE PLATE ETCHING

Date: 1918

Manufacturer: A.H. Heisey & Co., Newark, OH

Colors: Crystal only

Notes: This etching was designed by Josef Balda for Heisey. All the cameos in this etching have the same motif, a fairy in a leafy bower. The 4164 jug may be plain or have cut flutes on the neck.

STEMWARE:

NO. 3333 OLD GLORY

Burgundy, 3 oz.	$30.00
Claret, 4½ oz.	30.00
Cocktail, 3 oz. or 2½ oz.	28.00
Comport, High Footed, 6".	76.00
Cordial, 1 oz.	85.00
Finger Bowl (3309)	15.00
Goblet, 8 oz. or 9 oz.	30.00
Grapefruit, Footed	32.00
Grape Juice, 6 oz.	32.00
Parfait, 4½ oz.	35.00
Pousse Café, ¾ oz.	75.00

Saucer Champagne, 5½ oz.	35.00
Sherry, 2 oz.	35.00
Soda, Footed, 12 oz. (No. 3476).	35.00
Sundae or Sherbet, 5½ oz.	18.00
Wine, 2 oz.	45.00

ACCESSORIES:

Bar, 2 oz. (2052)	$25.00
Candy Jar & Cover, 1 lb. (4291).	120.00
Comport, High Footed, 5" (3800)	95.00
Iced Tea, Footed & Handled,	
12 oz. (3476)	50.00
Jug, 63 oz. (4164)	165.00
Nappy, 5" (3946).	24.00
Nappy, 8" (3946).	35.00
Oyster Cocktail, 4½ oz. (3542)	18.00
Plate, 6", 7" or 8" (4182)	12.00
Soda, 5 oz. (2401)	20.00
Soda, 8 oz. or 10 oz. (2351)	22.00
Soda or Iced Tea, 12 oz. or	
14 oz. (2351)	28.00
Tumbler, 10 oz. (2930)	22.00

Original Catalog Illustration:
No. 413 Renaissance etching on
No. 3333 Old Glory stems

SPARTA

Date: 1932

Manufacturer: Morgantown Glass Works, Morgantown, WV

Colors: Crystal. Ritz Blue bowl, Crystal stem

Notes: "...Unusual artistry is shown in the 'Sparta' design of classic figures that decorates the wide Platinum border." —Original company description.

STEMWARE:

NO. 7643 GOLF BALL

Goblet.	$165.00

Original Catalog Illustration:
Sparta decoration on No. 7643
Golf Ball goblet

HUMANS, FAIRIES, & ANIMALS *(continued)*

Illustration of No. 455
Sportsman etching

SPORTSMAN, NO. 455

ETCHING

Date: 1932

Manufacturer: A.H. Heisey & Co.,
Newark, OH

Colors: Crystal

Notes: Designed for Heisey by Carl Cobel.

Bar Bottle, 28 oz. (4033) $210.00
Bar Bottle, 28 oz. (4034) 210.00
Bar, 1½ or 2½ oz. (2052) 75.00
Cocktail Shaker, 1 qt. (4225) 185.00
Cocktail Shaker, 2 qt. (4225) 210.00
Cocktail, 3 oz. (3405) 65.00
Cocktail, 4 oz. (4002) 75.00
Decanter, 1 pt. (3397) 175.00
Decanter, 32 oz. (4027) 185.00
Decanter, 32 oz. (4035) 185.00
Decanter, Footed, 16 oz. (2401) 195.00
Decanter, Handled & Lipped,
   32 oz. (4037) 185.00
Goblet, 7 oz. (3307) 95.00

Goblet, 7 oz. (3308) 80.00
Goblet, 11 oz. (3308) 95.00
Goblet, 17 oz. (811¾) 145.00
Hors d'oeuvre, 13" (1401) 85.00
Ice Tub, Dolphin Footed
   (1401 or 1509) 175.00
Jug, 108 oz. (4163) 165.00
Mug, Beer, 12 oz. (4163) 95.00
Mug, Beer, 16 oz. (4163) 110.00
Old Fashioned (2401) 40.00
Plate, Round, 8½" (1401 or 1509) 25.00
Pretzel Jar (4163) . . . . 700.00+
Rock & Rye, 1 qt. (4225) 185.00
Saucer Champagne, 6 oz. (3308) 60.00
Soda, 7 oz. (2401) 30.00
Soda, 12 oz. (2401) 55.00
Soda, 12 oz. (603) 55.00
Soda, 14 oz. (2405) 55.00
Soda, 14 oz. (3397) 70.00
Toddy, 8 oz. (2351) 45.00
Wine, 2½ oz. (3397) 85.00

Detail of No. 270
Springtime etching

SPRINGTIME, NO. 270

DOUBLE PROCESS PLATE ETCHING

Date: Ca. 1927

Manufacturer: Monongah Glass Co.,
Fairmont, WV

Colors: Crystal

Notes: Most items had an optic. Original
company catalogs indicate the gold bands were
"24 carat Roman gold." This pattern was the
original inspiration for the Hocking depression
pattern now called Cameo.

STEMWARE:

NO. 7485

Brandy, ¾ oz. $65.00
Claret, 4 oz. 45.00
Cocktail, 2½ oz. 38.00
Goblet, 9 oz. 45.00
Sherbet, High Footed, 5½ oz. 40.00
Sherbet, Low Footed, 5½ oz. 23.00
Wine, 2½ oz. 45.00

ACCESSORIES:

Almond, Footed, 9 oz. (7806) $32.00
Almond, Individual, 1½ oz. (7806) 30.00

Confection Stand, 6"
   (comport) (7806) 40.00
Cream (8) 35.00
Decanter and cut Stopper, 26 oz.,
   cut flutes (41) 210.00
Finger Bowl (7811) 30.00
Ginger Ale, 7 oz. (9011) 22.00
Grape Juice, 5 oz. (9011) 20.00
Iced Tea, 10 oz. (9011) 28.00
Iced Tea, 13 oz. (9011) 32.00
Iced Tea, Handled, 12 oz. (9011) 45.00
Jug, Grape Juice, with cover,
   30 oz. (92-4) 200.00
Jug, Iced Tea with cover,
   60 oz. (92-6) 225.00
Jug, Water, 50 oz. (90-6) 170.00
Jug, Water, 60 oz. (8-6½) 180.00
Parfait, 5½ oz. (7851) 35.00
Plate, 6½" (10340) 20.00
Plate, 8½" (10340) 25.00
Sugar (6) 35.00
Water, 8 oz. (9011) 25.00
Water, 9 oz. (9011) 25.00
Whiskey, 2½ oz. (9011) 45.00

(continued) HUMANS, FAIRIES, & ANIMALS

SUNRISE MEDALLION, NO. 758

DOUBLE PLATE ETCHING

Date: Ca. 1930

Manufacturer: Morgantown Glass Works, Morgantown, WV

Colors: Crystal, Blue, Green, Pink. Nos. 7630 and 7642 also with Crystal bowl, Ebony stem.

Notes: The true name as shown in company literature was simply Sunrise, but it is now best known as Sunrise Medallion. "The lilting 'Sunrise' medallion No. 758 etched on Crystal bowls, enhanced by Ebony feet is available in a complete service."—Catalog quote, 1931.

STEMWARE:

NO. 7630 (EXAMPLES ALSO KNOWN IN NO. 7664 QUEEN ANNE STEMWARE.)
Champagne	$35.00
Cocktail	40.00
Cordial	190.00
Finger Bowl, Footed	40.00
Goblet	80.00
Iced Tea, Footed	70.00

Juice, Footed	38.00
Parfait	85.00
Sherbet	25.00
Wine	60.00

ACCESSORIES:
Cream	$250.00
Cup & Saucer	125.00
Iced Tea (flat)	60.00
Jug	450.00
Juice (flat)	45.00
Plate, 6"	25.00
Plate, 7½"	30.00
Plate, 8½"	40.00
Sugar	250.00
Tumbler, Footed, 11 oz. (7606 or 7654½)	80.00
Vase, 6"	295.00
Vase, 10" (45)	275.0
Vase, Bud, 10"	245.00

STEMWARE:

NO. 7664
Cocktail	$165.00
Cordial	350.00
Goblet	200.00
Saucer Champagne (Tall Sherbet)	170.00

NO. 7654½ LEGACY
Goblet	$200.00

Original Catalog Illustration: No. 758 Sunrise Medallion etching on No. 7630 goblet

SUPERBA

Date: 1931

Manufacturer: Morgantown Glass Works, Morgantown, WV

Colors: Crystal. Crystal with Black

Notes: "These tall pieces with their hand-twisted stems cased with Black are unusual examples of the glass working art. The Oriental etching in this two tone effect is in keeping with the striking shape it embellishes." —From early catalog.

TINKERBELL, NO. 756

PLATE ETCHING

Date: 1930s

Manufacturer: Morgantown Glass Company, Morgantown, WV

Colors: Crystal, Azure

Maria Medicine Set (24)	$500.00

Original Catalog Illustration: Superba etching on No. 7664 goblet

Catalog Illustration: No. 756 Tinkerbell etching on No. 24 Maria medicine set

CHARMIAN

PLATE ETCHING WITH GOLD INLAY

Date: 1924

Manufacturer: U.S. Glass Co., Tiffin, OH

Colors: Crystal. Amber

STEMWARE:
NO. 14196
Café Parfait	$50.00
Claret	50.00
Finger Bowl	20.00
Goblet	58.00
Oyster Cocktail	20.00
Saucer Champagne	45.00
Sundae (sherbet)	25.00
Wine	58.00

ACCESSORIES:
Grapefruit (251)	$55.00
Jug, 64 oz. (110)	500.00
Oil & Stopper (179)	195.00
Plate, 8" (8833)	22.00
Plate, Finger Bowl	20.00
Table, 10 oz. (tumbler) (354)	32.00
Tumbler, 12 oz. (iced tea) (354)	35.00
Vase, Bud, 10" (185)	85.00

Original Charmian etching with Gold inlay over Iris medallion on No. 14196 goblet

Original catalog assortment of Charmian etching

Chapter 27
Ivy

Ivy

Sand Carving

Date: 1940s

Manufacturer: Unknown

Colors: Crystal

Notes: While the actual manufactuer of these pieces is unknown, the sand-carved designs were done by Dorothy C. Thorpe, an independent California designer. Thorpe headed her own design studio and contracted with glass companies to make glass to her designs. Her creations are usually marked with her initials, DTC in block letters.

Goblet $45.00
Plate 40.00

Original Ad: Ivy sand-engraving

Ivy, No. 1003

Engraved Gray Cutting

Date: 1949

Manufacturer: A.H. Heisey & Co., Newark, OH

Colors: Crystal

STEMWARE
No. 5040 Lariat (blown)
Claret, 4 oz. $50.00
Cocktail, 3½ oz. 32.00
Cordial, Tall, 1 oz. 170.00
Finger Bowl 25.00
Goblet, 10 oz. 50.00
Iced Tea, Footed 12 oz. 40.00
Juice, Footed, 5 oz. 25.00
Sherbet, 5½ oz. 25.00
Wine, 2½ oz. 50.00

ACCESSORIES
Plate, Salad, 8" 20.00

Catalog Illustration: No. 1003 Ivy cutting on No. 5040 Lariat goblet

IVY *(continued)*

Original Catalog Illustration: No. 516 Plantation Ivy etching on No. 5067 Plantation goblet

Original Catalog Illustration:
No. 516 Plantation Ivy etching on assorted candlesticks

Original Catalog Illustration:
No. 516 Plantation Ivy etching on assorted bowls

PLANTATION IVY, No. 516

PLATE ETCHING

Date: 1950

Manufacturer: A.H. Heisey & Co., Newark, OH

Colors: Crystal

Notes: Designed by Horace King. With a new deep-etched effect resembling a carving or engraving, "Heisey's new PLANTATION IVY pattern harmonizes with modern dinnerware, producing an effect of rare beauty."—Trade journal description. For matching stemware, see No. 5067 Plantation. Most pressed tableware pieces are in the No. 1567 Plantation pattern. Others are No. 1519 Waverly.

STEMWARE

No. 5067 PLANTATION (BLOWN)

Claret	$65.00
Cocktail, 4½ oz.	45.00
Cordial, 1 oz.	180.00
Goblet, 10 oz.	50.00
Oyster Cocktail, 4 oz.	25.00
Sherbet, 6½ oz.	30.00
Soda, 5 oz. (juice)	45.00
Soda, 12 oz. (iced tea)	75.00
Wine, 3 oz.	60.00

ACCESSORIES

Bowl, 2-compartment Dressing, 8½" (1567)	60.00
Bowl, Crimped, 9½" (1519)	55.00
Bowl, Crimped, 12" (1519)	60.00
Bowl, Floral, 12" (seahorse feet) (1519)	85.00
Bowl, Gardenia, 13" (1519)	55.00
Bowl, Salad, 7" (1519)	50.00
Bowl, Salad, 9" (1519)	58.00
Butter & Cover, ¼ lb. (1567)	150.00
Butter & Cover, Round, 5" (1567)	180.00
Candlesticks, 1-light, pr. (1567)	255.00
Candlesticks, 2-light, pr. (1567)	270.00
Candlesticks, 3-light, pr. (1567)	300.00
Celery or Celery & Olive, 13" (1567)	65.00
Cheese & Cover, Footed, 5" (1567)	95.00
Comport & Cover, 5" (1567)	120.00
Cream & Sugar, pr. (1567)	120.00
Cup & Saucer (1567)	60.00
Gardenia, Footed, 11½" (1519)	55.00
Honey, Footed, 6½" (1567)	65.00
Jelly, 2-handled or Footed, 6½" (1567)	45.00
Lamp, Hurricane, 1-light (1567)	1,800.00
Mayonnaise (1567)	70.00
Mayonnaise, Rolled Foot (1567)	90.00
Oil & Stopper (1567)	190.00
Pitcher, Ice Lip, ½ gal. (1567)	480.00
Plate, Mayonnaise (1567)	60.00
Plate, Salad, 7" or 8" (1519)	65.00
Plate, Sandwich, 11" (1567)	75.00
Plate, Sandwich or Torte, 14" (1567)	85.00
Plate, Torte, 10½" (1567)	70.00
Relish, 3-compartment, 11" (1567)	65.00
Relish, 4-compartment, Round, 8" (1567)	70.00
Relish, 5-compartment, Oval, 13" (1567)	110.00
Salt & Pepper, pr. (1567)	160.00
Salver, Footed, 13" (1567)	200.00
Syrup Bottle (1567)	155.00
Tray for Sugar & Cream (1567)	100.00
Vase, Footed, 5" (1519)	70.00

Chapter 28
MEDALLIONS & SHIELDS

Medallions and Shields comprise decorations which have distinct portions that could be interpreted as such. Be aware that many double plate etchings having medallions with figures in them are illustrated and listed in Chapter 25 Humans, Fairies and Animals.

CHEROKEE ROSE

PLATE ETCHING

Date: 1950s

Manufacturer: U.S. Glass Co., Tiffin, OH

Colors: Crystal

Notes: Note that the floral chain forms an S shape. It is likely other pieces were made. The centerpieces are floral bowls.

STEMWARE:
NO. 17399 OR 17403

Claret, 4 oz.	$50.00
Cocktail, 3½ oz.	35.00
Cordial, 1 oz.	70.00
Goblet, 9 oz.	40.00
Iced Tea, 10½ oz.	40.00
Parfait, 4½ oz.	65.00
Saucer Champagne, 5½ oz.	35.00
Sherry, 2 oz.	58.00
Sundae, 5½ oz. (sherbet)	28.00
Tumbler, Footed, 5 oz. (juice)	25.00
Tumbler, Footed, 8 oz. (water)	30.00
Wine, 3½ oz.	45.00

ACCESSORIES:

Bell, Table (9743 or 9742)	$160.00
Bowl, Nut, 6" (5902)	35.00
Bowl, Salad, 10" (5902)	80.00
Candlesticks, 2 Light, pr. (5902)	145.00
Celery Tray, 10½" (5902)	65.00
Centerpiece, Cone, 13" (5902)	80.00
Centerpiece, Crimped, 12" (5902)	80.00
Centerpiece, Flared, 12½" (5902)	80.00
Comport, 6" (15082)	60.00
Cream (5902)	40.00
Finger Bowl (14196)	30.00
Mayonnaise (5902)	50.00
Nappy, 7" (5902)	45.00
Oyster Cocktail, 4½ oz. (14196)	27.00
Pitcher (5859)	145.00
Plate, 6" (5902)	18.00
Plate, Center-handled Cake, 12½" (5902)	90.00
Plate, Lily, 13½" (5902)	100.00
Plate, Mayonnaise (5902)	18.00
Plate, Salad, 8" (5902)	20.00
Plate, Sandwich, 14"	125.00
Relish, 3-part, 6½" (5902)	65.00
Relish, 3-part, 12½" (5902)	80.00
Sugar (5902)	40.00
Vase, Bud, 6" (14185)	40.00
Vase, Bud, 8" (14185)	55.00
Vase, Bud, 10" (14185)	60.00
Vase, Bud, 11" (15082)	65.00
Vase, Flared, 12" (5855)	125.00
Vase, Tear Drop, 8½" (5856)	95.00
Vase, Tub, 9¼" (17350)	90.00
Vase, Urn, 11" (5943)	120.00

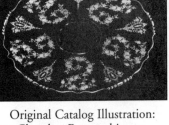

Original Catalog Illustration:
Cherokee Rose etching on
pressed sandwich plate

Original Catalog Illustration:
Cherokee Rose etching on
No. 15399 parfait

DAVID

PLATE ETCHING

Date: 1931

Manufacturer: Central Glass Works, Wheeling, WV

Colors: Crystal with stem in color

Notes: Certainly other stems were produced, but exact listings are not available. Name of decoration given by Hazel Marie Weatherman.

Goblet	$35.00

Original Catalog Illustration:
David plate etching

MEDALLIONS & SHIELDS *(continued)*

Original Catalog Illustration:
June Night etching on Jug

JUNE NIGHT

PLATE ETCHING

Date: 1950s

Manufacturer: U.S. Glass Co., Tiffin, OH

Colors: Crystal

Notes: It is likely other pieces were made. The centerpieces are floral bowls.

STEMWARE:

NO. 17392 OR NO. 17471

Claret	$60.00
Cocktail	35.00
Cordial	65.00
Goblet	40.00
Iced Tea	38.00
Juice	30.00
Oyster Cocktail	28.00
Parfait	48.00
Saucer Champagne	40.00
Sherry	62.00
Wine	50.00

ACCESSORIES:

Bell, Table (9743 or 9742)	$150.00
Bowl, Large (526)	150.00
Bowl, Nut, 6" (5902)	45.00
Bowl, Salad, 10" (5902)	140.00
Candlesticks, 2-light, pr. (5902)	150.00
Celery Tray, 10½" (5902)	65.00
Centerpiece, Cone-shaped, 12½" (5902)	110.00
Centerpiece, Crimped, 12" (5902)	150.00
Centerpiece, Shallow, 12½" (5902)	140.00
Comport, Tall, 6" (15082)	65.00
Cream (5902)	42.00
Finger Bowl (14196)	35.00
Jug, 60 oz. (5959)	195.00
Jug (14194)	195.00
Mayonnaise (5902)	70.00
Nappy, 7" (5902)	80.00
Oyster Cocktail, 4½ oz. (14196)	28.00
Plate, 6" (5902)	32.00
Plate, Cake (5902)	60.00
Plate, Center-handled Cake, 12½" (5909)	55.00
Plate, Lily or Floater, 13½" (5902)	60.00
Plate, Mayonnaise (5902)	30.00
Plate, Salad, 8" (5902)	35.00
Plate, Sandwich, 14" (5902)	70.00
Relish, Small 3-part, 6½" (5902)	50.00
Relish, Large 3-part, 12½" (5902)	130.00
Salt & Pepper, pr. (2)	60.00
Seafood Cocktail Set (6021)	85.00
Sugar (5902)	42.00
Vase, Bud, 6" (14185)	42.00
Vase, Bud, 8" (14185)	57.00
Vase, Bud, 10" (14185)	65.00
Vase, Bud, 11" (15082)	65.00
Vase, Flared, 12" (5855)	80.00
Vase, Tear Drop, 8½" (5856)	95.00
Vase, Tub, 9¼" (17350)	70.00
Vase, Urn, 11" (5943)	75.00

Original Catalog Illustration:
No. 628 Marlborough cutting on
No. 33 Kent goblet

MARLBOROUGH, NO. 628

ROCK CRYSTAL CUTTING

Date: 1930s

Manufacturer: Duncan & Miller Glass Co., Washington, PA

Colors: Crystal

STEMWARE:

NO. 33 KENT

Claret, 4½ oz., 6¾" high	$30.00
Cocktail, 4 oz., 6" high	30.00
Cordial, 1 oz., 3¾" high	70.00
Finger Bowl, 4½"	15.00
Goblet, 10 oz., 7¾" high	45.00
Iced Tea, Footed, 12 oz., 7" high	38.00
Orange Juice, Footed, 6 oz., 5¼" tall	24.00
Oyster Cocktail, 4 oz., 4" high	20.00
Saucer Champagne, 6 oz., 6¾" high	40.00
Wine, 3 oz., 6" high	45.00

ACCESSORIES:

Bowl, Deep Salad, 9" (33)	$55.00
Bowl, Flared, 12" (36)	68.00
Bowl, Low Foot, 13" (30)	68.00
Candlestick, Low, 3" pr. (115)	95.00
Candlesticks, 2-light, pr. (30)	115.00
Candy Box & Cover, 3-compartment, 6½" (106)	85.00
Celery & Relish, Oblong, 2-handled, 12" (30)	45.00
Cream (38)	40.00
Finger Bowl (30)	15.00
Iced Cocktail Set, 2- or 3-piece (30)	85.00
Mayonnaise Set (8)	85.00
Nappy, 2-handled, 6" (30)	35.00
Plate, 2-handled, 6" (30)	35.00
Plate, Bread & Butter, 6" (30½)	22.00
Plate, Dessert, 7½" (30½)	25.00
Plate, Salad, 8½" (30½)	25.00
Plate, Sandwich, 2-handled, 11" (30)	65.00
Plate, Torte, 13" (33)	80.00
Relish, 2 Handled, 2-compartment, 6" (30)	35.00
Sugar (38)	40.00
Vase, 10" (506)	90.00
Vase, Flip, Flared 8" (30)	80.00

(continued) MEDALLIONS & SHIELDS

OLD COLONY, NO. 448

PLATE ETCHING

Date: 1930

Manufacturer: A. H. Heisey & Co., Newark, OH

Colors: Crystal, Flamingo, Sahara, Crystal with Moongleam stem and foot, Moongleam with Crystal stem and foot, Alexandrite

Notes: One of Heisey's most popular etchings in its day. Found on a wide variety of pieces. Prices are for items in Crystal. For Flamingo, Sahara, Moongleam, add 100%. For Alexandrite add at least 250%. No. 1401 refers to Empress pattern; No. 1509, Queen Ann. Items with an asterisk (*) indicate pieces with dolphin feet.

No. 448 Old Colony etching on No. 2930 tumbler

STEMWARE:

NO. 3380 OLD DOMINION

Bar, 1 oz.	$35.00
Bar, 2 oz.	25.00
Claret, 4 oz.	25.00
Cocktail, 3 oz.	20.00
Comport, 7"	55.00
Cordial, 1 oz.	70.00
Frappe, 5 oz. (short or tall)	18.00
Goblet, 10 oz. (short or tall)	25.00
Grapefruit, Footed	25.00
Oyster Cocktail, 4 oz.	15.00
Parfait, 5 oz.	25.00
Saucer Champagne, 6 oz. (short)	18.00
Saucer Champagne, 6 oz. (tall)	20.00
Sherbet, 6 oz.	18.00
Soda or Iced Tea, 12 oz.	18.00
Soda, Footed, 5 oz. (juice)	15.00
Soda, Footed, 8 oz. (water)	15.00
Soda, Footed, 16 oz.	20.00
Tumbler, Footed, 10 oz.	15.00
Wine, 2½ oz.	35.00

NO. 3389 DUQUESNE

Claret, 4 oz.	$25.00
Cocktail, 3 oz.	24.00
Cordial, 1 oz.	70.00
Goblet, 9 oz.	25.00
Grapefruit, Footed	25.00
Oyster Cocktail, 4 oz.	18.00
Parfait, 5 oz.	28.00
Saucer Champagne, 5 oz.	25.00
Sherbet, 5 oz.	18.00
Soda, Footed, 12 oz.	15.00
Tumbler, Footed, 10 oz.	15.00
Wine, 2½ oz.	32.00

NO. 3390 CARCASSONNE

Bar, Footed, 2 oz.	$30.00
Claret, 4 oz.	27.00
Cordial, 1 oz.	55.00
Flagon, 12 oz.	35.00
Goblet, 11 oz. (short)	28.00
Goblet, 11 oz. (tall)	30.00
Morning After, 10½ oz.	30.00
Oyster Cocktail, 3 oz.	17.00
Saucer Champagne, 6 oz.	22.00
Sherbet, 6 oz.	18.00
Soda or Iced Tea, Footed, 12 oz.	18.00
Wine, 2½ oz.	30.00

NO. 3397 GASCONY

Cocktail, 3 oz.	$22.00
Decanter & Stopper, 1 pt.	150.00
Goblet, Low Foot, 11 oz.	55.00
Oyster Cocktail, 4 oz.	22.00
Pitcher, Tomato Juice	85.00
Saucer Champagne, 6 oz.	40.00
Sherbet, 6 oz.	18.00
Soda, Footed, 5 oz. (juice)	24.00
Soda, Footed, 12 oz. (iced tea)	40.00
Tumbler, Footed, 10 oz.	42.00
Wine, 2½ oz.	42.00

ACCESSORIES:

Baker, Oval (1183)	$45.00
Bouillon Cup & Plate (1401)	55.00
Bowl, Flared, Footed, 13" (1401)	85.00
Bowl, Floral, 2 Handled, Footed, 8½" (1401)	45.00
Bowl, Floral, 11" * (1401 or 1509)	75.00
Bowl, Salad, 2-handled, Round or Square, 10" (1401)	75.00
Candlesticks, 1-light, 6", pr. (135)	125.00
Candlesticks, 2-light, 5", pr. (134)	95.00
Celery Tray, 10" (1401)	30.00
Celery Tray, 13" (1401)	35.00
Cocktail Shaker, 1 qt. (4225)	95.00
Cocktail Shaker, 2 qt. (4225) Crystal only	110.00
Cocktail, 4 oz. (4002)	22.00
Comport, Oval, Footed, 7" (1401 or 1509)	45.00
Cream Soup, 2-handled & Plate (1401)	60.00
Cream * (1401 or 1509)	30.00
Cream, Individual (1401 or 1509)	30.00
Cup & Saucer (1183)	30.00
Cup & Saucer, After Dinner (1401)	85.00
Cup & Saucer, Round or Square (1401 or 1509)	35.00
Dessert, Oval, 2-handled, 10" (1401)	35.00
Dish, Oval Vegetable, 10" (1401)	35.00
Grapefruit, 6" (1401)	20.00
Hors d'oeuvre, 2-handled, 13" (1401)	75.00
Ice Tub (500)	75.00
Ice Tub * (1401 or 1509)	85.00

Jelly, 2-handled, Footed, 6" (1401 or 1509)	22.00
Jug, 73 oz. (4164)	145.00
Jug, 3 pt. * (1401 or 1509)	175.00
Mayonnaise, 5½" * (1401 or 1509)	35.00
Mint, Footed, 6" or 7" (1401 or 1509)	22.00
Mug, 16 oz. (4163) Crystal only	95.00
Mustard & Cover (1401)	85.00
Nappy, 4½" (1401 or 1509)	12.00
Nappy, 8" (1401 or 1509)	30.00
Nappy, Footed, 7½" (1401)	35.00
Nut Dish, Individual * (1509)	25.00
Oil, Footed, 4 oz. (1401)	70.00
Pickle & Olive, 2-compartment, 13" (1401)	35.00
Plate, 6" (3350)	15.00
Plate, 7" (1183)	15.00
Plate, 10" (1183)	85.00
Plate, Muffin, 2-handled, Round or Square, 12" (1401)	70.00
Plate, Round or Square, 10½" (1401 or 1509)	110.00
Plate, Round or Square, 6" or 7" (1401 or 1509)	18.00
Plate, Round or Square, 8" or 9" (1401 or 1509)	20.00
Plate, Round, 12" (1401)	75.00
Plate, Round, 4½" (1401)	12.00
Plate, Sandwich, 2-handled, Round or Square, 12" (1401 or 1509)	85.00
Platter, Oval, 14" (1401)	70.00
Preserve, 2-handled, Footed, 5" (1401)	20.00
Relish, Triplex, 7" (1401 or 1509)	30.00
Salt & Pepper (1401 or 1509)	70.00
Sandwich Tray, Center-handled, Round or Square, 12" (1401)	100.00
Soda, 5 oz. (2401)	12.00
Soda, 8 oz. (2351)	15.00
Soda, 12 oz. (2351)	18.00
Sugar * (1401 or 1509)	30.00
Sugar, Individual (1401 or 1509)	30.00
Tumbler, 10 oz. (2930)	18.00
Tumbler * (1401)	135.00
Vase, Bud, 8" (4205)	65.00
Vase, 9" * (1401)	110.00

169

MEDALLIONS & SHIELDS *(continued)*

Palais Versailles etching
with gold encrustation on
No. 17594 goblet

PALAIS VERSAILLES

ETCHING WITH ENCRUSTED GOLD

Date: 1954

Manufacturer: U.S. Glass Co., Tiffin, OH

Colors: Crystal

Notes: The large cut oval punties are etched and gold filled. Tiffin used the same motif for other cuttings: large cut ovals, cut ovals and etchings. These are different cuttings from Palais Versailles. This pattern was chosen by Elvis Presley as his stemware.

STEMWARE:
No. 17594
Claret	$110.00
Cocktail	90.00
Cordial	135.00
Goblet	110.00
Iced Tea, Footed	100.00
Saucer Champagne	90.00
Tumbler, Footed (juice)	100.00
Wine	125.00

ACCESSORIES:
Comport (5501)	$195.00
Finger Bowl	45.00
Plate, 8"	30.00

Original Catalog Illustration: No. 280 Trojan etching on baker

TROJAN, NO. 280

PLATE ETCHING

Date: 1929

Manufacturer: Fostoria Glass Co., Moundsville, WV

Colors: Gold Tint/Topaz, Rose

Notes: Trojan is etched primarily on No. 2375 Fairfax blanks.

STEMWARE:

No. 5099	Rose	Topaz
Claret	$72.00	$60.00
Cocktail	40.00	35.00
Cordial	115.00	95.00
Goblet	45.00	38.00
Iced Tea, Footed	40.00	35.00
Juice, Footed or Oyster Cocktail	36.00	30.00
Parfait	60.00	50.00
Saucer Champagne/High Sherbet	36.00	30.00
Sherbet, Low	30.00	26.00
Tumbler, Footed, 9 oz.	30.00	25.00
Whiskey, Footed	50.00	42.00
Wine	72.00	60.00

ACCESSORIES:

	Rose	Topaz
Ashtray, Large (2350)	$58.00	$45.00
Ashtray, Small (2350)	36.00	30.00
Baker, 9" (2375)	—	75.00
Bonbon (2375)	—	20.00
Bowl, "A", 12" (2394)	65.00	52.00
Bowl, 10" (2395)	120.00	85.00
Bowl, 12" (2375)	65.00	55.00
Bowl, Combination (2415)	235.00	185.00
Candlesticks, 2", pr. (2394)	55.00	48.00
Candlesticks, 3", pr. (2375)	68.00	50.00
Candlesticks, 5", pr. (2395½)	145.00	130.00
Candy Jar & Cover, ½ lb. (2394)	245.00	185.00
Celery, 11½" (2375)	48.00	35.00
Comport, 6" (2400)	40.00	35.00
Cream (2375½)	27.00	24.00
Cream Soup & Plate, Footed, pr. (2375)	44.00	38.00

	Rose	Topaz
Cream, Tea (2375½)	75.00	65.00
Cup & Saucer, After Dinner (2375)	65.00	48.00
Cup & Saucer, Footed (2375½)	30.00	24.00
Dessert, Large 2-handled (2375)	95.00	85.00
Fruit, 5" (2375)	25.00	22.00
Ice Bucket (2375)	90.00	75.00
Jug, Footed, 7 (5000)	415.00	300.00
Lunch Tray, Handled (2375)	45.00	40.00
Oil, Footed (2375)	375.00	275.00
Plate, Cake, 2-handled (2375)	42.00	38.00
Plate, Chop, 13" (2375)	58.00	48.00
Plate, Dinner, 9" (2375)	35.00	25.00
Plate, Dinner, 10" (2375)	85.00	68.00
Plate, Luncheon, 8" (2375)	20.00	18.00
Plate, Sauce Boat or Salad, 7" (2375)	12.00	10.00
Platter, 12" (2375)	80.00	70.00
Platter, 15" (2375)	185.00	165.00
Relish, 3-compartment (2350)	55.00	50.00
Relish, 8½" (2375)	—	25.00
Salt & Pepper, Footed, pr. (2375)	120.00	95.00
Sauce Boat (2375)	125.00	110.00
Sugar (2375½)	28.00	22.00
Sugar Pail, (2378)	200.00	145.00
Sugar, Tea (2375½)	65.00	50.00
Sweetmeat (2375)	22.00	20.00
Vase, 8" (2417)	160.00	135.00
Vase, 8" (4105)	240.00	190.00
Vase, 9" (2369)	—	245.00
Whipped Cream (2375)	20.00	18.00
Whipped Cream Pail (2378)	150.00	130.00

(continued) MEDALLIONS & SHIELDS

VERSAILLES, NO. 278

PLATE ETCHING

Date: 1928

Manufacturer: Fostoria Glass Co., Moundsville, WV

Colors: Crystal, Azure, Gold Tint, Green, Rose, Topaz

Notes: Versailles is etched on No. 2375 Fairfax blanks. Not all items were made in all colors since this was a popular Fostoria etching for many years. For crystal deduct 50% from Rose prices.

Original Catalog Illustration:
No. 278 Versailles etching on footed sugar and cream

STEMWARE: No 5098	Rose, Green, Topaz	Azure
Claret, 4 oz., 6" tall	$60.00	$70.00
Cocktail, 3 oz., 5⅛" tall	35.00	45.00
Cordial, ¾ oz., 3⅞" tall	120.00	140.00
Goblet, 9 oz., 8¼" tall	40.00	50.00
Iced Tea, Footed, 12 oz., 6" tall	40.00	50.00
Juice, Footed, 5 oz., 4⅜" tall	30.00	38.00
Oyster Cocktail, 5 oz., 3¾" tall	22.00	28.00
Parfait, 6 oz., 5¼" tall	42.00	52.00
Saucer Champagne/High Sherbet, 6 oz., 6" tall	37.00	42.00
Sherbet, Low, 6 oz., 4½" tall	25.00	35.00
Tumbler, Footed, 9 oz., 5¼" tall	27.00	35.00
Whiskey, Footed, 2½ oz., 2⅞" tall	48.00	58.00
Wine, 2½ oz., 5⅜" tall	60.00	70.00

No. 5099	Topaz Gold Tint
Claret, 4 oz., 6" tall	$60.00
Cordial, ¾ oz., 3⅞" tall	120.00
Goblet, 9 oz., 8¼" tall	40.00
Iced Tea. Footed, 12 oz., 5⅞" tall	40.00
Juice, Footed, 5 oz., 4½" tall	30.00
Oyster Cocktail, 4½ oz., 3½" tall	22.00
Parfait, 5½ oz.	42.00
Saucer Champagne/High Sherbet, 6 oz., 6⅛" tall	37.00
Sherbet, Low, 6 oz., 4¼" tall	25.00
Tumbler, Footed, 9 oz., 5⅜" tall	27.00
Whiskey, Footed, 2¾ oz., 2⅞" tall	48.00
Wine, 2½ oz., 5½" tall	60.00

ACCESSORIES:	Rose, Green Topaz, Gold Tint	Azure
Baker, 9" (2375)	$65.00	$145.00
Bonbon (2375)	22.00	32.00
Bouillon, Footed (2375)	22.00	40.00
Bowl, "A", 12" (2394)	45.00	75.00
Bowl, 12" (2375)	50.00	85.00
Candlesticks, 2", pr. (2394)	50.00	65.00
Candlesticks, 3", pr. (2375)	45.00	85.00

	Rose, Green Topaz, Gold Tint	Azure
Candlesticks, pr. (low) (2375½)	40.00	75.00
Candy Box & Cover, 3-compartment (2351)	185.00	—
Celery, 11½" (2375)	45.00	110.00
Centerpiece, 12" (2375)	65.00	100.00
Cereal, 6" (2376)	25.00	35.00
Comport, 7" (2375)	38.00	95.00
Cream (2375½)	20.00	28.00
Cream Soup, Footed (2375)	27.00	38.00
Cream, Tea (2375½)	55.00	75.00
Cup & Saucer, After Dinner (2375)	55.00	75.00
Cup & Saucer, Footed (2375½)	25.00	35.00
Dish, Lemon (2375)	350.00	460.00
Fruit, 5" (2375)	25.00	40.00
Ice Bucket (2375)	75.00	115.00
Lunch Tray, Handled, 11" (2375)	35.00	52.00
Mayonnaise (2375)	30.00	40.00
Plate, Bread & Butter, 6" (2375)	6.00	8.00
Plate, Cake, 10" (2375)	30.00	42.00
Plate, Cream Soup or Mayonnaise (2375)	10.00	18.00
Plate, Dinner, 9" (2375)	30.00	50.00
Plate, Dinner, 10" (2375)	75.00	115.00
Plate, Luncheon, 8" (2375)	10.00	17.00
Plate, Salad, 7" (2375)	9.00	14.00
Plate, Sauceboat (2375)	30.00	65.00
Platter, 12" (2375)	90.00	120.00
Platter, 15" (2375)	130.00	195.00
Relish, 8½" (2375)	35.00	—
Salt & Pepper, pr. (2375)	110.00	180.00
Sauceboat (2375)	90.00	170.00
Sugar & Cover, Footed (2375½)	185.00	250.00
Sugar Pail (2378)	168.00	265.00
Sugar, Tea (2375½)	50.00	68.00
Sweetmeat (2375)	18.00	25.00
Vase, 8" (2417)	185.00	—
Vase, 8" (4100)	150.00	285.00
Vase, Footed Fan, 8½" (2385)	140.00	265.00
Whipped Cream Pail (2378)	150.00	200.00
Whipped Cream (2375)	20.00	26.00

MITERS

Chapter 29

Miters are V-shaped grooves cut into glassware. This is a very versatile decoration and can be used to form many motifs. Other chapters also contain mitered cuttings which are done in other specific shapes.

Original Catalog Illustration: No. 1011 Bijou rock crystal engraving on No. 3725 goblet

BIJOU, NO. 1011

ROCK CRYSTAL ENGRAVING

Date: 1940s

Manufacturer: Cambridge Glass Co., Cambridge, OH

Colors: Crystal

STEMWARE:

No. 3725

Claret, 4½ oz.	$18.00
Cocktail, 2½ oz.	15.00
Cordial, 1 oz.	50.00
Goblet, 9 oz.	20.00
Iced Tea, Footed, 12 oz.	15.00

Oyster Cocktail, 4½ oz.	10.00
Sherbet, Low, 7 oz.	10.00
Sherbet, Tall, 7 oz.	12.00
Tumbler, Footed, 5 oz. (juice)	12.00
Wine, 2½ oz.	18.00

ACCESSORIES:

Old Fashioned Cocktail, 7 oz. (321)	$12.00
Salad Plate, 7½" (555)	10.00
Tumbler, 1½ oz. (whiskey) (321)	15.00
Tumbler, 12 oz. (497)	12.00
Tumbler, 14 oz. (iced tea) (497)	12.00

Caribbean cutting on No. 17687 goblet

CARIBBEAN

CUTTING

Date: 1950s

Manufacturer: Tiffin Art Glass Corp., Tiffin, OH

Colors: Crystal

Notes: "Dancing flames of cut crystal to capture your imagination..."—Original Tiffin Brochure.

STEMWARE:

No. 17687

Champagne/Sherbet	$30.00
Claret	35.00

Cocktail	30.00
Cordial	70.00
Goblet	35.00
Iced Tea	30.00
Juice	20.00

ACCESSORIES:

Finger Bowl	$15.00
Nappy, Dessert	15.00
Plate, Salad, 8"	18.00

Original Catalog Illustration: Formal rock crystal engraving on No. A56 Today goblet

FORMAL

ROCK CRYSTAL ENGRAVING

Date: 1950s

Manufacturer: Cambridge Glass Co., Cambridge, OH

Colors: Crystal

STEMWARE:

No. A56 TODAY

Claret	$25.00
Cocktail	20.00

Cordial	65.00
Goblet	25.00
Iced Tea, Footed, 12 oz.	22.00
Sherbet	15.00
Tumbler, Footed, 5 oz. (juice)	15.00
Wine	25.00

ACCESSORIES:

Plate, Salad, 8" (556)	$10.00

HYDE PARK

CUTTING

Date: 1950s

Manufacturer: Tiffin Art Glass Corp., Tiffin, OH

Colors: Crystal

Notes: "The inherent dignity of masterful styling emanates from this regal cutting design."—Original Tiffin Brochure.

STEMWARE:

No. 17687

Champagne/Sherbet	$30.00
Claret	35.00

Cocktail	30.00
Cordial	70.00
Goblet	35.00
Iced Tea	30.00
Juice	20.00

ACCESSORIES:

Finger Bowl	$15.00
Nappy, Dessert	15.00
Plate, Salad, 8"	18.00

Hyde Park cutting on
No. 17687 goblet

KILLARNEY, No. 686

ROCK CRYSTAL CUTTING

Date: 1940s

Manufacturer: Duncan & Miller Glass Co., Washington, PA

Colors: Crystal

STEMWARE:

No. 5323 ALDEN

Claret, 5 oz., 5¼" tall	$30.00
Cocktail, Liquor, 3½ oz., 4¼" tall	30.00
Finger Bowl, 4½"	15.00
Goblet, 10 oz., 6" tall	45.00
Ice Cream, Footed, 6 oz., 3" tall (sherbet)	17.00
Iced Tea, Footed, 13 oz., 5¾" tall	35.00
Orange Juice, Footed, 5 oz., 4¼" tall	24.00
Oyster Cocktail, 4½ oz., 3¼" tall	18.00
Saucer Champagne or Tall Sherbet, 6 oz., 4¼" tall	38.00
Wine, 3 oz., 4¾" tall	45.00

ACCESSORIES:

Bowl, Deep Salad, 9" (33)	$55.00
Bowl, Flared, 12" (36)	68.00

Bowl, Low Foot, 13" (30)	68.00
Candlestick, Low, 3" pr. (115)	75.00
Candlesticks, 2-light, pr. (30)	115.00
Candy Box & Cover, 3-compartment, 6½" (106)	85.00
Celery & Relish, Oblong, 2-handled, 12" (30)	45.00
Cream (38)	40.00
Finger Bowl (30)	15.00
Iced Cocktail Set, 2 pc. or 3 pc. (30)	85.00
Mayonnaise Set (8)	85.00
Nappy, 2-handled, 6" (30)	35.00
Plate, 2-handled, 6" (30)	35.00
Plate, Bread & Butter, 6" (30½)	22.00
Plate, Dessert, 7½" (30½)	25.00
Plate, Salad, 8½" (30½)	25.00
Plate, Sandwich, 2-handled, 11" (30)	65.00
Plate, Torte, 13" (33)	80.00
Relish, 2 Hdld, 2-compartment, 6" (30)	35.00
Sugar (38)	40.00
Vase, 10" (506)	90.00
Vase, Flip, Flared 8" (30)	80.00

Original Catalog Illustration:
No. 686 Killarney cutting on
No. 5323 Alden goblet

MODERNIST

CUTTING

Date: 1932

Manufacturer: Dunbar Glass Co., Dunbar, WV

Colors: Crystal. Bermuda Green and Rose Pink are likely. The following are possible: Steigel Green, Cobalt Blue and Ruby.

Notes: Only a few pieces are documented. This cutting also probably came on stemware, but that is uncertain. For pieces in color, add at least 50%.

Bedroom Set (tumble up) (6115)	$75.00
Iced Tea (6020)	18.00
Jug & Cover (6020)	85.00
Sandwich, Center-handled (6320)	45.00
Vase (6114)	48.00

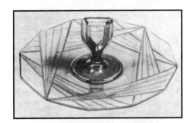

Original Ad: Modernist cutting
on handled sandwich

MITERS *(continued)*

L to R: Original Catalog Illustrations:
Neptune cutting on goblet and No. 1018 Plaza
rock crystal engraving on No. 3725 tall sherbert

NEPTUNE

GRAY CUTTING

Date: 1952

Manufacturer: Libbey Glass Co., Toledo, OH

Colors: Crystal

Notes: Designed by Freda Diamond.

Cocktail	$10.00
Cordial	35.00
Goblet	15.00
Sherbet	9.00
Wine	15.00

PLAZA, NO. 1018

ROCK CRYSTAL ENGRAVING

Date: 1940s

Manufacturer: Cambridge Glass Co., Cambridge, OH

Colors: Crystal

Notes: This was possibly made on the entire stem line, and possibly pressed accessories.

STEMWARE:
NO. 3725

Goblet	$30.00
Sherbet, Low	15.00
Sherbet, Tall	20.00

Original Catalog Illustration:
Repose cutting on goblet

REPOSE

GRAY CUTTING

Date: 1952

Manufacturer: Libbey Glass Co., Toledo, OH

Colors: Crystal

Notes: Designed by Freda Diamond.

Cocktail	$10.00
Cordial	35.00
Goblet	15.00
Sherbet	9.00
Wine	15.00

Royal Splendor cutting on
No. 17679 goblet

ROYAL SPLENDOR

CUTTING

Date: 1950s

Manufacturer: Tiffin Art Glass Corp.,
Tiffin, OH

Colors: Crystal

Notes: "Superbly crafted geometric design reflects the radiance of true crystal." —Original Tiffin Brochure.

STEMWARE:
NO. 17679

Champagne/Sherbet	$30.00
Claret	35.00

Cocktail	30.00
Cordial	70.00
Goblet	35.00
Iced Tea	30.00
Juice	20.00

ACCESSORIES:

Finger Bowl	$15.00
Nappy, Dessert	15.00
Plate, Salad, 8"	18.00

WARWICK, NO. 637

CUTTING

Date: 1930s

Manufacturer: Duncan & Miller Glass Co., Washington, PA

Colors: Crystal

STEMWARE:

NO. 30 YORK

Cocktail, Liquor	$30.00
Goblet	45.00
Iced Tea, Footed	38.00
Oyster Cocktail	17.00
Saucer Champagne or Tall Sherbet	40.00
Wine	45.00

ACCESSORIES:

Bowl, Deep Salad, 9" (33)	$55.00
Bowl, Flared, 12" (36)	68.00
Bowl, Low Foot, 13" (30)	68.00
Candlesticks, Low, 3", pr. (115)	75.00
Candlesticks, 2-light, pr. (30)	115.00
Candy Box & Cover, 3-compartment, 6½" (106)	85.00
Celery & Relish, Oblong, 2-handled, 12" (30)	45.00
Cream (38)	40.00
Finger Bowl (30)	15.00
Iced Cocktail Set, 2- or 3-piece (30)	85.00
Mayonnaise Set (8)	85.00
Nappy, 2-handled, 6" (30)	35.00
Plate, 2-handled, 6" (30)	35.00
Plate, Bread & Butter, 6" (30½)	22.00
Plate, Dessert, 7½" (30½)	25.00
Plate, Salad, 8½" (30½)	25.00
Plate, Sandwich, 2-handled, 11" (30)	65.00
Plate, Torte, 13" (33)	80.00
Relish, 2-handled, 2-compartment, 6" (30)	35.00
Sugar (38)	40.00
Vase, 10" (506)	90.00
Vase, Flip, Flared 8" (30)	80.00

Original Catalog Illustration: No. 637 Warwick on No. 30 York goblet

WEDDING RINGS

ROCK CRYSTAL ENGRAVING

Date: 1940s

Manufacturer: Cambridge Glass Co., Cambridge, OH

Colors: Crystal

STEMWARE:

NO. 7966 TRUMPET

Claret, Tall, 4 oz.	$25.00
Cocktail, Low, 4½ oz.	18.00
Cocktail, Tall, 3½ oz.	20.00
Cordial, Low, 1 oz.	40.00
Cordial, Tall, 1 oz.	50.00
Goblet, Footed, 12 oz.	25.00
Goblet, Tall, 9 oz.	30.00
Goblet, Tall, 10 oz. (7966/2)	32.00
Iced Tea, Footed, 12 oz.	22.00
Juice, Footed, 5 oz.	15.00
Sherbet, Low, 6 oz.	15.00
Sherbet, Tall, 6 oz.	24.00
Sherry, Tall, 2 oz.	45.00
Tumbler, Footed, 10 oz.	20.00
Wine, Low, 3 oz.	20.00

ACCESSORIES:

Bowl, Salad, 10" (P427)	$40.00
Cocktail Shaker (P101)	110.00
Comport, 5½" (533)	25.00
Cream (P254)	20.00
Decanter (1529)	95.00
Ice Tub (671)	65.00
Jug, Martini, 32 oz. (3900/114)	85.00
Mayonnaise (1532)	25.00
Oil & Stopper (P290)	65.00
Old Fashioned Cocktail, 9 oz. (321)	12.00
Plate, Cabaret, 13½" (P166)	42.00
Plate, Mayonnaise (1532)	15.00
Plate, Salad, 8" (556)	15.00
Relish, 3 pt. (P1498)	30.00
Salt & Pepper, pr. (P360)	50.00
Sugar (P254)	20.00
Tumbler, 14 oz. (497)	15.00
Vase (1528)	38.00

Original Catalog Illustration: Wedding Rings rock crystal engraving on No. P290 oil

Chapter 30

MITERS & PUNTIES

Miter cuts are those which are grooves cut into the glass. Punties are circles or ovals cut into the glass.
Several patterns contain both these motifs. Following are a few examples of this category of decoration.

Original Catalog Illustration:
No. 701 Concord rock crystal
cutting on No. 5323
Alden goblet

CONCORD, NO. 701

ROCK CRYSTAL CUTTING

Date: 1940s

Manufacturer: Duncan & Miller Glass Co.,
Washington, PA

Colors: Crystal

STEMWARE

NO. 5323 ALDEN
Claret, 5 oz., 5¼" tall. $30.00
Cocktail, Liquor, 3½ oz., 4¼" tall 30.00
Finger Bowl, 4½" 15.00
Goblet, 10 oz., 6" tall. 40.00
Ice Cream, Footed, 6 oz.,
   3" tall (sherbet). 18.00
Iced Tea, Footed, 13 oz., 5¾" tall 35.00
Orange Juice, Footed, 5 oz., 4¼" tall . . . 22.00
Oyster Cocktail, 4½ oz., 3¼" tall. 18.00
Saucer Champagne or Tall Sherbet,
   6 oz., 4¼" tall. 38.00
Wine, 3 oz., 4¾" tall 40.00

ACCESSORIES
Bowl, Deep Salad, 9" (33) $55.00
Bowl, Flared, 12" (36) 68.00
Bowl, Low Foot, 13" (30). 68.00
Candlesticks, Low, 3", pr. (115) 75.00

Candlesticks, 2-light, pr. (30) 115.00
Candy Box & Cover, 3-compartment,
   6½" (106) 85.00
Celery & Relish, Oblong, 2-handled,
   12" (30) 45.00
Comport, 6" (5317). 65.00
Comport, Tall, 7½" (8) 65.00
Cream (38) 40.00
Finger Bowl (30) 15.00
Iced Cocktail Set, 2- or 3-piece (30) 85.00
Mayonnaise Set (8) 82.00
Nappy, 2-handled, 6" (30) 35.00
Plate, 2-handled, 6" (30) 35.00
Plate, Bread & Butter, 6" (30½) 22.00
Plate, Dessert, 7½" (30½) 25.00
Plate, Salad, 8½" (30½) 25.00
Plate, Sandwich, 2-handled, 11" (30) . . . 65.00
Plate, Torte, 13" (33) 80.00
Relish, 2-handled, 2-compartment,
   6" (30) 35.00
Salad Dressing Set, 2-compartment,
   6", 2-piece (30). 55.00
Sugar (38) 40.00
Vase, 10" (506) 90.00
Vase, Flip, Flared 8" (30) 80.00

Original Catalog Illustration:
No. 1017 Euclid rock crystal
engraving on No. 3750 goblet

EUCLID, NO. 1017

ROCK CRYSTAL ENGRAVING

Date: 1940s

Manufacturer: Cambridge Glass Co.,
Cambridge, OH

Colors: Crystal

STEMWARE:

NO. 3750
Claret, 4½ oz. $18.00
Cocktail, 3½ oz. 15.00
Cordial, 1 oz. 50.00

Goblet, 10 oz. 18.00
Iced Tea, Footed, 12 oz. 15.00
Oyster Cocktail, 5 oz. 10.00
Sherbet, Low, 6 oz. 10.00
Sherbet, Tall, 6 oz. 12.00
Tumbler, Footed, 5 oz. (juice). 12.00
Wine, 3 oz. 18.00

ACCESSORIES:
Plate, Salad, 7½" (555) $12.00

HOLIDAY

ROCK CRYSTAL CUTTING

Date: 1950s

Manufacturer: Duncan & Miller Glass Co., Washington, PA

Colors: Crystal

STEMWARE

No. D3 DUNCAN PHYFE

Cocktail, Liquor, 3½ oz.	$30.00
Goblet, 10 oz.	45.00
Iced Tea, Footed, 14 oz.	38.00

Orange Juice, Footed, 5 oz.	24.00
Oyster Cocktail, Footed, 4½ oz.	18.00
Saucer Champagne or Tall Sherbet, 5 oz.	40.00
Wine or Claret, 4 oz.	45.00

ACCESSORIES

Plate, 6" (30½)	$17.00
Plate, 7½" (30½)	17.00
Plate, 8½" (30½)	20.00

Original Catalog Illustration: Holiday cutting on No. D3 Duncan Phyfe goblet

JUNO, NO. 688

ROCK CRYSTAL CUTTING

Date: 1940s

Manufacturer: Duncan & Miller Glass Co., Washington, PA

Colors: Crystal

STEMWARE

No. 5317 CATHAY

Claret, 5 oz., 5¾" tall	$30.00
Cocktail, Liquor, 3½ oz., 4" tall	30.00
Cordial, 1 oz., 3½" tall	70.00
Finger Bowl, 4½"	15.00
Goblet, 10 oz., 6¼" tall	45.00
Ice Cream, Footed (sherbet), 5 oz., 3½" tall	16.00
Iced Tea, Footed, 12 oz., 6½" tall	35.00
Juice, Orange, Footed, 5 oz., 4¾" tall	24.00
Oyster Cocktail, 4½ oz., 3½" tall	18.00
Saucer Champagne, 5 oz., 4½" tall	40.00
Tumbler, Footed, 9 oz., 5½" tall	36.00
Wine, 3 oz., 5" tall	45.00

ACCESSORIES

Bowl, Deep Salad, 9" (33)	$55.00
Bowl, Flared, 12" (36)	68.00

Bowl, Low Foot, 13" (30)	68.00
Candlestick, Low, 3" pr. (115)	75.00
Candlesticks, 2 Light, pr. (30)	115.00
Candy Box & Cover, 3-compartment, 6½" (106)	85.00
Celery & Relish, Oblong, 2-handled, 12" (30)	45.00
Cream (38)	40.00
Finger Bowl (30)	15.00
Iced Cocktail Set, 2 or 3 piece (30)	85.00
Mayonnaise Set (8)	85.00
Nappy, 2-handled, 6" (30)	35.00
Plate, 2-handled, 6" (30)	35.00
Plate, Bread & Butter, 6" (30½)	22.00
Plate, Dessert, 7½" (30½)	25.00
Plate, Salad, 8½" (30½)	25.00
Plate, Sandwich, 2-handled, 11" (30)	65.00
Plate, Torte, 13" (33)	80.00
Relish, 2-handled, 2-compartment, 6" (30)	35.00
Sugar (38)	40.00
Vase, 10" (506)	90.00
Vase, Flip, Flared 8" (30)	80.00

Original Catalog Illustration: Juno cutting on No. 5317 Cathay goblet and saucer champagne

SUNDOWN

ROCK CRYSTAL CUTTING

Date: 1950s

Manufacturer: Duncan & Miller Glass Co., Washington, PA

Colors: Crystal

Notes: No. 30½ refers to Pall Mall pattern.

STEMWARE

No. D7 CHALICE

Cocktail, Liquor	$30.00
Goblet	42.00

Iced Tea, Footed	35.00
Juice, Footed	24.00
Saucer Champagne or Tall Sherbet	38.00
Seafood Cocktail	16.00
Wine or Claret	42.00

ACCESSORIES

Plate, 7½" (30½)	$17.00
Plate, 8½" (30½)	17.00

Original Catalog Illustration: Sundown cutting on No. D7 Chalice goblet

Chapter 31

MITERS & SQUARES

This chapter contains miter cuttings which form squares as the primary motifs of the decorations.

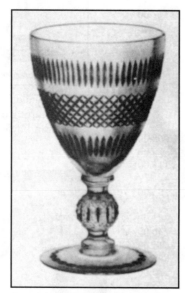

Original Catalog Illustration:
No. 629 rock crystal engraving on No. 1066 Aurora goblet

NO. 629

ROCK CRYSTAL ENGRAVING

Date: 1930s

Manufacturer: Cambridge Glass Co., Cambridge, OH

Colors: Crystal

NO. 1066 AURORA
Claret, 4½ oz.	$20.00
Cocktail, 3½ oz.	15.00
Cordial, 1 oz.	50.00
Goblet	20.00
Iced Tea, Footed, 12 oz.	18.00
Sherbet, Tall, 7 oz.	12.00
Tumbler, Footed, 5 oz.	15.00
Wine, 3 oz.	20.00

PICKWICK

ROCK CRYSTAL CUTTING

Date: 1950s

Manufacturer: Duncan & Miller Glass Co., Washington, PA

Colors: Crystal

Notes: No. 30½ refers to Pall Mall pattern.

STEMWARE:
NO. D3 DUNCAN-PHYFE
Cocktail, Liquor, 3½ oz.	$28.00
Goblet, 10 oz.	45.00
Iced Tea, Footed, 14 oz.	35.00
Orange Juice, Footed, 5 oz.	25.00
Oyster Cocktail, Footed, 4½ oz.	16.00
Saucer Champagne or Tall Sherbet, 5 oz.	38.00
Wine or Claret, 4 oz.	45.00

ACCESSORIES:
Hi Ball	$15.00
Plate, 6" (30½)	17.00
Plate, 7½" (30½)	17.00
Plate, 8½" (30½)	17.00

Original Catalog Illustration:
Pickwick cutting on No. D3 Duncan-Phyfe goblet

Chapter 32
MODERN

METEOR, NO. 726

CUTTING

Date: 1933

Manufacturer: Fostoria Glass Co., Moundsville, WV

Colors: Crystal

STEMWARE
NO. 4024 VICTORIAN

Claret/Wine, 3½ oz., 4½" tall $32.00
Cocktail, 4 oz., 3⅝" tall 26.00
Cordial, 1 oz., 3⅛" tall 60.00
Goblet, 10 oz., 5⅝" tall 32.00
Goblet, 11 oz., 6⅞" tall 32.00
Iced Tea, Footed, 12 oz., 5½" tall 32.00
Juice, Footed, 5 oz., 4¼" tall 28.00
Oyster Cocktail, 4 oz., 3⅜" tall 20.00
Rhine Wine, 3½ oz., 5⅞" tall 32.00
Saucer Champagne, 6½ oz., 4½" tall . . . 30.00
Sherbet, 5½ oz., 3⅞" tall 24.00
Sherry, 2 oz., 3⅞" tall 32.00
Tumbler, Footed, 8 oz., 4¾" tall 28.00
Whiskey, Footed, 1½ oz., 2½" tall 27.00

ACCESSORIES
Bowl, Footed, 10" (4024) $45.00
Candlesticks, 6" (4024) 42.00
Comport, 5" (4024) 20.00
Decanter, Footed (6011) 85.00
Finger Bowl (869) 10.00
Jug, Footed (6011) 75.00
Old Fashioned Cocktail (1184). 9.00
Oyster Cocktail, 4 oz. (4024) 10.00
Plate, 6" or 7" (2337). 10.00
Plate, 8" (2337) 12.00
Plate, 11" (2337) 35.00
Rhine Wine, 3½ oz. (4024) 25.00
Sherbet, 5½ oz. (4024) 15.00
Sherry, 2 oz. (4024) 25.00
Tumbler, 10 or 12 oz. (701) 12.00

Original Catalog Illustration:
Fostoria Meteor Cutting
on No. 726 goblet

RONDO, NO. 1081

ROCK CRYSTAL ENGRAVING

Date: 1950s

Manufacturer: Cambridge Glass Co., Cambridge, OH

Colors: Crystal

STEMWARE
No. 7966
Cocktail, Low $14.00
Cordial, Low 50.00
Goblet, Low 18.00
Sherbet, Low 10.00
Wine, Low. 18.00

ACCESSORIES
Bowl, 10" (P427) $28.00
Bowl, Oval, 11" (P384) 35.00
Bowl, Salad, 8" (P426) 32.00
Candlesticks, 1-light, 6" pr. (628) 42.00
Celery (P247) 27.00
Cocktail Shaker, 32 oz. (101) 100.00

Comport, 5½" (P533) 24.00
Comport, Blown, 5" (3700) 32.00
Cream (P254) 20.00
High Ball, 12 oz. (497) 15.00
Ice Tub (P671) 45.00
Jug, 76 oz. (3900/115) 90.00
Jug, Martini, 32 oz. (3900/114) 55.00
Mayonnaise (P1532) 45.00
Mayonnaise, 2-pt. (P1491) 28.00
Oil & Stopper, 6 oz. (P290) 45.00
Old Fashioned Cocktail, 9 oz. (321) 13.00
Plate, Cabaret, 13½" (P166) 40.00
Plate, Mayonnaise (P1532). 12.00
Plate, Salad, 7½" (555) 12.00
Relish, 3 part (P1498) 27.00
Salt & Pepper, pr. (P360) 45.00
Sugar (P254) 20.00
Vase, 6" (572) 28.00
Vase, 8" (6004) 27.00
Vase, Footed, 11" (278) 50.00

Rondo
rock crystal engraved
by Cambridge

Original Catalog Illustration:
No. 1081 Rondo cutting on
No. 7966 low goblet

MODERN *(continued)*

Original Catalog Illustration: No. 8P Tomorrow rock crystal engraving on No. A45 Today goblet

TOMORROW, NO. 8P

ROCK CRYSTAL ENGRAVING

Date: 1950s

Manufacturer: Cambridge Glass Co., Cambridge, OH

Colors: Crystal

STEMWARE
NO. A56 TODAY

Claret	$25.00
Cocktail	20.00
Cordial	65.00
Goblet	25.00
Iced Tea, Footed, 12 oz.	22.00
Sherbet	15.00
Tumbler, Footed, 5 oz. (juice)	15.00
Wine	25.00

ACCESSORIES

Plate, Salad, 8" (556)	$15.00

Original Catalog Illustration: No. 765 Vichy etching

VICHY, NO. 765

PLATE ETCHING

Date: 1930s

Manufacturer: Cambridge Glass Co., Cambridge, OH

Colors: Crystal

Notes: An asterisk (*) indicates stems with cut flutes. These should have 15% added to the value.

STEMWARE
NO. 3129

Brandy, ¾ oz.	$60.00
Champagne, Hollow Stem, 6 oz. *	28.00
Champagne, Saucer, 6 oz.	22.00
Champagne, Tall, 5 oz.	25.00
Claret, 4 oz.	25.00
Cocktail, 3½ oz.	22.00
Cordial, 1 oz.	60.00
Goblet, 10 oz.	25.00
Hoch, Tall, 6 oz.	25.00
Pousse-Café, 1 oz.	60.00
Roemer, 5 oz.	25.00
Sherbet, Low, 6 oz.	15.00
Sparkling Burgundy, Hollow Stem, 4 oz. *	28.00
Wine, 2 oz.	25.00
Wine, Burgundy, 2 oz.	25.00

ADDITIONAL ITEMS

Finger Bowl	$15.00
Plate, Finger Bowl	8.00
Sherry, 1½ oz. (7966) *	25.00
Sherry, 2 oz. (7966) *	25.00

Chapter 33
MORNING GLORY

MORNING GLORY

HAND SCULPTURED DECORATION

Date: 1947

Manufacturer: Chartiers Crystal—a division of Duncan & Miller

Colors: Crystal

Notes: Chartiers was a "budget" line of Duncan & Miller.

Brandy	$35.00
Cocktail, Liquor	18.00
Goblet	22.00
Iced Tea	20.00
Juice, Orange	15.00
Oyster Cocktail	9.00
Sherbet	9.00
Whiskey Sour	12.00
Wine	25.00

Original Ad: Morning Glory
hand-sculptured decoration on iced tea

MORNING GLORY, NO. 12

CARVING

Date: 1939

Manufacturer: Fostoria Glass Co., Moundsville, WV

Colors: Crystal, Amber

Notes: This decoration is done by sand blasting or sand carving. Fostoria also made a Morning Glory etching.

Ashtray, Oblong, 3½" x 2¾" (2427)	$15.00
Bowl, 7" (315)	30.00
Bowl, 9" (315)	35.00
Bowl, Footed, 9¼" (6023)	55.00
Bowl, Oblong Shallow, 11", (2596)	40.00
Candlesticks, 6", 1-light, pr. (2324)	60.00
Cigarette Box & Cover, 2-pt., 7"x 3⅛" (2427)	45.00
Ice Bowl, 4¾" x 6" (4123)	55.00
Lunch Tray, Handled	55.00
Plate, 6" or 7" (2337)	16.00
Plate, 8" (2337)	18.00
Plate, Cake, 2-handled, 9½" (2419)	40.00
Plate, Torte, 16" (2364)	50.00
Vase, 10" (5100)	90.00
Vase, Heavy, 5" (4128½)	75.00
Vase, Heavy, 8" (4132½)	85.00

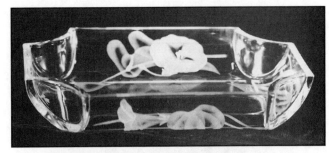

Morning Glory carving on No. 2596 oblong bowl

Morning Glory carving on torte plate

181

MORNING GLORY *(continued)*

Original catalog Illustration: Morning Glory etching

Detail of Morning Glory etching

MORNING GLORY, NO. 313

PLATE ETCHING

Date: 1931

Manufacturer: Fostoria Glass Co., Moundsville, WV

Colors: Crystal; Amber feet, Crystal bowls

Notes: Not all items were made with Amber feet. Prices are for both varieties.

STEMWARE:

NO. 6007
Claret, 4 oz., 5⅜" tall $35.00
Cocktail, 3½ oz., 4⅝" tall 24.00
Cordial, 1 oz., 3⅝" tall 65.00
Goblet, 10 oz., 7½" tall 28.00
Oyster Cocktail, 4½ oz., 3⅛" tall 12.00
Saucer Champagne, 5½ oz., 5⅜" tall
    (high sherbet) 22.00
Sherbet, Low, 5½ oz., 4" tall 15.00
Tumbler, Footed, 2 oz., 2¾" tall
    (bar or whiskey) 27.00
Tumbler, Footed, 5 oz., 4¼" tall (juice) 18.00
Tumbler, Footed, 9 oz., 5⅛" tall (water) 20.00
Tumbler, Footed, 12 oz., 5⅝" tall (iced tea) 24.00
Wine, 3 oz., 5" tall 38.00

ACCESSORIES:
Baker, 10" (2440) $45.00
Bonbon (2470) 27.00
Bowl, 10½" (2470½) 45.00
Candlesticks, 5½", pr. (2470½) 75.00
Celery, 11½" (2440) 30.00
Cream, Footed (2440) 24.00
Cup & Saucer (2440) 30.00
Cup & Saucer, After-dinner (2440) 45.00
Dish, Lemon (2470) 30.00
Finger Bowl (869) 15.00
Jug (2270) 95.00
Olive, 6½" (2440) 25.00
Pickle, 8½" (2440) 32.00
Plate, Bread & Butter, 6" (2440) 15.00
Plate, Cake (2470) 42.00
Plate, Dinner, 9" (2440) 45.00
Plate, Dinner, 10" (2440) 75.00
Plate, Luncheon, 8" (2440) 20.00
Plate, Salad, 7" (2440) 18.00
Plate, Torte, 13" (2440) 55.00
Platter, 12" (2440) 50.00
Relish, 3-part (2470) 40.00
Relish, 4-part (2419) 45.00
Sugar, Footed (2440) 24.00
Sweetmeat (2470) 30.00
Tray for Sugar & Cream (2470) 65.00
Vase, 7" (2440) 85.00
Vase, 7½" (2467) 90.00

CHAPTER 34
ORCHIDS

ORCHID, NO. 507

PLATE ETCHING

Date: 1940

Manufacturer: A.H. Heisey & Co., Newark, OH

Colors: Crystal only

Notes: Numbers following listings are original Heisey pattern numbers. Orchid was Heisey's most popular etching. Orchid continued in Heisey's line until its closing in 1957 when a reduced line was continued by Imperial Glass Corp. of Bellaire, Ohio, for a few years. The following original numbers and names will help you identify the blanks: No. 1495 Fern, No. 1509 Queen Anne, No. 1519 Waverly, No. 1540 Lariat, No. 1951 Cabochon. No. 942 Harvester and No. 947 Enchantress were also found on Nos. 5022 and 5025. "So fashionable, so delightfully feminine, this lovely Orchid pattern in sparkling hand wrought crystal by Heisey…rare, jewel-like beauty to highlight the most fastidious table setting… elegance to charm the most discerning guests." —Heisey pattern folder

STEMWARE:

NO. 5022 GRACEFUL/NO. 5025 TYROLEAN
Bell, Dinner	$150.00
Claret, 4½ oz.	110.00
Cocktail, 4 oz.	58.00
Cordial, 1 oz.	145.00
Finger Bowl	30.00
Goblet, Low Stem, 10 oz.	45.00
Goblet, Tall Stem, 10 oz.	55.00
Oyster Cocktail, 4 oz.	50.00
Saucer Champagne, 6 oz.	45.00
Sherbet, 6 oz.	25.00
Sherry, 2 oz.	135.00
Soda, Footed, 5 oz. (juice)	65.00
Soda, Footed, 12 oz. (iced tea)	80.00
Wine, 3 oz.	95.00

NO. 5089 PRINCESS
Claret, 4 oz.	$75.00
Cocktail, 3½ oz.	45.00
Cordial, 1 oz.	100.00
Goblet, 10 oz.	45.00
Iced Tea, Footed, 12 oz.	60.00
Juice, Footed, 5 oz.	45.00
Oyster Cocktail, 2½ oz.	25.00
Saucer Champagne, 5½ oz.	38.00
Wine, 2½ oz.	55.00

ACCESSORIES:

NO. 1519 UNLESS NOTED OTHERWISE
Ashtray, 3" (1435)	$35.00
Bar, 2½ oz. (2052)	70.00
Basket, Handled & Footed, 8½" (1540)	1200.00+
Bottle, French Dressing, 8 oz. (5031)	200.00
Bowl, Combination Dressing, 7" (1509)	60.00
Bowl, Crimped, 12"	95.00
Bowl, Flared, 8½" (1509)	75.00
Bowl, Flared, 11"	125.00
Bowl, Floral, 10"	90.00
Bowl, Floral, 13"	125.00
Bowl, Floral, Crimped, 9½"	90.00
Bowl, Floral, Crimped, 13"	100.00
Bowl, Floral, Seahorse Footed, 11"	175.00
Bowl, Floral, 2-handled, Footed, 8½" (1509)	75.00
Bowl, Fruit or Salad, Footed, 9"	140.00
Bowl, Fruit, Shallow, Footed	125.00
Bowl, Gardenia (485)	70.00
Bowl, Gardenia, 9" (1509)	75.00
Bowl, Gardenia, 10"	90.00
Bowl, Gardenia, 13"	85.00
Bowl, Lily, 9" (1509)	120.00
Bowl, Oval Dressing, 2-compartment, 6½"	80.00
Bowl, Oval Dressing, 2-compartment, 8"	95.00
Bowl, Oval, 4-footed, 11"	135.00
Bowl, Salad, 7" or 9"	85.00
Bowl, Salad, 9" (485)	75.00
Bowl, Sauce, Footed, 7½" (1509)	65.00
Bowl, Shallow, Rolled Edge, 11"	90.00
Bowl, Sunburst, 9" (1509)	95.00
Bowl, Sunburst Floral, 10" (1509)	110.00
Butter & Cover, ¼ lb. (1951)	350.00
Butter Dish & Cover, 6"	195.00
Candelabra & Prisms, 1-light, pr. (1509)	275.00
Candelabra & Prisms, 2-light, pr. (1495)	250.00
Candleholder, Deep Epergnette, 6", pr.	350.00+
Candlestick, 1-light, Blown, pr. (5026)	700.00+
Candlestick, 1-light, pr. (112)	95.00
Candlestick, 2-light, 5", pr. (134)	120.00
Candlestick, 2-light, pr. (1615)	270.00

Original Company Brochure: No. 507 Orchid etching on No. 5025 Tyrolean stems

Original Company Brochure: No. 507 Orchid etching on No. 4164 ice jug

ORCHIDS *(continued)*

Original Company Brochure:
No. 507 Orchid etching on
No. 1519 torte plate

Original Company Brochure:
No. 507 Orchid etching on
No. 4036 cocktail shaker

Original Company Brochure:
No. 507 Orchid etching on
No. 1519 ice bucket

Candlestick, 3-light (142 or 1519) . . . 180.00
Candy & Cover, High Footed,
    Seahorse handles, 5" 260.00
Candy Box & Cover, Low,
    6" (Bow Finial) 195.00
Celery Tray, 12" or 13" 65.00
Centerpiece, Gardenia or Fruit, 13" . . 450.00+
Cheese, Footed, 5½" (1509) 65.00
Cheese & Cracker, 2 pc., 12" (1509) . . 145.00
Cheese & Cracker, 2 pc., 14" 145.00
Chocolate & Cover, 5" 200.00
Cigarette Box & Cover (1489) 150.00
Cigarette Holder & Cover,
    Seahorse handles 195.00
Cigarette Holder (4035) 95.00
Cocktail Icer & Liner (3304) 260.00
Cocktail Shaker, 1 pt. (4225) 300.00
Cocktail Shaker, 1 qt. (4036 or 4225) . . 295.00
Cocktail, 4 oz. (4002) 65.00
Comport, Blown, 5½" (5027) 100.00
Comport, Footed, Oval, 7" 145.00
Comport, Low Footed, 6" . . . . 400.00+
Comport, Low Footed, 6½" 65.00
Comport, Nut, Oval, Footed, 7" 95.00
Cordial, 1 oz. (4090) 300.00
Cream & Sugar, Footed, pr. 90.00
Cream, Individual 50.00
Cup & Saucer (1509 or 1519) 60.00
Decanter, 1 pt. (4036½) 350.00
Decanter, Footed, 1 pt. (4036) 375.00
Epergne Bowl, Footed,
    with 4233 vase (1187) 700.00
Honey or Cheese, Footed, 6½" or 7" . . 65.00
Ice Bucket, 2-handled 250.00
Ice Cube Bucket, Dolphin
    Footed (1509) 245.00
Jelly, Footed, 6½" or 7" 70.00
Jug, Ice, ½ gal. (3484 or 5034) 600.00
Jug, Ice, 73 oz. (4164) 600.00
Lamp, Hurricane, Square Base,
    1-light (1503) . . . . 600.00+
Lemon & Cover, Oval, 6" . . . . 400.00+
Lemon Dish & Cover,
    Dolphin Finial, 6½" (1509) 325.00
Marmalade & Cover (4121) 275.00
Mayonnaise, 1 Handle, 5½",
    1- or 2-compartment 65.00
Mayonnaise, Footed, 5½" 65.00
Mayonnaise, Footed, Rolled Edge,
    5" (1540) 70.00
Mayonnaise, Twin, 6" (1495) 60.00
Mint, Footed, 5½" (1509 or 1519) 45.00
Mint, Footed, 8" (1509) 70.00
Mustard & Cover (1509) 155.00
Nappy, 4½" (1509) 40.00
Nappy, 8" (1509) 75.00
Oil, Footed, 3 oz. 195.00
Plate, 6", 7" or 8" (4182) 18.00
Plate, Cheese & Sandwich, 2 pc., 11" . . 150.00
Plate, Demi-Torte, 11" (1509 or 1519) . . 75.00
Plate, Mayonnaise, 7" 25.00
Plate, Mayonnaise, 8" (1495) 25.00
Plate, Salad, 7" or 8" 25.00

Plate, Sandwich, 10" (1509) 90.00
Plate, Sandwich, 11" 90.00
Plate, Sandwich, 14" 100.00
Plate, Sandwich, 14" (485) 70.00
Plate, Sandwich, Center-handled,
    12" (1509) 90.00
Plate, Sandwich, Round, 2-handled,
    12" (1509) 80.00
Plate, Service, 10½" (dinner)
    (1509 or 1519) 180.00
Plate, Snack Rack & Center,
    16" (1509) 130.00
Plate, Torte, 14" (485) 70.00
Plate, Torte, 14", plain or rolled edge . . 115.00
Relish, 3-compartment, 11" (1495) . . . 90.00
Relish, 3-compartment, 11" (1509) . . . 80.00
Relish, 5 O'clock, 11" (1509) 90.00
Relish, Oblong, 3-compartment, 11" . . 75.00
Relish, Round, 3-compartment, 7" 70.00
Relish, Round, 4-compartment,
    8" or 9" 85.00
Relish, Triplex, 7" (1509) 65.00
Salt & Pepper, pr. (1519/1605) 100.00
Salt & Pepper, pr. (42) 95.00
Salt & Pepper, pr. (57) 110.00
Salver or Cake Plate, Footed, 13½" . . . 280.00
Salver, Footed, 12" 270.00
Sandwich, Center-handled, 14" 100.00
Sauce, Footed, 5½" (1509) 45.00
Sherry, 2 oz. (4090) 200.00
Sherry, 2½ oz. (3311) 110.00
Sherry, Oval, 1 pt. (4037) 260.00
Soda or Iced Tea, 12 oz. (3484) 60.00
Soda, 10 oz. (4052) 60.00
Soda, 6, 7 or 12 oz. (2351 or 2401) . . . 60.00
Sugar, Individual 50.00
Tankard, Ice, ½ gal. (5032) 600.00
Toast & Dome (1519/3806) 300.00
Tray, for Individual
    Cream & Sugar (1509) 80.00
Tumbler, Luncheon, 10 oz. (3389) 60.00
Vase, 6" (4191) 300.00
Vase, 7" or 8" (5034 or 4191) 350.00
Vase, 8", 9" or 10" (4198 or 4192½) . . 400.00+
Vase, 12" (4191) . . . . 400.00+
Vase, 12" or 14" (4198) . . . . 500.00+
Vase, Ball, 7" (4045) . . . . 500.00+
Vase, Bud, 8" (4205) 210.00
Vase, Crimped Top, 7" (1540) 125.00
Vase, Fan, Footed, 7" 110.00
Vase, Flip, 10½" (4057) . . . . 450.00+
Vase, Footed, 7" 110.00
Vase, Footed, 9" (5012) 200.00
Vase, Square Footed Bud,
    8" or 10" (5012) 210.00
Vase, Square Footed Bud, 12" (5012) . . 250.00
Vase, Square Top, 7" (1540) 125.00
Vase, Straight, 7" (1540) 125.00
Vase, Swing, Footed, 12+" (1540) . . . . 600.00+
Vase, Swing, Footed,
    less than 12" (1540) . . . . 450.00+
Vase, Violet, 4" 130.00
Whipped Cream, 6" (1495) 60.00

Chapter 35
POPPIES

The poppy motif became extremely popular, especially for realistic etchings, after World War I, when the poem In Flanders Fields *gained great popularity.*

FLANDERS

PLATE ETCHING

Date: 1928

Manufacturer: U.S. Glass Co., Tiffin, OH

Colors: Crystal, Mandarin, Rose

Notes: For prices of Crystal pieces, deduct 35% from Mandarin prices.

STEMWARE:

No. 15024	Rose	Mandarin
Café Parfait	$95.00	$70.00
Claret	140.00	95.00
Cocktail	45.00	37.00
Cordial	120.00	90.00
Goblet	55.00	32.00
Saucer Champagne	40.00	30.00
Sundae (sherbet)	32.00	20.00
Wine	85.00	48.00

Accessories:	Rose	Mandarin
Almond, Individual	$70.00	$60.00
Bonbon, Handled (5831)	55.00	40.00
Bouillon, 2-handled	140.00	88.00
Bowl, Footed, 11"	100.00	75.00
Candleholder, pr. (5831)	145.00	90.00
Candy Box & Cover	295.00	195.00
Candy Jar & Cover, Footed	295.00	150.00
Celery Tray (5831)	75.00	55.00
Celery, 11"	70.00	50.00
Centerpiece, Bowl (5831)	95.00	75.00
Cheese & Cracker, 2-piece	125.00	95.00
Comport, Small (583)	70.00	40.00
Cream & Sugar, pr. (5831)	240.00	185.00
Cup & Saucer (5831)	100.00	75.00
Finger Bowl (185)	45.00	30.00
Grapefruit (251)	140.00	85.00
Jug & Cover (194)	400.00	325.00
Mayonnaise	75.00	50.00
Nappy, Handled (5831)	75.00	55.00
Oil & Stopper	325.00	250.00
Oyster Cocktail (196)	45.00	30.00
Plate, Dinner, 10"	95.00	68.00
Plate, Mayonnaise	25.00	15.00
Plate, Salad, 7½" (5831)	20.00	17.00
Relish, 3-compartment	70.00	50.00
Salt & Pepper, pr.	350.00+	300.00
Table, Tumbler (020)	85.00	65.00
Vase, Bud	90.00	55.00
Vase, Footed, Cupped Rim	275.00	200.00

Original Catalog Illustration:
Flanders etching on No. 15024 stemware

Original Catalog Illustration:
Flanders etching on No. 194 jug & cover

Original Catalog Illustration: Flanders etching on centerpiece

POPPIES *(continued)*

L to R: Original Catalog Illustrations:
Gloria etching on No. 3011 Cambridge Nude stem
Gloria etching on No. 3120 goblet

Original Catalog Illustration:
Gloria etching on dinner plate

GLORIA, NO. 746

PLATE ETCHING

Date: Ca. 1930

Manufacturer: Cambridge Glass Co., Cambridge, OH

Colors: Crystal, Mandarin Gold, Peach Blo, Green, Emerald Green, Amber, Blue, Heatherbloom

Notes: When found on Ebony glass with silver deposit decoration it is called No. D971-S.

STEMWARE:
No. 3011 CAMBRIDGE NUDE, CRYSTAL ONLY

Cocktail, 3½ oz.	$350.00
Comport, Flared, 7"	350.00
Goblet, Banquet, 11 oz.	350.00
Goblet, Table, 11 oz.	300.00
Sherbet, Tall, 7 oz.	300.00

No. 3120

	Crystal	Colors
Claret, 4½ oz.	$37.00	$70.00
Cordial, 1 oz.	75.00	150.00
Goblet, 9 oz.	20.00	32.00
Sherbet, Low, 6 oz.	14.00	20.00
Sherbet, Tall, 6 oz.	15.00	22.00
Tumbler, Footed, 5 oz.	15.00	25.00
Tumbler, Footed, 10 oz.	18.00	25.00
Tumbler, Footed, 12 oz.	22.00	38.00

No. 3130

Goblet, 8 oz.	$24.00	$35.00
Sherbet, Low, 6 oz.	14.00	22.00
Sherbet, Tall, 6 oz.	18.00	26.00
Tumbler, Footed, 2½ oz. (used with 3400/79 Cocktail Shaker)	35.00	60.00
Tumbler, Footed, 5 oz.	15.00	22.00
Tumbler, Footed, 10 oz.	16.00	25.00
Tumbler, Footed, 12 oz.	20.00	30.00
Wine, 2½ oz.	24.00	50.00

No. 3135

Cordial, 1 oz.	$78.00	$160.00
Finger Bowl	25.00	40.00
Fruit Salad, 6" (no stem)	11.00	20.00
Goblet, 8 oz.	22.00	37.00
Oyster Cocktail, 4½ oz.	15.00	20.00
Plate, Finger Bowl	8.00	12.00
Sherbet, Low or Tall, 6 oz.	15.00	20.00
Tumbler, Footed, 5 oz.	15.00	22.00
Tumbler, Footed, 10 oz.	17.00	24.00
Tumbler, Footed, 12 oz.	20.00	35.00

ACCESSORIES:

	Crystal	Colors
Baker, 10" (3400/51)	$45.00	$90.00
Basket, 2-handled, 6" (3400/1182)	22.00	36.00
Bonbon, 2-handled, 5¼" (3400/1179)	22.00	36.00
Bonbon, 2-handled, 5¼" (3400/1180)	22.00	36.00
Bonbon, Crimped, Footed, 5" (3400/25)	18.00	30.00
Bonbon, Flared, Footed, 5½" (3400/26)	18.00	30.00
Bowl, 2-handled, Footed, Keyhole stem, 9½" (3400/29)	65.00	110.00

(continued) **POPPIES**

	Crystal	Colors
Bowl, 2-handled, 9½" (3400/34)	65.00	100.00
Bowl, 2-handled, 10" (3400/1185)	45.00	80.00
Bowl, 4-toed, 12" (3400/5)	40.00	72.00
Bowl, 12" (3400/4)	45.00	80.00
Bowl, 13" (3400/1)	42.00	80.00
Bowl, Fruit, 11" (3400/1188)	42.00	85.00
Bowl, Oval, 12" (3400/1240)	45.00	85.00
Bowl, Salad, 2-handled, 9" (3400/21)	42.00	75.00
Butter & Cover, 5½" (3400/52)	150.00	325.00
Candlesticks, 6" (3400/1192)	60.00	90.00
Candlesticks, 1-light, pr. (3400/627)	55.00	85.00
Candy Box & Cover, 7" (3400/9)	78.00	137.00
Celery & Relish Service, 12" (3400/67)	55.00	80.00
Cereal, 6" (3400/53)	22.00	37.00
Cereal, Square, 6" (3400/82)	20.00	35.00
Cheese & Cracker, 2-piece, 11½" (3400/6)	45.00	80.00
Cocktail Shaker (3400/78)	125.00	245.00
Comport, 4" (3400/15)	15.00	30.00
Comport, 4-toed, 5" (3400/74)	22.00	40.00
Comport, 4-toed, 6" (3400/13)	24.00	45.00
Comport, Tall, 6" (3400/14)	40.00	85.00
Comport, Low, Keyhole stem, 7" (3400/28)	35.00	62.00
Comport, Tall, Keyhole stem, 7" (3400/29)	40.00	85.00
Cranberry, 4-toed, 3½" (3400/70)	30.00	65.00
Cream (3400/68)	18.00	30.00
Cream, Footed, 6" (3400/16)	17.00	30.00
Cream or Syrup, Tall (3400/39)	22.00	40.00
Cream Soup (3400/55)	30.00	55.00
Cream Soup, Square (3400/85)	35.00	65.00
Cup & Saucer (3400/54)	18.00	30.00
Cup & Saucer, 4-toed, Square (3400/50)	35.00	85.00
Cup & Saucer, After Dinner (3400/69)	78.00	125.00
Cup & Saucer, After Dinner, Square (3400/83)	85.00	135.00
Cup & Saucer, Square (3400/75)	35.00	85.00
Finger Bowl, Footed (3025)	22.00	32.00
Fruit Saucer, 5½" (3400/56)	18.00	32.00
Fruit Saucer, Square (3400/81)	30.00	42.00
Ice Pail (3400/851)	55.00	100.00
Jug & Cover, 64 oz. (1205)	195.00	330.00
Mayonnaise (3400/11)	35.00	62.00
Nut, Individual, 4-toed, 3" (3400/71)	65.00	85.00
Oil & Stopper, Tall, Footed (3400/79)	105.00	200.00
Pickle, 2-handled, 8¾" (3400/86)	20.00	32.00
Pickle Tray, 9" (3400/59)	20.00	42.00
Plate, 2-handled, 6" (3400/1181)	12.00	18.00
Plate, 2-handled, 11" (3400/35)	25.00	32.00
Plate, Bread & Butter, Round, 6" (3400/60)	9.00	12.00
Plate, Bread & Butter, Square, (3400/1174)	9.00	12.00
Plate, Cake, Footed, Salver, 11" (3400/707)	95.00	250.00
Plate, Chop or Salad, 14" (3400/65)	50.00	95.00
Plate, Dinner, Square (3400/1177)	75.00	98.00
Plate, Dinner, 9½" (3400/63)	75.00	98.00

Original Catalog Illustration:
Gloria etching on butter and cover

	Crystal	Colors
Plate, Mayonnaise (3400/11)	10.00	15.00
Plate, Salad, Round, 8½" (3400/62)	12.00	18.00
Plate, Salad, Square, (3400/1176)	12.00	18.00
Plate, Salad, 2-handled, 10" (3400/22)	24.00	45.00
Plate, Sandwich, 2-handled, 11½" (3400/8)	28.00	50.00
Plate, Service (3400/1178)	55.00	85.00
Plate, Tea, 7½" (3400/61)	12.00	16.00
Platter, 11½" (3400/57)	68.00	130.00
Relish Tray, 2-compartment, Center keyhole (3400/1093)	30.00	42.00
Relish Tray, 4-compartment, Center keyhole (3400/862)	35.00	58.00
Relish, 2-compartment, 2-handled, 8¾" (3400/88)	22.00	38.00
Relish, 2-compartment, 2-handled (3400/90)	24.00	40.00
Relish, 3-compartment, 3-handled (3400/91)	26.00	44.00
Salt & Pepper, pr. (3400/18)	52.00	95.00
Salt & Pepper, Short, pr. (3400/76)	50.00	90.00
Salt & Pepper, Tall, pr. (3400/77)	60.00	140.00
Sugar (3400/68)	18.00	30.00
Sugar, Footed, 6" (3400/16)	17.00	30.00
Sugar Shaker (3400/40)	195.00	320.00
Tray, 2-handled, 9" (1071)	18.00	30.00
Tray, Sandwich, Center Keyhole, 11" (3400/10)	35.00	48.00
Tumbler, 8 oz. (497)	22.00	45.00
Tumbler, 9 oz. (321)	22.00	40.00
Tumbler, 12 oz. (499)	22.00	40.00
Tumbler, 14 oz. (3400/100)	22.00	45.00
Vase, 10" (1284)	85.00	178.00
Vase, 10" (3400/23)	85.00	175.00
Vase, Keyhole stem, 10" (1305)	65.00	135.00
Vase, 11" (1242 or 1297)	65.00	128.00
Vase, 11" (1299)	80.00	150.00
Vase, 12" (3400/17)	65.00	130.00
Vase, Keyhole stem, 12" (1238)	75.00	140.00
Vase, Keyhole stem, 14" (1239)	90.00	195.00
Vase, Oval, 9" (1228)	95.00	175.00

POPPIES *(continued)*

Original Catalog Illustration:
No. 309 Legion etching on assortment

LEGION, NO. 309

PLATE ETCHING

Date: Ca. 1929

Manufacturer: Fostoria Glass Co., Moundsville, WV

Colors: Crystal, Rose, Topaz

Notes: No. 2375 refers to Fairfax blanks, and No. 2440 refers to Lafayette blanks.

STEMWARE:

NO. 6000, CRYSTAL ONLY
Cocktail, 3½ oz., 3¾" tall. $17.00
Goblet, 10 oz., 6¼" tall 20.00
Oyster Cocktail, 4 oz., 2⅞" tall. 10.00
Saucer Champagne, 6 oz., 4¾" tall 18.00
Sherbet, Low, 6 oz., 3⅞" tall. 12.00
Tumbler, Footed, 5 oz., 3⅝" tall (juice). . . . 15.00
Tumbler, Footed, 13 oz., 5¼" tall (iced tea). . 18.00
Wine, 3 oz., 4¼" tall 25.00

ACCESSORIES:	Crystal	Colors
Bowl, "B," 10½" (2440)	$30.00	$45.00
Bowl, 12" (2470)	34.00	50.00
Bowl, Salad, 12" (2440)	34.00	50.00
Candlesticks, 3", pr. (2375).	30.00	45.00
Candlesticks, 5½", pr. (2470)	48.00	65.00
Cream & Sugar, Footed, pr. (2375½).	36.00	60.00
Cup & Saucer, Footed (2375½).	20.00	38.00
Dish, Lemon (2470)	15.00	24.00
Plate, Bread & Butter, 6" (2375)	7.00	10.00
Plate, Cake, 10" (2470).	35.00	48.00
Plate, Dinner, 9" (2375)	32.00	48.00
Plate, Luncheon, 8" (2375)	12.00	16.00
Plate, Salad, 7" (2375).	10.00	15.00
Plate, Torte, 13" (2440).	35.00	55.00
Relish, 4-part, Oval (2470)	25.00	48.00
Sweetmeat (2470)	18.00	30.00
Tumbler, 9 oz. (4076)	20.00	38.00
Vase, 7" (2440).	40.00	70.00

Original Catalog Illustration:
Poppy etching on covered jug

POPPIES

ETCHING

Date: 1930s

Manufacturer: U.S. Glass Co., Tiffin, OH

Colors: Crystal

STEMWARE:

NO. 14196
Cocktail, 2½ oz. $40.00
Goblet, 9 oz. 50.00
Saucer Champagne. 45.00
Sundae (sherbet) 20.00
Tumbler, Footed & Handled, 12 oz.. . . . . 45.00
Wine, 2 oz. 50.00

ACCESSORIES:
Candlesticks, 10", pr. (9288) $70.00
Comport, High, 7" (9705). 60.00
Comport, Low, 10" (9705). 65.00
Finger Bowl (14196) 25.00
Iced Tea, 12 oz. (354). 30.00
Iced Tea, Handled, 12 oz. (354) 45.00
Jug & Cover, Tall (115) 210.00
Jug, Tall, 3 pt. (114). 190.00
Oil & Stopper (14194). 145.00
Oyster Cocktail (13630). 20.00
Plate, Finger Bowl (8814). 15.00
Tankard & Cover, Tall, Footed (14194). . 210.00
Tumbler, Table, 10 oz. (354). 25.00
Vase, Bud, 8½" (14194). 65.00
Vase, Bud, 10½" (14194). 75.00

ROGENE, NO. 269

DEEP PLATE ETCHING

Date: 1920s or 1930s

Manufacturer: Fostoria Glass Co., Moundsville, WV

Colors: Crystal

STEMWARE:
NO. 5082

Claret, 4½ oz., 5¾" tall	$45.00
Cocktail, 3 oz., 4½ oz. tall	35.00
Cordial, ¾ oz., 3¾" tall	85.00
Fruit, 5 oz., 3¾" tall (low sherbet)	22.00
Goblet, 9 oz., 7⅝" tall	45.00
Parfait, 6 oz.	40.00
Saucer Champagne, 5 oz., 5¼" tall	42.00
Wine, 2¾ oz., 5⅛" tall	45.00

ACCESSORIES:

Almond, Footed (4095)	$25.00
Bedroom Set, 2-piece (tumble up) (1697)	150.00
Comport, 5" (5078)	35.00
Cream (185)	50.00
Finger Bowl (766)	15.00
Grapefruit & Liner (both etched) (945½)	55.00
Jelly & Cover (825)	65.00
Jug, Footed, No. 7 (4095)	125.00
Jug, No. 7 (318)	125.00
Marmalade & Cover (1968)	80.00
Mayonnaise, Footed (2138)	50.00
Nappy, 5" (5078)	20.00
Oil with Cut Neck, 5 oz. (1465)	95.00
Oyster Cocktail (837)	20.00
Plate, 6" (2283)	15.00
Plate, 7" (2283)	18.00
Plate, Mayonnaise	18.00
Sugar (185)	50.00
Tumbler, 2½ oz. (887)	55.00
Tumbler, 5 oz. (889)	38.00
Tumbler, 8 oz. (889)	45.00
Tumbler, 13 oz. (889)	50.00
Tumbler, Footed, 2½ oz. (4095)	60.00
Tumbler, Footed, 5 oz. (4095)	45.00
Tumbler, Footed, 10 oz. (4095)	65.00
Tumbler, Footed, 13 oz. (4095)	70.00
Tumbler, Handled, 12 oz. (837)	70.00
Tumbler, Table (4076)	45.00

Original Catalog Illustration:
No. 269 Rogene etching on
jelly and cover

SHIRLEY, NO. 331

PLATE ETCHING

Date: 1939

Manufacturer: Fostoria Glass Co., Moundsville, WV

Colors: Crystal

Notes: No. 2496 indicates Baroque blanks.

STEMWARE:
NO. 6017 SCEPTRE

Claret, 4 oz., 5⅞" tall	$50.00
Cocktail, 3½ oz., 4⅞" tall	32.00
Cordial, ¾ oz., 3⅞" tall	60.00
Goblet, 9 oz., 7⅜" tall	35.00
Iced Tea, 12 oz. 6" tall	35.00
Juice, 5 oz., 4¾" tall	32.00
Oyster Cocktail, 4 oz., 3⅝" tall	28.00
Saucer Champagne, 6 oz., 5½" tall	35.00
Sherbet, 6 oz., 4½" tall	25.00
Tumbler, Footed, 9 oz., 5½" tall	35.00
Wine, 3 oz., 5½" tall	55.00

ACCESSORIES:

Celery, 11" (2496)	$18.00
Cream Soup (2496)	20.00
Cream, Footed, 3¾" (2496)	18.00
Cream, Individual, 3⅛" (2496)	22.00
Cup & Saucer, Footed (2350½)	20.00
Dish, Vegetable, 9½" (2496)	25.00
Finger Bowl (766)	12.00
Fruit, 5" (2496)	12.00
Ice Bucket, 4⅜" x 6½" (2496)	50.00
Jug, Footed, 53 oz., 8⅞" tall (6011)	125.00
Pickle, 8" (2496)	18.00
Plate, 6" or 7" (2337)	8.00
Plate, 8" (2337)	10.00
Plate, Cake, 2-handled, 10" (2496)	30.00
Plate, Cream Soup (2496)	10.00
Platter, Oval, 12" (2496)	35.00
Salt & Pepper, 2¾", pr. (2496)	65.00
Sugar, Footed, 3½" (2496)	18.00
Sugar, Individual, 2⅞" (2496)	22.00

Original Catalog Illustration:
No. 331 Shirley etching on
footed jug

Chapter 36
PUNTIES

Punties are rounds or ovals cut and often polished into the glass.

Original Catalog Illustration: Cretan cutting
on D5 Duncan Scroll goblet

CRETAN

ROCK CRYSTAL CUTTING

Date: 1950s

Manufacturer: Duncan & Miller Glass Co., Washington, PA

Colors: Crystal

Notes: Probably designed by James Rosati. No. 30½ refers to Pall Mall pattern.

STEMWARE:
NO. D5 DUNCAN SCROLL
Cocktail, Liquor $30.00
Goblet 45.00
Iced Tea, Footed 35.00
Juice, Footed. 25.00
Saucer Champagne or Tall Sherbet. 40.00
Seafood Cocktail. 18.00
Wine or Claret 45.00

ACCESSORIES:
Plate, 7½ " (30½) $17.00
Plate, 8½ " (30½) 17.00

Original Catalog Illustration: Dawn cutting
on D5 Duncan Scroll goblet

DAWN

ROCK CRYSTAL CUTTING

Date: 1950s

Manufacturer: Duncan & Miller Glass Co., Washington, PA

Colors: Crystal

Notes: Probably designed by James Rosati. No. 30½ refers to Pall Mall pattern.

STEMWARE:
NO. D5 DUNCAN SCROLL
Cocktail, Liquor $30.00
Goblet 45.00
Iced Tea, Footed 35.00
Juice, Footed. 25.00
Saucer Champagne or Tall Sherbet. 40.00
Seafood Cocktail. 18.00
Wine or Claret 45.00

ACCESSORIES:
High Ball $15.00
Plate, 7½" (30½) 17.00
Plate, 8½" (30½) 17.00

FLEUR-DE-LIS

ROCK CRYSTAL CUTTING

Date: 1950s

Manufacturer: Duncan & Miller Glass Co., Washington, PA

Colors: Crystal

Notes: Probably designed by James Rosati. Almost certainly matching pressed plates were made, and possibly other pieces.

STEMWARE:
NO. D5 DUNCAN SCROLL
Cocktail, Liquor	$28.00
Goblet	40.00
Iced Tea, Footed	32.00
Juice, Footed	22.00
Saucer Champagne or Tall Sherbet	35.00
Seafood Cocktail	15.00
Wine or Claret	40.00

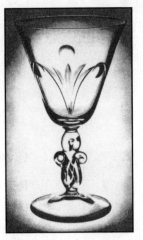

Original Catalog Illustration:
Fleur-de-Lis cutting on No. D5 Duncan Scroll goblet

HAWTHORNE

ROCK CRYSTAL CUTTING

Date: 1950s

Manufacturer: Duncan & Miller Glass Co., Washington, PA

Colors: Crystal

Notes: Probably designed by James Rosati. No. 30½ refers to Pall Mall pattern.

STEMWARE:
NO. D5 DUNCAN SCROLL
Cocktail, Liquor	$28.00
Goblet	40.00
Iced Tea, Footed	32.00
Juice, Footed	22.00
Saucer Champagne or Tall Sherbet	35.00
Seafood Cocktail	15.00
Wine or Claret	40.00

ACCESSORIES:
Plate, 7½" (30½)	$17.00
Plate, 8½" (30½)	17.00

Original Catalog Illustration:
Hawthorne cutting on No. D5 Duncan Scroll goblet

TERRACE

POLISHED CUTTING

Date: 1952

Manufacturer: Libbey Glass Co., Toledo, OH

Colors: Crystal

Notes: Designed by Freda Diamond.

STEMWARE:
Cocktail	$10.00
Cordial	35.00
Goblet	15.00
Sherbet	9.00
Wine	15.00

Original Ad: Terrace cutting on goblet

Chapter 37
ROSES

Some roses are quite realistic and detailed while others are more stylized.

Original Catalog Illustration:
No. 1074 Cambridge Rose
rock crystal engraving on
No. 3700 Dunkirk Iced Tea

CAMBRIDGE ROSE, NO. 1074

ROCK CRYSTAL ENGRAVING

Date: 1940s

Manufacturer: Cambridge Glass Co.,
Cambridge, OH

Colors: Crystal

Notes: Line numbers preceded by the letter
P indicate Pristine blanks.

STEMWARE:
NO. 3700 DUNKIRK

Claret, 4½ oz.	$20.00
Cocktail, 3 oz.	15.00
Cordial, 1 oz.	50.00
Goblet, 9 oz.	20.00
Iced Tea, Footed, 12 oz.	15.00
Oyster Cocktail, 4½ oz.	10.00
Sherbet, Low, 6 oz.	11.00

Sherbet, Tall, 6 oz.	15.00
Tumbler, Footed, 5 oz. (juice)	12.00
Wine, 2½ oz.	20.00

ACCESSORIES:

Bowl, 12" (P430)	$38.00
Candlesticks, 3½", pr. (628)	55.00
Candy Box & Cover (P 306)	50.00
Cream (P254)	20.00
Mayonnaise (1532)	25.00
Plate, 14" (P125)	50.00
Plate, Mayonnaise (1532)	10.00
Plate, Salad, 7½" (555)	15.00
Plate, Salad, 8" (556)	15.00
Relish, 3 Part, 10" (P214)	35.00
Sugar (P254)	20.00
Vase, Footed, 11" (278)	75.00

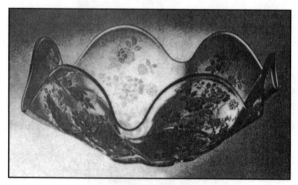

Original Catalog Illustration:
Charmaine Rose etching on crimped bowl

CHARMAINE ROSE

ETCHING

Date: 1950s

Manufacturer: Duncan & Miller Glass Co., Washington, PA

Colors: Crystal

STEMWARE:
NO. 5375 DIAMOND

Cocktail, Liquor, 3½ oz., 5" tall	$32.00
Cordial, 1 oz., 4¼" tall	75.00
Goblet, 9 oz., 7¼" tall	50.00
Iced Tea, 12 oz., 6½" tall	38.00
Orange Juice, 5 oz., 4¾" tall	27.00
Oyster Cocktail, 4½ oz., 3¾" tall	20.00
Saucer Champagne, 5½ oz., 5½" tall	42.00
Wine, 3 oz., 5¾" tall	50.00

ACCESSORIES:

Bowl, Crimped, 10½" (115)	$75.00
Bowl, Oval, 10" (115)	85.00
Candlesticks, 2-light, 7" pr. (3)	100.00
Candlesticks, Low, 1-light, 3", pr. (115)	75.00
Candy Box & Cover, 8" (115)	85.00
Cheese & Cracker, 2-handled, 11" (115)	70.00
Comport, High Footed, 5½" Tall (115)	75.00
Cream, 7 oz., 3" Tall (115)	45.00

Mayonnaise, Crimped, 5½" (115)	50.00
Nappy, Round, 1-handled, 5½" (115)	35.00
Plate, 2-handled, 7½" (115)	18.00
Plate, Torte, 14" (30)	65.00
Relish, Oblong, 3-compartment	55.00
Relish, Round, 2-compartment, 2-handled, 6" (115)	50.00
Sandwich Tray, 2-handled (115)	55.00
Sugar, 7 oz., 3¾" Tall (115)	45.00
Vase, Crimped, 5" (115)	65.00

DOLLY MADISON ROSE, NO. 1015

ENGRAVED GRAY CUTTING

Date: 1949

Manufacturer: A.H. Heisey & Co., Newark, OH

Colors: Crystal

Notes: Made to match Castleton China's Dolly Madison Rose. No. 1951 refers to pressed Cabochon.

STEMWARE:
NO. 4091 KIMBERLY

Bell, Dinner	$220.00
Claret	70.00
Cocktail	50.00
Cordial	175.00
Finger Bowl or Dessert Dish (3309)	25.00
Goblet, Low	60.00
Goblet, Tall	70.00
Iced Tea, Footed	45.00
Juice, Footed	30.00
Saucer Champagne	60.00
Sherbet, Low	30.00
Wine	70.00

ACCESSORIES:

Ashtray (1489)	$50.00
Ashtray, Individual	40.00
Beverage	25.00
Cigarette Box & Cover, King Size (1489)	100.00
Cigarette Box & Cover, Regular (1489)	85.00
Cigarette Holder	65.00
Cream & Sugar, pr. (1951)	100.00
Cup & Saucer	65.00
Mayonnaise (1951)	45.00
Mayonnaise, 2-compartment (1951)	45.00
Mint, Footed (1951)	55.00
Oyster or Fruit Cocktail (3542)	22.00
Plate, Mayonnaise	18.00
Plate, Salad	22.00
Plate, Sandwich	50.00
Salt & Pepper, pr. (1615 or 1951)	150.00

Original Catalog Illustration: No. 1015 Dolly Madison Rose cutting

HEISEY ROSE, NO. 515

PLATE ETCHING

Date: 1949

Manufacturer: A.H. Heisey & Co., Newark, OH

Colors: Crystal

Notes: This rose etching was designed by Jane Phillips to be used on Heisey's new Rose stemware featuring a sculptured rose as the stem. By 1951 Heisey described the etching as "Hand-etched Heisey Rose, representing elegant decor on fine crystal, is ideal for traditional interiors." After A.H. Heisey & Co. ceased business in 1957, Imperial Glass Corporation continued to make some pieces of Heisey Rose, including most of the stem line. Line numbers refer to patterns as follows: No. 1509 Queen Anne, No. 1519 Waverly and No. 1951 Cabochon. Cocktail shakers were fitted with all glass plain, rooster head or horse head stoppers. The two figural stoppers add considerably to the value of the shakers.

Original Brochure: No. 515 Heisey Rose on No. 5072 Rose stem goblet

STEMWARE:
NO. 5072 ROSE

Bell, Dinner	$225.00
Claret, 4 oz.	155.00
Cocktail, 4 oz.	70.00
Cordial, 1 oz.	200.00
Finger Bowl	35.00
Goblet, 9 oz.	60.00
Iced Tea, Footed, 12 oz.	60.00
Juice, Footed, 5 oz.	45.00
Oyster Cocktail, 3½ oz.	60.00
Sherbet, 6 oz.	50.00
Wine, 3 oz.	140.00

ACCESSORIES:
NO. 1519 UNLESS NOTED OTHERWISE

Ashtray, 3" (1435)	$42.00
Bowl, Combination Dressing, 7" (1509)	60.00
Bowl, Floral, 11"	75.00
Bowl, Floral or Fruit, Crimped, 12"	85.00
Bowl, Floral, 13"	100.00
Bowl, Floral, 3 Footed, 11", Seahorse feet	175.00
Bowl, Floral, Crimped, 13"	120.00
Bowl, Floral, Crimped, 9½"	80.00
Bowl, Gardenia, 10"	80.00

Bowl, Gardenia, 13"	90.00
Bowl, Lily, 7" (1509)	60.00
Bowl, Oval, 4-footed, 11" (1519 originally 1495)	155.00
Bowl, Salad, 7"	58.00
Bowl, Salad, 9"	68.00
Butter & Cover, ¼ lb. (1951)	325.00
Butter Dish & Cover, Square, 6"	200.00
Candlesticks, 1-light, pr. (112)	100.00
Candlesticks, 1-light, pr. (134)	180.00
Candlesticks, 2-light, pr. (1615)	250.00
Candlesticks, 3-light, pr. (142)	210.00
Candlesticks, 3-light, pr.	210.00

193

ROSES *(continued)*

Candy & Cover, High Footed, Seahorse handles, 5" 195.00
Candy Box & Cover, 6¼" (1951) 170.00
Candy Box & Cover, Low, 6", Bow knot finial 145.00
Celery Tray, 12" or 13" 70.00
Cheese & Cracker, 2-piece, 11", 12" or 14" (1509 or 1519) . . . 165.00
Chocolate & Cover, 5", Wave finial 170.00
Cigarette Holder, Blown (4035) . . 140.00
Cocktail Icer & Liner (3304) 200.00
Cocktail Shaker, 1 qt. (4036) 210.00
Cocktail Shaker, 1 qt. (4225) 210.00
Comport, Low Foot, 6½" 70.00
Comport, Oval, Footed, 7" 80.00
Cream & Sugar, Footed, pr. 80.00
Cream, Footed, Individual 45.00
Cup & Saucer 75.00
Decanter & Stopper, 1 pt. (4036½) 210.00
Epergnette, Deep, 6" 195.00
French Dressing Bottle & Stopper, 8 oz. (5031) 235.00
Gardenia Centerpiece & Epergnette, 13" 145.00
Gardenia Centerpiece with Vase, 13" (2 Styles) 180.00
Gardenia Centerpiece, 13" 95.00
Honey or Cheese, Footed, 6½" 70.00
Ice Bucket, Dolphin Footed (1509) 315.00
Ice Tub, 2-handled . . . . 495.00+
Jelly, 2-handled, Footed, 6" (1509) 60.00
Jelly, Footed, 6½" 70.00
Jug, 73 oz. (4164) . . . . 625.00+
Lamp, Hurricane with 12" Globe (1567 or 301) . . . . . 500.00+
Lemon & Cover, 6½", Dolphin finial (1509) 190.00
Lemon or Candy & Cover, Oval, 6" 185.00
Mayonnaise, 1-handled, 5½" (1519 originally 1495) 65.00
Mayonnaise, Footed, 5½" 65.00
Mint, Footed, 5¾" (1951) 80.00
Mint, Footed, 6" (1509) 42.00
Oil, Footed, 8 oz. 195.00
Plate, Cake, Footed, 13½" 325.00
Plate, Demi-Torte, 11" 85.00
Plate, Salad, 7" or 8" 28.00
Plate, Sandwich, 11" 60.00
Plate, Sandwich 14" 125.00
Plate, Sandwich, Center-handled, 14" 240.00
Plate, Service, 10½" 185.00
Plate, Torte, 14" 100.00
Relish, 3-compartment, 11" 70.00
Relish, 3-compartment, Round, 7" . . 75.00
Relish, 4-compartment, Round, 9" . . 75.00
Salt & Pepper, Footed 95.00
Salver, Footed, 12" . . . . 350.00+
Sugar, Footed, Individual 45.00
Tray for Individual Cream & Sugar (1509) 65.00
Vase, 8" or 10", Blown (4198) . . . 150.00
Vase, Fan, Footed, 7" 135.00
Vase, Footed, 7" 125.00
Vase, Bud, Square Footed, 8" or 10" (5012) 160.00
Vase, Bud, Square Footed, 12" (5012) 195.00
Vase, Violet, Footed, 3½" 125.00

Original Catalog Illustration:
No. 316 Midnight Rose plate etching on assorted pieces

MIDNIGHT ROSE, NO. 316

PLATE ETCHING

Date: 1933

Manufacturer: Fostoria Glass Co., Moundsville, WV

Colors: Crystal

STEMWARE:
NO. 6009

Claret-Wine, 3¾ oz., 5⅜" tall $32.00
Cocktail, 3¾ oz., 4¾" tall 22.00
Cordial, 1 oz., 3¾" tall 60.00
Goblet, 9 oz., 7⅝" tall 28.00
Iced Tea, Footed, 12 oz., 5⅞" tall 20.00
Oyster Cocktail, 4¾ oz., 3¾" tall 12.00
Saucer Champagne or High Sherbet, 5½ oz., 5⅝ " tall. . 24.00
Sherbet, Low, 5½ oz., 4⅜" tall 17.00
Tumbler, Footed, 5 oz., 4⅜" tall (juice) 17.00
Tumbler, Footed, 9 oz., 5¼" tall (water) 17.00

ACCESSORIES:
NO. 2440 UNLESS NOTED OTHERWISE

Bonbon, Handled, 5" $18.00
Bowl, 7" (2470½) 35.00
Bowl, 10½" (2470½) 50.00
Bowl, Oblong, 11" (2481) 55.00
Brandy Inhaler (906) 45.00
Candlesticks, 5", pr. (2481) 50.00
Candlesticks, 5½", pr. (2470½) . . . 50.00
Candlesticks, Duo, pr. (2472) 55.00
Candlesticks, Trindle, pr. (2482) . . . 65.00
Candy Jar & Cover (4099) 40.00
Celery, 11½" 26.00
Champagne, Hollow Stem (795) . . . 18.00
Cream & Sugar, Footed, pr. 48.00
Cup & Saucer 20.00
Dish, Oval Sauce, 6½" 27.00
Finger Bowl (869) 14.00
Jug, Ice (2464) 55.00
Lemon, Handled, 5" 18.00
Mayonnaise, 6½" 25.00
Old Fashion Cocktail, Sham, 7 oz. (1184) 13.00
Olive, 6½" 18.00
Pickle, 8½" 22.00
Plate, Bread & Butter, 6" 11.00
Plate, Cake (2475) 35.00
Plate, Dinner, 9" 35.00
Plate, Luncheon, 8" 24.00
Plate, Oval Cake, 10½" 40.00
Plate, Salad, 7" 16.00
Plate, Torte, 13" 50.00
Relish, 2- or 3-part, Handled 28.00
Relish, 4-part. (2470) 40.00
Relish, 4-or 5-part (2419 or 2462) . . 45.00
Sherry, 2 oz. (846) 25.00
Sweetmeat, Handled, 4½" 20.00
Tray for Sugar & Cream (2470) . . . 35.00
Tray, Oval, 8½" 45.00
Tumbler (2464) 24.00
Vase, 6½" or 7½" (4111 or 2467) . . 55.00
Vase, 7½" (4110) 50.00
Vase, 8½" (4112) 65.00
Vase, 10" (2470) 80.00
Whiskey, Sham, 1¾ oz. (887) 18.00

MORNING ROSE

CUTTING

Date: 1950s

Manufacturer: Tiffin Art Glass Corp., Tiffin, OH

Colors: Crystal

Notes: See also Tiffin Rose below. "The dewy freshness of early morn... in this version of the Tiffin Rose"—original brochure.

STEMWARE:
No. 17684
Champagne/Sherbet $30.00
Claret. 35.00
Cocktail 30.00
Cordial 70.00
Goblet 35.00
Iced Tea 30.00
Juice 20.00

ACCESSORIES:
Finger Bowl $15.00
Nappy, Dessert 15.00
Plate, Salad, 8" 18.00

Morning Rose cutting on No. 17684 goblet

ROSE

CUTTING

Date: 1951

Manufacturer: Fostoria Glass Co., Moundsville, WV

Colors: Crystal

Notes: "Even supposing you don't recognize handblown crystal on sight, there's no mistaking the handwork in this design. Fostoria's Rose is cut by hand, petal by petal. (She loves me, she loves me not, she loves me!) The single flower, bold and beautiful, is rendered on a graceful, bell-like shape and notice the turned-spool stems. Rose fits into any decor, traditional or modern a wise choice for gifts, or for yourself." Certainly other pressed accessories were made, but cannot be documented at this time.

STEMWARE:
No. 6036 RUTLEDGE
Claret-Wine, 3¼ oz., 4¾" tall $28.00
Cocktail, 3½ oz., 4⅛" tall 21.00
Cordial, 1 oz., 3¼" tall 50.00
Goblet, 9½ oz., 6⅞" tall 28.00
Iced Tea, Footed, 12 oz., 6⅛" tall 24.00
Juice, Footed, 5 oz., 4⅝" tall 17.00
Oyster Cocktail, 4 oz., 3¾" tall 12.00
Parfait, 5½ oz., 5⅞" tall 24.00
Sherbet, High, 6 oz., 4¾" tall 24.00
Sherbet, Low, 6 oz., 4⅛" tall 18.00

ACCESSORIES:
Cream & Sugar, pr. $84.00
Cream, Individual 38.00
Cup & Saucer 60.00
Plate, Salad, 7½" or 8½" 15.00
Relish, 2-part, 8" 65.00
Relish, 3-part, 11" 75.00
Salt & Pepper, pr. 80.00
Sugar, Individual 38.00

Would a quick look tell you Fostoria's "Rose" is made by hand?

Original ad:
No. 827 Rose cutting

ROSES *(continued)*

Original Catalog Illustration:
Roses etching on jug

ROSES

ETCHING

Date: Ca. 1914

Manufacturer: U.S. Glass Co., Tiffin, OH

Colors: Crystal

STEMWARE:
No. 14180
Claret, 4 oz.	$25.00
Cocktail, 3½ oz.	20.00
Cordial, 1 oz.	75.00
Goblet, 9 oz.	48.00
Parfait, Café, 5¾ oz.	40.00
Saucer Champagne, 6½ oz.	40.00
Sundae, 6 oz. (sherbet)	20.00
Wine, 2½ oz.	45.00

ACCESSORIES:
Bonbon, Low Foot, 6" (14153)	$40.00
Decanter, 1 qt. (14179)	240.00
Iced Tea, 14 oz. (354)	28.00
Iced Tea, Handled, 14 oz. (354)	40.00
Jug, 2 qt. (107)	200.00
Oil & Stopper (14179)	150.00
Oyster Cocktail (13630)	20.00
Tumbler, 2½ oz. (bar) (354)	40.00
Tumbler, 5 oz. (juice) (354)	20.00
Tumbler, 10 oz. or 12 oz. (354)	25.00
Vase, Bud, 6" (19)	50.00
Vase, Bud, 10" (19)	65.00

Tiffin Rose Cutting

Tea Rose etching

TIFFIN ROSE AND TEA ROSE

CUTTING OR ETCHINGS

Date: 1950s

Manufacturer: Tiffin Art Glass Corp., Tiffin, OH

Colors: Crystal

Notes: Tea Rose etching and Tiffin Rose etching items are valued the same as those for Tiffin Rose cutting.

STEMWARE:
No. 17680
Claret	$30.00
Cocktail	20.00
Cordial	50.00
Goblet	30.00
Iced Tea, Footed	28.00
Saucer Champagne	24.00
Tumbler, Footed (juice)	18.00
Wine	30.00

ACCESSORIES:
Bowl, Large (526)	$60.00
Bowl, Medium (526)	48.00
Bowl, Nut, 6" (5902)	35.00
Bowl, Salad, 10" (5902)	55.00
Bowl, Small (526)	35.00
Candlesticks, 2-light, pr. (5902)	75.00
Celery Tray (5902)	30.00
Centerpiece, Cone shape, 12½ " (5902)	55.00
Centerpiece, Crimped, 12" (5902)	50.00
Centerpiece, Shallow, 13" (5902)	50.00
Comport, Tall (15082)	65.00
Cream (5902)	24.00
Finger Bowl	14.00
Jug (14194)	95.00
Jug, 60 oz. (5959)	95.00
Mayonnaise (5902)	25.00
Nappy, 7" (5902)	20.00
Nappy, Dessert	20.00
Plate Lily or Floater (5902)	32.00
Plate, Cake, Center-handled (5909)	35.00
Plate, Handled Cake (5902)	45.00
Plate, Mayonnaise, 6" (5902)	14.00
Plate, Salad, 8" (5902)	18.00
Plate, Sandwich, 14" (5902)	40.00
Relish, 3-part, large (5902)	38.00
Relish, 3-part, small (5902)	32.00
Salt & Pepper, pr. (2)	65.00
Seafood Cocktail Set (6021)	85.00
Vase, Bud, 6" (14185)	50.00
Vase, Bud, 8" (14185)	60.00
Vase, Bud, 10" (14185)	85.00
Vase, Bud, 11" (15082)	90.00

Chapter 38
SATIN FINISH

Satin Finish is a treatment to decorate glass in which all or some portions of the pieces are subjected to acid and leave a semi-opaque, satiny finish. Companies made items completely satin finish or with portions left clear—some of them quite effective in their presentation.

U.S. Glass was probably the largest producer of satin glass as it offered much of its line in the 1920s with satin finish. Actually many of these pieces are much more difficult to find in bright or shiny finish.

ECHEC

ETCHING

Date: 1925

Manufacturer: U.S. Glass Co., Tiffin, OH

Colors: Black

Notes: "In this decoration we have achieved the unusual by combining both satin and brilliant finish in a bold square pattern edged with gold bands." —Original ad. The decoration is square alternating satin and shiny in a checkerboard motif. Other items were made.

Cheese & Cracker, 10",
   2-piece (320) $130.00
Compote, Cupped, 8" (15179) 138.00
Flower Holder (16261) 200.00
Plate, Cake, Center-handled,
   10" (320) 125.00
Rose Bowl, Footed, 7½" (8098) 145.00
Vase, Dahlia, Cupped,
   10½" (15151) 200.00
Vase, Dahlia, Cupped, 8" (15151) . . . 170.00

Original Ad: Echec etching from 1920s U.S. Glass advertisement

KIMBERLY

ETCHING

Date: 1926

Manufacturer: U.S. Glass Co., Tiffin, OH

Colors: Black, Ruby

Notes: "Acres of diamonds at Kimberly which is the world's greatest diamond mine. Out of the mine of our experience and skill we have developed this decoration, aptly named Kimberly." —1926 ad. The decoration is a diamond pattern separated by clear lines and covers the entire item. Prices are for Ruby—for Black deduct 50%. Other pieces were certainly made.

Basket . . . . $500.00+
Bonbon, Low Foot, 5" (330) 125.00
Bowl, Floral, 8½" (320) 195.00
Bowl, Footed, 8½" (330) 235.00
Candlesticks, 10", pr. (320) 325.00
Candy & Cover, Conic (330) 225.00
Compote, 5½" (330) 210.00
Plate, Cake, Center-handled,
   10" (179) 210.00
Vase, Bud, 10" (9723) 185.00
Vase, Wall (320) 225.00

Kimberly decoration on Conic covered candy

SATIN FINISH *(continued)*

No. 4044 New Era plate, nut cup, goblet and soda in Satin Finish

STEMWARE:

NO. 3418 SAVOY PLAZA

Cocktail, 3½ oz.	$35.00
Cordial, 1 oz.	120.00
Finger Bowl	20.00
Goblet, 10 oz.	60.00
Oyster Cocktail, 3½ oz.	25.00
Saucer Champagne, 6 oz.	38.00
Sherry, 1½ oz.	120.00
Soda, Footed, 12 oz. (iced tea)	30.00
Soda, Footed, 5 oz. (juice)	25.00
Wine, 3 oz.	75.00

NO. 4044 NEW ERA

Claret, 4 oz.	$50.00
Cocktail, 3½ oz.	24.00
Cordial, 1 oz.	100.00
Goblet, 10 oz.	50.00
Oyster Cocktail, 3½ oz.	20.00
Pilsner, 8 oz.	75.00
Pilsner, 10 oz.	85.00
Pilsner, 12 oz.	90.00
Saucer Champagne, 6 oz.	35.00
Sherbet, 6 oz.	22.00
Soda, Footed, 5 oz. (juice)	24.00
Soda, Footed, 12 oz. or 14 oz. (iced tea)	35.00
Soda or Tumbler, Footed, 8 oz. (water)	30.00
Wine, 3 oz.	50.00

Original Catalog Illustration: Assortment of Silver Mist

SATIN FINISH

ETCHING

Date: 1936

Manufacturer: A.H. Heisey & Co., Newark, OH

Colors: Crystal

Notes: Heisey used satin finish as a decoration in several ways and on many pieces in the 1930s. The 1930s focused primarily on pieces with satin finish accents. But the company also made pieces, including some animals, in all-over satin finish.

ACCESSORIES:

Bowl, Floral, 11" (4044)	$95.00
Bowl, Floral, Oval (1445)	185.00
Bowl, Floral, Oval, 12" (1447)	90.00
Candelabra, 2-light, pr. (402)	900.00+
Candlesticks, 1-light, pr. (1445)	325.00
Candlesticks, 2-light, pr. (1428)	120.00
Candlesticks, 2-light, pr. (1445)	345.00
Candlesticks, 2-light, pr. (1447)	385.00
Candlesticks, 2-light, pr. (4044)	295.00
Celery Tray, 13" (4044)	50.00
Cigarette Holder (1428)	60.00
Cocktail Shaker, 2 qt. (4225)	85.00
Cream & Sugar, pr. (4044)	110.00
Cup & Saucer (4044)	65.00
Cup & Saucer, After Dinner (4044)	120.00
Decanter & Stopper (4036)	100.00
Hors d'oeuvre, Base, Center & Cover (1184)	145.00
Nut or Ashtray, Individual (4044)	55.00
Plate, 10" (4044)	120.00
Plate, Bread & Butter, 5½" (4044)	30.00
Plate, Salad, 7" (4044)	42.00
Relish, 3-compartment, 13" (4044)	50.00
Relish, 5-compartment (Star) (1466)	90.00
Rock & Rye, 28 oz. (4044)	175.00
Vase, Horn of Plenty, 7" (1428)	60.00
Vase, Horn of Plenty, 9" (1428)	75.00
Vase, Horn of Plenty, 11" (1428)	100.00
Vase, Individual (1428)	60.00

SILVER MIST

MATTE FINISH

Date: 1934

Manufacturer: Fostoria Glass Co., Moundsville, WV

Colors: Crystal

STEMWARE:

NO. 4024

Claret-Wine, 3½ oz., 4½" tall	$30.00
Cocktail, 4 oz., 3⅝" tall	24.00
Cordial, 1 oz., 3⅛" tall	50.00
Goblet, 10 oz., 5⅝" tall	28.00
Goblet, 11 oz., 6⅛" tall	28.00
Iced Tea, Footed, 12 oz., 5½" tall	28.00
Juice, Footed, 5 oz., 4¼" tall	25.00

Oyster Cocktail, 4 oz., 3⅜" tall 17.00
Rhine Wine, 3½ oz., 5⅞" tall 30.00
Saucer Champagne, 6½ oz., 4½" tall 26.00
Sherbet, 5½ oz., 3⅞" tall 20.00
Sherry, 2 oz., 3⅞" tall 30.00
Tumbler, Footed, 8 oz., 4¾" tall 25.00
Whiskey, Footed, ... 25.00

ACCESSORIES:
Ashtray (2419, 2457, 2520 or 2534) . . . $10.00
Bird (2521) 60.00
Bitters Bottle (2494) 65.00
Bonbon (2517) 20.00
Bowl, Handled, 9" (2536) 50.00
Bowl, Handled, 10" (2484) 55.00
Bubble Ball, 4" or 5" 50.00
Bubble Ball, 6" or 7" 55.00
Bubble Ball, 8" or 9" 65.00
Candlesticks, 2-light, pr, (2484) 90.00
Candlesticks, 5½", pr. (2535) 65.00
Candlesticks, Duo, pr. (2472 or 2496) . . 90.00
Candlesticks, Trindle, pr. (2496) 110.00
Candy Jar & Cover (4099) 85.00
Cigarette (5092) 35.00
Cigarette Box & Cover, Large (2391) . . . 45.00
Cocktail Shaker, Gold Top
    (2518, 2518½, 2525 or 2525½) . . . 110.00
Cocktail, Footed, 3 oz. (2518) 24.00
Cocktail, Footed, 4 oz. (4115½) 24.00
Cologne & Stopper (2519) 65.00
Cordial (4024) 50.00
Cordial Bottle (2494) 90.00
Cream (2497½) 32.00
Decanter (2494 or 2518) 95.00
Dish, Sauce, 6½" (2440) 15.00
Elephant 110.00
Fish Canape (2492) 45.00

Lemon (2517) 30.00
Mayonnaise (2513) 40.00
Mayonnaise, 2-part (2440) 40.00
Mint, Handled, 4" (2513) 18.00
Nappy, 4½" (2538) 7.00
Nappy, 6" (2538) 8.00
Nappy, 11" (2538) 15.00
Old Fashioned Cocktail, Sham, 7 oz. . . 18.00
Pelican (2531) 95.00
Penguin (2531) 90.00
Plate, 6", 7" or 8" (2510) 14.00
Polar Bear (2531) 95.00
Preserve, Handled, 5" (2513) 18.00
Puff & Cover (2519) 65.00
Relish, 2- or 3-part (2513) 30.00
Relish, 4 Part (2419) 38.00
Relish, 5 Part (2419) 40.00
Relish, Handled, 2-part (2440) 30.00
Relish, Handled, 3-part (2440) 32.00
Seafood Cocktail (Fish) (2497) 45.00
Seal (2531) 95.00
Sherry (4024) 30.00
Sugar (2497½) 32.00
Sweetmeat (2517) 35.00
Tray, Oval, 8½" (2440) 32.00
Tumbler, Sham, 10 oz. or 12 oz. (701) . . 22.00
Vase, 4" (4103) 35.00
Vase, 5½" (2489) 40.00
Vase, 6" (2404) 40.00
Vase, 6½" (2523) 45.00
Vase, 8" (2522) 55.00
Vase, 9" (2428) 55.00
Vase, 13" (2428) 70.00
Vase, Bud, 8" (5088) 50.00
Whiskey, 1¾ oz. (887) 22.00
Whiskey, 2 oz. (2518) 22.00
Wine, 5 oz. (2518) 30.00

Original Catalog Illustration:
Silver Mist decoration on
No. 4024 stemware

VELVA

SATIN FINISH

Date: 1937

Manufacturer: U.S. Glass Co., Tiffin, OH

Colors: Crystal, Regal Blue, Black

Notes: The line number on which Velva decoration appears is No. 15363 Continental (from original company material). Velva is gaining popularity, especially with Art Deco collectors. For Blue items add 30% to 40%.

Bowl, 10" $200.00
Bowl, Cupped 140.00
Bowl, Oval, 11" 185.00
Bowl, Rolled Edge 120.00
Candleholders, 2-light, pr. 350.00
Candlesticks, 1-light, 6", pr. 145.00

Candy Box & Cover 135.00
Candy Jar & Cover 190.00
Comport 125.00
Cream 60.00
Goblet 90.00
Iced Tea 65.00
Mayonnaise 75.00
Plate, Mayonnaise 25.00
Plate, Oval, 15" 170.00
Relish, 2-compartment 70.00
Relish, Rectangular, 5-part 95.00
Salver 120.00
Sugar 60.00
Sundae, High Foot 75.00
Vase, 10½" 225.00

Velva decoration on
No. 15363 Continental bowl

199

Chapter 39
STARS

Stars in various forms have long been used for glassware decoration, especially in cuttings. Most glass companies made a six-pointed or eight-pointed star cutting with minor rays between the major miters. We have not included these cuttings. Most were first made prior to the 1920s although they continued during this period. These cuttings were primarily made on very plain blanks, making it virtually impossible to attribute them correctly.

Original Catalog Illustration:
No. 728 Embassy cutting on
No. 4024 Victorian goblet

EMBASSY, NO. 728

CUTTING

Date: 1933

Manufacturer: Fostoria Glass Co., Moundsville, WV

Colors: Crystal

Notes: Probably plates and accessory pieces were made to match.

STEMWARE:
NO. 4024 VICTORIAN
Claret-Wine, 3½ oz., 4½" tall $32.00
Cocktail, 4 oz., 3⅝" tall 26.00
Cordial, 1 oz., 3⅛" tall 60.00

Goblet, 10 oz., 5⅝" tall 32.00
Goblet, 11 oz., 6⅞" tall 32.00
Iced Tea, Footed, 12 oz., 5½" tall 32.00
Juice, Footed, 5 oz., 4¼" tall 28.00
Oyster Cocktail, 4 oz., 3⅜" tall 20.00
Rhine Wine, 3½ oz., 5⅞" tall 32.00
Saucer Champagne, 6½ oz., 4½" tall . . . 30.00
Sherbet, 5½ oz., 3⅞" tall 24.00
Sherry, 2 oz., 3⅞" tall 32.00
Tumbler, Footed, 8 oz., 4¾" tall 28.00
Whiskey, Footed, 1½ oz., 2½" tall 27.00

Original Catalog Illustration:
No. 727 National cutting on
No. 4024 Victorian goblet

NATIONAL, NO. 727

CUTTING

Date: 1933

Manufacturer: Fostoria Glass Co., Moundsville, WV

Colors: Crystal

Notes: Probably plates and accessory pieces were made to match.

STEMWARE:
NO. 4024 VICTORIAN
Claret-Wine, 3½ oz., 4½" tall $32.00
Cocktail, 4 oz., 3⅝" tall 26.00
Cordial, 1 oz., 3⅛" tall 60.00

Goblet, 10 oz., 5⅝" tall 32.00
Goblet, 11 oz., 6⅞" tall 32.00
Iced Tea, Footed, 12 oz., 5½" tall 32.00
Juice, Footed, 5 oz., 4¼" tall 28.00
Oyster Cocktail, 4 oz., 3⅜" tall 20.00
Rhine Wine, 3½ oz., 5⅞" tall 32.00
Saucer Champagne, 6½ oz., 4½" tall . . . 30.00
Sherbet, 5½ oz., 3⅞" tall 24.00
Sherry, 2 oz., 3⅞" tall 32.00
Tumbler, Footed, 8 oz., 4¾" tall 28.00
Whiskey, Footed, 1½ oz., 2½" tall 27.00

Original Catalog Illustration: No. 108 cutting on No. 3400 Candlewick stemware

NO. 108

CUTTING

Date: 1930

Manufacturer: Imperial Glass Corp., Bellaire, OH

Colors: Crystal

Notes: Most likely many other pieces in Candlewick were cut with this design.

STEMWARE:

NO. 3400 CANDLEWICK

Claret, 5 oz.	$60.00
Cocktail, 4 oz.	25.00
Cordial, 1 oz.	55.00
Goblet, 9 oz.	37.00
Oyster Cocktail, 4 oz.	22.00
Parfait, 6 oz.	48.00
Saucer Champagne or Sherbet, 6 oz.	28.00
Sherbet, Low, 5 oz.	22.00
Tumbler, Footed, 9 oz.	25.00
Tumbler, Footed, 12 oz. (iced tea)	23.00
Tumbler, Water, Footed, 10 oz.	23.00
Wine, 4 oz.	30.00

ACCESSORIES:

Bowl, Salad (400/75B)	$45.00
Butter, Covered, Round, 5½" (400/144)	48.00
Decanter & Stopper (400/163)	275.00
Finger Bowl (3400)	20.00
Marmalade & Cover (400/89)	50.00
Plate, Dinner, 10½" (400/10D)	55.00
Plate, Marmalade (400)	15.00
Plate, for Salad Set (400/75B)	25.00
Tray, Handled, Mint, 9" (400/149D)	35.00
Vase, Fan, 8" (400/87F)	40.00

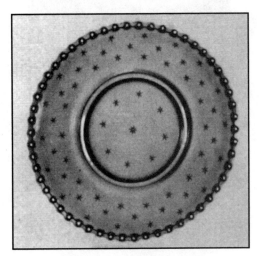

Original Catalog Illustration:
No. 108 cutting on dinner plate

Original Catalog Illustration:
No. 108 cutting on fan vase

No. 10 Scotch Thistle etching on high sherbet or saucer champagne

SCOTCH THISTLE, NO. 10

ETCHING

Date: 1920s

Manufacturer: Central Glass Co., Wheeling, WV

Colors: Crystal

Notes: Very similar, or the same as, one of the Tiffin etchings called "Special Thistle." Tiffin may have continued this etching after Central closed, but this is speculation. Scotch Thistle is the original Central name. Central made a full line of this but company literature indicates that only the following items were made. However, this should be taken with a grain of salt since this is a policy that was in force only when this specific information was printed, and may not have been followed during the many years of production. Most items were available in optic or plain. An asterisk (*) indicates items made with Cut 17—a cut star bottom and cut flutes.

STEMWARE:
NO. 528
Brandy, ¾ oz. $75.00
Champagne, Tall, 5 oz. 22.00
Claret, 4 oz or 5 oz. 30.00
Cocktail, 3 oz. 22.00
Cordial, 1 oz. 75.00
Custard, Handled, 4½ oz. (punch cup) 15.00
Goblet, 8 oz. 25.00
Goblet, 10 oz. 30.00
Saucer Champagne, 6 oz. 22.00
Sherbet, 4½ oz. 15.00
Sherry, 2 oz. 75.00
Wine, 3 oz. 35.00

ACCESSORIES:
Ale, 6½ oz. (68) $22.00
Almond Dish, Individual (112). 18.00
Almond Dish, Large, 4½" (112) 25.00
Bell Tumbler, 8 oz. (228 or 301) 20.00
Bottle, Salad (496) 50.00
Boudoir (tumble up) (946) * 175.00
Bowl, Berry, Low Foot, 4½" (62) 22.00
Bowl, Berry, Low Foot, 6" or 7" (62) 30.00
Comport, Tall, 5" or 6" (67) 45.00
Concave, Tumbler, 8 oz. 20.00
Decanter, 24 oz., cut neck (530) 165.00
Decanter, Handled, cut neck (530) 185.00
Decanter, qt. (729 or 983) 150.00
Finger Bowl, 14 oz. (530). 20.00
Horseradish Jar, Optic (949). 65.00

Catalog Illustration: No. 10 Scotch Thistle etching

(continued) **THISTLES**

Iced Tea, Handled, 11 oz. (734) 35.00
Jug (7, 20) * 95.00
Jug, 54 oz. (50) 95.00
Jug & Cover, 80 oz. (11) 135.00
Marmalade & Cover (284) 65.00
Oil & Stopper (112) 95.00
Plate for Marmalade (284) 12.00
Plate, 5" or 6", cut star bottom (530) 17.00
Plate, Finger Bowl, 6" (530) 12.00
Plate, Sherbet, 5" (530) 12.00
Salt, Individual (112) 22.00
Sherbet, Large, 6 oz. (528) 17.00

Sherbet, Small, 4½ oz. (7809) 15.00
Teapot (733) 275.00
Tumbler, 2½ oz. (whiskey) (530) * 45.00
Tumbler, 4 oz. or 5 oz. (530) * 16.00
Tumbler, 5 oz. (841) 16.00
Tumbler, 5½ oz. (530) * 16.00
Tumbler, 8 oz. (530) * 20.00
Tumbler, 9 oz. or 10 oz. (871 or 1096) 22.00
Tumbler, 10 oz. (table) (530) * 20.00
Tumbler, 11 oz. (530) * 20.00
Tumbler, 12 oz. (530) * 22.00
Tumbler, 14 oz. (530) * 25.00

THISTLE

ETCHING

Date: 1930s

Manufacturer: U.S. Glass Co., Tiffin, OH

Colors: Crystal

Notes: This is a separate pattern from Tiffin's Special Thistle. This etching was done exclusively by Tiffin.

STEMWARE:
NO. 14180
Café Parfait $25.00
Cocktail, 3½ oz. 20.00
Cordial, 1 oz. 65.00
Goblet, 9 oz. 27.00
Peach Melba 20.00
Saucer Champagne 20.00
Sundae, Sherbet 15.00

ACCESSORIES:
Finger Bowl (1080) $15.00
Jug & Cover, 2 qt. (117) 135.00
Oil & Stopper (14179) 100.00
Plate, Finger Bowl (8814) 10.00
Tumbler, Table (354) 20.00
Tumbler, Whiskey, 2½ oz. (354) 35.00
Tumbler, Juice, 5 oz. (354) 18.00
Tumbler, 7 oz. (354) 20.00
Tumbler, 12 oz. (354) 22.00
Tumbler, Handled, 12 oz. (354) 32.00
Tumbler, 14 oz. (354) 24.00

Original Catalog Illustration: Thistle Goblet, Café Parfait, Saucer Champagne, Cocktail, Cordial, and Peach Melba

Chapter 41

TREES & LEAVES

Trees comprise a few decorations on glass, but leaves are used as a motif for many. These are often quite stylized, but sometimes are realistic.

Detail of Byzantine etching

BYZANTINE

PLATE ETCHING

Date: 1931

Manufacturer: U.S. Glass Co., Tiffin, OH

Colors: Crystal, Mandarin with Crystal Trim. Crystal with Ebony Trim. Rare in Mandarin with Black Trim. When decorated with platinum encrusted band, it is called Leaf-Byzantine (ca. 1932).

Notes: Blown bowl, pressed stem. Made wide optic. A very stylized etching reminiscent of leaves. Pieces were made with gold encrustation in the etching, especially on Ebony blanks. Add 25% to 50% for Leaf-Byzantine on 15048.

STEMWARE:

NO. 15037 OR NO. 17507

Café Parfait	$42.00
Cocktail	32.00
Cordial	75.00
Goblet	38.00
Iced Tea	32.00
Saucer Champagne	32.00
Sundae (sherbet)	20.00
Wine	38.00

ACCESSORIES:

Candleholders, pr. (5831)	$45.00
Centerpiece (bowl) (5831 or 8177)	90.00
Comport, Small (5831)	50.00
Cream (5831)	40.00
Cup & Saucer (5831)	45.00
Finger Bowl (002)	18.00
Jug (128)	95.00
Mayonnaise (5831)	38.00
Nappy, Handled (5831)	25.00
Oyster Cocktail (196)	20.00
Plate, Mayonnaise (5831)	15.00
Plate, Salad, 7½" (5831)	15.00
Sugar (5831)	40.00

Original Catalog Illustration:
Cadena etching on jug with cover

CADENA

PLATE ETCHING

Date: 1920s

Manufacturer: U. S. Glass Co., Tiffin, OH

Colors: Crystal. Mandarin or Rose with Crystal Trim

STEMWARE:

NO. 15065	Crystal	Colors
Cocktail	$20.00	$30.00
Cordial	75.00	110.00
Goblet	24.00	40.00
Oyster Cocktail	15.00	28.00
Saucer Champagne	20.00	35.00
Sundae (sherbet)	17.00	25.00
Table (tumbler)	22.00	35.00

ACCESSORIES:

	Crystal	Colors
Candleholders, pr. (5831)	$60.00	$85.00
Centerpiece (bowl) (5831)	38.00	60.00
Creme Soup (5831)	24.00	38.00
Cup & Saucer (5831)	38.00	80.00
Finger Bowl (041)	18.00	28.00
Grapefruit (251)	25.00	58.00
Jug & Cover (194)	275.00	395.00
Mayonnaise (5831)	30.00	50.00
Nappy, Handled (5831)	15.00	27.00
Pickle Tray (5831)	20.00	35.00
Plate, 6" (8814)	8.00	12.00
Plate, 7½" (5831)	12.00	16.00
Plate, Creme Soup (5831)	8.00	12.00
Plate, Mayonnaise	12.00	16.00

CHINTZ, NO. 338

PLATE ETCHING

Date: 1942

Manufacturer: Fostoria Glass Co., Moundsville, WV

Colors: Crystal

Notes: Made to match Spode's Rosebud china pattern. Made on No. 2496 Baroque dinnerware.

STEMWARE:

NO. 6026 GREENBRIAR

Claret-Wine, 4½ oz., 5⅜" tall	$27.00
Cocktail, 4 oz., 5" tall	19.00
Cocktail, Footed, 4 oz., 3⅝" tall	17.00
Cordial, 1 oz., 3⅞" tall	55.00
Goblet, 9 oz., 7⅝" tall	30.00
Goblet, Low, 9 oz., 6⅞" tall	22.00
Iced Tea, Footed, 13 oz., 6" tall	20.00
Juice, Footed, 5 oz., 4¾" tall	16.00
Oyster Cocktail, 4 oz., 3⅝" tall	12.00
Saucer Champagne, 6 oz., 5½" tall	22.00
Sherbet, Low, 6 oz., 4⅜" tall	17.00

ACCESSORIES:

Bottle, Salad Dressing & Stopper, 6½" (2083)	$350.00
Celery, 11" (2496)	40.00

Cream & Sugar, pr. (2496)	40.00
Cream, Individual (2496)	25.00
Cream Soup (2496)	80.00
Cup, Footed, & Saucer (2496)	30.00
Dish, Vegetable, 9½" (2496)	75.00
Finger Bowl, 4½" (869)	40.00
Fruit, 5" (2496)	32.00
Jug, Footed, 9¾" (5000)	390.00
Luncheon Tray, Center-handled, 11" (2375)	50.00
Mayonnaise (2496)	50.00
Oil & Stopper, 3½ oz. (2496)	120.00
Pickle, 8" (2496)	35.00
Plate, 6" (2496)	12.00
Plate, 7½" or 8½" (2496)	20.00
Plate, 9½" (2496)	65.00
Plate, Cream Soup (2496)	15.00
Plate, Mayonnaise (2496)	20.00
Platter, Oval, 12" (2496)	110.00
Salt & Pepper shaker, pr. (2496)	100.00
Sugar, Individual (2496)	25.00
Tray for Sugar & Cream (2496)	30.00
Vase, 5" (4108 or 4128)	90.00
Vase, Footed, 6" (4143)	110.00
Vase, Footed, 7½" (4143)	150.00

Original Catalog Illustration:
No. 338 Chintz etching
on assortment

FERN

ROCK CRYSTAL CUTTING

Date: 1950s

Manufacturer: Duncan & Miller Glass Co., Washington, PA

Colors: Crystal

Notes: No. 30½ refers to Pall Mall pattern.

STEMWARE:

NO. D1 MANDARIN

Cocktail, Liquor, 3½ oz.	$28.00
Goblet, 11 oz.	40.00

Iced Tea, Footed, 14 oz.	32.00
Orange Juice, Footed, 5 oz.	20.00
Oyster Cocktail, Footed, 4½ oz.	15.00
Saucer Champagne or Tall Sherbet, 5 oz.	35.00
Wine or Claret, 4 oz.	40.00

ACCESSORIES:

Plate, 6" (30½)	$15.00
Plate, 7½" or 8½" (30½)	17.00

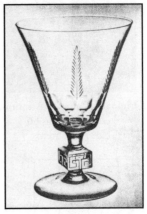

Original Catalog Illustration:
Fern cutting on No. D1
Mandarin goblet

FERN, NO. 305

PLATE ETCHING

Date: 1929

Manufacturer: Fostoria Glass Co., Moundsville, WV

Colors: Crystal, Amber, Green, Rose. Ebony with Gold Rim. No. 4020 pieces made with Crystal bowls with square Ebony bases. Available on No. 2419 Mayfair table service in Crystal and Rose only.

Notes: For items in colors, add 50%.

STEMWARE:

NO. 4020

Cocktail, 4 oz., 3⅝" tall	$18.00
Goblet, 11 oz., 5¾" tall	30.00
Iced Tea, Footed, 16 oz., 6" tall	25.00
Juice, Footed, 5 oz., 4⅛" tall	24.00
Sherbet, Low, 5 oz. or 7 oz., 3" tall	22.00
Sherbet, Tall, 7 oz., 4⅜" tall	30.00
Tumbler, Footed, 10 oz., 5" tall	22.00
Tumbler, Footed, 13 oz., 5¼" tall	28.00
Whiskey, 2 oz., 2⅛" tall	30.00
Wine, 3 oz.	25.00

Original Catalog Illustration:
No. 305 Fern etching on
No. 4020 footed tumbler

TREES & LEAVES *(continued)*

Original Catalog Illustration:
No. 305 Fern etching on
No. 5098 footed tumbler

Original Catalog Illustration:
Fernlee etching on
No. 7627 Stems

Original Catalog Illustration:
No. 783 Francis First cutting
on No. 5326 Deauville goblet

Original Catalog Illustration:
Governor Clinton cutting on
No. D1 Mandarin goblet

No. 5098

Claret, 4 oz., 6" tall $25.00
Cocktail, 3 oz., 5⅛" tall 18.00
Cordial, ¾ oz., 3⅞" tall 60.00
Goblet, 10 oz., 8¼" tall 30.00
Juice, Footed, 5 oz., 4⅜" tall 22.00
Oyster Cocktail, 5 oz., 3¾" tall 16.00
Parfait, 6 oz., 5¼" tall 25.00
Sherbet, High, 6 oz., 6" tall 30.00
Sherbet, Low, 6 oz., 4⅛" tall 22.00
Wine, 2½ oz., 5⅜" tall 25.00
Water, Footed, 9 oz., 5¼" tall 28.00

FERNLEE

PLATE ETCHING

Date: 1931

Manufacturer: Morgantown Glass Works,
Morgantown, WV

Colors: Crystal. Crystal bowl with Black
filament stem

Notes: Called Jonquil by the company when
made in Topaz. "Fernlee etching is bright with
the flowing leaves in satin effect."—original
company description. Expect to find other
items than those listed. For filament stems,
add 100%.

FRANCIS FIRST, NO. 783

ROCK CRYSTAL CUTTING

Date: 1940s

Manufacturer: Duncan & Miller Glass Co.,
Washington, PA

Colors: Crystal

Notes: It is likely that matching pressed ware
was made, but we cannot document any at this
time. Expect to find plates at least.

STEMWARE:
NO. 5326 DEAUVILLE
Claret, 4½ oz., 6¾" high $30.00
Cocktail, Liquor, 3½ oz., 5¼" high 30.00

GOVERNOR CLINTON

ROCK CRYSTAL CUTTING

Date: 1950s

Manufacturer: Duncan & Miller Glass Co.,
Washington, PA

Colors: Crystal

Notes: No. 30½ refers to Pall Mall pattern.

STEMWARE:
NO. D1 MANDARIN
Cocktail, Liquor, 3½ oz. $30.00
Goblet, 11 oz. 45.00

ACCESSORIES:
Cream & Sugar, pr. (4020) $60.00
Cup & Saucer, After Dinner
   (2350/2419) 25.00
Cup & Saucer, Footed, Crystal only
   (2350½/2419) 22.00
Dish, Lemon (2375) 30.00
Finger Bowl (4021 or 4121) 12.00
Jug, Footed, (4020) 95.00
Plate, 6" 8.00

STEMWARE:
NO. 7672
Goblet $60.00
Goblet, Luncheon 55.00
Liquor 85.00
Sherbet, Low 25.00
Sherbet, Tall 48.00
Wine 60.00
Tumbler (9074) 50.00

Cordial, 1 oz., 5" high 70.00
Finger Bowl, 4½" 15.00
Goblet, 9 oz., 7¾" high 45.00
Goblet, Luncheon, 9 oz., 6" high 40.00
Ice Cream, 6 oz. (sherbet), 3¾" high . . . 17.00
Iced Tea, Footed, 13 oz., 6¾" high 38.00
Orange Juice, Footed, 5 oz., 4¾" high . . 24.00
Oyster Cocktail, 4½ oz., 4¼" high 18.00
Plate, Finger Bowl, 6" 15.00
Saucer Champagne, 6 oz., 6" high 40.00
Wine, 3 oz., 6¼" high 45.00

Iced Tea, Footed, 14 oz. 38.00
Orange Juice, Footed, 5 oz. 24.00
Oyster Cocktail, Footed, 4½ oz. 18.00
Saucer Champagne or
   Tall Sherbet, 5 oz. 38.00
Wine or Claret, 4 oz. 45.00

ACCESSORIES:
Plate, 6" (30½) $15.00
Plate, 7½" or 8½" (30½) 17.00

(continued) # TREES & LEAVES

INDIAN TREE

CAMEO ETCHING

Date: 1940s

Manufacturer: Duncan & Miller Glass Co., Washington, PA

Colors: Crystal

Notes: Made to match various Indian Tree designs on china, although catalog pages do not indicate this. Pattern names are as follows: No. 115 Canterbury, No. 117 Three Feathers, and No. 30 Pall Mall.

STEMWARE:

NO. 5326 DEAUVILLE

Claret, 4½ oz., 6¾" high	$32.00
Cocktail, Liquor, 3½ oz., 5¼" high	32.00
Cordial, 1 oz., 5" high	75.00
Finger Bowl, 4½"	18.00
Goblet, 9 oz., 7¾" high	50.00
Goblet, Luncheon, 9 oz., 6" high	38.00
Ice Cream, Sherbet, 6 oz., 3¾" high	17.00
Iced Tea, Footed, 13 oz., 6¾" high	38.00
Orange Juice, Footed, 5 oz., 4¾" high	25.00
Oyster Cocktail, 4½ oz., 4¼" high	20.00
Plate, Finger Bowl, 6"	10.00
Saucer Champagne, 6 oz., 6" high	45.00
Wine, 3 oz., 6¼" high	50.00

ACCESSORIES:

NO. 115 UNLESS NOTED OTHERWISE

Basket, Oval Handled, 10"	$85.00
Basket, Oval Handled, 11½"	95.00
Bowl, Crimped, 10½"	60.00
Bowl, Shallow Salad, 12"	65.00
Candlesticks, 1-light, 3", pr.	72.00
Candlesticks, 2-light, 5", pr. (30)	70.00
Candy Box & Cover, 3-compartment, 8"	90.00
Comport, High Foot, 5½" tall	65.00
Cream, 7 oz., 3¾" tall	40.00
Cream, Individual, 2¾" tall	45.00
Mayonnaise, Crimped, 5½"	38.00
Nappy, 2-handled, Round, 6"	28.00
Olive, 2-handled, Oval, 6"	28.00
Plate, 6" or 7½"	12.00
Plate, 14"	75.00
Plate, Mayonnaise, Handled, 7½"	15.00
Plate, Salad, 8½"	16.00
Plate, Sandwich, 2-handled 11"	45.00
Relish, 3-handled, 3-compartment, 9"	40.00
Sugar, 7 oz, 3" tall	40.00
Sugar, Individual, 2½" tall	45.00
Tray, Sugar & Cream, Oval	38.00
Vase, Bud, Footed, 9" (506)	65.00
Vase, Cornucopia, 8" (117)	78.00

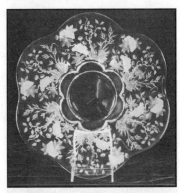

Indian Tree etching on plate

Original Catalog Illustration: Indian Tree etching on cornucopia case

JULIE

CUTTING

Date: 1950s

Manufacturer: Tiffin Art Glass Corp., Tiffin, OH

Colors: Crystal

Notes: "A graceful sweep, destined for harmony with many new china patterns."—Original Tiffin Brochure.

STEMWARE:

NO. 17684

Champagne/Sherbet	$30.00
Claret	35.00
Cocktail	30.00
Cordial	70.00
Goblet	35.00
Iced Tea	30.00
Juice	20.00

ACCESSORIES:

Finger Bowl	$15.00
Nappy, Dessert	15.00
Plate, Salad, 8"	18.00

Original Catalog Illustration: Julie cutting on No. 17684 goblet

TREES & LEAVES *(continued)*

Original Catalog Illustration: No. 329 Lido etching of No. 6011 footed jug

LIDO, NO. 329

PLATE ETCHING

Date: 1937

Manufacturer: Fostoria Glass Co., Moundsville, WV

Colors: Crystal, Azure

Notes: "No. 2496 designates Baroque blanks. Feathery fronds of wind-blown palms form the symmetrical motif of this Fostoria Golden Jubilee Master-Etching. It is modern in conception and subtle in execution."—From a Fostoria ad, 1937. For accessory pieces in Azure, add 25% to Crystal items.

STEMWARE:

NO. 6017 SCEPTRE	Crystal	Azure
Claret, 4 oz., 5⅞" tall	$30.00	$40.00
Cocktail, 3½ oz., 4⅞" tall	25.00	30.00
Cordial, ¾ oz., 3⅞" tall	55.00	68.00
Goblet, 9 oz., 7⅜" tall	28.00	35.00
Oyster Cocktail, 4 oz., 3⅝" tall	18.00	22.00
Sherbet, High, 6 oz., 5½" tall (saucer champagne)	18.00	27.00
Sherbet, Low, 6 oz., 4½" tall	20.00	25.00
Tumbler, Footed, 5 oz., 4¾" tall (juice)	20.00	24.00
Tumbler, Footed, 9 oz., 5½" tall (water)	20.00	24.00
Tumbler, Footed, 12 oz., 6" tall (iced tea)	25.00	30.00
Tumbler, Footed, 14 oz., 6½" tall (iced tea)	25.00	30.00
Wine, 3 oz., 5½" tall	32.00	38.00

ACCESSORIES:

Bonbon, 3-toed, 7⅜" (2496)	$18.00
Bowl, Nut, Cupped, 3-toed, 6¼" (2496)	25.00
Candy Box & Cover, 3-part, 6¼" (2496)	75.00
Celery, 11" (2496)	27.00
Cheese & Cracker, 2 piece, 11" (2496)	50.00
Comport, 5½" (2496)	27.00
Comport, 6½", 5¾" tall (2496)	30.00
Cream, Footed, 3¾" tall (2496)	15.00
Cream, Individual, 3⅛" tall (2496)	18.00
Cup & Saucer, Footed (2496)	25.00
Dish, Serving, 2-handled, 8½" (2496)	50.00
Finger Bowl (766)	20.00
Ice Bucket, 4⅜" x 6½" (2496)	70.00
Jelly & Cover, 7½" (2496)	62.00
Jug, Footed, 53 oz. (6011)	145.00
Mayonnaise (2496½)	32.00
Nappy, Handled, 3-cornered, 4⅝" (2496)	16.00
Nappy, Handled, Flared, 5" (2496)	16.00
Nappy, Handled, Regular, 4⅜" (2496)	16.00
Nappy, Handled, Square, 4" (2496)	16.00
Oil & Stopper, 3½ oz., 5½" tall (2496)	95.00
Old Fashioned Cocktail, 7½ oz., 3⅛" tall (4132)	18.00
Pickle, 8" (2496)	20.00
Plate, 6" or 7" (2496)	10.00
Plate, 8" (2496)	15.00
Plate, Cake, 2-handled, 10" (2496)	35.00
Plate, Mayonnaise (2496½)	15.00
Plate, Torte, 14" (2496)	50.00
Salt & Pepper, 2¾" tall, pr. (2496)	60.00
Sugar, Footed, 3½" tall (2496)	15.00
Sugar, Individual, 2⅞" tall (2496)	18.00
Sweetmeat, Square, 6" (2496)	22.00
Tidbit, 3-toed, Flat, 8¼" (2496)	24.00
Tray, Sugar & Cream, 6½" (2496)	17.00
Tumbler, Sham, 4 oz., 3½" tall (4132)	10.00
Tumbler, Sham, 5 oz., 3¾" tall (4132)	10.00
Tumbler, Sham, 7 oz., 4⅛" tall (4132)	14.00
Tumbler, Sham, 9 oz., 3¾" tall (4132)	15.00
Tumbler, Sham, 12 oz., 4⅞" tall (4132)	17.00
Tumbler, Sham, 14 oz., 5⅜" tall (4132)	20.00
Whiskey, Sham, 1½ oz., 2⅛" tall (4132)	25.00

Original Ad: Pomona cutting on No. 17507 goblet

POMONA

CUTTING

Date: 1952

Manufacturer: Tiffin Glass Co., Tiffin, OH

Colors: Crystal

Notes: "All stemware items available in this new pattern"—according to original ad.

STEMWARE:

NO. 17507	
Goblet	$35.00

(continued) TREES & LEAVES

SPRAY

ROCK CRYSTAL CUTTING

Date: 1950s

Manufacturer: Duncan & Miller Glass Co., Washington, PA

Colors: Crystal

Notes: No. 30½ refers to Pall Mall pattern.

STEMWARE:

NO. D7 CHALICE
Cocktail, Liquor	$26.00
Goblet	40.00
Iced Tea, Footed	35.00
Juice, Footed	22.00
Saucer Champagne or Tall Sherbet	35.00
Seafood Cocktail, Footed	18.00
Wine or Claret	40.00

ACCESSORIES:
High Ball	$12.00
Plate, 6½" (30½)	12.00
Plate, 7½" (30½)	12.00

Original Catalog Illustration:
Spray rock crystal cutting on No. D7 Chalice goblet

TEMPO, NO. 1029

ROCK CRYSTAL ENGRAVING

Date: Ca. 1940s

Manufacturer: Cambridge Glass Co., Cambridge, OH

Colors: Crystal

STEMWARE:

No. 3700
Claret, 4½ oz.	$25.00
Cocktail, 3 oz.	20.00
Cordial, 1 oz.	65.00
Goblet	25.00
Iced Tea	22.00
Oyster Cocktail, 4½ oz.	15.00
Sherbet, Low	15.00
Sherbet, Tall	25.00
Tumbler, Footed, 5 oz.	18.00
Tumbler, Footed, 12 oz.	20.00
Wine, 2½ oz.	25.00

ACCESSORIES:
Bonbon, 2-handled, 5½" (1180)	$15.00
Bonbon, Footed, 2-handled, 7" (3900/130)	20.00
Candlesticks, 2-light, 6", pr. (3900/72)	55.00
Celery & Relish, 3-part, 9" (3900/125)	30.00
Celery & Relish, 3-part, 12" (3900/126)	35.00
Comport (blown), 5⅜" (3121)	42.00
Comport, 5½" (3900/136)	30.00
Comport, Low, 6½" (P54)	32.00
Cream (3900/41)	24.00
Cream, Individual (P253)	25.00
Icer, 2-piece (968)	85.00
Jug, 76 oz. (3900/115)	90.00
Mayonnaise (3900/129)	30.00
Mayonnaise, Divided (3900/111)	30.00
Plate, Low Footed, 8" (P56)	18.00
Plate, Bonbon, 8" (3900/131)	12.00
Plate, Cake, Handled, 13½" (3900/35)	35.00
Plate, Mayonnaise (3900/129)	12.00
Plate, Rolled Edge, 14" (3900/116)	40.00
Plate, Salad, 7½" (555)	16.00
Relish, 2-part, 6" (1497)	24.00
Sugar (3900/41)	24.00
Sugar, Individual (P253)	25.00
Vase, 8" (6004)	50.00
Vase, Bud, Footed, 10" (274)	60.00

Original Catalog Illustration:
No. 1029 Tempo rock crystal engraving on No. 3700 iced tea

TREES & LEAVES *(continued)*

Original Catalog Illustration:
No. 335 Willow etching on
footed creamer and sugar

WILLOW, No. 335

PLATE ETCHING

Date: 1939

Manufacturer: Fostoria Glass Co.,
Moundsville, WV

Colors: Crystal

Notes: Available on No. 2574 Raleigh table
ware. Made to complement the popular Blue
Willow china dinnerware.

STEMWARE:
No. 6023 COLFAX
Claret-Wine, 4 oz., 4¾" tall $20.00
Cocktail, 3¾ oz., 4⅜" tall 18.00
Cordial, 1 oz., 3⅜" tall 45.00
Goblet, 9 oz., 6⅜" tall 24.00
Iced Tea, 12 oz., 4¾" tall 21.00
Juice, Footed, 5 oz., 4½" tall 16.00
Oyster Cocktail, 4 oz., 3⅝" tall 10.00
Sherbet, Low, 6 oz., 4⅛" tall 15.00
Saucer Champagne, 6 oz., 4⅞" tall 20.00
Tumbler, Footed, 9 oz., 5⅛" tall 17.00

ACCESSORIES:
Bonbon, 5" (2574) $18.00
Celery, 10½" (2574) 20.00
Comport, Blown, 5", 4¾" tall (6023) . . . 22.00
Cream, Footed (2574) 20.00
Cream, Individual (2574) 25.00
Cup, Footed & Saucer (2574) 25.00
Dish, Serving, 8½" (2574) 35.00
Finger Bowl (766) 12.00
Jug, Footed, 53 oz. (6011) 95.00
Lemon, 2-handled plate, 6½" (2574) . . . 15.00
Oil & Stopper, 4¾ oz. (2574) 55.00
Olive, 6" (2574) 15.00
Pickle, 8" (2574) 18.00
Plate, Several sizes (2574) . . . . 15.00+
Plate, Various sizes (2574) 15.00
Plate, Sandwich (2574) 25.00
Relish, 3-part, 10" (2574) 30.00
Salt & Pepper, pr. (2574) 42.00
Sugar, Footed (2574) 20.00
Sugar, Individual (2574) 25.00
Sweetmeat, 5¼" (2574) 18.00
Whipped Cream, 5" (2574) 18.00

Original Catalog Illustration:
Willow cutting on No. D3
Duncan-Phyfe goblet

WILLOW

CUTTING

Date: 1950s

Manufacturer: Duncan & Miller Glass Co.,
Washington, PA

Colors: Crystal

Notes: Advertised as complementing several
sterling and china patterns.

STEMWARE:
No. D3 DUNCAN-PHYFE
Cocktail, Liquor, 3½ oz. $25.00
Goblet, 10 oz. 35.00
Iced Tea, Footed, 14 oz. 32.00
Orange Juice, Footed, 5 oz. 30.00
Oyster Cocktail, Footed, 4½ oz. 22.00
Saucer Champagne or
    Tall Sherbet, 5 oz. 30.00
Wine or Claret, 4 oz. 40.00

ACCESSORIES:
Bowl, Flared Flower, 12½" $85.00
Bowl, Salad, 10½" 100.00
Candlesticks, 2-light, pr. 145.00
Candy Box & Cover, 6" 100.00
Candy Jar & Cover 100.00
Celery & Relish, 5-compartment, 12" . . . 70.00
Celery & Relish, Oblong,
    3-compartment, 2-handled, 12" 85.00
Cheese & Cracker, 2-handled,
    2-piece, 11" 100.00
Comport, High Footed, 7½" 65.00
Cream & Sugar, pr. 76.00
Mayonnaise 65.00
Plate, 7½" or 8½" (30½) 32.00
Plate, Mayonnaise 18.00
Plate, Torte, 14" 110.00
Relish, 5-compartment, 10" 90.00
Sandwich Tray, 2-handled, 11" 90.00
Vase, Flip, 8" 75.00

Chapter 42
WHEAT

EMPIRE

ROCK CRYSTAL ENGRAVING

Date: 1930s

Manufacturer: Cambridge Glass Co., Cambridge, OH

Colors: Crystal

STEMWARE:

NO. 3500 GADROON

Claret, 4½ oz.	$28.00
Cocktail.	28.00
Cordial, 1 oz.	74.00
Finger Bowl.	20.00
Finger Bowl, Footed.	22.00
Goblet, Long Bowl.	30.00
Goblet, Short Bowl	35.00
Oyster Cocktail	22.00
Parfait, Café, 5 oz.	25.00
Sherbet, Low, 7 oz.	22.00
Sherbet, Tall, 7 oz.	25.00
Tumbler, 2½ oz.	22.00

Tumbler, Footed, 5 oz.	22.00
Tumbler, Footed, 10 oz.	24.00
Tumbler, Footed, 13 oz.	25.00
Wine, 2½ oz.	30.00
Wine, Low, 2½ oz.	30.00

ACCESSORIES:

Bowl, Floral, 11" (3500)	$50.00
Candlesticks, 2-light, Keyhole Stem, pr.	75.00
Cocktail Icer, 2-piece (968)	75.00
Compote, 6" tall	40.00
Mayonnaise, Divided	35.00
Plate, Bread & Butter, 6⅜" (3500)	11.00
Plate, Chop, 14" (3500)	35.00
Plate, Mayonnaise	15.00
Plate, Salad, 7½" (3500/167)	15.00
Plate, Salad, 8½" (3500/5)	15.00
Relish, 3-part, 12" (3500)	32.00

Wholesaler's Catalog Illustration: Empire rock crystal engraving on bowl

HARVEST, NO. 1053

ROCK CRYSTAL ENGRAVING

Date: 1940s

Manufacturer: Cambridge Glass Co., Cambridge, OH

Colors: Crystal

STEMWARE:

NO. 3750 CHARLESTON

Claret, 4½ oz.	$20.00
Cocktail, 2½ oz.	14.00
Cordial, 1 oz.	58.00
Goblet, 10 oz.	20.00
Iced Tea, Footed, 12 oz.	16.00
Juice, Footed, 5 oz.	12.00
Oyster Cocktail, 4½ oz.	9.00
Sherbet, Tall, 6 oz.	15.00
Sherry Wine, 2½ oz.	17.00

ACCESSORIES:

Bowl, 12" (P430)	$45.00
Bowl, Flower, 12" (P430)	45.00
Bowl, Oval, 11" (P384)	45.00
Bowl, Salad, 10" (P427)	40.00
Candlesticks, 2-light, Keyhole Stem, pr. (647)	70.00

Original Catalog Illustration: No. 1053 Harvest rock crystal engraving on candy box

Candlesticks, Calla Lily, pr. (P499)	65.00
Candy Box & Cover (P306)	45.00
Candy Box & Cover, 3-part, 7" (103)	45.00
Celery & Relish, 5-part, 10" (P212)	32.00
Celery & Relish, 5-part, 12" (3900/120)	35.00
Celery & Relish, 5-part, 12" (P418)	35.00
Celery (P247)	27.00
Comport, Tall, 6" (532)	45.00
Cream (P254)	20.00
Hurricane Lamp (1613)	95.00
Jug, 76 oz. (3900/115)	90.00
Jug, Martini, 32 oz. (3900/114)	85.00
Plate, 14" (P125)	45.00
Plate, Crescent Salad, 8" (P454)	20.00
Plate, Mayonnaise (1491)	12.00
Plate, Salad, 7½" (555)	12.00
Plate, Salad, 8" (556)	12.00
Relish, 2-piece, 12" (P419)	22.00
Salad Dressing, Twin (1491)	35.00
Sugar (P254)	20.00
Tray, Relish, 3-part, 12" (P215)	35.00
Vase, Footed, 11" (278)	55.0

Original Catalog Illustration: No. 1053 Harvest rock crystal engraving on footed vase

WHEAT *(continued)*

Original Catalog Illustration:
Mesa cutting on No. D2 Riviera goblet

MESA

ROCK CRYSTAL CUTTING

Date: 1950s

Manufacturer: Duncan & Miller Glass Co., Washington, PA

Colors: Crystal

Notes: No. 30½ refers to Pall Mall pattern.

STEMWARE:
NO. D2 RIVIERA
Brandy, 1½ oz........................$48.00
Cocktail, Liquor, 3½ oz..................26.00
Goblet, 10 oz. 40.00
Iced Tea, Footed, 14 oz. 35.00
Orange Juice, Footed, 5 oz................22.00
Oyster Cocktail, Footed, 4½ oz............17.00
Saucer Champagne or Tall Sherbet, 6 oz.......35.00
Wine or Claret, 4 oz. 40.00

ACCESSORIES:
Plate, 6" (30½) $12.00
Plate, 7½" (30½)......................15.00
Plate, 8½" (30½).......................15.00

Original Catalog Illustration:
Wheat cutting on No. D7 Chalice goblet

WHEAT

ROCK CRYSTAL CUTTING

Date: 1950s

Manufacturer: Duncan & Miller Glass Co., Washington, PA

Colors: Crystal

Notes: No. 30½ refers to Pall Mall pattern.

STEMWARE:
NO. D7 CHALICE
Cocktail, Liquor.....................$26.00
Goblet...............................48.00
Iced Tea, Footed......................35.00
Juice, Footed 22.00
Saucer Champagne or Tall Sherbet 35.00
Seafood Cocktail, Footed 17.00
Wine or Claret........................40.00

ACCESSORIES:
High Ball............................$12.00
Plate, 7½" (30½)......................15.00
Plate, 8½" (30½).......................15.00

Chapter 43
WREATHS

BLAIR HOUSE

CUTTING

Date: 1950s

Manufacturer: Tiffin Art Glass Corp., Tiffin, OH

Colors: Crystal

Notes: Note the polished mirror effect on the interior of the wreath—a decorative treatment used often by Tiffin, especially in their popular Palais Versailles decoration. Note also the air-trap bubble in the stem—another Tiffin feature. "Destined to become a cherished heirloom of lustrous grandeur."—Original Tiffin Brochure.

STEMWARE:
NO. 17594

Champagne/Sherbet	$30.00
Claret	35.00
Cocktail	30.00
Cordial	70.00
Goblet	35.00
Iced Tea	30.00
Juice	20.00

ACCESSORIES:

Finger Bowl	$15.00
Nappy, Dessert	15.00
Plate, Salad, 8"	18.00

Original Tiffin Brochure:
Blair House cutting on No. 17594 goblet

COLONIAL MIRROR, NO. 334

PLATE ETCHING

Date: 1939

Manufacturer: Fostoria Glass Co., Moundsville, WV

Colors: Crystal

STEMWARE:
NO. 6023 COLFAX

Claret-Wine, 4 oz., 4¾" tall	$20.00
Cocktail, 3¾ oz., 4⅜" tall	18.00
Cordial, 1 oz., 3⅜" tall	45.00
Goblet, 9 oz., 6⅜" tall	20.00
Iced Tea, 12 oz., 4¾" tall	18.00
Juice, Footed, 5 oz., 4½" tall	15.00
Oyster Cocktail, 4 oz., 3⅝" tall	10.00
Saucer Champagne	15.00
Sherbet, Low	12.00
Tumbler, Footed, 9 oz.	14.00

Detail of Colonial Mirror etching

WREATHS *(continued)*

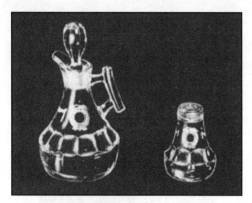

Original Catalog Illustration:
No. 334 Colonial Mirror on oil & stopper and salt shaker

ACCESSORIES:
Bonbon, 5" (2574)	$18.00
Celery, 10½" (2574)	20.00
Comport, Blown, 5", 4¾" tall (6023)	22.00
Cream & Sugar, Footed, pr. (2574)	40.00
Cream, Individual (2574)	25.00
Cup, Footed & Saucer (2574)	25.00
Dish, Serving, 8½" (2574)	35.00
Finger Bowl (766)	12.00
Jug, Footed, 53 oz. (6011)	95.00
Lemon, 6½" (2 handled plate) (2574)	15.00
Oil & Stopper, 4¾ oz. (2574)	55.00
Olive, 6" (2574)	15.00
Pickle, 8" (2574)	18.00
Plate (several sizes) (2574)	15.00+
Plate, Sandwich (2574)	25.00
Relish, 3 part, 10" (2574)	30.00
Salt & Pepper, pr. (2574)	42.00
Sugar, Individual (2574)	25.00
Sweetmeat, 5¼" (2574)	18.00
Whipped Cream, 5" (2574)	18.00

Original Ad: Lenox etching on
No. 6017 footed tumbler

LENOX

PLATE ETCHING

Date: 1937

Manufacturer: Fostoria Glass Co.,
Moundsville, WV

Colors: Crystal

Notes: "A formal but friendly design to live with the best families for years and years; a Master Etching for an evening of romance in congenial company."—From Fostoria ad, 1937.

STEMWARE:
NO. 6017
Claret, 4 oz.	$25.00
Cocktail, 3½ oz.	20.00
Cordial, ¾ oz.	45.00
Goblet, 9 oz.	28.00
Oyster Cocktail, 4 oz.	18.00
Saucer Champagne/High Sherbet, 6 oz.	20.00
Sherbet, Low, 6 oz.	18.00
Tumbler, Footed, 5 oz.	17.00

Tumbler, Footed, 9 oz.	15.00
Tumbler, Footed, 12 oz.	18.00
Tumbler, Footed, 14 oz.	20.00
Wine, 3 oz.	28.00

ACCESSORIES:
Cream & Sugar, Footed, pr. (2350½)	$44.00
Finger Bowl (766)	15.00
Jug, Footed (6011)	90.00
Plate, 6" (2337)	13.00
Plate, 7" (2337)	17.00
Plate, 8" (2337)	22.00
Tumbler, Sham, 5 oz. (4132)	9.00
Tumbler, Sham, 7 oz. (4132)	11.00
Tumbler, Sham, 9 oz. (4132)	15.00
Tumbler, Sham, 12 oz. (4132)	18.00
Tumbler, Sham, 14 oz. (4132)	20.00
Whiskey, Sham, 1½ oz. (4132)	18.00
Whiskey Sour, Sham, 4 oz. (4132)	14.00

Original Catalog Illustration:
No. 738 plate etching on
mayonnaise set

NO. 738

PLATE ETCHING

Date: 1930s or 1940s

Manufacturer: Cambridge Glass Co.,
Cambridge, OH

Colors: Crystal. Possibly others.

ACCESSORIES:
Basket, 11" (977)	$85.00
Bowl, 8½" (971)	25.00
Bowl, 10" (984)	35.00
Bowl, 11" (855 or 856)	40.00
Bowl, 12" (842)	45.00

Candlesticks, 1-light, 4", pr. (627)	75.00
Candlesticks, 1-light, 4", pr. (878)	75.00
Cheese & Cracker, 11", 2-piece (868)	50.00
Compote, 11½" (877)	50.00
Compote, Tall, 7" (1090)	45.00
Cream & Sugar, pr. (867)	40.00
Mayonnaise (873)	25.00
Plate, 2-handled, 11" (972)	25.00
Plate, Mayonnaise (873)	15.00
Sandwich Tray, Handled, 11" (870)	25.00

Chapter 44
CATARACT SHARPE MANUFACTURING CO.

This company produced many rock crystal (polished) cuttings during the 1930s and the 1940s. The firm was strictly a decorating company, producing no glass of its own. Blanks were purchased from Libbey Glass Co. and possibly others.

Designs were marketed as Rock Sharpe Crystal and were meant as low-cost examples of cut stemware to appeal to brides and housewives. Stems were often complex to add to the attractiveness.

Little accurate documentation is now known about the company. Original line numbers are not known for either the stem lines or the cuttings. In the following list, the numbers used are the same as used in the book: A Collection of American Crystal *by Bob Page and Dale Frederickson. These numbers are strictly an identification guide. Captions list original names and dates.*

Following are several examples of Rock Sharpe designs. Comments below are from original descriptions in company advertising. All cuttings are valued at approximately $20 to $35 each for goblets.

Chantilly 1940

Cranbrook 1940

Empire Wreath 1940
"Substantial shape and sturdy construction. This design is especially effective with pottery table settings. Harmonizes with Early American furnishings."

Groton 1940
"A well planned traditional design and pattern that can be at home in any period dining room. Its fragile appearance is deceiving."

CATARACT SHARPE MANUFACTURING CO. *(continued)*

Interlaken 1939
"Clear as an Alpine Lake! It's **Interlaken** in Rocke Sharpe Crystal. It rings to a finger tap like Swiss bells. Floral design, with a counter-motif of curves and lattice-like cuttings. The distinctive ornament in the stem, too, makes this glass one of interest in a collection of rare beauty."

Marlowe 1940
"Graceful, with a luminous brilliance that reflects dancing lights like fireflies at dusk, and has a silvery bell-like ring. Dramatic deeply chiseled design, even the hand-cut stem glitters with flashing fire."

Marshfield 1940
"Tall and graceful, with a deep hand-cut, original floral design, this goblet can be counted on to impress the most critical guests."

Newgate 1940
"Newgate, once the gateway to old London, now a sparkling, hand-cut addition to the Rock Sharpe Crystal collection. You'll love this enchanting design, reminiscent of English court splendor; the glittering depths of the diamond-cut stem flashing color and fire."

No. 1017-1 1937

No. 2013-1 1940
"Growing popularity of Regency interiors makes this goblet much in demand. It gets its elegance from careful designing rather than ornamentation."

Oradea 1940

Royale 1939
"A name fitting the regal splendor of this new design in the Rock Sharpe Crystal collection. Brilliant motif of royal palm fronds in glass that might grace a Bourbon table. Hand-cut stem ornament sparkles like a crown jewel."

Chapter 45
LOTUS DECORATING CO.

This company made no glass of its own, but bought blanks from many companies. It opened in 1912 and went out of business a few years ago. In the 1930s it often combined glass of several companies and placed the same decoration on each, creating "sets" of glassware from several companies, leading to much confusion for today's collectors.

Lotus did many decorations in rock crystal cuttings, plate etchings, and gold and platinum bands. In later years, silkscreen decorations and enameled motifs were widely used. It also did special 50th-anniversary pieces and 25th-anniversary commemoratives in gold and silver.

Since most of the stemware decorated by Lotus is of uncertain origin, we have listed Lotus decorations in alphabetical order.

BOUQUET

CUTTING

Done on stemware with blown bowls and pressed stems. Advertised as American Beauty Crystal. "Note how the glass artisan has hand cut this flowery design to blend with a hand shaped stem. Glistening true-ringing lead crystal is handblown and handmade."
—Original company description.

STEMWARE:

Champagne, Hollow Stem	$18.00
Claret	18.00
Cocktail	15.00
Cordial	40.00
Goblet	20.00
Iced Tea, Footed	18.00
Oyster Cocktail	10.00
Saucer Champagne	15.00
Sherbet, Low	10.00
Tumbler, Footed	15.00

ACCESSORIES:

Plate, Salad, 8"	$12.00

Bouquet cutting from original pattern folder

CALL OF THE WILD

PLATE ETCHING

Date: 1930

Colors: Black

Notes: Items were available with etching and also with silver encrustation in the etching. Many of the forms are from Duncan & Miller.

Bowl, Duncan (6750)	$65.00
Candlesticks, 1-light, pr., Duncan, several styles (6650)	60.00
Candlesticks, 2-light, pr. Duncan (6650)	75.00
Candy Box & Cover, Duncan (5050)	120.00
Compote (7150)	65.00
Decanter (0850)	155.00
Mayonnaise & Plate (6450)	85.00
Vase, Duncan (7550)	125.00
Vase, Flared, Duncan (0650)	110.00

Original Ad:
Call of the Wild etching

LOTUS DECORATING CO. *(continued)*

Carlton Rose cutting from original pattern folder

CARLTON ROSE

ROCK CRYSTAL CUTTING

Done on stemware with blown bowls and pressed stems. A modern low-priced range, rock crystal cutting. "All handmade crystal that will add beauty to any table setting and afford a graceful addition to any decoration theme."—Original company description.

Claret, 5 oz. $18.00
Cocktail, 3½ oz. 15.00
Cordial, 1 oz. 40.00
Goblet, 11 oz. 20.00
Iced Tea, Footed, 12 oz. 18.00
Juice, Footed, 5 oz. 15.00
Plate, Salad, 8". 12.00
Sherbet, 6 oz. 10.00

Cheryl cutting from original pattern folder

CHERYL

CUTTING

Done on stemware with blown bowls and pressed stems. "Sunburst pattern that literally makes your table appointments sparkle like diamonds with its radiance."—Original company description.

Claret $15.00
Cocktail. 12.00
Cordial 35.00
Goblet. 18.00
Iced Tea, Footed. 15.00
Juice, Footed 12.00
Plate, Salad, 8". 12.00
Sherbet 9.00

Dawn cutting from original pattern folder

DAWN

ROCK CRYSTAL CUTTING

Found on stems with blown bowls and pressed stems. Made in crystal. Fresh and crystal clear as the name implies. "The angular shape of the bowl is very high and the decorative cut pattern fits to perfection."—Original description

Claret $15.00
Cocktail. 12.00
Cordial 35.00
Goblet. 18.00
Iced Tea, Footed. 15.00
Juice, Footed 12.00
Plate, Salad, 8". 12.00
Sherbet 9.00

(continued) LOTUS DECORATING CO.

DEBUT

CUTTING

Done on stemware with blown bowls and pressed stems. "The happiness of springtime is heralded in this beautiful goblet with its floral spray. Notice the harmony between the design and the shape of the bowl."—Original company description.

```
Claret . . . . . . . . . . . . . . . . . . . . . . . . . . . . . $15.00
Cocktail. . . . . . . . . . . . . . . . . . . . . . . . . . . . 12.00
Cordial . . . . . . . . . . . . . . . . . . . . . . . . . . . . 35.00
Goblet. . . . . . . . . . . . . . . . . . . . . . . . . . . . . 18.00
Iced Tea, Footed. . . . . . . . . . . . . . . . . . . . . 15.00
Juice, Footed . . . . . . . . . . . . . . . . . . . . . . . 12.00
Plate, Salad, 8". . . . . . . . . . . . . . . . . . . . . . 12.00
Sherbet . . . . . . . . . . . . . . . . . . . . . . . . . . . . 9.00
```

Debut cutting from original pattern folder

DUCHESS

CUTTING

Done on stemware with blown bowls and pulled stems. "Sparkling deep polished cuttings as only Lotus craftsmen achieve. Modern shaped bowl creates gay appearance."—Original company description.

```
Claret (for all wines). . . . . . . . . . . . . . . . . . $15.00
Goblet. . . . . . . . . . . . . . . . . . . . . . . . . . . . . 18.00
Iced Tea. . . . . . . . . . . . . . . . . . . . . . . . . . . . 15.00
Juice, Footed . . . . . . . . . . . . . . . . . . . . . . . 12.00
Plate, 8". . . . . . . . . . . . . . . . . . . . . . . . . . . 12.00
Sherbet (also for Champagne). . . . . . . . . . . . . 9.00
```

Duchess cutting from original pattern folder

FLORENCE

CUTTING

Done on stemware with blown bowls and pulled stems. "Tulip shaped bowl with sparkling polished cuttings captures light refractions with every facet. Crystal jewels for table settings." —Original company description.

```
Claret (for all wines). . . . . . . . . . . . . . . . . . $15.00
Goblet. . . . . . . . . . . . . . . . . . . . . . . . . . . . . 18.00
Iced Tea. . . . . . . . . . . . . . . . . . . . . . . . . . . . 15.00
Juice, Footed . . . . . . . . . . . . . . . . . . . . . . . 12.00
Plate, 8". . . . . . . . . . . . . . . . . . . . . . . . . . . 12.00
Sherbet (also for champagne) . . . . . . . . . . . . . 9.00
```

Florence cutting from original pattern folder

219

LOTUS DECORATING CO. *(continued)*

L to R: Gloria cutting from original pattern folder
Kent cutting from original pattern folder

GLORIA

CUTTING

Made on stemware with blown bowls and pressed stems. "Hand cut and hand polished. Notched stem on beautiful full lead crystal." —Original company description.

Claret (for all wines)	$18.00
Cocktail	15.00
Cordial	40.00
Goblet	20.00
Iced Tea	18.00
Juice	15.00
Plate, 8"	12.00
Sherbet (also for champagne)	10.00

KENT

CUTTING

Done on stemware with blown bowls and pressed stems. "Happy the hostess who sets her table with Kent. Splendidly executed bands of decorative cutting will reflect myriad lights." —Original company description.

Claret	$15.00
Cocktail	12.00
Cordial	35.00
Goblet	18.00
Iced Tea, Footed	15.00
Juice, Footed	12.00
Plate, Salad, 8"	12.00
Sherbet	9.00

LA FURISTE

PLATE ETCHING

Date: 1930

Notes: Patent No. 71974 design patent. Many stemware and decorative items also made.

Goblet	$55.00

MARLENE

CUTTING

Done on stemware with blown bowls and pulled stems. "Superbly crafted geometric design on fine crystal baroque shape. This delicate stem completes the continental look."—Original company description.

Claret (for all wines)	$15.00
Goblet	18.00
Iced Tea	15.00
Juice, Footed	12.00
Plate, 8"	12.00
Sherbet (also for Champagne)	9.00

L to R: La Furiste etching on goblet
Marlene cutting from original pattern folder

(continued) LOTUS DECORATING CO.

MEADOW TREE, NO. 95-7

GRAY CUTTING

Date: 1953

Colors: Crystal

Notes: "Lotus craftsmen have created the Meadow Tree cutting appropriately fashioned to harmonize with the many chinaware patterns and to accentuate any decorative theme. Available in all Stemware, Footed Tumblers, Salad Plates and other essential items."
—Original ad, November 1953

STEMWARE:

Claret, 4 oz. $18.00
Cocktail, 4 oz. 15.00

Cordial, 1¼ oz. 55.00
Goblet, 11 oz. 20.00
Iced Tea, Footed, 12 oz. 18.00
Juice, Footed, 6 oz. 15.00
Sherbet, 6½ oz. 10.00
Sherry Wine, 2½ oz. 20.00

ACCESSORIES:

Cup & Saucer $45.00
Plate, Bread & Butter, 6" 12.00
Plate, Salad, 8" 15.00

Original ad: No. 95-7 Meadow
Tree cutting

No. 1012

PLATE ETCHING

Colors: Rose stem and foot, Crystal bowl.
Green stem and foot, Crystal bowl.

STEMWARE:

No. 27

Goblet, 9 oz. $22.00
Sherbet, High, 5 oz. 20.00
Sherbet, Low, 5 oz. 14.00
Wine, 2½ oz. 22.00
Cocktail, 3½ oz. 20.00

ACCESSORIES:

Bonbon, 2-handled, 6½" (86) $25.00
Bonbon, Crimped, 6½" (103) 25.00
Bonbon, Flared, 6½" (103) 25.00
Bowl, Bell, Handled, 9" (201) 50.00
Cake, Handled, 10" (200) 35.00
Celery, 2-handled, 11" (201) 35.00
Cheese & Cracker, 10" (200) 50.00

Cheese, 2-handled, 6½" (86) 25.00
Cream (87) 30.00
Cup & Saucer (21) 45.00
Decanter, 1 qt. (21) 95.00
Iced Tea, Footed, 12 oz. (24) 18.00
Jug, 4 pt. (24) 95.00
Mayonnaise (103) 35.00
Mint, 2-handled, 6" (86) 25.00
Olive, 2-handled, 7" (86) 25.00
Plate, Bread & Butter, 6" (60) 12.00
Plate, Dinner, 9" (60). 40.00
Plate, Salad, 7½" or 8" (60) 15.00
Plate, Service, 12" (60). 75.00
Sandwich, 2-handled, 11" (201) 35.00
Sugar (87) 30.00
Tumbler, Footed, 2¾ oz. (24). 35.00
Tumbler, Footed, 7 oz. (24) 15.00
Tumbler, Footed, 10 oz. (24) 15.00

Original Company Brochure:
No. 1012 etching

SERENITY

CUTTING

Done on stemware with blown bowls and pressed stems. "Beautiful hand cutting on handblown, true-ringing lead crystal. A rare jewel in this day of mechanization. Blends well with the modern or traditional."—Original company description.

STEMWARE:

Champagne, Hollow Stem $18.00
Claret 18.00
Cocktail. 15.00

Cordial 40.00
Goblet. 20.00
Iced Tea, Footed. 18.00
Oyster Cocktail 10.00
Saucer Champagne. 15.00
Sherbet, Low 10.00
Tumbler, Footed 15.00

ACCESSORIES:

Plate, Salad, 8" $12.00

Original pattern folder:
Serenity cutting on assortment

221

LOTUS DECORATING CO. *(continued)*

Spruce cutting from original ad

SPRUCE, NO. C20

CUTTING

Date: 1955

Colors: Crystal

Notes: "A stunning new line that is rich in beauty...modern in design and it is available in complete table settings. Hand made and hand cut full lead glass with striking 'Spruce' motif."—Original Ad, 1955. Other items not documented.

Goblet	$20.00
Sherbet	12.00

Vignette cutting from original pattern folder

VIGNETTE

CUTTING WITH PLATINUM BAND

Done on stems with blown bowls and pulled stems. "Edged with a band of purest platinum, this goblet, with its beautifully restrained wreath, brings prestige to your table. Only the most skilled craftsmen can achieve this perfection."—Original company description.

STEMWARE:

Claret, 4 oz.	$12.00
Cocktail, 3½ oz.	10.00

Cordial, 1 oz.	25.00
Goblet, 11 oz.	15.00
Iced Tea, Footed, 12 oz.	14.00
Juice, Footed, 5 oz.	10.00
Sherbet, 5½ oz.	8.00

ACCESSORIES:

Plate, Salad, 8"	$9.00

Windsor cutting from original pattern folder

WINDSOR

GRAY CUTTING

Done on stemware with blown bowls and pulled stems. "Hand-made grey cutting ethereal design on tulip shaped rock crystal has that expensive look of cherished heirlooms." —Original company description.

STEMWARE:

Claret (for all wines)	$12.00
Goblet	15.00

Iced Tea	14.00
Juice, Footed	10.00
Sherbet/Champagne	8.00

ACCESSORIES:

Plate, 8"	$9.00

Vase with Lotus sticker

We have not been able to locate information about this piece with its brocade-type etching. The vase has an original Lotus company sticker.

Value: $30.00

Winslo cutting from original pattern folder

WINSLO

ROCK CRYSTAL CUTTING

Done on stemware with blown bowls and pressed stems. "Those who choose Winslo may rest assured that they have selected a pattern of enduring dignity. Notice that the design of the bowl is echoed in the base."—Original company description.

STEMWARE:

Claret	$15.00
Cocktail	12.00
Cordial	35.00
Goblet	18.00
Iced Tea, Footed	15.00
Juice, Footed	12.00
Sherbet	9.00

ACCESSORIES:

Plate, Salad, 8"	$12.00

Part III
DECORATIVE ACCESSORIES

Many groups of collectible glass can be termed decorative accessories, meaning those items not used for setting a table or for holding beverages. These pieces are most often decorative in nature, although they also have usable functions such as vases, candy jars and others. In the following chapters we have listed several categories which can form interesting and varied collections. Most companies made items in these basic categories so that there is great variety available to the collector. These decorative items are so popular, originally with glass companies, and now with collectors that many of these categories have had books written about them.

We have chosen several categories to suggest to you the many possibilities of collecting: baskets, boudoir glass, candlesticks and console sets, candy jars, figurines, smoking items and vases. You will find some interesting new items not before presented in glass books.

Enjoy collecting your particular category. The possibilities in each category are almost endless.

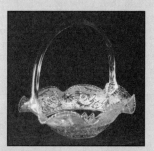

Duncan & Miller Glass Co.
Early American Sandwich Basket

Baskets—During the mid-teens, glass baskets for flowers or fruit first began to appear in quantity. Many companies designed baskets, from small and delicate to large and massive. At first, most of the baskets were made simply as a one-item pattern, but later companies began adding a basket, or many, to their standard pattern lines. For examples of this, examine listings in many of Duncan & Miller's lines such as Early American Sandwich or Canterbury. Baskets also began to change functions in later years. Instead of the usual flower vases, now items such as candy, nuts, mints and other things were suggested as suitable for serving from a small basket. U.S. Glass made tiny baskets for holding individual servings of nuts or mints at table settings. Baskets come in a huge variety of colors, from crystal to pastels and on to deep colors, including black. Decorations on baskets also are varied. U.S. Glass produced many with its wonderful satin finish. Companies such as Westmoreland made baskets in a variety of enameled decorations. Cuttings and etchings were also very popular, and were made by many companies, sometimes developed specifically for baskets only.

Boudoir Items—This chapter will introduce you to the varied items available primarily for use in the bedroom. Most common are the dresser sets and night sets or tumble ups. Dresser or vanity sets were usually comprised of a covered powder box and one or two colognes and often had a matching glass tray. Extended sets also might have a ring tree, a candlestick or other small items made to match. New Martinsville made a number of different styles of dresser sets in crystal and various colors, including combinations of colors and colors combined with crystal. Many attractive dresser sets were made more appealing with fanciful, elaborate stoppers for the colognes or perfumes. Decorations are sometimes found on dresser sets, but often color alone and pattern in the glass were considered enough to attract the buyer. Night sets or tumble ups were usually delicate blown-glass bottles holding about two cups with a relatively narrow neck over which a small tumbler could be placed upside down. This was an effective way to have water available in a guest room overnight and still have it protected from any dust or dirt. Fenton and Morgantown produced tumble ups in many desirable colors. Morgantown also combined its opaque colors to make attractive tumble ups with one color for the bottom and another for the tumbler. Dunbar created some very interestingly shaped tumble ups much different from the standard shape used by most other companies. As with other items of this time period, colors and decorations added immeasurably to the appeal of these sets.

Morgantown Glass Company Maria Medicine Set

L to R: Paden City No. 444 candy jar
Fostoria crown candy box

Duncan & Miller Glass Co.
sculptured floral cigarette box and ashtray

Candy Jars and Boxes—These items, too, became standard items for most glass companies. Who could resist having an attractive glass jar or box to serve candy from? They made perfect gifts to the bride or hostess. Candy jars are usually footed or pedestaled and have a lid. Candy boxes are usually low and flat on the bottoms, and likewise have lids. Candy boxes also often have internal dividers so that two or three kinds or candy could be served from the same container. As with most other items, these pieces were sometimes part of standard lines, but often were simply a standard shape made by the company. Colors and decorations abound as well as shapes.

Smoking Items—With the emphasis on smoking as being bad for one's health, the production of ashtrays, cigarette boxes and other smoking paraphernalia has declined. However, in the 1930s and 1940s especially, there was a great market for ashtrays and the like. Most companies produced a variety of these items. Examples can range from very simple designs to elaborate ones. Some particularly attractive examples are the sculptured designs made by Duncan & Miller, especially when these are found in opalescent colors. Ashtrays were made in a great variety of colors and some may be decorated. Also ashtrays were often used as souvenirs, either with inscriptions or decals added. Some glass companies such as New Martinsville also used ashtrays as a company promotion with their name in the bottom of the trays. Sizes of ashtrays range from small individual trays to huge, massive coffee table sized trays popular in the 1950s. Covered cigarette boxes, cigarette urns and lighters were also made to match ashtrays and add dimension to a smoking collection.

A.H. Heisey Mallards

L to R: Morgantown Glass Co. Engagement and Catherine vases, U.S. Glass Co. openwork vase

Figurines—One of the most attractive categories to today's collectors are glass animals and figurines. Many companies made at least some animals, and a few companies made rather extensive numbers of them. Fostoria, New Martinsville and Heisey made many types of animals, all of which are eagerly collected today. At least Heisey's (and possibly other companies) gained the distinction of being used in Tennessee Williams' play, *The Glass Menagerie* when it was produced on Broadway. Most animals are made in solid crystal glass, but some are also made in colors.

Vases—What homemaker can not have a vase or several? Immense numbers of glass vases were made by glass companies in a myriad of shapes, colors and decorations. Vases are available in simple, utilitarian styles or in very elaborate shapes and forms. Sizes of vases can also range from bud vases meant to hold one bloom or a tiny bouquet to massive vases meant for large arrangements. This category is almost endless in its possibilities for collecting. The styles alone would form a huge collection. Adding colors, sizes and decorations to the mix simply makes the possibilities endless.

Chapter 46
BASKETS

Glass baskets became popular in the teens and were made by most tableware companies. The ability to press a basket with handle attached required expert innovation by mold makers. Duncan & Miller was able to patent its method of doing this, and most companies followed with pressed handled baskets of their own.

Baskets are a form of vase, but collectors have made a niche for them alone. Many, many varieties exist, but the following list gives a sampling of those available to the collector. Note: Additional illustrations follow the company price listings.

CAMBRIDGE GLASS CO.

Some of Cambridge's baskets were fitted with an interior flower block.

No. 41, Optic, Crystal, 6"	$40.00
No. 42, Colonial, Crystal, 8"	55.00
No. 73, Cake, Crystal, 9"	65.00
No. 122, Crystal, 5"	35.00
No. 124, Crystal, 9" (same shape as No. 125)	60.00
No. 125, Crystal, 12"	75.00
No. 193, Crystal, 7"	42.00
No. 220, Crystal, 9"	55.00
No. 221, Crystal, 9"	55.00
No. 222, Crystal, 12"	75.00
No 223, Crystal, 12"	75.00
No. 231, Crystal, 11"	70.00

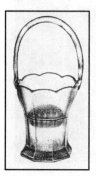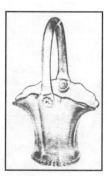

Cambridge Glass Co.
L to R: No. 222, No. 231, No. 122

DUNCAN & MILLER GLASS CO.

Canterbury, Handled, Crystal, 10" or 11½" (115)	$75.00
Canterbury, Handled, Straight or Crimped, Pink Opalescent, 3" (115)	75.00
Canterbury, Handled, Straight or Crimped, Crystal, 4½" (115)	35.00
Early American Sandwich, Regular or Crimped, Handled, Crystal, 12" (41)	250.00
Early American Sandwich, Tall-handled, Crystal, 6" (41)	95.00
Hobnail, Tall-handled, Blue Opalescent, 10" (118)	130.00
Flower design, Amber	85.00
Flower design, Pink	110.00

Duncan & Miller Glass Co.
Two examples of Canterbury No. 115

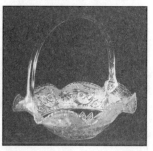

Duncan & Miller Glass Co.
L to R: Flower Design, Early American Sandwich No. 41

BASKETS *(continued)*

A.H. Heisey Glass
Co. Lariat Orchid
Etch No. 1540

Imperial Glass Corp.
L to R: No. 300, No. 698

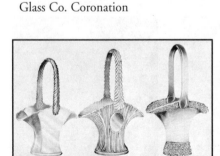

Original Catalog
Illustration: Indiana
Glass Co. Coronation

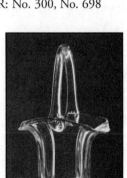

New Martinsville Glass Co.
No. 136 Square

L to R: Morgantown Glass Co.
Clayton and Ashley baskets

U.S. Glass Co.
No. 9574

Westmoreland Glass Co. No. 750

A.H. HEISEY GLASS CO.

Double Rib & Panel, Moongleam (417) $225.00
Lariat, Orchid Etch, Crystal (1540) . . . . 1200.00+

IMPERIAL GLASS CORP.

No. 252, Crystal, 13" $70.00
No. 300, Crystal, 10" 50.00
    With Nos. 2, 9 or 206 Cutting 60.00
No. 300, Rose, 10" 75.00
No. 363, Daisy 50.00
No. 698, Green, 10" 75.00
No. 714, Grape Design, Crystal, 10" 55.00
Twisted Optic, Crystal (313) 55.00

INDIANA GLASS CO.

Coronation, Handled, Crystal, 12" $35.00

NEW MARTINSVILLE GLASS CO.

No. 132, Square, Crystal, 14" $35.00
No. 136, Square, Crystal, 11" 35.00
Janice, Red 175.00
Janice, Crystal with Blue Handle 110.00

MORGANTOWN GLASS CO.

Ashley, Old Amethyst, 10" (36-4354) $800.00
Clayton, Amethyst, 10" (4357½) 750.00
Jennie, Amethyst with Crystal, 4½" (20) 675.00
Patrick, Red, 8" 700.00
Patrick, Ritz Blue, 8" (19-4358) 700.00
Patrick, Yellow, 8" 600.00

U.S. GLASS CO.

No. 9574, Blue Satin $125.00
No. 15151, Crystal with Green Handle 90.00
See next page for other U.S. Glass/Tiffin baskets. Most
likely these baskets were made at another U.S. Glass
factory, but were cut at Tiffin.

WESTMORELAND GLASS CO.

No. 750, Crystal, 3" or 4" $30.00
No. 750, Crystal, 5" or 6" 30.00
No. 750, Crystal, 7" or 8" 35.00
No. 752, Crystal, 5" 45.00
No. 752, Crystal, 6" or 7" 60.00
No. 752, Crystal with Engraved
    Medallion, 7" 75.00
No. 755, Crystal, 6" 45.00

(continued) **BASKETS**

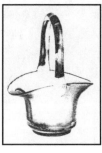 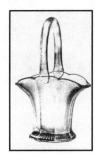 

Cambridge Glass Co.
L to R: No. 41 Optic, No. 125 Optic, No. 42 Colonial

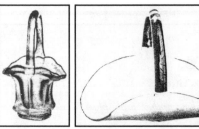

Cambridge Glass Co.
L to R: No. 122, No. 73 Cake, No. 221

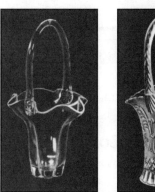 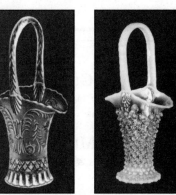

Duncan & Miller Glass Co.
L to R: Canterbury No. 115, Early American Sandwich
No. 41, Hobnail No. 118

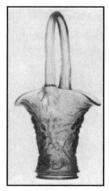 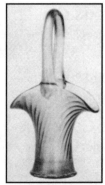 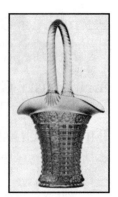

Imperial Glass Corp.
L to R: No. 714, Twisted Optic No. 313, No. 252

U.S. Glass Co.
No. 15151

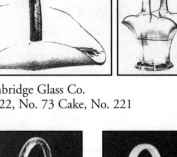

New Martinsville
Glass Co., Janice

A.H. Heisey Glass Co.
Original Catalog Illustration:
Double Rib & Panel No. 417

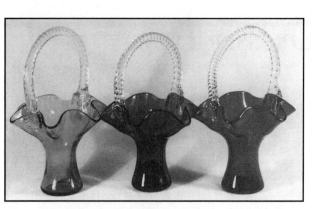

Morgantown Glass Co. Patrick

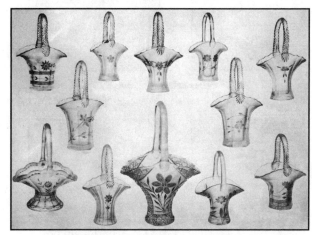

Assorted U.S. Glass Co./Tiffin Baskets

227

Chapter 47
BOUDOIR ITEMS

*Boudoir items comprise a wide variety of styles, colors and items. Most companies made at least a small number of boudoir items; and many made a large number. This chapter contains dresser sets (colognes and powder boxes), clocks, lamps and night sets or tumble ups. While examples of all these are shown, they only begin to suggest the wide variety of items available. **Note: Additional illustrations follow the company price listings.***

CLOCKS

McKee Glass Co. tambour mantel clock

McKEE GLASS CO.
Tambour Mantel Clock, Green . . . . $500.00+

Prices will vary due to colors: amber, pink, blue. Made both in key wind and electric.

DRESSER ITEMS

L to R: Cambridge Glass Co. vanity set,
Duncan & Miller Glass Co. Hobnail cologne and puff box

L to R: Co-operative Flint Glass Co. puff box
Fenton Art Glass Co. Swirled Feather cologne and powder box

L to R: A.H. Heisey Glass Co. Yeoman puff box
Imperial Glass Corp. My Lady Set

CAMBRIDGE GLASS CO.
Cologne, 1½ oz., Decoration 485, Gold Trim (206). . . $85.00
Vanity Set, Crystal 65.00

DUNCAN & MILLER GLASS CO.
Hobnail Puff Box & Cover, 4" (118) $26.00
Hobnail Cologne & Stopper, 8 oz. (118) 32.00
Perfume Bottle & Stopper, 7" tall (129) 60.00
Puff Box & Cover, 4" (129) 45.00

CO-OPERATIVE FLINT GLASS CO.
No. 387 Puff Box, Crystal. $45.00

FENTON ART GLASS CO.
Swirled Feather Cologne (2005), Rose Opalescent . . . $150.00
Swirled Feather Powder Box (2005), Rose Opalescent. . . 95.00

A.H. HEISEY GLASS CO.
Yeoman Puff Box, Flamingo (1186) $150.00

IMPERIAL GLASS CORP.
Hobnail Covered Powder, Green Opalescent $50.00
My Lady Set—Tray, Powder Box, Cologne,
   Crystal (169). 110.00
   With Nos. 16 or 216 decoration 140.00

(continued) # DRESSER ITEMS

JEANNETTE GLASS CO.

Duck Powder Jar, Marigold Carnival $30.00
Poodle Dog Powder Jar, Marigold Carnival 30.00
Scottie Dog Powder Jar, Marigold Carnival 30.00

Jeanette Glass Co. poodle, scottie and duck powder jars.

NEW MARTINSVILLE GLASS CO.

Cologne, Blue (10) $45.00
Geneva Cologne, Rose 85.00
Geneva Puff Box, Rose 65.00
Judy Cologne, Crystal with Jade 40.00
Judy Puff Box, Crystal with Jade 50.00
Leota Puff Box, Crystal with Green 35.00
Leota Cologne, Crystal with Green 40.00
Puff Box, Blue (10) 45.00

L to R: New Martinsville Glass Co. No. 10 puff box,
Geneva cologne and puff box

PADEN CITY GLASS MFG. CO.

Cologne, Black (499) $65.00
Cologne, Crystal (503) 25.00
Cologne, 4 oz., Green (501) 35.00
Cologne, 5 oz., Blue (500) 75.00
Cologne, 5 oz., Amber (502) 30.00
Puff Box & Cover, Amber (201) 27.00
Puff Box & Cover, Blue (503-5) 40.00
Puff Box & Cover, Green (209) 30.00
Puff Box & Cover, Mulberry (198-4) 50.00
Vamp Dresser Set, Crystal 70.00
Vanity Set, Moon Set, Crystal 90.00
Vanity Set, Sun Set, Crystal (215) 135.00
Vanity Tray, 10", Green (499) 38.00

L to R: Paden City Mfg. Co.
Vamp dresser set and Moon Set vanity set

U.S. GLASS CO.

Dresser Set, Crystal. $95.00
Milady Set, Blue Satin 275.00
Cologne, Unknown Number, Green with Opaque . . . 200.00+
Cologne, Unknown Number, Green Satin 150.00
Cologne, Unknown Number, Green Satin 150.00
Cologne, Unknown Number, Green Satin 150.00

L to R: U.S. Glass Co. Assorted colognes

WESTMORELAND GLASS CO.

Cologne, 1 oz., Crystal (1801) $35.00
Cologne, 1 oz., Triangular Foot &
   Stopper, Crystal (1856) 35.00
Cologne, 1 oz., Crystal (1901) 35.00
Colonial, Jewel Box & Cover, Footed, Crystal (1700). . . 35.00
Colonial, Pomade Box & Cover, Crystal (1700). 30.00
Colonial, Puff Box & Cover or Hair
   Receiver, Crystal (1700). 35.00
Dresser Set, Crystal (1701) 85.00
Lotus Cologne, ½ oz., Crystal (1921) 40.00
Puff Box, 3½" or 4½", Crystal (1900/1, 1900/2). 22.00
Puff & Powder Box, Combination, Crystal (1900). 35.00

UNDETERMINED MANUFACTURER

Powder Box, Crystal Satin. $68.00
Similar to Consolidated's Ruba Rombic, but simpler in style.
Crackle Set, Crystal 45.00
Mascot, Pink Satin 60.00

L to R: Westmoreland Glass Co. No. 1856 cologne, Lotus
cologne and Undetermined Manufacturer crackle set

BOUDOIR ITEMS *(continued)*

L to R: Cambridge Glass Co. cologne
Paden City Glass Co. Cologne No. 502 and No. 501

L to R: Paden City Mfg. Co.
No. 499, No. 500 and No. 503 colognes

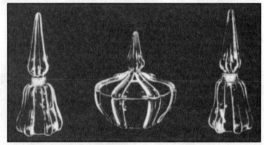

Duncan & Miller Glass Co. No. 129 perfumes and puff

L to R: Westmoreland Glass Co.
No. 1901 Cologne, Puff or hair receiver and Colonial jewel

L to R: Paden City Mfg. Co.
No. 209, No. 201 and No. 198 puff boxes

L to R: Westmoreland Glass Co. Colonial Puff or hair receiver,
No. 1901 Puff and Combination puff & powder

 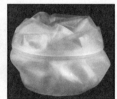 

L to R: Imperial Hobnail puff box
Undetermined Manufacturer powder box and Mascot puff box

U.S. Glass Co. Milady set

Paden City Mfg. Co. Sun Set vanity set

L to R: Undetermined Manufacturer amber lamps
Imperial Glass Co. No 805 tumble up

U.S. Glass Co. Dresser set

L to R: Paden City Glass Mfg. Co. guest set
Morgantown Glass Co. night set and Trudy night set

New Martinsville Glass Co. Judy Colognes and puff

L to R: New Martinsville Glass Co. guest set
Unknown Manufacturer deep blue tumble up

New Martinsville Glass Co. Leota colognes and puff

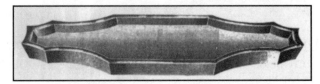

Paden City Mfg. Co. No. 499 vanity tray

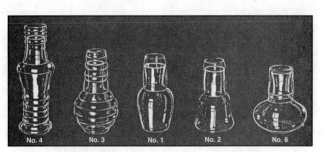

Louie Glass Co. assorted tumble ups

LAMPS

L to R: McKee Glass Co. Danse De Lumiere lamp,
New Martinsville Glass Co. lamp,
Undetermined Manufacturer fluted column lamp

MCKEE GLASS CO.

Danse De Lumiere, made in Rose Pink, Canary, Blue, Amber or Crystal with satin finish.

Crystal $500.00
Colors 900.00

NEW MARTINSVILLE GLASS CO.

Lamp, Crystal. $35.00

UNDETERMINED MANUFACTURER

Many varieties of lamps were made, the following will give you some idea as to what you may expect to find.

Amber, Crystal bases, pr. $45.00
Green, straight fluted column, pr. 75.00

NIGHT SETS, TUMBLE UPS & OTHERS

L to R: Dunbar Glass Co. No. 4082 Tumble Up
Imperial Glass Co. guest room set
Louie Glass Co. No. 3 tumble up

L to R: Morgantown Glass Co. Maria medicine set
New Martinsville Glass Co. guest jug and tumbler

L to R: Paden City Mfg. Flapper guest set
U.S. Glass Co. No. 6712 Night cap set
Undetermined Manufacturer hand-painted cherries tumble up

DUNBAR GLASS CO.

No. 4082, Rose Pink $55.00

IMPERIAL GLASS CORP.

No. 805 with No. 217 Cutting, Green. $50.00
Guest Room Set, No. 650 with
    No. 2 Cutting, Crystal. 55.00

LOUIE GLASS CO.

No. 1, Pink $40.00
No. 2, Green 40.00
No. 3, Iridized Marigold 50.00
No. 4, Crystal. 40.00
No. 6, Crystal. 30.00

MORGANTOWN GLASS CO.

Maria, Medicine Set, Azure, Cut (24) $500.00
Night Set, Green 70.00
Trudy, Jade Green Opaque 130.00

NEW MARTINSVILLE GLASS CO.

Guest Jug & Tumbler, Green (140) $75.00
Guest Set: Tray, Covered Pitcher, Tumbler, Pink (728). . 120.00

PADEN CITY GLASS MFG. CO.

Guest Set, 2 pc., Green (499) $28.00
Flapper Guest Set, Pink 95.00

U.S. GLASS CO.

No. 6712, 2-piece Night Cap Set, Green $28.00

UNDETERMINED MANUFACTURER

Crystal with Hand-painted Cherries $35.00
Deep Blue 110.00

Chapter 48
CANDLESTICKS, CONSOLE BOWLS & CONSOLE SETS

Included in this chapter are candlesticks, floral bowls and console sets—a pair of candlesticks and a center bowl, sometimes with a separate base. Console sets were popular in the late 1920s and into the 1940s. Candlesticks remain popular, but often very fine center bowls find little interest among today's collectors. For a period re-creation of dining room accessories, nothing can replace the console set. Note: Additional illustrations follow the company price listings.

CANDLESTICKS

L to R: Cambridge Glass Co. No. 72 candlestick
Consolidated Glass Co. Catalonian candlestick

Duncan & Miller Glass Co. Tear Drop candlesticks

L to R: Fostoria Glass Co.
Flame candlestick & No. 1490 engraved candlestick

CAMBRIDGE GLASS CO.
No. 72, with Rose Point etching, Crystal, pr. $55.00

CONSOLIDATED GLASS CO.
Catalonian, l-light, pr., Green $70.00

DUNCAN & MILLER GLASS CO.
No. 120-C, 3-light, Milk Glass, each . . . . $700.00+
Black, 2-light, Cut, pr. 125.00
Canterbury, 1-light, 6", pr. (115) 20.00
Canterbury, 3-light, 6", pr. (115) 40.00
Early American Sandwich, 1-light, w/Prisms,
   10", pr., Crystal (41) 225.00
Early American Sandwich, 2-light, 5", pr.,
   Crystal (41). 175.00
Early American Sandwich, 1-light, pr., Chartreuse 55.00
Grandee, 3-light, pr. (14) 95.00
Hobnail, 1-light, 4", pr. (118) 25.00
Laguna Hurricane Lamp, ea., Green 150.00
Pall Mall, 2-light, 6", pr. (30) 50.00
Pall Mall, Square, Solid, 2", pr., Crystal (30) 25.00
Pall Mall, Square, 3", pr., Crystal (31) 30.00
Pall Mall, Triangular, Solid, 2", pr., Crystal (30). 35.00
Radiance, pr., Blue 65.00
Sculptured, Chrysanthemum, pr.,
   Cape Cod Opalescent 325.00
Tear Drop, 1-light, 2 styles, pr., Crystal 25.00
Tear Drop, 2-light, Crystal, pr. 45.00
Three Feathers, 1-light, Green, pr. 70.00

FOSTORIA GLASS CO.
No. 1490, Engraved, pr., Crystal $95.00
Flame, 2-light, Gold Lace etch, pr., Crystal 125.00

CANDLESTICKS *(continued)*

L to R: A.H. Heisey Glass Co.
Kohinoor candlestick and Mercury candlestick

L to R: Imperial Glass Corp.
Original Art: No. 153 candlestick and Vinelf candlestick
New Martinsville Glass Co. Moondrops candlestick

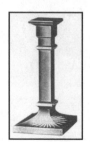

L to R: Paden City Glass Co. Original Catalog illustrations:
No. 110, 113, 114, 117 candlesticks

L to R: U.S. Glass Co.
No. 5831 candlestick and plum 2-light candlestick

L to R: Verlys Glass Co. Water lily candlestick
Westmoreland Glass Co. Lotus candlesticks

A.H. HEISEY GLASS CO.

Grape Cluster, 1-light, pr., Crystal (1445) $295.00
Kohinoor, 2-light, prisms, pr., Crystal, (1488) 750.00
Mercury, 1-light, pr., Moongleam, (112) 75.00
Miss Muffet, pr., with or without diamond optic,
    Moongleam (118) 95.00
Overlapping Swirl, 1-light, pr., Flamingo (121) 80.00
Pembroke, 1-light, pr., Moongleam (105) 250.00
Trident, 2-light, pr., Crystal (134) 60.00

IMPERIAL GLASS CORP.

No. 153, pr., Crystal. $25.00
No. 635, 8¼", pr., Crystal 70.00
Vinelf, Milk Glass, pr.. . . . . 70.00

NEW MARTINSVILLE GLASS CO.

No. 10, Handled, 4", pr., Crystal $30.00
No. 10-3, 3", pr., Green 35.00
Moondrops, 3-light, pr., Pink (37) 80.00
Radiance, 2-light, pr., Blue (42) 125.00

PADEN CITY GLASS CO.

*Many of these candlesticks were made in blue, green, amber and
mulberry according to old company information.*

No. 108, 4", Handled, pr., Crystal. $40.00
No. 109 or No. 110, 9", pr., Crystal 75.00
No. 111, 9", pr., Crystal 75.00
No. 112 or No. 113, 3½", pr., Crystal. 32.00
No. 112, No. 113, 5½", pr., Crystal 38.00
No. 112 or No. 113, 7", pr., Crystal 45.00
No. 112 or No. 113, 8½", pr., Crystal. 70.00
No. 114, 6¼", pr., Crystal 40.00
No. 114 or No. 115, 7", pr., Crystal 45.00
No. 115, 9", pr., Crystal 75.00
No. 116, 7", pr., Crystal 45.00
No. 116, 9½", pr., Crystal 80.00
No. 117, 8½", pr., Crystal 75.00
No. 118, 1½", pr., Crystal 20.00
No. 119, 3", pr., Crystal 25.00
No. 120, 3," Jumbo, pr., Crystal 25.00
No. 198, 7½", pr., Crystal 65.00
No. 207, 10", pr., Crystal 80.00
Party Line, 4½", pr., Green (191) 55.00

U.S. GLASS CO.

No. 10, Low, Reflex Green, Enamel décor, pr. $40.00
No. 13, Black, pr.. . . . . 50.00
No. 75, 9½", Amberina Satin, pr.. . . . . 100.00
2-light, Yellow, pr. (5831).. . . . . 130.00
2-light, 6⅜", Plum, pr.. . . . . 90.00

VERLYS GLASS CO.

Water Lily Candlesticks, pr., Crystal Satin $90.00

WESTMORELAND GLASS CO.

Lotus, 1-light, Black Satin, pr.. . . . . $80.00

L to R: Duncan & Miller Glass Co.
Early American Sandwich Candlestick
A.H. Heisey Glass Co. Pembroke candlestick

L to R: Duncan & Miller Glass Co. No. 120-C candlestick
A.H. Heisey Glass Co. Grape cluster candlesticks

Duncan & Miller Glass Co. Canterbury candlestick

L to R: Duncan & Miller Glass Co. Grandee candlestick
A.H. Heisey Glass Co. Trident candlestick

Duncan & Miller Glass Co.
Early American Sandwich candlesticks

L to R: A.H. Heisey Glass Co.
Miss Muffet candlestick and Overlapping Swirl candlestick

Duncan & Miller Glass Co. Hobnail candlesticks

L to R: Duncan & Miller Glass Co.
Three Feathers candlestick and Radiance candlesticks

235

CANDLESTICKS *(continued)*

 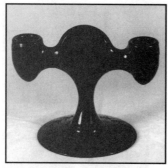

L to R: U.S. Glass Co. No. 75 candlesticks
Duncan & Miller Glass Co. black candlestick

L to R: Duncan & Miller Glass Co. Laguna hurricane lamp
New Martinsville Glass Co. Radiance candlestick

L to R: New Martinsville Glass Co.
Original Catalog Illustration: No. 10-3 candlestick
Duncan & Miller Glass Co. Sculptured candlestick

L to R: U.S. Glass Co. No. 10 and No. 13 candlesticks

L to R: Paden City Glass Co. Original Catalog illustrations:
No. 108 candlestick and No. 119 candlestick

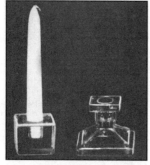 

L to R: Duncan & Miller Glass Co. Pall Mall candlesticks
New Martinsville Glass Co. No. 10 candlestick

L to R: Paden City Glass Co. Original Catalog illustrations:
No. 118 and No. 120 candlesticks

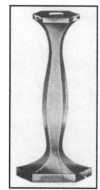 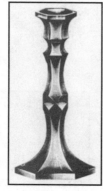 

L to R: Paden City Glass Co. Original Catalog illustrations:
No. 109, No. 111 and No. 112 candlesticks

L to R: Paden City Glass Co. Original Catalog illustrations:
No. 115 and No. 116 candlesticks

CONSOLE BOWLS

CAMBRIDGE GLASS CO.

Georgian, Amberina with Black base $85.00

DUNCAN & MILLER GLASS CO.

No. 16, Ritz Blue $85.00
Unknown number, Green 75.00
Viking Boat, Crystal 295.00

A.H. HEISEY GLASS CO.

Columbia, Crystal $75.00

IMPERIAL GLASS CORP.

Vinelf compote, Milk Glass. $75.00

TIFFIN ART GLASS CO.

Empress, Crystal with Ruby trim. $150.00

U.S. GLASS CO.

No. 310, Amberina Satin $60.00
No. 315, High Footed, Black Satin 75.00
No. 315, Low Footed, Black Satin. 60.00
Carrera, Orange (opaque) 110.00

L to R: Cambridge Glass Co. Georgian console bowl
Duncan & Miller Glass Co. Viking boat console bowl

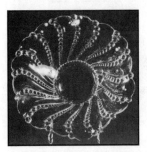

L to R: A.H. Heisey Glass Co. Columbia console bowl
Imperial Glass Corp. Original Art: Vinelf compote

L to R: Tiffin Art Glass Co. Empress console bowl
U.S. Glass Co. Carrera console bowl

CONSOLE SETS

CENTRAL GLASS WORKS

Console Set, Black $100.00

CHARTIERS (DIVISION OF DUNCAN & MILLER)

Ivy Decorated, Crystal $85.00

CO-OPERATIVE FLINT GLASS CO.

No. 471 & 449, Crystal $80.00

Central Glass Works Original Ad: console set

Chartiers (Division of Duncan & Miller Glass Co.)
Ivy decorated console set

Co-Operative Flint Glass Co. No 471 and 449 console set

237

Console Sets *(continued)*

Duncan & Miller Glass Co. Pharoah console set

Fenton Art Glass Co. No. 549 console set

Fostoria Glass Co. No. 2395 June etching console set

Imperial Glass Co. No. 320 Cut 15 console set

Indiana Glass Co. Original Ad: No. 301 Garland console set

Westmoreland Glass Co. No. 1930 console set

Duncan & Miller Glass Co.

Early American Sandwich, Chartreuse (41) $140.00
Pharaoh, Green 245.00
Venetian, Ruby Red 225.00

Fenton Art Glass Co.

No. 549 Candlesticks, Floral Bowl & Plateau, Jade. . . $275.00

Fostoria Glass Co.

June Etching, Azure (2394) $200.00
June Etching, Azure (2395) 270.00
This set was not made in Crystal.

Imperial Glass Corp.

No. 320, Cut 15, Crystal $155.00
No. 6869, 4 candlesticks and bowl,
   Cut 201, Crystal 125.00

Indiana Glass Co.

Crystal, Amber Stain $125.00
Garland, No. 301, Crystal, Satin Fruit 125.00

Lancaster Glass Co.

Jody, Topaz, Decorated No. 27 (354, 355) $75.00

U.S. Glass Co.

No. 66, Candlesticks, Console Bowl w/Black Base,
   Blue Satin $165.00
No. 66, Candlesticks, pedestal foot, No. 315 Bowl,
   Black Satin 175.00
No. 315, Compote, Unknown No. Candlesticks,
   Canary Satin 120.00
No.15179, Low Footed Bowl with glass candles,
   Black Satin 400.00
Cascade, Crystal (15365) 300.00

Westmoreland Glass Co.

No. 1930, Crystal $85.00

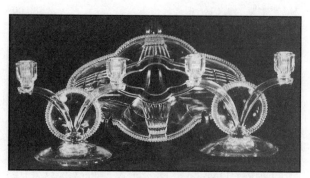

U.S. Glass Co. Cascade console set

(continued) CONSOLE BOWLS & SETS

Duncan & Miller Glass Co. No. 16 console bowl

Fostoria Glass Co. No. 2394 June etching console set

Duncan & Miller Glass Co. Unknown No. console bowl

U.S. Glass Co. No. 66 console set

U.S. Glass Co. No. 310 console bowl

Duncan & Miller Glass Co. Venetian console set

U.S. Glass Co. No. 315 compote with unknown candlesticks

Duncan & Miller Glass Co.
Early American Sandwich console set

239

Chapter 49

CANDY JARS & BOXES

This chapter contains examples of covered candy jars (tall) and covered candy boxes (low). The following list is only a small sampling of what can be found in this interesting collectible. Prices given are for items exactly as described. Different colors or decorations can change values. Generally speaking, candy jars are tall and slender, usually with a foot. Candy boxes are usually flat on the bottom and are broad and short.

If measurements are known, candy jars and boxes are measured as follows: height including lid, width across top of box, diameter of foot. An asterisk (*) indicates items that may be Co-Operative Flint Glass Co. **Note: Additional illustrations follow the company price listings.**

L to R: Beaumont Glass Co. Leaf finial candy jar
Cambridge Glass Co. Pristine candy box

L to R: Co-Operative Flint Glass Co. candy jar
Dunbar Glass Co. Candy jar

BEAUMONT GLASS CO.

Leaf Finial, 10⅛" tall, 3⁹/₁₆" wide,
    3⅞" square foot, Ferlux (moonstone) $50.00

CAMBRIDGE GLASS CO.

No. 96 Plain, ½ lb. 8¾" tall, 3¾" wide, 3¼" foot,
    Primrose, Opaque Yellow $60.00
Pristine 5⅛" tall, 5¾" wide, 3½" foot, Crystal (306) . . . 30.00
Cambridge Square, Ebon, Black Satin 65.00
No. 3400, Blue. 85.00

CO-OPERATIVE FLINT GLASS CO.

½ lb., 8¾" tall, 3⅞" wide, 3¼" foot, Green $40.00

DUNBAR GLASS CO.

1 lb., 10" tall, 4⅜" wide, 3¾" foot, Pink $50.00

DUNCAN & MILLER GLASS CO.

No. 106, 3-compartment, 4" tall, 6¼" wide,
    6¼" foot, Green $60.00
No. 115, Canterbury, 3-handled, 3-compartment,
    8", Crystal. 35.00
Caribbean, Amber 100.00
Early American Sandwich Bonbon & Cover,
    7½" tall, Crystal (41) 55.00
Early American Sandwich Urn & Cover,
    12", Crystal (41) 200.00
Pall Mall, Rectangular, 8", Crystal (30) 45.00

Duncan & Miller Glass Co. No. 106 Candy box

Duncan & Miller Glass Co. Caribbean candy box

(continued) Candy Jars & Boxes

Fostoria Glass Co.

Century, $7\frac{1}{8}$" tall, $4\frac{5}{8}$" wide, $3\frac{5}{8}$" foot, Crystal (2630) $35.00
Crown, $5\frac{3}{4}$" tall, $5\frac{3}{8}$" wide, $3\frac{1}{8}$" foot, Gold (2749) . . . 75.00
Diadem, ½ lb., $5\frac{1}{2}$" tall, $5\frac{1}{4}$" wide, $2\frac{7}{16}$" foot, Green (2430) 60.00
Flame, $4\frac{3}{4}$" tall, $6\frac{1}{2}$" wide, $4\frac{3}{16}$" foot, Gold Tint (2545) 100.00
Horizon, $3\frac{7}{8}$" tall, $5\frac{1}{8}$" wide, $2\frac{1}{2}$" foot, Spruce Green (2650) 50.00
No. 2219, ¼ lb., 8" tall, $3\frac{1}{4}$" wide, $2\frac{3}{4}$" foot, Crystal with iridescent finish 50.00
No. 2219, ½ lb., $8\frac{5}{8}$" tall, $3\frac{3}{4}$" wide, $3\frac{1}{8}$" foot, Crystal with iridescent finish 50.00
No. 2219, 1 lb., $11\frac{1}{4}$" tall, $4\frac{5}{8}$" wide, $3\frac{7}{8}$" foot, Crystal with iridescent finish 60.00
No. 2250, ¼ lb., $5\frac{3}{4}$" tall, $4\frac{1}{8}$" wide, $2\frac{11}{16}$" foot, Crystal with orange enamel 40.00
No. 2250, ½ lb., $6\frac{3}{8}$" tall, $4\frac{7}{8}$" wide, $3\frac{1}{4}$" foot, Blue . . 50.00
No. 2250, 1 lb., $7\frac{1}{2}$" tall, $5\frac{13}{16}$" wide, $3\frac{5}{8}$" foot, Green 60.00
No. 2331, 3-compartment, $5\frac{1}{4}$" tall, 7" wide, $6\frac{11}{16}$" foot, Rose with Versailles etching 250.00
No. 2380, 6" tall, 7" wide, $3\frac{3}{16}$" foot, Orchid with spiral optic 85.00
No. 2380, Rose, plain 75.00
No. 2394, ½ lb. $5\frac{3}{4}$" tall, $6\frac{1}{2}$" wide, 3-footed, Topaz . . 60.00
No. 2395, $5\frac{3}{4}$" tall, 7" wide, $3\frac{9}{16}$" foot, Amber 80.00
No. 2413, $9\frac{1}{8}$" tall, 7" wide, $3\frac{3}{16}$" foot, Green 125.00

A.H. Heisey Glass Co.

Yeoman, Cut Rose decoration, Crystal (1184) $75.00

Imperial Glass Corp.

Many Imperial jars and boxes of the 1930s were made in Crystal, Amber, Green and Rose.

Crocheted Crystal, $6\frac{3}{4}$" tall, $6\frac{1}{4}$" wide, $3\frac{3}{4}$" foot, Blue $35.00
No. 148/1 Candy Box, Crystal 35.00
No. 645/3 Candy Box, Crystal 35.00
No. 685/1 Candy Jar, Crystal 35.00
No. 717 Candy Box, Crystal, Cut No. 16 . . . . . 45.00
Twisted Optic, 9" tall, $4\frac{1}{4}$" wide, $3\frac{1}{8}$" foot, Rose Marie (313) 55.00

Indiana Glass Co.

Old English, ½ lb. Candy Jar, Green (172) $60.00

L to R: A.H. Heisey Glass Co. Yeoman candy jar
Imperial Glass Corp. Crocheted candy jar

L to R: Fostoria Glass Co.
Crown candy box and Flame candy box

Fostoria Glass Co. No. 2250 candy jars

Fostoria Glass Co. No. 2380 candy jars

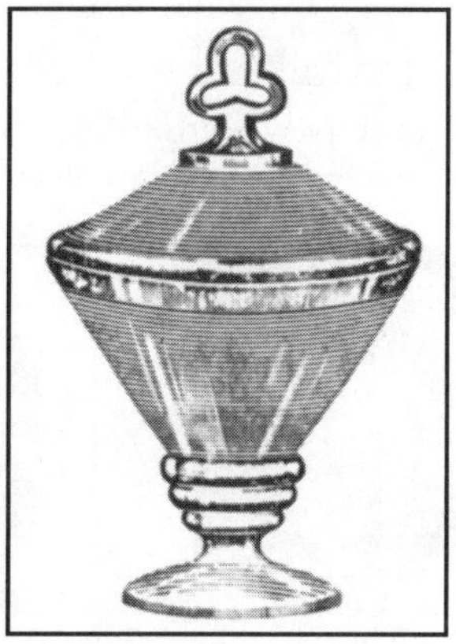

L to R: Imperial Glass Corp. Twisted Optic candy jar
Indiana Glass Co. Old English candy jar

CANDY JARS & BOXES *(continued)*

Lancaster Glass Co. Star Joiner candy box

L to R: Louie Glass Co. Original Ad No. 51, No. 1, No. 2 candy jars and McKee Glass Co. Rectangular candy jar

L to R: Morgantown Glass Co. Guilford and Wilmont candy jars

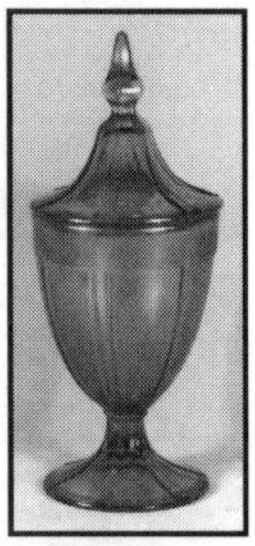

L to R: New Martinsville Glass Co. No. 149/1 candy jar, No. 472 candy jar, Northwood Glass Co. Colonial candy jar

L to R: Paden City Mfg. Co. No. 444 candy jar, No. 503 candy jar, No. 701 candy jar

LANCASTER GLASS CO.

No. 83, 7⅞" tall, 5 3/16" wide, 3⅜" foot, Crystal Stretch with Enamel decor	$35.00
Star Joiner, 4¼" tall, 6¾" wide, 3-footed, Blue	45.00

LOUIE GLASS CO.

No. 51, Crystal	$40.00
No. 1, Crystal	30.00
No. 2, Crystal	30.00
Spiral Optic, depending on size	10.00 to 30.00

MCKEE GLASS CO.

Rectangular, Green, Gold decoration	$65.00

MORGANTOWN GLASS CO.

Guilford, 8½" tall, 4 7/16" wide, 3¾" foot, Nanking Blue (14)	$250.00
Helga, 4½" tall, 4½" wide, Ritz Blue (2938)	350.00
Maureen, 6½" tall, 4½" wide, Ritz Blue (9074)	375.00
Wilmont, 7¼" tall, 4 9/16" wide, 3⅜" foot, Steel Blue (128)	45.00

NEW MARTINSVILLE GLASS MFG. CO.

No. 149/1 8½" tall, 3 9/16" wide, 3⅛" foot, Amber	$30.00
No. 149/3 ½ lb., 8¼" tall, 5⅛" wide, 3¼" foot, Green	40.00
No. 149/3 ½ lb., 8¼" tall, 5⅛" wide, 3¼" foot, Crystal	35.00
No. 472, 9⅙" tall, 4 3/16" wide, 3⅞" foot, Crystal	50.00

NORTHWOOD GLASS CO.

Colonial, Blue Iridescent	$75.00

PADEN CITY GLASS MFG. CO.

No. 180 Candy Jar & Cover, Plain or Optic, Crystal	$35.00
No. 198 Bonbon & Cover, 7", Green	45.00
No. 444, 9¾" tall, 6¾" wide, 3¾" foot, Crystal with Rose Cascade etching	55.00
No. 503 ½ lb., 8¾" tall, 3¾" wide, 3⅛" foot, Mulberry	60.00
No. 503 Candy Box & Cover, Low Foot, 6", Blue	45.00
No. 503 Candy Jar & Cover, ½ lb., Amber	30.00
No. 700 ½ lb., Amber	40.00
No. 701, 7⅞" tall, 5 3/16" wide, 3 9/16" foot, Blue	45.00
No. 801 Candy Jar & Cover, ¼ lb., Crystal	35.00
No. 801 Candy Jar & Cover, ½ lb., Crystal	40.00
No. 801 Candy Jar & Cover, 1 lb., Crystal	45.00

Paden City Mfg. Co. No. 700 candy box

(continued) # Candy Jars & Boxes

U.S. Glass Co.

Heart Bonbon, Green Satin. $85.00
Oval, Black Satin with gold enamel decor (15319). 90.00
No. 314 Bonbon, 6 1/4" tall, 6 1/6" wide, 3 1/4" foot, Rose 40.00
No. 330 Bonbon, 6" tall, 3 9/16" wide, 2 15/16" foot, Reflex Green Satin with Handpainted Parrot 65.00
No. 345, 3 7/8" tall, 6 1/4" wide, 6 1/4" foot, Rose Satin, Handpainted decoration 65.00
No. 9557, Blown, 1/2 lb., 8 11/16" tall, 3 1/2" wide, 3" foot, Blue with Canary foot. 85.00
No. 15179, 1/2 lb., 9 5/8" tall, 3 1/2" wide, 3 1/2" foot, Blue Satin 70.00
No. 15179, 1/2 lb., Emerald Green Satin 85.00
No. 15531, Conic, 7 3/4" tall, 6 5/8" wide, 3 1/8" foot, Emerald Green Satin 60.00
No. 15531, Conic, 7 3/4" tall, 6 5/8" wide, 3 1/8" foot, Emerald Green with optic 60.00
Velva, 7" tall, 6 3/16" wide, 3 15/16" foot, Regal Blue with Satin highlights. 225.00

Westmoreland Glass Co.

No. 1700 1 lb., 8" tall, 3 5/16" wide, 3" foot, Crystal, Elaborate Handpainted decoration $50.00
No. 1795 1 lb., 10 3/4" tall, 5 5/8" wide, 4 5/8" foot, Crystal, Elaborate Handpainted decoration. 40.00
No. 1854-1 Chocolate Box, Crystal. 40.00
No. 1854-2 Chocolate Box, Crystal. 40.00
No. 1855 Chocolate Box & Cover, Crystal 40.00

Undetermined Manufacturer

1/2 lb., 9 1/4" tall, 3 15/16" wide, 3 5/16" foot $45.00
Blown, 7 1/8" tall, 5 3/8" wide, 4 3/16" foot, Blue 50.00
Blown, 7 3/4" tall, 4 1/8" wide, 2 3/4" foot, narrow swirl optic, Amber 35.00
Bubble (possibly 1970s), 7" tall, 4 1/2" wide, 3" foot, Crystal with Satin highlights 25.00
Colonial, Patent dated 10-7-19, 10" tall, 4 7/8" wide, 3 13/16" foot, Crystal 50.00
Crystal with Gray Cutting. 45.00
Disk stem with Fleur de Lys finial, 9 1/4" tall, 5 3/4" wide, 3 1/4" foot, Blue *. 50.00
Low Footed with Fleur de Lys finial, 7" tall, 7 5/8" wide, 3 5/16" foot, Pink with etched band *. 50.00
Spiral Optic, 1/2 lb., 9 1/8" tall, 3 9/16" wide, 3 1/2" foot, Green 40.00
Urn Shape, Marked Iowa State Fair 1924, 8 1/2" tall, 3 3/4" wide, 3 1/8" foot, Dull Green 50.00

U.S. Glass Co. Oval candy box

L to R: U.S. Glass Co. No. 9557 candy jar and Velva candy jar

L to R: Westmoreland Glass Co.
No. 1700 candy jar and No. 1795 candy jar

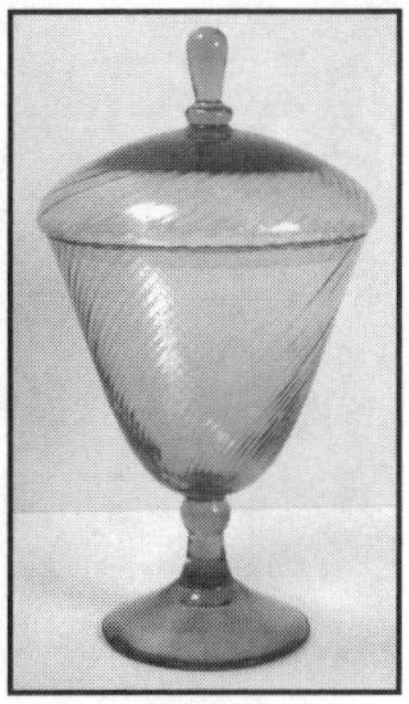

L to R: Unknown disc stem candy jar
Unknown blown swirl optic candy jar

CANDY JARS & BOXES *(continued)*

L to R: Cambridge Glass Co. No. 96 plain candy jar
Fostoria Glass Co. No. 22413 candy jar

Fostoria Glass Co. No. 2219 candy jars

L to R: Cambridge Glass Co.
Cambridge square candy box and No. 3400 candy box

L to R: Fostoria Glass Co.
Diadem candy box and Century candy jar

L to R: Duncan & Miller Glass Co.
Pall Mall candy box and Canterbury candy box

L to R: Fostoria Glass Co.
No. 2394 candy jar and No. 2395 candy jar

L to R: Duncan & Miller Glass Co.
Early American Sandwich urn and bonbon

L to R: Fostoria Glass Co.
No. 2331 candy box and Horizon candy box

(continued) CANDY JARS & BOXES

L to R: Imperial Glass Corp.
No. 68511 candy jar and No. 717 candy jar

L to R: Lancaster Glass Co. No. 83 candy jar
New Martinsville Glass Co. No. 149/3 candy jar

L to R: Imperial Glass Corp.
No. 64513 candy box and No. 14811 candy box

L to R: Morgantown Glass Co. No. 1854-1 Chocolate box
Paden City Glass Mfg. Co. No. 198 bonbon

L to R: Morgantown Glass Co.
Helga candy box and Maureen candy jar

L to R: Morgantown Glass Co.
No. 1854-2 chocolate box and No. 1855 chocolate box

Louie Glass Co. Original Ad Spiral Optic candy jars

L to R: Paden City Mfg. Co.
No. 180 candy jar and No. 801 candy jar

CANDY JARS & BOXES *(continued)*

L to R: U.S. Glass Co.
No. 314 bonbon and No. 330 bonbon

L to R: Unknown candy jar and Unknown urn shape candy jar

L to R: U.S. Glass Co. No. 345 candy box and Heart bonbon

L to R: U.S. Glass Co. No. 15531 Conic candy jar and
No. 15531 Conic with optic candy jar

L to R: Unknown colonial candy jar and
Unknown crystal candy jar with gray cutting

L to R: Unknown bubble candy box and
Unknown blown candy jar

 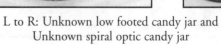

L to R: Unknown low footed candy jar and
Unknown spiral optic candy jar

Chapter 50
FIGURINES

Figurines, both human and animals, are eagerly sought by many collectors. Many companies made figurines in almost endless variety, both in Crystal and colors. Some favorites, like the New Martinsville seals, were continued by Viking Glass without the balanced balls on their noses. Imperial Glass continued most of the Heisey figurines, at first in Crystal, then Caramel Slag and other Imperial colors. Since the 1980s the Heisey Collectors of America have continued the reproduction of the Heisey animals. Remember that Heisey made animals only in crystal with very few in pale amber or cobalt. All other colors are reproductions. Pilgrim animals shown are hand-made and so vary in exact shape. Other companies made very similar animals.

We have included some animals of very recent production mainly for identification, especially from Viking Glass. While out of the time frame of this book, we felt that proper identification was more important than strict date guidelines. An asterisk ( )indicates figures made in original Heisey molds but reproduced by other companies. A double asterisk (**) indicates a set of Duncan & Miller figurines.*
Note: Additional illustrations follow the company price listings.

CAMBRIDGE GLASS CO.
Frog, Amber. $20.00
Heron Flower Holder, 12", Crystal (1111). 150.00
Sea Gull Flower Frog (1138) 95.00
Swan, 8½", Mandarin (many sizes & colors) 95.00

CO-OPERATIVE FLINT GLASS CO.
Frog with Cover, Crystal. $125.00

DUNCAN & MILLER GLASS CO.
Bird of Paradise, 13", Crystal (30) . . . . $900.00+
Cart, Crystal Satin ** 195.00
Donkey, Crystal Satin ** 285.00
Dove, Crystal 285.00
Duck, Solid, Crystal (30) 95.00
Duck Ashtray, 4", Crystal (30) 45.00
Duck Ashtray, 4", Ruby (30) 165.00
Duck Cigarette Box & Cover, 6", Crystal (30). 85.00
Goose, Crystal 350.00
Heron, 7", Crystal (30). 150.00
Peon, Crystal Satin ** 310.00
Ruffed Grouse, 7½", Crystal (30) . . . . 1000.00+
Sailfish, Blue Opalescent (30) . . . . 600.00+
Sailfish Crystal Satin (30) 350.00
Swan Handled Oval Bowl, 10" or 11", Crystal (30) 75.00
Swan Handled Oval Bowl, Pall Mall line,
   6", Crystal (30) 50.00
Swan, Open, 10½", Crystal (30½) 65.00
Swan, Open, 12", Ruby (30½) 275.00
Swan, Open, 3½", Crystal (30½) 50.00
Swan, Open, 6", Crystal (30½). 25.00
Swan, Open, 7", Crystal (30½") 35.00
Swan, Solid, 3", Crystal 30.00
Swan, Solid, 5", Crystal 40.00
Swan, Solid, 7", Crystal 95.00
Swan, Spread Wing, Opalescent 140.00
Tropical Fish Candlesticks, Blue Opalescent, pr. . . . . 1,500.00+

L to R: Cambridge Glass Co. swan
Co-Operative Flint Glass Co. frog

L to R: Duncan & Miller Glass Co. peon with donkey and cart
Duncan & Miller Glass Co. ruffed grouse

L to R: Duncan & Miller Glass Co.
sailfish and spread wing swan

FIGURINES *(continued)*

L to R: Fenton Art Glass Co. bunny and Fostoria Glass Co. duck

L to R: A.H. Heisey Glass Co.
doe head book end and flying mare

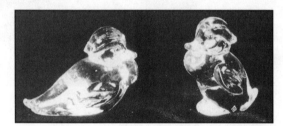

A.H. Heisey Glass Co. ducklings

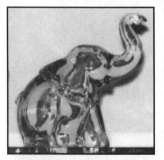

L to R: A.H. Heisey Glass Co. small crystal elephant and Oscar

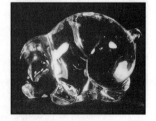

L to R: A.H. Heisey Glass Co. scottie and sow

FENTON ART GLASS CO.

Bird, Happiness, Custard Satin with HP Roses. $65.00
Bunny, Crystal Satin. 35.00
Duckling, Light Blue Satin, HP flowers. 35.00
Elephant, Small, French Opalescent * 60.00
Frog, Turquoise Satin 22.00
Whale, White Satin, HP flowers 35.00

FOSTORIA GLASS CO.

Duck, Small, Crystal, 3 styles, ea. $35.00
Eagle book ends, Crystal, pr. (2585) 250.00
Goldfish, Crystal, 2 styles 195.00
Lyre, book ends, pr. (2601) 145.00

A.H. HEISEY GLASS CO.

Airedale, Crystal $600.00
Clydesdale, Crystal 500.00
Doe Head, book ends, Crystal, pr. 2000.00
Dolphin, Match Holder, Crystal 190.00
Donkey, Crystal 400.00
Duckling, Wood, Crystal, 2 styles, ea. 185.00
Elephant, Large, Crystal 500.00
Elephant, Small, Crystal 295.00
Fish, book ends, Crystal, pr. 300.00+
Fish Bowl, Crystal 650.00
Giraffe, Crystal, 2 styles, ea. 265.00
Goose, Wings Down, Crystal 500.00
Goose, Wings Half, Crystal. 125.00
Goose, Wings Up, Crystal. 145.00
Hen, Crystal. 550.00
Horse Head book ends, Crystal Satin, pr.. . . . . 350.00
Horse, Show, Crystal. . . . . 1800.00+
Madonna, Crystal Satin (1) 120.00
Mallard, Wings Down, Crystal 350.00
Mallard, Wings Half, Crystal. 250.00
Mallard, Wings Up, Crystal. 225.00
Mare, Flying, Crystal . . . . 1800.00+
Oscar, Crystal. 140.00
Pheasant, Asiatic, Crystal 400.00
Pony, Balking, Crystal. 255.00
Pony, Kicking, Crystal. 235.00
Pony, Standing, Crystal. 100.00
Pony, Standing, Light Amber . . . . 700.00+
Rabbit, Paperweight, Crystal (ears shortened). 180.00
Rooster, Vase, Crystal 100.00
Rooster, Fighting, Crystal 225.00
Scottie, Crystal. 150.00
Sow, Crystal. . . . . 850.00+

L to R: A.H. Heisey Glass Co. hen and fish bowl

HOUZE GLASS CO.
Pony, Rocker Blotter, Yellow $95.00
Scottie, Rocker Blotter, Jadeite 75.00

IMPERIAL GLASS CORP.
Elephant, Medium, Caramel Slag * $70.00
Pony, Balking, Caramel Slag * 200.00
Pony, Kicking, Caramel Slag * 200.00
Pony, Standing, Caramel Slag * 65.00

L.E. SMITH GLASS CO.
Scottie, Crystal Satin. $65.00
Swan Dish with flower frog, Green Satin (3) 70.00

NEW MARTINSVILLE GLASS CO.
Bear, Baby, 3", Crystal (487) $75.00
Bear, Mama, 4", Crystal (488). 260.00
Bear, Papa, 4", Crystal (489) 300.00
Chick, 1", Crystal (667) 35.00
Hen, 5", Crystal (669) 85.00
Pig, Large, 6½" long, Crystal (762) 400.00
Rooster, 7½", Crystal (668) 100.00
Squirrel book ends, 4½", Crystal, pr. (674) 140.00
Swan, Crystal with Blue (4521-2SJ) 70.00
Swan, Crystal with Ruby (4551-1SJ) 70.00
Swan, Ruby with Crystal. 70.00
Swan Bowl, Square, Crystal (4541) 65.00

PILGRIM GLASS CO.
Mouse, Amber $30.00
Snail, Olive Green 35.00
Whale, Olive Green 30.00

PRINCESS HOUSE
Cat, Crystal $40.00

L to R: Houze Glass Co. pony and Scottie rocker blotters

L.E. Smith Glass Co. Swan dish with flower frog and Scottie

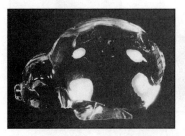

L to R: New Martinsville Glass Co. pig and squirrel book end

L to R: Pilgrim Glass Co. whale, mouse and snail

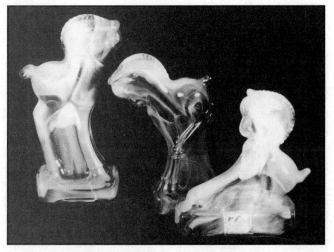

L to R: Imperial Glass Corp. caramel slag
standing pony, kicking pony and balking pony

L to R: New Martinsville Glass Co. swan bowl
Princess house cat

FIGURINES *(continued)*

Tiffin Art Glass Corp. pheasant with paperweight bases

L to R: U.S. Glass Co. cats and tall frog candlestick

L to R: Viking Glass Co. cygnet and seals

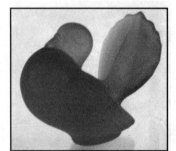

L to R: Westmoreland Glass Co.
dog doorstop and pouter pigeon

TIFFIN ART GLASS CORP.

Faun Flower Floater, Copen Blue. $395.00
Pheasant with Paperweight Base,
    Copen Blue, 2 styles . . . . 500.00+

U.S. GLASS CO.

Cat, Sassie Suzy, Black Satin $225.00
Cat, Small, Black Satin 195.00
Frog Candlesticks, Tall, Black Satin, pr. 350.00
Frog Candlesticks, Short, Black Satin, pr. 210.00
Moose book ends, Amber Satin, pr. 550.00
Moose Pin Tray, Black Satin 125.00

VIKING GLASS CO.

Bunny, 2 styles, Ruby, ea. * $45.00
Cat, Black 25.00
Cygnet, Ruby * 35.00
Dog, Black 25.00
Pony, Balking, Ruby * 140.00
Pony, Kicking, Ruby * 140.00
Pony, Standing, Ruby * 140.00
Rabbit, Crystal 40.00
Rabbit, Mother, Ruby * 95.00
Seal, 7", Crystal 40.00
Seal, Baby, 4½", Crystal 30.00
Sparrow, Ruby * 55.00
Tiger Paperweight, Ruby * 95.00

WESTMORELAND GLASS CO.

Dog, Doorstop, Blue Satin (78). $450.00
Dog, Small, Crystal (75) 40.00
Duck, Individual Salt (1) 25.00
Owl, Continued by Degenhart (1) 35.00
Owl, book end, Crystal, pr. 250.00
Pouter Pigeon, Amber Satin (9). 35.00
Starfish, Candlesticks, Almond, pr. 55.00

Viking Glass Co. bunnies and mother rabbit

(continued) FIGURINES

L to R: Cambridge Glass Co.
heron flower holder and sea gull flower frog

Duncan & Miller Glass Co. dove

L to R: Cambridge Glass Co. frog
Duncan & Miller Glass Co. goose

Duncan & Miller Glass Co. ducks

Duncan & Miller Glass Co. bird of paradise

L to R: Duncan & Miller Glass Co. heron and swans

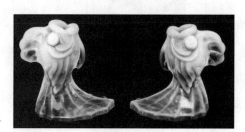

Duncan & Miller Glass Co. tropical fish candlesticks

Duncan & Miller Glass Co. solid swans

251

FIGURINES (continued)

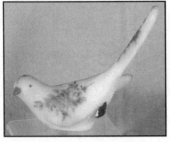

L to R: Fenton Art Glass Co. happiness bird and duckling

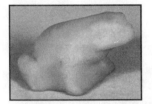
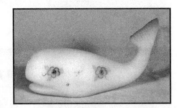

L to R: Fenton Art Glass Co. frog and whale

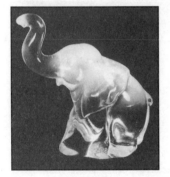

L to R: Fenton Art Glass Co. elephant and
Fostoria Glass Co. goldfish

L to R: Fostoria Glass Co. eagle book end and lyre book ends

A.H. Heisey Glass Co. mallards

L to R: A.H. Heisey Glass Co. fighting rooster and rooster vase

A.H. Heisey Glass Co. rabbit paperweight

L to R: A.H. Heisey Glass Co. clydesdale and donkey

L to R: A.H. Heisey Glass Co. giraffe, Madonna and
Asiatic pheasant

(continued) FIGURINES

L to R: A.H. Heisey Glass Co.
large crystal elephant and horse head book end

L to R: A.H. Heisey Glass Co. geese

L to R: A.H. Heisey Glass Co. show horse and standing pony

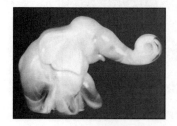

L to R: Imperial Glass Co. caramel slag elephant
New Martinsville baby bear

L to R: A.H. Heisey Glass Co. kicking pony and balking pony

New Martinsville Glass Co. hen and chicks and rooster

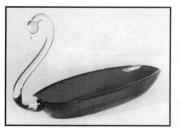

L to R: New Martinsville Glass Co.
swan and No. 4551-1SJ swan

L to R: A.H. Heisey Glass Co. airedale and fish book end

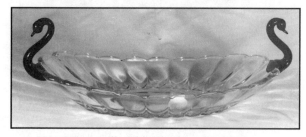

New Martinsville Glass Co. No. 4521-2SJ swan

FIGURINES *(continued)*

L to R: Tiffin Art Glass Corp. fawn flower floater

L to R: U.S. Glass Glass Co.
short frog candlestick and moose pin tray

L to R: Viking Glass Co.
standing pony, kicking pony and balking pony

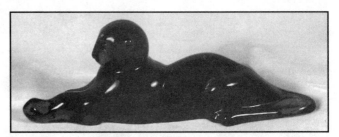

Viking Glass Co. tiger paperweight

L to R: Viking Glass Co. dog and cat

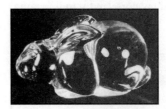

L to R: Viking Glass Co. rabbit and sparrow

L to R: Westmoreland Glass Co. owl book end and owl

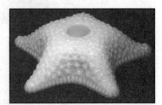

L to R: Westmoreland Glass Co. duck and starfish candlestick

Chapter 51
SMOKING ITEMS

Smoking items are becoming more collectible at this time. More collectors are becoming attracted to this sub-category of Depression/elegant glassware. While the ubiquitous ashtrays comprise much of what is available in this category, there are also cigarette boxes, cigarette holders, combination sets and others available. There is great diversity in this category, including many advertising or souvenir items. Prices given are for Crystal unless color is noted. **Note: Additional illustrations follow the company price listings.**

BROOKE GLASS CO.
Covered Cigarette Box, Ruby $35.00

CAMBRIDGE GLASS CO.
No. 618, Ashtray with Cigarette Holder, Crystal $45.00

DUNCAN & MILLER GLASS CO.
Ashtray, Card Suit, Shapes, Set of 4, 3",
   Crystal (123) $60.00
Ashtray, Cloverleaf, 5", Chartreuse 35.00
Ashtray, Club, 5", Crystal (12) 15.00
Ashtray, Individual, Crystal (50) 6.00
Ashtray, Oblong, 3" x 2½", Crystal (116) 8.00
Ashtray, Oval, 4", Crystal (32) 8.00
Ashtray, Oval, 5½", Crystal (32) 10.00
Ashtray, Oval, 7", Crystal (32) 15.00
Ashtray, Rectangular, Oval Center, 3½", Crystal (31) 8.00
Ashtray, Rectangular, Oval Center, 5", Crystal (31) 10.00
Ashtray, Rectangular, Oval Center, 6½", Crystal (31) . . . 15.00
Ashtray, 2½", Crystal (10) 18.00
Ashtray, 3", Crystal (100) 5.00
Ashtray, 4", Crystal (11) 15.00
Ashtray, 4½", Crystal (17) 6.00
Canterbury Cigarette Box & Cover,
   4½", Crystal (115) 35.00
Canterbury Cigarette Jar & Cover, Ashtray Top,
   4" tall, Crystal (115) 45.00
Canterbury Club Ashtray, 3", Crystal (115) 8.00
Canterbury Club Ashtray, 4½", Crystal (115) 12.00
Canterbury Club Ashtray, 5½", Crystal (115) 15.00
Caribbean Cigarette Jar & Cover, Amber 150.00
Cigarette Box & Cover, Crystal (116) 30.00

L to R: Brooke Glass Co. covered cigarette box
Cambridge Glass Co. No. 618 ashtray

L to R: Duncan & Miller Glass Co. cloverleaf ashtray and
No. 10 ashtray with gray cutting

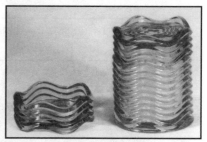

L to R: Duncan & Miller Glass Co. Canterbury cigarette jar
and Caribbean cigarette jar

Duncan & Miller Glass Co. No. 116 cigarette set

SMOKING ITEMS *(continued)*

L to R: Duncan & Miller Glass Co. No. 32 cigarette box
Duncan sculptured floral cigarette box

Duncan & Miller Glass Co. No. 50 cigarette set

L to R: Greensburg Glass Works elephant cigarette box,
elephant ashtray and dog ashtray

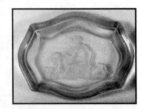

L to R: A.H. Heisey McArthur Hat ashtray
Yeoman Cupid and Psyche ashtray

L to R: Imperial Glass Corp. fish, zodiac, and duck ashtray

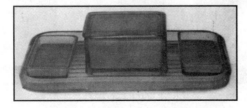

New Martinsville Glass Co. No. 10-2 cigarette set

Cigarette Box & Cover, Oval,
   4½" x 3½", Crystal (32) 22.00
Cigarette Box & Cover, 4½" x 3½", Crystal (100) 15.00
Cigarette Holder, Oval, 3", Crystal (12) 12.00
Cigarette Holder, urn-form, 2-handled,
   Square Foot, 3½", Crystal (539) 25.00
Cigarette Holder, urn-form, Square Foot, 3½",
   Crystal (538) 25.00
Cigarette Jar & Cover, Crystal (50) 20.00
Early American Sandwich Ashtray, Individual,
   2¾" sq., Crystal (41) 10.00
Early American Sandwich Cigarette Holder,
   3", Crystal (41) 35.00
Early American Sandwich Cigarette Box & Cover,
   3½", Crystal (41) 45.00
Sculptured Floral Cigarette Box, Crystal Satin 65.00
Sculptured Floral Ashtray, Crystal Satin 30.00

GREENSBURG GLASS WORKS

Dog Cigarette Box, Black (1) $50.00
Dog Ashtray, Pink (1) 45.00
Elephant Ashtray, Green (2) 45.00
Elephant Cigarette Box, Green (2) 50.00

A.H. HEISEY GLASS CO.

McArthur Hat Ashtray, Crystal $30.00
Yeoman Ashtray, Cupid & Psyche, Flamingo 40.00
Yeoman Ashtray, Irish Setter, Flamingo 40.00

IMPERIAL GLASS CORP.

West Virginia Centennial, Amber $35.00
Fish, Crystal 30.00
Duck, Crystal 30.00
Zodiac, Crystal 35.00
Eagle Cigarette Holder, Crystal 35.00
Eagle Ashtray, Crystal 35.00

NEW MARTINSVILLE GLASS CO.

Allah Smoker's Set—Tray, 2 Ashtrays,
   Cigarette Holder, Amethyst (149) $95.00
Van's Own Ashtray/Cigarette Holder
   Combination, Crystal (149) 30.00
Ashtray, Crystal (20) 55.00
Cigarette Set—Tray, Cigarette Box,
   2 Ashtrays, Amethyst (10-2) 50.00

New Martinsville Glass Co. Allah smokers set

(continued) # SMOKING ITEMS

PADEN CITY GLASS MFG. CO.

Ashtray (15) $15.00
Ashtray, Crystal (3)........................... 10.00
Ashtray, Crystal (14)........................... 9.00
Ashtray, Green (2) 25.00

U.S. GLASS CO.

Ashtray, Green $45.00
Reservoir Ashtray, Crystal 65.00
Twilight Ashtray............................. 95.00

WESTMORELAND GLASS CO.

Ashtray, Crystal (350)......................... $5.00
Ashtray, Crystal (351)......................... 20.00
Ashtray, Crystal (353)......................... 10.00
Ashtray, with Rooster Decoration, 4", Crystal (455).... 25.00
Ashtray or Individual Butter, Crystal (205) 7.00
Ashtray, Safety, Crystal (337).................. 15.00
Ashtray, Safety, Crystal (346).................. 15.00
Ashtray, 3 Cigar Rests, Crystal (343) 15.00
Ashtray, Candle, 6" x 4", Crystal (348) 30.00
Ashtray, Cigarette, 4" x 3", Crystal (347).......... 20.00
Ashtray or Pin Tray, 3" or 4", Crystal (454)......... 8.00
Ashtray, 3-cornered, Crystal (1800).............. 9.00
Ashtray Nest-4, Crystal (1834) 15.00
Ashtray Nest-4, Crystal (1835) 15.00
Cigarette Holder Ashtray, Crystal (349)........... 20.00
Cigarette Holder, Crystal (352)................. 20.00
English Hobnail Hat, Crystal (555)............... 15.00
Snuffer & Tray, Crystal (1850/344)............... 18.00

UNDETERMINED MANUFACTURER

Golfer, Green $45.00
Moondance, Green........................... 45.00

L to R: Paden City Mfg. Co. No. 3 ashtray and No. 15 ashtray

L to R: U.S. Glass Co. ashtray and Twilight ashtray

L to R: Westmoreland Glass Co.
No. 455 ashtray with rooster and No. 343 ashtray

Westmoreland Glass Co. No. 348 candle ashtray

Westmoreland Glass Co. English Hobnail hat

Undetermined Manufacturer golfer ashtray

L to R: Westmoreland Glass Co.
No. 1834 ashtray nest and No. 352 cigarette holder

SMOKING ITEMS(continued)

L to R: Duncan & Miller Glass Co. Early American Sandwich
cigarette holder and No. 12 oval cigarette holder

L to R: Duncan & Miller Glass Co.
No. 31 rectangular ashtray and No. 32 oval ashtray

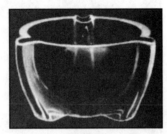

L to R: Duncan & Miller Glass Co.
Canterbury club ashtray and No. 12 club ashtray

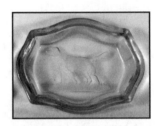

L to R: Greensburg Glass Works dog cigarette box
A.H. Heisey Yeoman Irish Setter ashtray

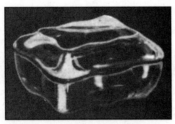

L to R: Duncan & Miller Glass Co.
urn-form cigarette holder and Canterbury cigarette box

L to R: Imperial Glass Corp. West Virginia centennial ashtray
Original art: eagle cigarette holder and ashtray

Duncan & Miller Glass Co. sculptured floral ashtray

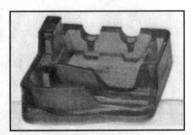

L to R: New Martinsville Glass Co. Van's own ashtray/cigarette
holder and No. 20 ashtray

(*continued*) SMOKING ITEMS

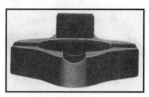 

L to R: Paden City Mfg. Co. No. 2 ashtray and No. 14 ashtray

 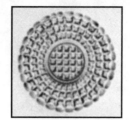

L to R: Westmoreland Glass Co. No. 205 butter or ashtray and No. 349 cigarette holder ashtray

New Reservoir Ash Tray

THIS is an item that fills a long felt want wherever men congregate. It's a "party" ash tray that sells on sight. Housewives, remembering burned tables and table cloths, appreciate at a glance its saving merits.

The upper tray empties its burden of ashes at a touch to the reservoir below. Smouldering stubs burn out in the confined atmosphere of the lower chamber.

Made in blue, canary and amber glass, satin finish, plain and also decorated in gold.

Top tilts all ashes into Lower Reservoir

UNITED STATES GLASS COMPANY

PITTSBURGH, PENNSYLVANIA

OFFICES IN ALL PRINCIPAL CITIES

Visit Our New Display and Sales Rooms—Pottery & Glass Bldg., 954 Liberty Ave., Pittsburgh, Pa.

U.S. Glass Co. Original Ad: reservoir ashtray

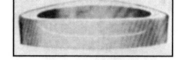 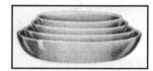

L to R: Westmoreland Glass Co.
No. 1800 3-cornered ashtray and No. 1853 ashtray nest

Westmoreland Glass Co. No. 347 cigarette ashtray and
No. 1850/344 snuffer and tray

L to R: Westmoreland Glass Co.
No. 337 safety ashtray and No. 353 ashtray

Westmoreland Glass Co. No. 351 ashtray

Westmoreland Glass Co. No. 346 safety ashtray

Undetermined Manufacturer Moondance ashtray

259

Chapter 52
VASES

Vases are some of the most versatile and enduring pieces made of glass. Glass companies produced hundreds of styles of vases from delicate tiny vases for one flower to large, heavy vases for huge bouquets.

Many of the styles shown here, especially the blown-ware vases, are common to several companies. Careful study is needed to differentiate them. The following list contains only a sampling of vases available from this time period. **Note: Additional illustrations follow the company price listings.**

  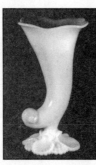

L to R: Bartlett Collins Glass Co. No. 385 vase with No. 210 cutting, No. 375 vase with No. 260 cutting Cambridge Glass Co. cornucopia vase

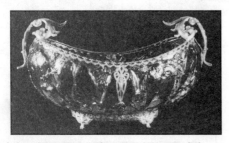

Consolidated Lamp & Glass Co. Love Birds banana boat

L to R: Duncan & Miller Glass Co. short and tall Three Feathers vase and urn vase

BARTLETT COLLINS GLASS CO.

These shapes are common to many companies. The safest way to attribute these is by a recognized decoration.

No. 252, No. 238 Cutting, Green	$25.00
No. 375, No. 260 Cutting, Green	25.00
No. 380, No. 9 Cutting, Nu-Rose, Pink	25.00
No. 385, No. 210 Cutting, Nu-Rose	25.00

CAMBRIDGE GLASS CO.

Cornucopia, Crown Tuscan	$145.00

CONSOLIDATED LAMP & GLASS CO.

Love Birds banana boat, in metal filigree	$700.00
Sunset	145.00
Vine, Custard with Gold Trim, No. 700	460.00

DUNCAN & MILLER GLASS CO.

No. 119, Flared, 8½", Crystal	$35.00
No. 120, Footed, 10", Crystal	35.00
No. 120, Footed, 5½", Crystal	15.00
No. 120, Footed, 12" or 14", Crystal	40.00
No. 120, Footed, 6", Crystal	15.00
No. 121, Flared and Cupped, 7", Crystal	35.00
No. 126, Footed, Crimped, 12," Crystal	45.00
No. 505, 8" or 10", Crystal	20.00
No. 505, 12", Crystal	25.00
No. 506, 10", Crystal	20.00
No. 506, 8", Crystal	15.00
No. 506, 12", Crystal	22.00
No. 506, Bud, 9", Crystal	20.00
No. 507, 12", Crystal	22.00
No. 507, 6" or 8", Crystal	15.00
No. 507, 10", Crystal	18.00
No. 508, 9", Crystal	20.00
No. 509, 9", Crystal	25.00
No. 510, 9" Bud, Crystal	25.00
No. 5200, 10", Crystal	35.00
No. 5200, 7" or 8", Crystal	25.00
Murano, Flared, 7", Milk Glass	300.00
Radiance, No. 5113, 6" or 9" Rose Bowl, Crystal	55.00
Three Feathers, Short, Blue Opalescent	85.00
Three Feathers, Tall, Blue Opalescent	185.00
Urn, Milk Glass with Green Handles	450.00

(continued) VASES

A.H. HEISEY GLASS CO.

Ball, 6", Saturn Optic, Crystal (4085) $55.00
Fogg Flower Box, Moongleam (501) 135.00
Oval, 9", Flamingo (4209) 90.00
Steele, Moongleam (4157) 95.00

IMPERIAL GLASS CORP.

*Many vases made by Imperial in the 1930s were available in
Crystal, Amber, Green and Rose.*

No. 304, Bud, 10" to 12" tall, Rose. $25.00
No. 598/2, 10½", Square, Green. 30.00
No. 743B, 5¼", Blue Opalescent 35.00
No. 6001, 10", Green. 30.00
No. 6002, 9", Round, Green. 30.00
Reeded, All-Over Gold Decoration 85.00
Twisted Optic, 7" to 8", made fan,
　　flared or rolled top, Rose 45.00

D.C. JENKINS GLASS CO.

No. 980, 80 oz., Crystal $20.00
No. 981, 80 oz., Crystal 20.00
No. 982, 80 oz., Crystal 20.00
No. 983, 80 oz., Crystal 20.00
No. 984, 80 oz., Crystal 20.00
No. 985, 80 oz., Crystal 20.00

L.E. SMITH GLASS CO.

Black with Silver Decoration $45.00

LOUIE GLASS CO.

No. 17, 10", Black $22.00
No. 20, 10", Black 90.00
No. 20, 10", Crystal with Multicolored Bands 55.00
No. 20, 10", Blue with Platinum Stripes & Handles . . . 90.00
No. 20, 10", Blue with Crystal Handles. 95.00
No. 20, 10", Topaz with Crystal Handles. 80.00
No. 34, 10", Crystal with Black Foot. 25.00
No. 49, 7", Black 18.00
No. 49, Blue with assorted advertisements 54.00
No. 88, 10", Black 24.00
No. 504, Black. 65.00
Any Shown in Ad, Crystal. 10.00
Baluster-form, Tall ruffled neck, Black, decorated. 30.00
Baluster-form, Rolled neck, Black 45.00
Blue in Metal Holder 50.00
Bulbous, Tall flared neck, Black. 12.00
Ovoid, Short flared neck, Black. 12.00
Ovoid, Tall ruffled neck, 4½", Black (2) 15.00
Ovoid, Tall ruffled neck, Black 15.00
Tapering, Cylindrical, Tall ruffled neck, Black 25.00
Unknown, Footed, Black 16.00

A.H. Heisey Glass Co. Fogg flower box

Imperial Glass Corp. Original Catalog Illustration:
L to R: No. 6001, No. 598/2 and No. 6002 vases

L to R: D.C. Jenkins Glass Co. No. 980 vase and
L.E. Smith Glass Co. vase

L to R: Louie Glass Co. No. 49 advertisement vase, No. 20
vase with platinum stripes and baluster-form rolled neck vase

L to R: Louie Glass Co. tall flared neck black vase, short flared
neck black vase and tall ruffled neck black vase

VASES *(continued)*

McKee Glass Co. Original Ad: assorted vases

L to R: Monongah Glass Co. vase
Morgantown Glass Co. Engagement and Catherine vase

L to R: Morgantown Glass Co.
Neapolitan witch ball and Squat vase

L to R: Phoenix Glass Co. Philodendron and Wild Rose vase

McKEE GLASS CO.

The following are shown in the accompanying 1931 ad in black. Some of these pieces were made in other colors including Skokie Green (jadeite). Prices are for items in black.

Bowl, Bulb, 5½" (26) $20.00
Bowl, Bulb, 7" (27) 25.00
Jardiniere, 3-footed, 5½" tall (25) 30.00
Vase, Footed, 8½" (23) 30.00
Vase, Triangular, 8½" (100) 115.00

MONONGAH GLASS CO.

Pink $32.00

MORGANTOWN

No. 7662½/28 9", Ebony with Crystal $150.00
Catherine, Jade (45) 170.00
Electra, 10", Handled, Ebony with Crystal (35½) 650.00
Engagement, Jade with Ebony (58½) 400.00
Jackson, 8", Ebony with Crystal (14½) 170.00
Media, 10", Jade (54) 135.00
Neapolitan Witch Ball, Jade or Spanish Red (64) 900.00
Petite, Green (46) 60.00
Saturn, Jade (70) 350.00
Serenade, 10", Jade (53) 150.00
Squat, Aquamarine (59) 120.00

NEW MARTINSVILLE GLASS CO.

Morning Dove, 9", Crystal (101) $95.00

PHOENIX GLASS CO.

Philodendron, Blue on Crystal $220.00
Pine Cone, Black Satin 175.00
Wild Geese, Slate Blue on Milk 285.00
Wild Rose, Crystal with Ruby Stain 270.00

New Martinsville Glass Co. Original Ad: Morning Dove vase

U.S. Glass Co. (Tiffin)

Aster, with Coralene Decoration $95.00
Bud, Black Satin 45.00
Canterbury, Twilight 85.00
Carrera, 8", Green 145.00
Cornucopia (5508) 75.00
Cornucopia, Spiral Optic, Copen Blue (6041) 175.00
Dahlia, 8", Black Satin 65.00
Flip, 10", sand carved (5859) 220.00
Flower Arranger, Black Satin 85.00
Iris, 6", Amber Satin (16254) 85.00
Iris, 6", Black Satin (16254) 100.00
Iris, 6", Canary with Enamel (16254) 120.00
Lily, 8", Black Satin 55.00
Open-work Comport, Orange (310) 55.00
Open-work, Black Satin (310) 85.00
Poppy, Large, Black Satin 95.00
Poppy, Small, Green Satin 85.00
Wall, Green Satin (320) 110.00

West Virginia Glass

No. 909, 5⅜", Crystal $10.00
No. 1331, 12½", Crystal 15.00
No. 7784, 10", Crystal 15.00

Westmoreland Glass Co.

No. 100, 10", Semi-Cut, Crystal $65.00
No. 102, 9½", Crystal 35.00
No. 103, 12½", Crystal 35.00
No. 104, 15", Crystal 50.00
No. 1708, 7", Footed, Crystal 25.00
No. 1709, 8", Crystal 35.00
No. 1709, 8", with Umbrella Handle, Crystal 50.00

L to R: U.S. Glass Co. dahlia, lily and flower arranger vases

L to R: U.S. Glass Co. open-work vase and carrera vase

U.S. Glass Co. cornucopia spiral optic vase and flip sand carved vase

West Virginia Glass Co. Original ad

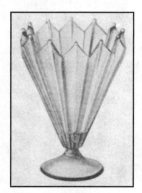

L to R: Westmoreland Glass Co.
No. 100 semi-cut vase and No. 1709 footed vase

263

VASES *(continued)*

L to R: Bartlett Collins Glass Co. No. 252 vase with
No. 238 cutting, No. 380 vase with No. 9 cutting
Consolidated Lamp & Glass Co. sunset vase

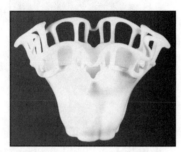

L to R: Consolidated Lamp & Glass Co. Vine vase
Duncan & Miller Glass Co. Murano vase

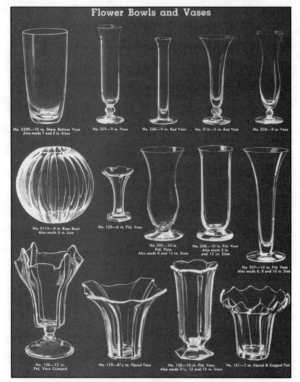

Duncan & Miller Glass Co.
Original Catalog Illustration: Assorted vases

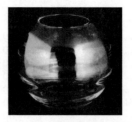

L to R: A.H. Heisey Glass Co. Ball vase and Steele vase

L to R: A.H. Heisey Glass Co. Oval vase
Imperial Glass Corp. No. 743B vase

L to R: Imperial Glass Corp. No. 304 bud vase and Reeded vase

Imperial Glass Corp.
Original Catalog Illustration: Twisted Optic vases

L to R: D.C. Jenkins Glass Co. No. 981 vase and No. 982 vase

(continued) VASES

L to R: D.C. Jenkins Glass Co.
No. 983, No. 984, and No. 985 vases

L to R: Louie Glass Co. No. 34 vase
No. 17 vase, No. 49 vase and unknown footed vase

L to R: Louie Glass Co. assorted black ruffled neck vases

L to R: Louie Glass Co. No. 504, No. 88 and No. 20 vases

Louie Glass Co. Original 1960 Ad

L to R: Louie Glass Co. No. 20 vase with multicolored bands
Morgantown Glass Co. Saturn vase

Louie Glass Co. vases in metal holder

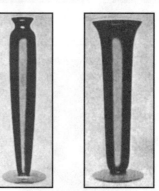

L to R: Morgantown Glass Co.
Media vase, No. 7662½ vase and Serenade vase

265

VASES (continued)

L to R: Morgantown Glass Co. No. 35½ vase and Jackson vase

L to R: U.S. Glass Co. assorted Iris vases and wall vase

L to R: Morgantown Glass Co. Petite vase and Electra vase

L to R: Phoenix Glass Co. Pine Cone vase and Wild Geese vase

L to R: U.S. Glass Co. Canterbury vase and Aster vase

L to R: Westmoreland Glass Co. No. 102 and No. 103 vases

L to R: U.S. Glass Co. cornucopia vase and small Poppy vase

L to R: Westmoreland Glass Co.
No. 104 vase and No. 1708 footed vase

L to R: U.S. Glass Co. bud vases and open-work comport

Chapter 53

LITTLE EXTRAS

This chapter contains many items from original sources that we just couldn't leave out of the book. Late additions are also listed. No attempt to price or make complete lists was made, as this is simply an identification guide. We have collected ads, catalogs and other original company material, including Imperial photographs, for many years. Glass manufacturers and decorating companies are also listed.

L to R: Bryce Bros. Glass Co. Original 1953 ad: Snowflake cutting made in 7 items and Consolidated Glass Co. Catalonian line vase, also recently made by Kanawha Glass

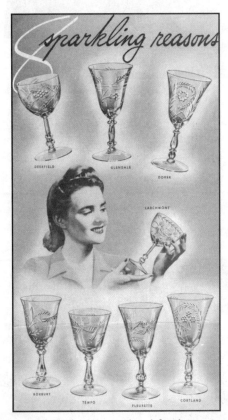

Cambridge Glass Co. 1943 ad for decorations

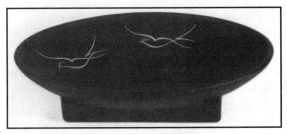

Cambridge Glass Co.
Cambridge Square in Ebon with gold birds

Cambridge Glass Co. night set

Central Glass Works Frances cream and sugar

LITTLE EXTRAS (continued)

Dunbar Glass Corp.
Original 1950 brochure of lamps

Dunbar Glass Corp.
Original 1950 brochure of assorted vases

Dunbar Glass Corp.
Original 1950 brochure of assorted vases

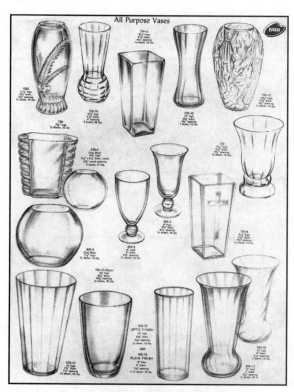

Dunbar Glass Corp.
Original 1950 brochure of assorted vases

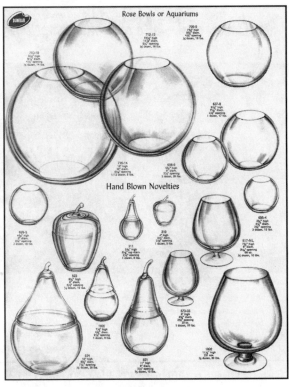

Dunbar Glass Corp.
Original 1950 brochure of assorted vases

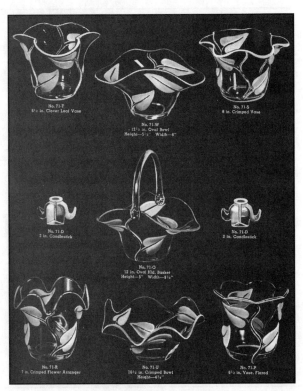

Duncan & Miller Glass Co.
American Way pattern on assorted pieces

Duncan & Miller Glass Co. Buttons and Bows stemware

L to R: Duncan & Miller Glass Co. Canterbury 2-light epergne
candelabrum and Dogwood sculptured opalescent plate

Duncan & Miller Glass Co. No. 5 vase and floral bowl

Duncan & Miller Glass Co. Sylvan opalescent console set

LITTLE EXTRAS *(continued)*

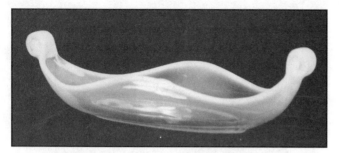

Duncan & Miller Glass Co. Floral opalescent bowl

Duncan & Miller Glass Co.
Canterbury bowl with sandblast decoration

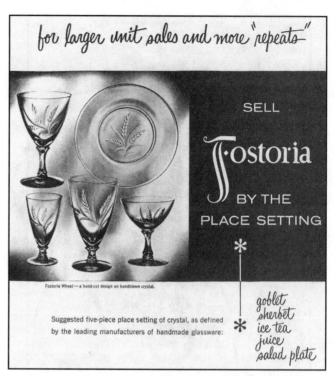

Fostoria Glass Co. Original 1953 ad of Wheat cutting

Duncan & Miller Glass Co. opalescent swan

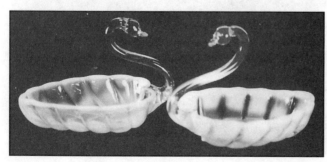

Duncan & Miller Glass Co. Sylvan opalescent swans

Gay Fad Studios located in Lancaster, Ohio specialized in
enameled decorations on glass. Original 1953 ad

(continued) LITTLE EXTRAS

Imperial Glass Co. Original ad of Black Suede assortment

The following photos are part of the Cathay line produced by Imperial Glass Company in conjunction with designer Virginia B. Evans. Many pieces are also signed by Virginia B. Evans. The original production was crystal with satin finish highlights. Later Imperial produced certain pieces in jade, ruby, verde green and possibly other colors.

Cathay by Imperial Dragon candleholders (5009), Lung ashtray (5005) and Wu Ling ashtray (5001)

Imperial Glass Co. Black Suede assortment

Cathay by Imperial
Fan sweetmeat box (5002) and Scolding bird (5024)

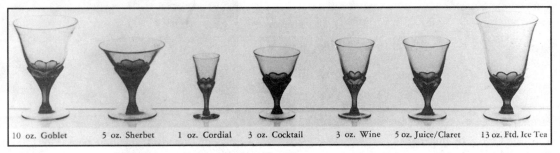

| 10 oz. Goblet | 5 oz. Sherbet | 1 oz. Cordial | 3 oz. Cocktail | 3 oz. Wine | 5 oz. Juice/Claret | 13 oz. Ftd. Ice Tea |

Imperial Glass Co. Blossom stemware

271

LITTLE EXTRAS (continued)

Cathay by Imperial Pavilion tray (5085), Pagoda (5001),
Butterfly ashtray (5006), Plum blossom ashtray (5007) and
Peach blossom mint or nut

Cathay by Imperial Shang candy jar (5002) and Man and
Woman candle servants (5033/5034)

Cathay by Imperial
Ming jar and cover (5019) and Yin and Yang ashtray (5004)

Cathay by Imperial Shen flower bowl

Cathay by Imperial
Wedding lamps (5027) and Celestial centerpiece

Cathay by Imperial Concubine book ends (5000), Plum
Blossom ashtray (5007) and Bamboo urn (5014)

Cathay by Imperial Pillow cigarette box (5018) and Lu Tung book holders (5030)

Imperial Jade green assortment from the 1980s. Most pieces are from Cathay molds

Imperial 1937 factory photo of Coronet pattern, also renamed Victorian and later Chroma

Imperial stemware

Cathay by Imperial 1950s Milk Glass assortments

Imperial 1950s Milk Glass serving pieces

Imperial Russel Wright Pinch stemware

LITTLE EXTRAS *(continued)*

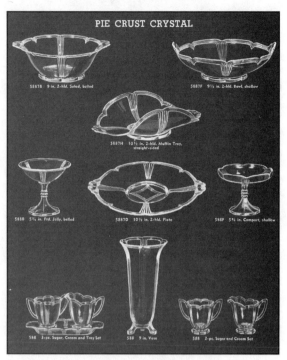

Imperial Pie Crust assortment (5887, 588)

Imperial 1951 cased glass vases

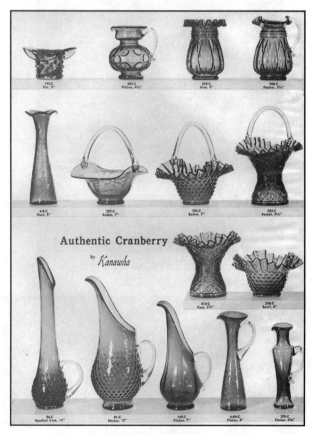

Kanawha Glass Co. Cranberry assortment

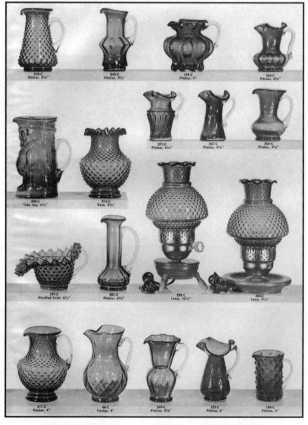

Kanawha Glass Co. Cranberry assortment

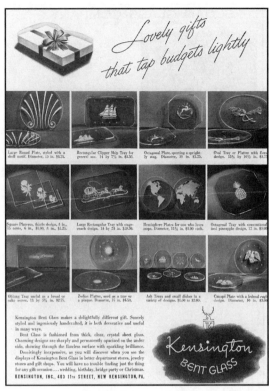

Kensington, Inc. 1943 ad of decorated Bent Glass assortment

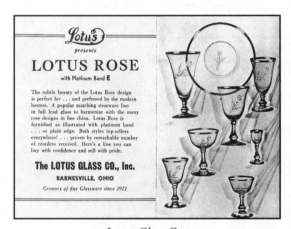

Lotus Glass Co.
1953 ad of Lotus Rose cutting with platinum bands

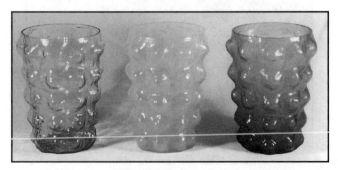

Morgantown Glass Works Snowball vases (1933)

L to R: McBride Glass Co. Cut stemware
Morgantown Glass Works Campbell candlestick (7950)

Monongahela Valley Cut Glass Co. (cutting company)
1953 ad of Sunburst cutting on No. 7113 stems

L to R: Morgantown Glass Works Ducal cutting on No. 7672
goblet, black filament and San Toy etching on No. 7669 goblet

LITTLE EXTRAS *(continued)*

Morgantown Glass Works
No. 329 needle etching on No. 7577 sherbet

Silver City Glass Co. (decorating company)
Duck silver deposit on cocktail set

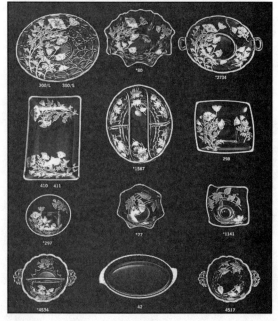

Silver City Glass Co. (decorating company) 1965 catalog
illustration: Flanders, Forest and Springtime sterling on crystal

Sloan Glass Co (cutting company)
Original company page of various cuttings

Sloan Glass Co (cutting company)
Original company page of various cuttings

(continued) LITTLE EXTRAS

U.S. Glass/Tiffin cut compotes: Pristine, Mirage, Gold Palais Versailles, Leland and Resplendent

U.S. Glass/Tiffin decorated goblets: Caribbean, Angelique (platinum band) or Minuet (gold band), Hyde Park, Anniversary Rose (gold band) or Bridal Rose (platinum band)

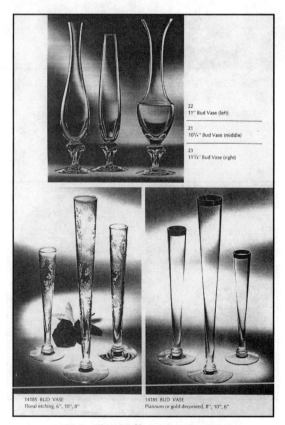

U.S. Glass/Tiffin assorted vases

U.S. Glass/Tiffin decorated goblets: Lisette, Westchester gold etched band, Marquis, Melissa, Delphi (gold band) or Riviera (platinum band), Mademoiselle

LITTLE EXTRAS *(continued)*

U.S. Glass/Tiffin Hawkes cutting on Tiffin blanks:
No. 7334 Heather, No. 17594 Hermitage,
No. 17863 Richelieu and No. 7240 Madison

Westmoreland Glass Co.
Black plates with Mary Gregory-type decoration

L to R: U.S. Glass/Tiffin Cordelia etching on No. 17067 goblet
West Virginia Glass Specialty Co.
Cranberry stain with clear sandblasted design

Washington Co. (decorating company)
1954 ad of enamel decorated salad sets

West Virginia Glass Specialty Co.
1963 ad of Snowy Holly decoration

INDEX

Please note that the Cambridge Glass Co. called their rock crystal cuttings rock crystal engravings even though they are not truly engravings. In the interests of preserving original terminology, we have retained their term in the following listing. Also be aware that several companies may have made patterns with the same names, so be sure to check all listings when trying to find your pattern.